In San Francisco in 1908, printer Henry Taylor decided to have a dinner party. He wrote and printed this poster-size invitation and gave it to seven lucky friends, who are called out in the text. The rainbow roll or split-fountain technique was first used in nineteenth-century type specimen books in France and the United States. But it later became hugely popular in counterculture California, thanks to the underground tabloid [The City of San Francisco Oracle](#) in the mid-1960s and the posters that the Colby printing company made in Los Angeles in the 1970s.

In 1971, designers John Van Hamersveld and Ed Thrasher got together to make this poster. Using a black-and-white photograph shot by Thrasher, Van Hamersveld applied the optically distorted type and then created the effect of the words "Southern California" disappearing into L.A.'s notorious smog. The image speaks volumes about the world's perception of Los Angeles at the time.

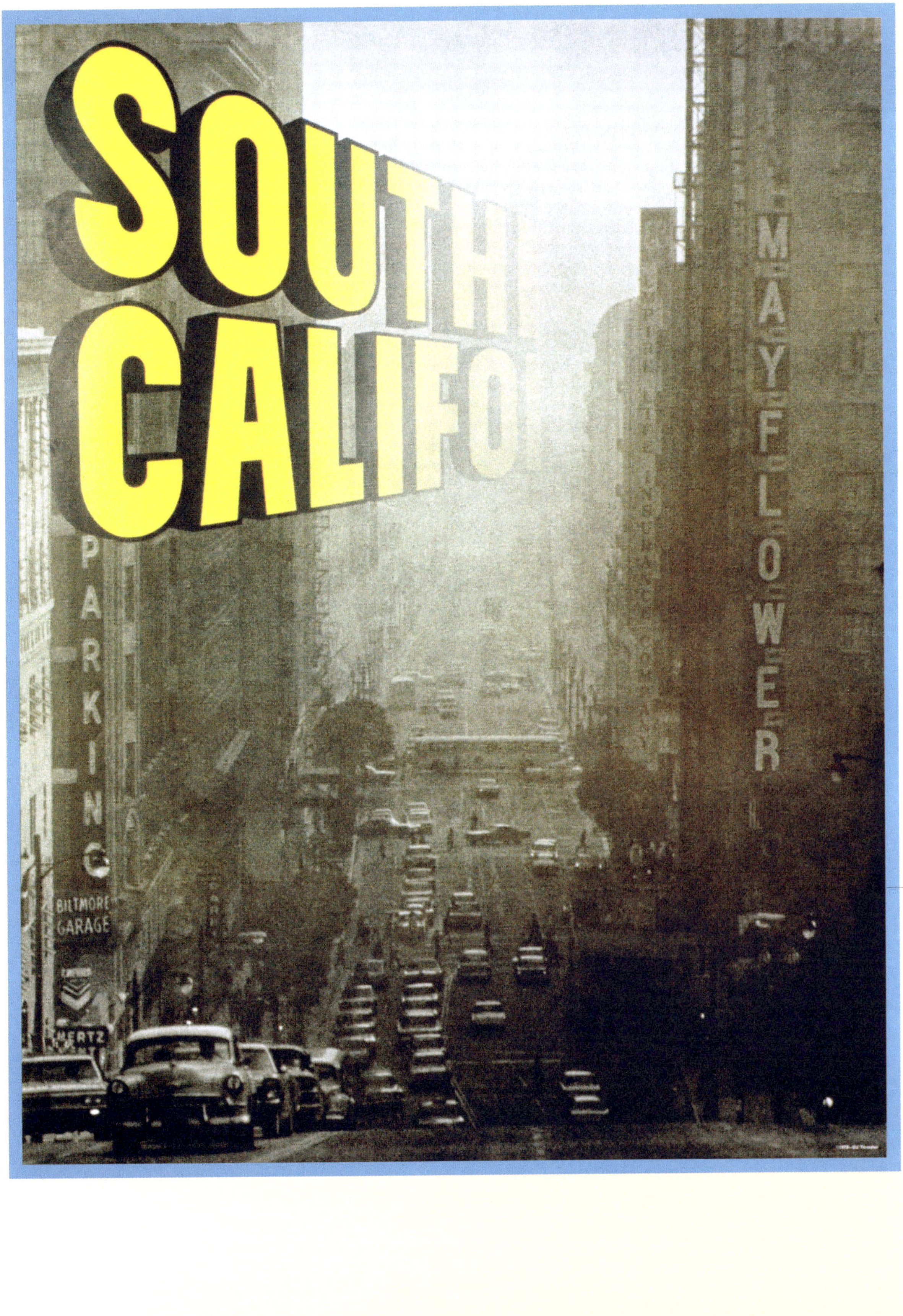
SOUTH
CALIFO
MAYFLOWER
PARKING
BILTMORE GARAGE
HERTZ

Following a chance meeting in the Midwest, architectural historian Reyner Banham asked designer Deborah Sussman to create a billboard advertising his 1972 BBC documentary, Reyner Banham Loves Los Angeles. In the film, Banham whimsically and lovingly tours the city, casting a fresh eye upon its virtues while guided by his robotic "Baede-kar" (a riff on the nineteenth-century Baedeker travel guides). About her design approach for the project, Sussman recalls, "there's kitsch and then there's Looney Tunes. I decided Looney Tunes, kitsch L.A." The same treatment was used for the film's titles. This photograph shows Banham (at right) and the BBC crew shooting the film's opening sequence.

Earthquakes   Mudslides
FIRES
AND RIOTS

CALIFORNIA &
GRAPHIC DESIGN
1936 → 1986

LOUISE   SANDHAUS

With texts by Denise Gonzales Crisp,
Lorraine Wild and Michael Worthington

Contents

Introduction: Greetings from the Left Coast! LOUISE SANDHAUS **10**

18 Sunbaked Modernism

INTRODUCTION The Sun Went to Their Heads **22**
DIAGRAM Influences & Intersections: Sunbaked Modernists **26**
ESSAY "Forward into the Past!" LORRAINE WILD **28**
REPRINT "California Modern," ALVIN LUSTIG, 1958 **36**
EXCERPT "Merle Armitage: His Many Loves and Varied Lives," WARD RITCHIE, 1982 **42**

The Work **48**

114 Industry & the Indies

INTRODUCTION For Your Viewing Pleasure **118**
DIAGRAM Influences & Intersections: The Indies and the Industry **122**
ESSAY "Out of Time: How to Make Motion Graphics in Southern California," MICHAEL WORTHINGTON **124**
REPRINT "The Artist as Design Scientist," GENE YOUNGBLOOD, 1970 **130**
REPRINT "Animation Mechanisms," JOHN WHITNEY, 1971 **134**
EXCERPT "Robert Abel: Video Surrealist," JEFFERY ALTSHULER, 1975 **140**

The Work **146**

210 Sixties alt Sixties

INTRODUCTION The Counterculture Was Never What It Used to Be **214**
DIAGRAM Influences & Intersections: The Alternative Sixties **218**
ESSAY "Orange," LORRAINE WILD **220**
DOCUMENT "Immaculate Heart College Art Department Rules," 1965/1968 **228**
COVER CA, 1967 **229**
EXCERPT "Rock Posters," DUGALD STERMER, 1967 **230**
EXCERPT "Communications," Whole Earth Catalog, 1970 **234**
EXCERPT "California Institute of the Arts: Prologue to a Community," Arts in Society, WALT DISNEY AND ROBERT W. CORRIGAN, 1970 **238**

The Work **242**

306 California Girls

    INTRODUCTION View from the Broads **310**

    DIAGRAM Influences & Intersections: California Girls **314**

    ESSAY "Water and Power," DENISE GONZALES CRISP **316**

    EXCERPT daisy with all the petals yes, SISTER CORITA KENT, 1966 **326**

    EXCERPT "No, kid, make it happy!" DUGALD STERMER, 1971 **328**

    EXCERPT "A Feminist Option," ROSE DENEVE, 1976 **332**

The Work **340**

Acknowledgments **401**
About the Contributors **403**
Selected Bibliography **404**
Index **410**

INTRODUCTION: GREETINGS FROM THE LEFT COAST!
Louise Sandhaus

Books on the history of graphic design abound. Many of the momentous and memorable creations from a rich past of professional output are well documented in lush, informative volumes that populate all sorts of shelves beyond those belonging to graphic designers. There are encyclopedic surveys, designer monographs, and examinations of the design proclivities of nations including Britain, Japan, Switzerland, the Netherlands, and, popularly and prolifically, Germany and its Bauhaus. Graphic design of the United States has also had its plentiful due, but, beyond a few exceptions (some significant), most publishing about American work serves up a melting pot. Until relatively recently, most of these volumes perpetuated the validation of twentieth-century modernism as the sole source of bona fide graphic design, capital G, capital D. Not until the graphics of Push Pin Studios, the nostalgic celebrations of Charles S. Anderson, and, the most influential, Denise Scott Brown and Robert Venturi's Learning from Las Vegas, did a much broader range of graphic languages receive serious consideration. The Walker Art Center's controversial 1989 exhibition Graphic Design in America: A Visual Language History continued this strain of investigation, in no small part by sparking responses such as the symposium series Eclecticism and Modernism organized by Steven Heller for the School of Visual Arts in New York. (Here, I first encountered psychedelic poster designer Victor Moscoso, considered persona non grata by the graphic design orthodoxy in which I resided. Ha!)

    Within this lively discussion, graphic design specific to California has yet to receive the spotlight, despite a rich and extensive history that, for the most part, confirms all the stereotypes and expectations of a freewheeling West Coast culture where anything goes and everyone does her or his own thing. The California New Wave aesthetic drew national attention in the eighties, yet exciting and revolutionary work from prior decades has remained hidden in plain sight. No book has set out to capture more widely the particular and visually ecstatic graphic design production of the Golden State. So this volume aims to help set the situation right: it offers a raucous gathering of more than 250 examples of smart, offbeat, innovative, groundbreaking graphic design projects from a distinctive yet underacknowledged heyday of the so-called Left Coast between 1936 and 1986 (which in no way suggests a lack of attention-worthy work outside that time span).

    So what makes California design deserving of special attention, and what, in the first place, makes it by definition "Californian?" Here's my theory: California has no terra firma—earthquakes, mudslides, fires, and the occasional civil uprising cause incessant upheaval and change. California is fluid. It has a sense of humor. It is a place of boundless reinvention and innovation, where the entertainment, aerospace, and high-tech industries all found a cozy home. A mecca of consumerism, it is also a place of great creativity, freedom, and social consciousness, where the status quo undergoes constant renovation. Without solid ground, tradition lacks secure footing; old rules go out the door and new motivations rush in, resulting in new and vibrant forms.

What Is This Book? What This Book Is Not!

I am not a design historian, critic, theoretician, or scholar, although at times I wear parts of these costumes. That said, this four-section book includes history, criticism, a bit of theory, and maybe even some "new knowledge" (academic-speak for "discoveries"). Its approach reflects, perhaps, a "California" way of presenting information—the kind both conceived and reflected in Reyner Banham's classic yet iconoclastic survey <u>Los Angeles: The Architecture of Four Ecologies</u>. Banham suggests that no traditional historical-narrative form could allow for an explanation of the uniqueness of Southern California's built environment. Thus, he had to invent a new way of telling. Likewise, so goes this book, but here the innovations around "telling" extend to "showing" by including the design of the book itself. That effort is in no small part assisted by Jens Gehlhaar's CIA Compendium typeface family, which he tailored for this project to manifest the text more visually.

To make sense of the work this volume includes—and excludes—the reader should imagine a dinner party that serves only desserts. This is not a comprehensive historical survey of California graphic design (no meat and potatoes here); it isn't even a look at the highlights of what is widely considered to be "important" California graphic design. The sugary offerings within these pages range from the obvious to the obscure. This is a heavily curated selection based on little more than the way the heart quickens when the eye encounters something radiant, wonderful, and new. One end of the buffet (to carry out the dessert metaphor), offers iconoclastic works that belie independence of thought—more rough than shiny, more ad hoc than prescribed, more unschooled than mandated. Back in the day, some of these projects might have

EARTHQUAKES, MUDSLIDES, FIRES & RIOTS

been deemed "provincial" or dismissed as trying to be something they aren't; now, through the panoramic lens with which we survey culture, they seem so vibrant as to leave us baffled as to how they possibly went ignored. At the other end are treats that have become California "classics," more or less acknowledged on a national, if not international, scale as design connected the Golden State. Some of these examples achieved mass popularity: think of John Van Hamersveld's blazing pink-and-orange Day-Glo poster for the surfer documentary The Endless Summer. Others have been celebrated within the field, such as Alvin Lustig's conceptual cover designs for New Directions books or April Greiman's legendary "Does it Make Sense?" issue of Design Quarterly—not the usual bound journal but a poster featuring a life-size scanned image of the designer herself in all her bit-mapped glory.

A Particular Timeline

In the decade-long process of assembling this book, people often asked me, why focus on these particular 50 years? My starting point, 1936, is anchored in the designs of the charismatic Merle Armitage, one of the first in a lineage of California graphic producers to veer off prescribed design pathways and give modernism his own inventive twist. When I first saw Armitage's work, I wasn't sure whether he did it out of genius, ignorance, or nonchalance, but the results can safely be described as idiosyncratic, dynamic, and elegant. At the time, I was working as an exhibition designer (with collaborator architects Tim Durfee and Iris Anna Regn) on the 2000–2001 survey Made in California: Art, Image & Identity 1900–2000, curated by Stephanie Baron and her vast collaborative team for the Los Angeles County Museum of Art. This ambitious millennial show looked at works of art in relation to media images of the state—from idyllic vacation ads to picture-perfect promos of the poolside postwar lifestyle to, eventually, news images of urban upheaval and turmoil—and questioned whether the art works confirmed, contradicted, or complicated the popular visual identity disseminated through media including the press, films, and literature.

    The pieces in this exhibition provoked a vivid recall of something I heard that California-based artist Billy Al Bengston once said along the lines of, "Fuck New York. Fuck Europe. We'll figure out what art is." This sentiment time and again seemed to get at an explanation of why the art and design produced "out here" looked so distinctive. It spoke to a chronology of California designers and their different relationships to the modernist impulse: early-twentieth-century Europeans, such as Oskar Fischinger, who, forced to emigrate, found a sunny incubator for the innovation inherent in the modernist directive to "make it new"; midcentury artists, such as the Eameses, who saw California as a place of liberation where they could continue to experiment, to push their work forward and avoid any chance of staleness; and those who came later, Bengston's generation and its inheritors, who rejected or subverted aspects of late '50s and early '60s modernism that had become part of a rote orthodoxy. In every case, California provided a valuable distance from the East Coast and European capitals; it offered an opportunity to draw from different sources, to suckle from a different breast.

A short time later, when my design team and I worked on the UCLA Hammer Museum's <u>World from Here: Treasures of the Great Libraries of Los Angeles</u>, my inkling was reinforced. First, it seemed significant that this stopper-of-a-show took notice of local gems. Also, I had the opportunity to take a close look at Armitage's <u>Stravinsky</u>, which is part of the UCLA Clark Library collection. To experience Armitage's work once again made Bengston's words rush back to me in full recognition that what I was seeing was the work of a designer who had transcended whatever design dictates were coming from the East Coast and across the pond telling us here, in California, what to do and how to do it. With that revelation, I began to wonder what else was there. And, of course, all this staggering work had existed all along. One just had to look for it, or see it through the right glasses—in this case, SUNglasses!

I chose to end this book's chronology 50 years later, with Greiman's autobiographical work from 1986, "Does It Make Sense?" Arguably the first piece of design to embrace the potential of the Apple Macintosh, it was part of a seismic upheaval within in the comfortable world of design, and it signaled that many of those who were riding the resulting wave were women. <u>California</u> women. This disruption within the insular zone of corporate modernism, the dominant national voice of graphic design in the late '80s, made room for new voices saying new things in new ways. Once again, just as I saw in the work of Armitage, a California designer had rejected the programmatic and opted, instead, for the different. And this time, the iconoclast was a woman who flouted not one but two rules—against embracing the computer as an aesthetic as opposed to a mere tool, and against using the designer, the self, as subject matter.

How This Book Is Structured

Within this span from Armitage to Greiman, four themes leapt out: "Sunbaked Modernism" explores what happens to European traditions in California; "Industry & the Indies" examines work created for the screen—including film titles, TV graphics, light shows, and video games—by Hollywood, the avant-garde, and an intersection of the two; "Sixties alt Sixties" highlights just some of what was going on beyond the psychedelic posters that became so synonymous with 1960s California graphic design; and, finally, "California Girls" presents what seems apparent to me, which is that the Golden State has more women wielding global influence in the substance and style of graphic design than anywhere else in the world.

Each section explores one of these themes. The design work that I have included is arranged chronologically to give a sense of evolution over the period from 1936 to 1986, although not every section starts and stops precisely with those dates. In addition to the designs themselves, each section contains the following: an introduction giving an overview of the perspective from which the examples were selected; a sampling of historical texts, either reprinted in full or excerpted; and a new essay, written especially for this book, in which a recognized designer/writer offers his or her insights. Given that graphic design is only just beginning to train scholars and writers, designers themselves have for years taken up the task of formulating the literature on which the field is now finding its roots and interpreting the significance and influence of its history and current developments. I chose Denise Gonzales Crisp, Lorraine Wild, and Michael Worthington as much for their deep knowledge about design and media as for their distinctive writing, which stylistically embraces the California lineage of Esther McCoy, Joan Didion, and Banham.

But the design work is the main show, taking on the role conventionally assigned to a text. Here, the written is subordinate to the visual; design projects dominate this book, with extended captions describing or "illustrating" how they may have been seen or understood from various design and cultural perspectives. (At the same time, the visual work is so strong that it performs on its own.)

Some Complications

One dilemma I encountered was whom to credit as responsible for certain projects. How do you ascertain authorship when, say, the maker was a hired gun for an ad agency and may have created the form but was not the sole generator of the idea, which may have been the case of the group Advertising Designers and others in the days before graphic designers worked independently? Or, how do you assign credit to individuals within a large team? In the example of the film TRON and many undertakings of Robert Abel and Associates, the weave of contributors is so tight it becomes hard to see the individual threads. In the sixties, the problem took on new dimensions: Sometimes design was a collective enterprise, such as the hippie newspaper Kaliflower. Other times, the maker was unacknowledged or "anonymous," as was standard with most output from the anticapitalist, anticompetition Diggers and the Communications Company. Or, if there was an identified maker, does "layout" constitute "design?" This was the question in trying to establish the designer of the Whole Earth Catalog. There were no easy answers. In the end, I've tried to identify the conceptualizers and visualizers, the ones mostly widely acknowledged for giving visual form to thought or for the planning and visual execution of a message—in other words, following widely embraced definitions of "graphic design."

Final Decisions

Of the hundreds of projects considered for this book, many were left on the proverbial cutting-room floor. The debate here boiled down to: Is this a historically important work versus is this fabulous and distinctive and sooooooo California? (And good-looking wins in California every time!) Or, can I get permission to use this? (The answer, sometimes, was no.) Or, if I have to choose between excluding an image and including it at small scale, is it worth it? It also was agonizing not to give a fuller voice to the schools and institutions in California that played a crucial role in shaping the designers whose work shines from these pages. To me, this meant talking about the plant but ignoring the seed.

Just as there are many more examples of highly interesting work from the '30s to the '80s than could be included here, so are there whole other movements to be explored that began and flourished around that end date: the punk scene; the California new wave; the emergence of the publisher and type foundry Emigre; the homegrown, hothouse, postmodern graphic experimentation going on within CalArts; and the debut of Wired magazine, for starters.

I hope others will continue the effort, to examine what's missing here and has been undeservedly overlooked. At the very least, this is a beginning, a tiny tick mark on so much history yet to be covered. Let's go!

> "There is science, logic, reason, there is thought verified by experience, and then there is California."

EDWARD ABBEY
"A VOICE CRYING IN THE WILDERNESS"
1989

INTRODUCTION: THE SUN WENT TO THEIR HEADS

"Sunbaked," according to the dictionary, means two things: "baked by exposure to the sun" and "excessively heated by the sun." Apply those definitions to modernism, with its cerebral tenets, and it warms up to the point of overheating, as in, "the sun went to his head." It's an apt way to characterize modern graphic design as realized in California and to suggest how environmental characteristics might have transformed chilly established approaches and ideas into sunbaked goodness.

    The story of Californian modernist design is one of a handmade, poolside, indoor-outdoor, playful-yet-purposeful aesthetic of invention, reinvention, and exuberant production in architecture, craft, furnishings, and fashion. Publicized at the time through the popular press, movies, and television, California modernism came to permeate America's on-the-go lifestyle of the postwar period and well beyond. Yet this sunny and significant episode in design history has largely remained in the dark—until recently. Thanks in part to the Pacific Standard Time exhibition and publication series on California postwar art and architecture, sponsored by the Getty Research Institute, some light—including substantial scholarship—has finally begun to shine on the West Coast chapter of the complex tale that is modernism. Graphic design innovations previously dismissed as regional and provincial when measured against highfalutin' European and East Coast standards have come to be recognized as fascinating inflections worthy of interest.

    The roots of graphic modernism in California are both imported and homegrown. East Coasters such as Saul Bass and Lou Danziger, midwesterners including Merle Armitage and Allen Porter, and Europeans such as Herbert Matter—all schooled in modern design—provided one strand. Another strand derived from California natives (or those whose longtime residence made them near natives), such as Ray Eames, Alvin Lustig, and John and Marilyn Neuhart, whose exposure to modernism came via many a worldly high-school teacher who preached its gospel and celebrated its foreign fruits—the European-produced work that, for years, served as the gold standard. Lustig, who was exposed to modern design through art instructor Harry Koblick, in turn inspired an entire generation of California designers through his own teaching at Pasadena's Art Center College of Design, among them Danziger, John Follis, Charles Kratka, and Fred Usher. Other designers, too, absorbed the influence of significant California schools and instructors. The Neuharts credit their education at Long Beach City College and the University of California, Los Angeles, while Don Birrell got his start at Chouinard Art Institute. Many of these students were World War II veterans who studied under the G.I. Bill. Others found their way into design through smaller institutions specializing in commercial trades such as lettering or printing. Here, we find Doyald Young and Jack Stauffacher. No matter where the exposure to modernism originated, the outcome gained vitality from the California heat and nourishment from a proximity to Latin and Asian cultures—influences we encounter in the forms and colors favored by designers such as Ray Eames, Alexander Girard, and the Neuharts. Ultimately, a new blend of creativity, artistry, ingenuity, and craft gained independence, unshackled from ball-and-chain allegiances to a prescribed, imported modern design.

 Emboldened by this freedom from tradition, important contributions to the field of graphic design took seed, flourished, and, in some cases, grew into revolutions. Lustig reinvented the standard approach to book-cover design, replacing literal illustrations with more symbolic language. Ken Parkhurst, working for Lustig, may have been the first designer to lend his talents to an annual report, while Follis is credited with establishing the field of environmental design—signage and wayfinding programs related to modernism's concern for serving pragmatic needs. Danziger and Keith Godard, colleagues at California Institute of the Arts, are widely regarded within the field as being the first in the United States to offer courses in the history of graphic design. In the remote outpost of Vacaville, off the stretch of highway between Sacramento and San Francisco, Birrell conceived the first shop for West Coast modern design, preceding even Girard's legendary interior-design retail establishment for Knoll in New York, Textiles & Objects, which combined folk art with modernist decor. Computer technology, one branch of which originated in California, also advanced the language of graphic design, especially in the work of motion-graphic designers such as John Whitney. It's a good bet that the first computer-generated logo came from California, as well.

The examples here represent some of the vivid tastes and flavors of the West Coast, as well as a design language that speaks not demurely but with a declarative California accent to enliven and advance the modernist conversation. In some cases, these works are well known but warrant a second look. Other projects have been widely recognized but for reasons other than their graphic design. The assessment of "beautiful" within modern graphic design is commonly attributed to refined works originating in New York and Europe. In California, modernism blossomed beyond borders of refinement into manifestations that, in their wonder and remarkability, demand a larger stage. Examples range from the grand—Kratka's vibrant abstract murals at the Los Angeles International Airport—to the small, such as the emphatic cover designs that Follis and Matter created for <u>Arts & Architecture.</u> Folk modernism is yet another strain that took hold in the West, with colorful, charming, and delightful variations of handmade and traditional crafts celebrated and transformed in the inspired hands of the Eameses, Girard, and the Neuharts. Along with Ward Ritchie and Stauffacher, the Neuharts also explored new approaches to letterpress, and the work they produced was diverse in its intentions and outcomes.

 It's worth remembering that until recently, the field of graphic design was largely the province of service providers such as type houses, printers, letterers, photographers, and illustrators—all employed as hired guns in advertising. Much of the commercial work shown on these pages can be traced to agencies, including the Gelvatex Paints ad by Danziger for the Dreyfus Agency and Young's typeface for Henry Dreyfuss and Associates. It isn't until 1950, when Bass opened his own L.A. studio, that we see graphic designers, for the most part, working directly with clients rather than through agency intermediaries. Book design, although not commonly associated with California, also found fertile territory here. In San Francisco and Los Angeles, the "fine press" production traditions associated most with the Arts and Crafts movement and, in particular, designer William Morris, comingled with the industry-minded methods of the Bauhaus. In the Bay Area, Stauffacher obsessively explored the use of type for abstract composition rather than readability, while farther south, Armitage—a theatrical impresario with no design training—exercised his full-bodied ego and renegade spirit toward creating new kinds of reading experiences such as starting a book on its cover or, in 1941, imagining what sort of typographic treatments, images, and materials might exist for books in the year 2000.

Complementing the information in this section are three essays that further illuminate the character of the region and its designers during the moment when modernism found its California footing. In the first text, design historian and graphic designer Lorraine Wild both avows and disavows the term "modernism" as it ping-pongs across different interpretations and meanings. The second is a reprint of Lustig's 1958 essay "California Modern," which sums up the ethos and spirit of design that might best define sunbaked modernism. It's an indelible and distinctive image. And, finally, we have Ritchie's playful and anecdote-rich 1982 essay about Armitage, whose big vision and DIY spirit fully embody the warmth, sizzle, and sunlit brilliance of design in the Golden State.

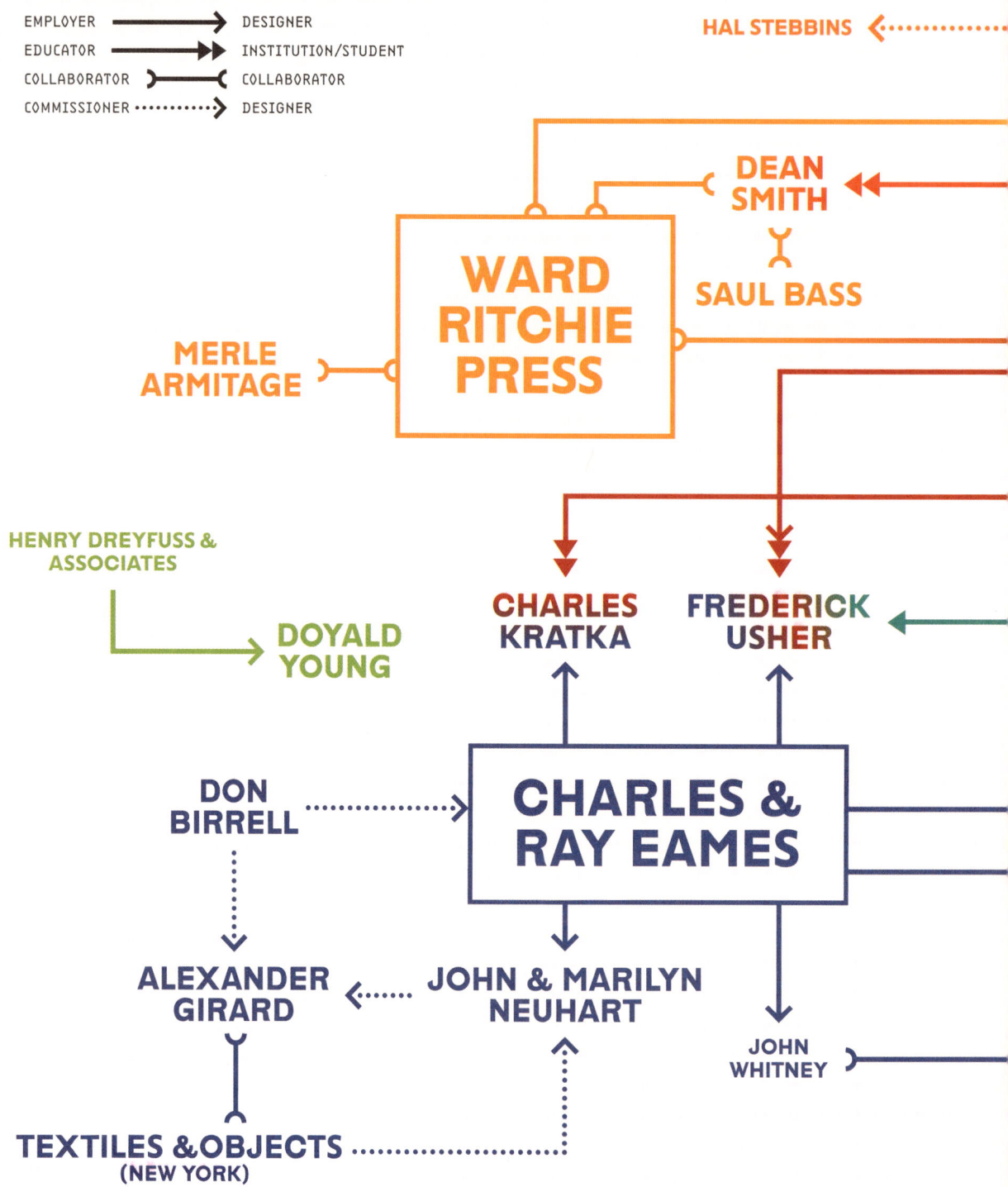

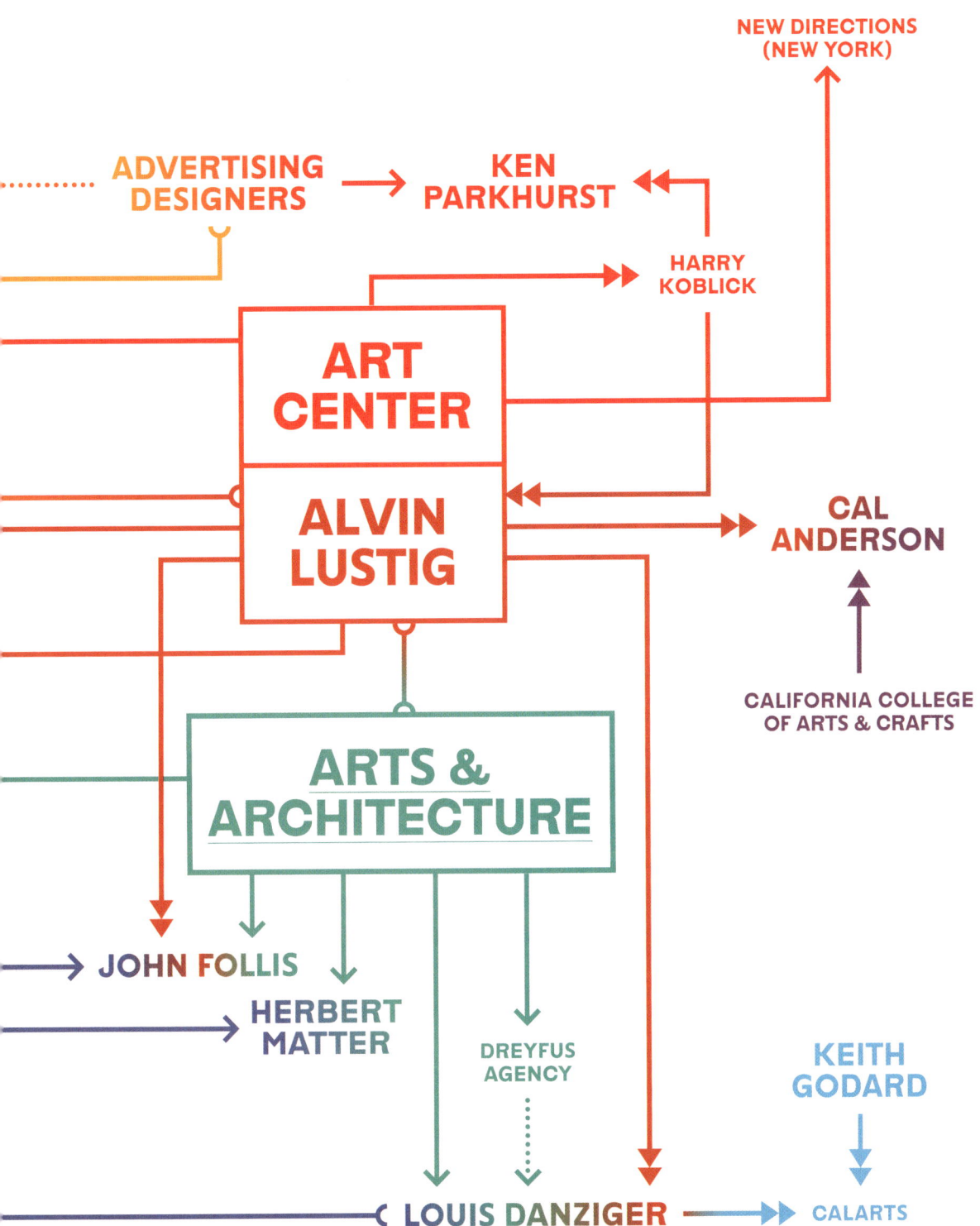

LORRAINE WILD

"FORWARD INTO THE PAST!"*

How can we really understand the history of ideas in graphic design? Can graphic design be understood in chronological periods, the way that, say, furniture or interiors are often classified or interpreted? Are the artifacts of graphic design simply too diverse to classify or too ephemeral to support a convincing narrative? For instance, after years of looking at the graphic design produced during the mid-twentieth century, one might argue that the modernist work is the work that matters. However, you can only hold onto that idea as long as you ignore the fact that 80 percent of the graphic design produced during that time (advertisements, billboards, books, sales collateral, exhibitions, point-of-sale, film titles, etc.) isn't what we now recognize as modern. Even the design that won awards or was documented as "important" during that time isn't <u>all</u> the work of the infamous émigrés or Paul Rand. A lot of the work of the past now looks, to our eyes, like banal, somewhat dated material, and that, in a nutshell, describes the problem that confounds every person seeking to talk about graphic design of the past: Do you want to just talk about the work that you like? Or do you want to talk about what was actually made? And if you admit that there is a problem with the work that was actually made, then you have to admit that in the past, just as now, there was tons of work produced that technically <u>was</u> graphic design, but is not really all that interesting.

* "Forward into the Past" is the title of a Firesign Theatre sketch that was first recorded in 1969 in Los Angeles.

And the operative word here is <u>tons</u>: that other than limited-edition books and prints, we are talking about innumerable artifacts. No collector can be sure of completion. For every piece reproduced in the graphic design history books (and it is remarkable, given the countless number of things, how few artifacts are repeatedly represented in the history books), you know there are endless numbers of lost or forgotten works, some quite justifiably so.

So what do you talk about? Do you talk about the work that led to more work that was interesting, worthy of our attention because the ideas or images in it were fertile and led to the next generation of work? (That is probably what has generated this volume on California design: the work that begot the work, that tells us something about the place and times in which it was begot.) Or do you talk about the unlettered stuff, the true vernacular, which might be interesting as a genre but not as specific individual works? One piece of the vernacular is, after all, just as wonderful as the next....

Or do you make it up?

II

If you look at American design before World War II (graphic design, but other forms, too), you see a lot of design dedicated to the future but informed by the past.

The 1920s brought Art Deco, a hybrid of silvery lines and zigzags pointing toward an imaginary future, embellishing images of luxury and comfort not deviant in any fundamental way from historic precedents of luxury or prestige. The DNA of Art Deco is split between the visual avant-garde of the 1920s (in many of its variations), the movies (borrowing from similar sources), and the fantasies of science fiction. Art Deco delivers a romantic, appealing idea and image that optimistically promises access to creature comforts to be enjoyed by all, secure in the notion that everything is up to date (and embellished with metallic foil for decorative impact).

Designers designing in the midst of the Depression delivered visions of a reflective, magnetic, electric, airbrushed, science-fiction Valhalla to distract from the failures of the grimy present. So the impulse behind Art Deco, describing the future as a shinier and more glamorous version of the present, morphs into the more mechanized and hygienic image of Moderne, or Streamlined, design as fast moving, scientific, efficient, and, most of all, workable. Images of transportation underline speed and convenience, and beckon to a future based in mobility. Yet genteel Americans during both decades, witnessing the inevitable crash and burn of the giant economic bubble of the '20s and the devastating scarcity of the '30s, clung to the familiar patterns of classical and Colonial design, popularizing a historical eclecticism in residential design and interior decoration. That historicist eclecticism strove to connect a legibility of narrative to a present that, in the face of economic collapse, was obviously disappointing (though now, the nostalgia of that historicist eclecticism is what seems much more random, since the narratives it refers to have basically been lost). Driving down the typical Los Angeles prewar street, with its three-bedroom English, New England(-ish), Prairie Bungalow, and Spanish Colonial homes, makes you realize that there might once have been a point behind the selection of the styles, a visual language that was popularly understood, but which today somehow seems like a decorative Esperanto that only the most adept followers can translate. In plan, those thousands of smallish houses of Los Angeles offer a pragmatic story of affordable middle-class housing; in elevation, they seem to tell someone else's story, not ours.

In the world of graphic design before World War II, then, much of the same dynamic was at work: Art Deco deployed to deliver promises of entertainment or eventual technological prowess; Depression-era streamlining instigated to lure worried customers into a technological future; historical eclecticism utilized to comfort consumers with messages about safety, security, acceptance, beauty, and calm. In fact, "hybridity" seems like a polite way to describe this concoction of seductive futuristic fantasies and dependable evocations of seemingly secure historical traditions; "neurotic" or perhaps even "paranoid" are adjectives that might get closer to the core of cultural complexity imaged by designers who put the styles to use, and the consumers of those products and images who routinely immersed themselves simultaneously in an imagined past and an imagined future for reasons that, in retrospect, seem either naive or cynical. But in all cases, the designers are using a known language as code to an audience. The Art Deco style, the Streamlined style (or, conversely, Cape Cod Shingle or Spanish Stucco) were invoked to elicit specific reactions on the part of their audiences. Raymond Loewy famously defined beauty as the trajectory of a sales curve, swooping upward; mimesis, after all, was the point.

III

That is why it is so surprising to see many designers switch gears after World War II, to see them—and their clients—snap awake to a less predetermined present.

"Sunbaked Modernism" in this context refers to the work of West Coast designers who were determined to abandon both the weary historicism and the unrequited futurism of the generation that preceded them. The optimism of the midcentury-modern work across all design media is palpable, and this material has been beloved for a good while now; and ironically, since it is the production of many designers answering contemporary problems, it turns out that it has many relevancies to design now. By concentrating on the present, the designers of the midcentury inadvertently delivered visions for the future, minus the futurism. And while we as designers and consumers now possess, post-postmodernism, a large closet stuffed with historical styles always there to be rummaged though, including something we now refer to as "midcentury," the canny observer cannot miss the fact that this most persuasive and now-looking work was produced for a "now" that is 60 to 70 years old. Those seeking an eternal fountain of design youth are beckoned to drink from it and gain enlightenment. (As I write this, Mick Jagger turns 70 and the radio is playing "Satisfaction," and I am confronted with another type of time travel offered by a rupture in the space/time/style continuum, if there is such a thing.)

While Stefan Sagmeister has offered us the unhelpful equation "Style=Fart," more thoughtful reflections on the problem(s) of style were offered by those closer to the argument. In the early 1950s, Alvin Lustig stated, more or less, that using a style that was distant to the content of a given problem (e.g., setting the Bible in sans-serif) was as pointless as believing that certain styles were more correct than others. In other words, the designer/artist brought his intentions to his work, and considered the content, and considered the audience, and the whole context of the problem, and then was free to use whatever in the world he deemed workable. In other words, to be a truly contemporary (if not modern) designer, in Lustig's mind, was to be free of the strictures of style—period. To be able to use it with abandon.

And isn't that what we are looking at when we see a copy of Merle Armitage's 1941 edition (for the Limited Editions Club) of Looking Backward? Edward Bellamy's novel (a futuristic socialist romance that takes place in the year 2000) is set in large gothic compressed fonts and Poster Bodoni and uses abstract and semiabstract illustrations (by Armitage's wife, the artist Elise) in a form that doesn't really look like Art Deco or Moderne or anything in any particular style. Perhaps as Armitage was trying to give form to Bellamy's vision of the future, he was consciously rejecting what in 1941 may have already appeared to be outworn prewar versions of the future, and therefore depicted times to come as a stylistic void. It's all concept, clothed in a visual form that is undefinable, other than not-seen-before.

Arts & Architecture magazine (in both "California…" and non-"California" iterations) displayed the same simplified, almost style-less typography in the interior of the publication. There was clearly a vacuuming of any reference to earlier Moderne typographic styles that clung, in those days, to a lot of graphic materials that documented architecture. The hands of so many of the designers who produced the imaginative covers for A&A were unrestrained when it came to personal compositions with metaphoric/abstract or simply abstract images (which they signed like artworks); but the rest of the magazine was plain, modest, free of any overt stylistic message. And this is not true of the contents of the magazine, which presented a cavalcade of new ideas and strong images of California architecture, product design, furniture, and all sorts of other objects. These things all had the remarkable new style that we still see as defining the midcentury, but the graphic design (at least that produced for A&A) took a much cooler and quieter stance.

And certainly the terse, disciplined work of Lou Danziger falls into the category of style as no style, or not seen before, across the entire range of his production, with few exceptions. He used his imagination to create metaphors and was able to employ the photograph in ways that seemed simultaneously documentary and expressive. But his typography is so stylistically restrained that it skirts our contemporary definition of "default"—though by the absolute grace of proportion and composition it misses that dubious state by a wide margin. However, he comes closest to it in his design for LACMA's 1971 Art and Technology project, a book that catalogues the work of a group of scientists

COVER OF <u>A REPORT ON THE ART AND TECHNOLOGY PROGRAM OF THE LOS ANGELES COUNTY MUSEUM OF ART, 1967–1971</u> (Los Angeles: Los Angeles County Museum of Art, 1971), designed by Lou Danziger

and artists engaging in serious, convention-busting collaborations without predetermined outcomes—an effort as forward looking as possible—and it is here that Danziger strips down his graphic delivery to one degree above zero. There are references (of course) in his design to the style-less-ness of technological charts, science textbooks, and the "objectivity" of the Swiss (by 1971, International/Corporate) typographic style and even the IBM Selectric setting of Stewart Brand's <u>Whole Earth Catalog</u> of 1968. And while late in the "midcentury" time frame, the logic that was behind Danziger's thinking was surely formed by the move away from definable styles and toward a Lustigian open-endedness of graphic language that depended upon some audience collaboration: the designer was free to invent, and the audience was invited to "get it."

SUNBAKED MODERNISM

IV

But shuffle the midcentury cards a bit differently and one happens upon an entirely different sort of graphic output that also read as being all about the present but did so using graphic typography and imagery that was all about the past. The works that fall into this category represent a pretty wide range, including almost all of the actual graphic design produced by the Eames Office (mostly by Deborah Sussman, John and Marilyn Neuhart, Fred Usher, and many others). Some examples are the several versions of the House of Cards project, the graphic design generated in support of the Day of the Dead film and exhibition (1957), the exhibition Mathematica (1960), and John Neuhart's poster for the Textiles & Objects shop (1961). These projects marry contemporary pictorial intensity with typography that references late-nineteenth- and early-twentieth-century commercial vernaculars, wood-type headlines, and densely cluttered compositions. This confounding relationship between a typography of the past and contemporary innovation turns out to provide a welcome mat for the audience into the new: a particular philosophy of Charles and Ray Eameses' "functional decoration," a playful pragmatism that acknowledges that it might take some seduction to bring a popular audience to modernism's door.

The Eameses' shift from staid historical eclecticism toward a more motley cultural eclecticism was "fun" (a term the couple used frequently themselves), democratic, even "global," and thereby ripe for innovative commercial use by other savvy designers. Marget Larsen's art direction for the Joseph Magnin store and Don Birrell's Nut Tree are happy retail versions of the combination of bright colors, density, ethnic hodge-podge, and retro typography.

However—it wasn't really retro. There is nothing "stylistic" about that typography, no purity, particularly in the settings or the combination of the type with the use of bold color. This is the interesting thing about the use of older vernacular typography: it is not obedient to or a replica of any actual antique typographic style. If there is any reminder of the past, it is of a vernacular (again) of an undefined but very pragmatic time—like the design of nineteenth-century machinery, where it is all pure function. You can argue that the appearance of the commercial wood typography in this period is pretty pure visual expression of function as well. So its reappearance in the mid-twentieth century is not meant to make people more comfortable or to harken back to some utopia of the past but to reassert (or revisualize) the pragmatic energy of the new.

And maybe that's the weird link between the quotation of historical typography in a lot of advanced and new design of the 1950s and the historical typography used by various designers of the 1960s counterculture: the use of wood type and other nineteenth-century typographic forms in psychedelic posters and other underground communications of all kinds is remarkable and stubborn. It is true that Bay Area psychedelic concert posters were deliberately "unreadable," that the style was a code, an early version of micromarketing. Like the projects in the Eames Office, there was nothing inherent in the concerts that the posters were announcing that called for historicist typography, and the typography itself is somewhat disguised by the clashing colors. However, you also see historical typography used in a lot of antiwar and other left-wing communications of the '60s and '70s. The ironic use of nostalgia, which is often what this typography signals, was quickly cracked as a sort of code for youth and began to appear in aboveground marketing for the younger generation. This may well be why truly oppositional anti-mainstream groups such as the Diggers or the Black Panthers avoided the same "functional decoration": they didn't want to go near that which had morphed so quickly into a mainstream style.

V

All this is speculation. There are no traces, no arguments; all you can do is look! And note, perhaps, the dumping of all manner of historical quotation for that brief period in the early 1980s when bit-mapping and all sorts of shiny, Day-Glo swooshing and splattering took over: our brief return to a Streamlined adoration of the machine, only this time it is processing speed and not a speeding train that holds all the promise of the future. And that lasted about five minutes, only to be more or less put to rest by the reanimation of historical quotation, via postmodern theory, across all design media again; an example of ever shortening cycles in stylistic approaches to design, the existence of which so many designers deny.

CALIFORNIA MODERN: There are diverse influences acting on Southern California, which, if properly synthesized, could produce great design.

We, who live and work in California, share the sense of exhilaration and growth that charges the very air. What is happening here? Is it just another boom following perpetual boom? Will a great and noble architecture raise its head to the sun or will we glut ourselves with cheap plaster husks? Will the land sprawl away from us into planless confusion? Do we as designers and architects have any special opportunities or responsibilities to ourselves or the community? Is this the "new world" really getting itself built, or are these the last gestures of a tinseled unreality? Is our search for the New to end in great monuments of creative originality or mere architectural sensationalism?

It is common practice today to place the word "California" in front of almost any vagrant word and thus achieve a magic combination hopefully intended to make the heart jump and the purse strings fly open. The word "California" alone produces a wide range of emotional response, ranging from a snarl of contempt to ecstatic eye-rolling. I shall deal in this article with "California Modern" or any other phrase that implies something unique or special about modern design in this area. I maintain that something flies into your mind when the magic phrase "California Modern" is uttered, and I intend to examine this vision. It probably ranges from a picture of some of the best domestic architecture in the world to an overstuffed overripe kind of lushness that is particularly localized in this area.

It is certainly no secret that this area is particularly well suited for the development of modern architecture. The climate, the freedom from tradition, the heightened sense of life—all of these factors contribute to make a unique architectural opportunity. Is there, however, developing in this specific region a mature architecture reflecting the best features of the area, or are we being inundated by heavy-handed perversions of badly digested basic principles? I think we can safely say that both processes are taking place. Unfortunately, however, the majority of the work is still, at best, a rather hectic scrambling of clichés and ill-digested forms. That quality in our environment which gives us freedom also limits us by failing to impose disciplines.

One of the strongest factors in California's favor is its freedom from European tradition. This lack of continuity with

Western civilization is also one of the qualities deplored by the outsider. We lose the rigor and economy of thinking and acting that has characterized European thought and, reveling in our new-found freedom, often commit excesses that are somewhat horrifying. It is impossible for an area as young and unfettered as this to avoid making extravagant gestures, some of which do not come off. However, if we intend to take full advantage of our opportunity and are honestly seeking a real and even great architecture we must stop a moment and take stock.

Most of our excesses can be traced directly to an insufficient understanding of the basic aims and tendencies in modern architecture. It is not the intention of this paper to attempt to trace the development of this movement or to evaluate the contribution of the great pioneers such as Frank Lloyd Wright, Louis Sullivan, Mies van der Rohe and Le Corbusier, but rather to goad the reader into a more discerning self-criticism and recognition of his responsibilities. My theme is that no matter how wondrous the physical opportunities are, without a clear understanding of the basic principles and even conflicts inherent in the movement, nothing but architectural hash will be produced. Our opportunity lies in synthesis, and synthesis demands understanding of all the factors involved. It is probably true that the form modern architecture has taken in the rest of the world is not quite what we seek here; nevertheless, we are in no position to take liberties with it at least until we understand the factors involved. The prevalent willingness to "try anything," instead of becoming a liberating force, often only produces a form of architectural sensationalism.

We are in no danger of producing a sterile and barren architecture. Our threat lies in the other direction. Reacting to the exuberance and richness of the area we are inclined to encase poorly articulated skeletons in heavy surface effects that have nothing to do with design integrity. This is true whether it is a chair or a building we are examining. It is certainly true that the skeletal approach which has characterized most good European design is probably not sufficient for us psychologically. At the same time we must at least understand the necessity for honestly revealed structure which is one of the prerequisites of good design. In our anxiety to appear sufficiently "rich" we camouflage our bad skeletons with endless textures and materials. Poor craftsmanship, paucity of imagination and an inability to think simply and structurally are covered with a heavy gravy of surface effects.

We do want rich and handsome buildings; but lightly and honestly expressed structure is the only skeleton on which the flesh hangs well.

During the last seventy-five years there has been evolving a concept of building which has placed human needs, structural honesty and a new understanding of space before any other stylistic considerations. This development has been diverse and often conflicting. Vital personalities and pioneers have made their great contributions to the swelling stream of a growing tradition. This new tradition, at first either denied or ignored, has emerged as the basis of a new architecture throughout the world. Like all rebellion, this development has often been self-conscious and even incomplete. We in California, especially the younger designers, have the great opportunity to inherit this treasure of beliefs, ideas, and discoveries and to carry further their logical development. We cannot take these researches for granted or dismiss them with superficial understanding. If we are going to develop an architecture worthy of the terrain and the potential living pattern, we must be stern in our self-criticism and ask ourselves many questions.

Are these forms we are using integrated and honestly conditioned by the problem we are solving, or are they simply the residue of past solutions? Is this design in front of me just fashion, gesture and expediency, or is it at least an attempt at reflection of the organic quality of nature itself? We all can ask ourselves these questions, whether we are designers of buildings or chairs.

Although I am asking for a bit of soul-searching on the part of the designers, it is also true that some self-scrutiny would do no harm to the manufacturers, especially in the field of home furnishings. With only a few exceptions, the planning and production of furniture in the local area is done with remarkable shortsightedness. Eastern designs are brazenly stolen, thickened up and sold as "California" modern. Designs just "grow," and rarely is a trained designer consulted. With the East languishing for California designs, we continually affront them with half-baked reflections of their own work.

As to any sort of coordinated program of research and design, such as made the California clothing fashions a world-wide influence, so far there is nothing visible. This is not true of ceramics and textiles. Although they are usually produced by individuals or small concerns, they have made a distinct mark and often represent California at its best. These small industries reflect a care for craftsmanship and design quality which is rarely seen in the more ambitious manufacturing.

If we have truly digested the basic principles, we are then in a position to synthesize and add to their growth. California offers every opportunity for this growth. Everything about it is attuned to a magnificent flowering of architecture. All the elements that architecture was denied in the past are now sought by the new architecture in just that region where they abound. Sun, light, air, vista and natural growth surround us. If we can measure the richness of these natural advantages against an intellectually clarified understanding of the precepts of modern architecture, then will we produce something truly unique and worthy of the name California.

84

4

MERLE ARMITAGE
HIS MANY LOVES AND VARIED LIVES

Here are some intimate details not generally known of Armitage's life. He was a colorful impresario, lothario, and maverick designer. Armitage was in the forefront of those who were toppling tradition in book design during the thirties. His retinue of wives also reveals his versatility.

I CAN'T RECALL exactly when I first met Merle Armitage. It was well over sixty years ago and probably at the bookshop of Jake Zeitlin. An interesting and creative group of young iconoclasts used to gather there to look at books and exchange ideas. Of all the frequenters, Armitage was undoubtedly the most dynamic and outspoken. He was a renegade from the East who was vocally critical of the local culture. In a talk he gave to the California Art Club on March 4, 1929, he had harsh words for his newly adopted community: "Arriving in California from New York, I was appalled by the anemic, colorless art being produced in this remote and provincial Los Angeles area. Moral, social, and sentimental values were utterly confused with aesthetic values."

This talk made a great impression on those who gathered at the bookshop, and it was decided it should be published under Zeitlin's imprint. The title of the book was *The Aristocracy of Art*.

Typographically it was brutally bold, conceived by Grace Marion Brown with help from Grant Dahlstrom and Armitage. Its bold treatment undoubtedly influenced Armitage's style when he began designing books a few years later. Its publication aroused a good deal of interest and helped start the "small renaissance" in art, letters, and printing that developed, incredibly, in southern California during the Depression years of the 1930s.

Most of Armitage's activities and accomplishments have been recorded in two autobiographies and in books by his friends. What I remember are the more intimate aspects of his life and our long years of friendship.

He was an able and driving man, full of enthusiasm and energy. He was continually delving into and promoting a variety of activities. He was raised in the Midwest and had little formal education, but having an inquiring mind and a rambling curiosity, he absorbed an incredible knowledge of music, art, and literature. His friendships eventually encompassed a who's who in the arts. While still in his teens, he migrated to New York to work with the impresario and promoter, Charles L. Wagner. With foresight and imagination, these two promoted the United States careers of many who were to become household names — John McCormack, Amelita Galli-Curci, Mary Garden, Rosa Ponselle, Feodor Chaliapin, Leopold Stokowsky, Martha Graham, Arnold Schoenberg, and Igor Stravinsky.

Armitage was accused of occasionally using unethical schemes to get newspaper publicity for his clients in the cities where they were scheduled to appear. He admitted to planting occasional fictitious gossip to keep his clients' names in the news, but denied any responsibility for an episode that salvaged a tour he was handling for a Russian opera company. The tour had begun on the West Coast with little success and was in deep financial trouble by the time it arrived in Chicago.

...Armitage, sitting in his office in the old Louis Sullivan–designed Philharmonic Auditorium Building in Los Angeles with few scheduled events to occupy his time, began writing about artists he'd known. He soon converted his jottings into books, and in 1932 he wrote, designed, and printed books on Warren Newcombe, Maier-Krieg, Rockwell Kent, and Richard Day. He also compiled a book of the photographs of Edward Weston. He then induced Alfred A. Knopf and E. Weyhe to publish these books.

Thus was born a maverick designer who has had a considerable influence on the appearance of the modern book. Earlier he had been responsible for printed pieces done to promote his clients' theatrical appearances and shows. His book design followed the bold and flamboyant style he had used in these pieces. He was considered by traditional designers to be an outlaw and was often criticized, but he could not have cared less. He helped liberate American book typography from convention.

During the promotion of his book on Eugene Maier-Krieg, Merle visited Maier-Krieg's studio often. On these visits, Merle would sometimes drop by my studio, which was only a few blocks away. I had just returned from my apprenticeship in Paris to start The Ward Ritchie Press in a small printing studio behind my family home in South Pasadena. Merle and I would chat and exchange ideas about the craft in which we were both comparative novices.

I have never known a man with such drive and energy. He was overflowing with ideas for books to write or compile — books on Stravinsky, Schoenberg, Martha Graham, Millard Sheets, Picasso, Paul Klee, Jean Charlot, and on and on. He reveled in his new avocation and remarked to his friend Henry Miller, "I write books so I can design them." Miller, himself a maverick, surprisingly answered, "But your books have no tradition." That is true, but they were innovative, bold in concept with great variety in content and design.

Merle was an accomplished publicist, not only for his clients but for himself. He decided that his new career needed more exposure. He wrote to me, "Coming out of a clear sky, the firm of E. Weyhe, who have published about half of the 21 books I have designed, want me to do a book on them, and have suggested a title *21 — An Adventure in Book Designing*. There will be articles by a number of critics and bookmen and I would be very pleased if you could contribute to it. As you know, my approach has been to let the punishment fit the crime or let the subject of the book dictate its design and format. I have the greatest respect for book tradition, but believe in many cases certain forms are outmoded and empty, and when they are perpetuated, they tend to draw the spirit of the book back into periods of the past which have no identification with today."

The book was published under the title *Designed Books*. In addition to my article and those of a half-dozen friends such as Carl Zigrosser, Edwin Corle, and Manuel Komroff, it contained page reproductions from each of the books Armitage had designed up to the point of the book's publication in 1938. While most of the contributions were paeans of praise, as Merle wished from his friends, I attempted to analyze the factors involved in his break with tradition and how it evolved.

Merle sent copies of the book to many influential people, including George Macy, the director of the Limited Editions Club. Macy had started the club in 1928, just before the 1929 panic. The collecting of press books was then in vogue. His plan was to issue an edition of a classic each month to 1,500 subscribers. Each edition was to be illustrated by a well-known artist and printed by one of the world's fine printers. Macy was a superb salesman in print. His announcements of forthcoming books so whetted the appetites of his subscribers that his club weathered the Depression without too many problems.

While Macy was basically a conservative bookman, the innovative and modern designs of Armitage's books interested him.

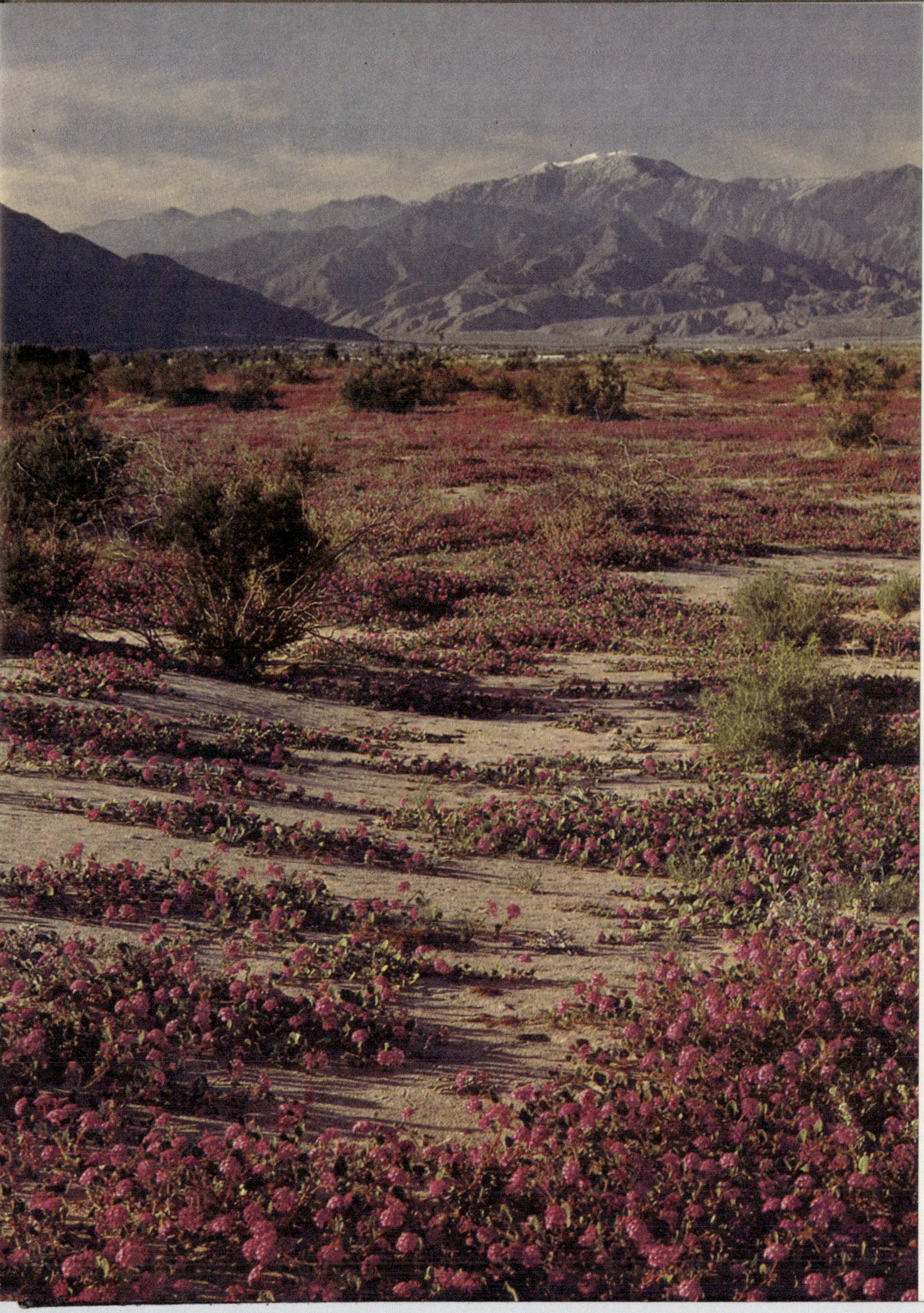

↑ Don Birrell at the Nut Tree, Vacaville, mid-1950s
← "Sand-verbena blooms in the Coachella Valley," from <u>Beautiful California</u>, 1971

Merle Armitage [1893–1975]. IGOR STRAVINSKY, 1936, 6 x 8 IN. Armitage, who lived primarily in Southern California from 1923 until his death in 1975, was a theater impresario who wore many significant hats—including that of book designer. With experience designing publicity materials for the performers he represented but no training in the book arts, he rejected traditional and modern typography and forged his own take on design. ¶ For Stravinsky, Armitage prints the beginning of a polemic about art on the cover and continues it inside, where he features an abundance of Stravinsky portraits—eight in all—shot by the young modernist photographer Edward Weston. Pose after pose of the great maestro testifies to the designer's appreciation of Weston as much as of Stravinsky. Rather than merely rejecting the tradition of the single dignified image, Armitage also seems to be winking at the notion of the celebrity portrait. ¶ A self-described bad boy of design, Armitage saw himself as revolutionizing the traditional book experience of looking, holding, and reading. Rather than offering an expected "final word" on the artist's practice, he fashioned an imaginative interrogation of Stravinsky's oeuvre with 11 texts by 11 writers—a bouquet, rather than a summation, of ideas.

STRAWINSKY

Strawinsky has said of his work, "There is nothing to discuss, nor to criticize; one does not criticize anybody or anything that is functioning. A nose is not manufactured; a nose just *is*. Thus, too, my art."

This is absolutely true—for Strawinsky.

It is true of any creative artist. The job is conceived; it is executed; and there it is, take it or leave it; the artist is not concerned for his attention has departed from that work and is probably concentrated on a new work, a work which, in the career of a Strawinsky, may be completely antithetical to the momentary comments of critics. There is no such thing as static art or static criticism, but the artist is always a pace ahead of the critic. He takes his hurdle by intuition, inspiration, genius, what you will—but the critic takes it with a more deliberate behaviorism of experience, reaction, comparison and logical decision. The artist is not geared to this pragmatic ratio and he breaks free and denies the value of comment, analysis, and discussion—denies the very reactions that his own intuitive white-hot speed have made inevitable.

It is impossible for Igor Strawinsky to create music in this world without creating the by-product of criticism. This book contains eleven critiques of his art, comments ranging from 1922 to 1936, some of which

PORTRAITS BY
EDWARD WESTON

Alvin Lustig [1915–1955] **and Ward Ritchie** [1905–1996]. <u>**THE GHOST IN THE UNDERBLOWS**</u>, 1940, 6 ¼ x 9 ⅛ IN. Ward Ritchie was an independent and adventurous publisher and printer who got his start just as modern design was gaining a foothold in Los Angeles. Alvin Lustig, whose celebrated career included time working for Ritchie, played a crucial role in giving American design a modern face. Lustig recognized California as a place free from the burden of the European cultural ideals that dominated the East Coast, and he credited this liberation for his ability to "see freshly and unencumbered."[1] Their collaboration on <u>The Ghost in the Underblows</u>, a suite of books that contains the poem of this name by Alfred Young Fisher, was a project financed by collector subscriptions.[2] Ritchie, who printed the book at his press, requested that Lustig design a different type-ornament composition for each of the 10 books. ¶ According to Ritchie, while others had used "printer's flowers" for centuries, nothing comparable to Lustig's arranging the texts themselves in decorative designs in lieu of illustrations had ever been done. "He created a new art form, virile, abstract, and colorful," Ritchie recalled.[3] In the end, Fisher's poem never found success equal to the design of its publication.

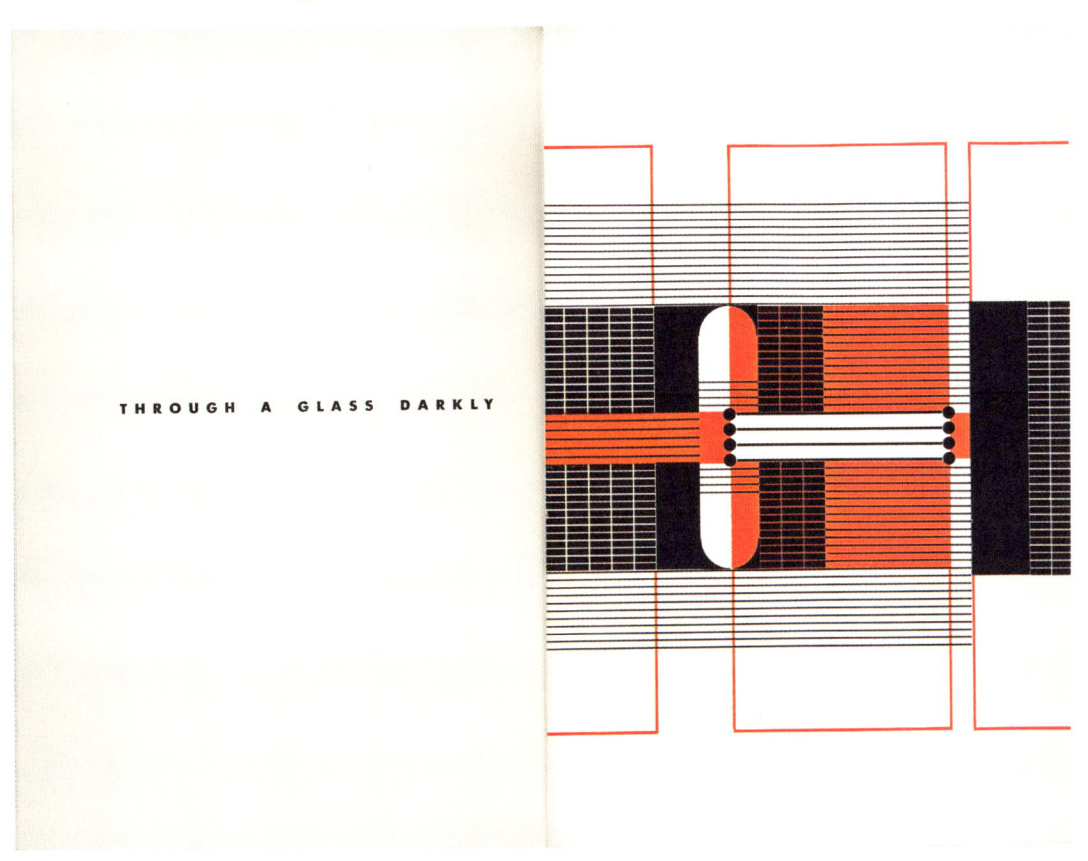

THE GHOST IN THE UNDERBLOWS

BY ALFRED YOUNG FISHER
EDITED WITH AN INTRODUCTION BY
LAWRENCE CLARK POWELL · DESIGNED BY
ALVIN LUSTIG AND PRINTED BY THE
WARD RITCHIE PRESS AT LOS ANGELES
CALIFORNIA · NINETEEN HUNDRED AND FORTY

THROUGH A GLASS DARKLY

Merle Armitage. <u>LOOKING BACKWARD</u>, **1941, 6 ¾ x 9 IN.**
Armitage received a commission from the bibliophiles of the Limited Editions Club to reinterpret Edward Bellamy's novel <u>Looking Backward</u> (1888), in which the protagonist falls into a deep, hypnotic sleep and finds himself transported 113 years into the future. In a fantastical leap of graphic production that matches the science-fiction theme, Armitage tried to imagine what books might look like in the year 2000—a vision that featured a shocking-yellow cover made from a new DuPont binding linen that was both "washable and vermin-proof." Meticulously printed by Ward Ritchie Press, the book included 14 vibrantly colored illustrations by Elise (Cavanna) printed on stock embossed with a custom watermark of the story's "time spiral." Armitage enclosed the volume in a slipcase made of an early clear plastic (Plasticle) that was quite expensive at the time.[4]

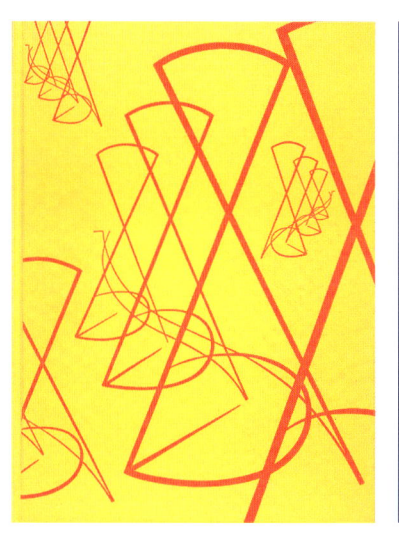

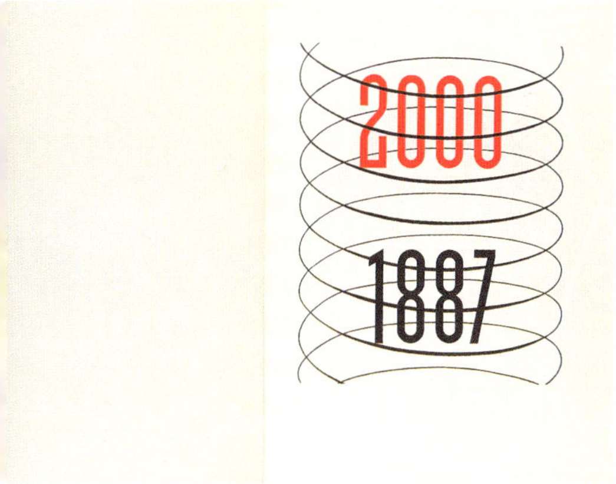

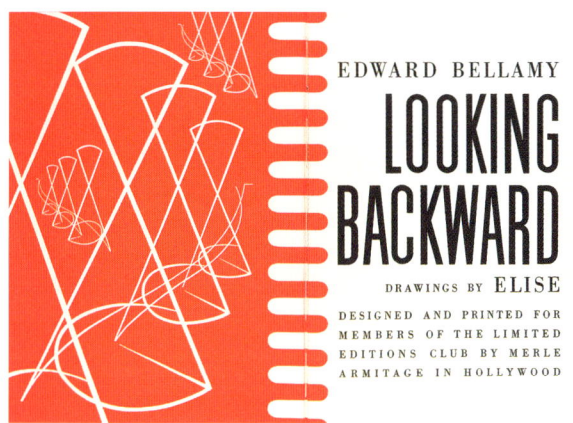

EDWARD BELLAMY
LOOKING BACKWARD
DRAWINGS BY ELISE

DESIGNED AND PRINTED FOR
MEMBERS OF THE LIMITED
EDITIONS CLUB BY MERLE
ARMITAGE IN HOLLYWOOD

2000
1887

SUNBAKED MODERNISM

Alvin Lustig. The embodiment of an independent mind, Lustig was one of a handful of California designers who became widely influential through diverse practices that included 2- and 3-D design, teaching, and writing. As an educator, he spawned a generation of designers in Los Angeles, including Lou Danziger, John Follis, Charles Kratka, and Fred Usher, who were stimulated by the way he connected design to larger ideas in the culture beyond art and commerce, including sociology and psychology. ¶ These three projects represent only a small sample of Lustig's prolific hand. Lustig embraced his California roots, acknowledging the "sense of exhilaration and growth that charged the very air" and provided a "heightened sense of life."[5] ¶ **NEUROTICA LOGO, 1947.** Composed of a scrappy blotch with scratchy nervous type, this logo emblemized a small independent publication of particular interest to the Beats—one group among many in California that proposed an alternative to mainstream culture. The logo suggests a rent in the fabric of refinement and dignity that serves as a peephole to a conversation that lies beyond. ¶ **GRAPHIC PATTERN, 1950, 42 x 28 IN.** Lustig often sketched patterns evocative of African artifacts for his textile designs, but this bit of "Lustigiana" never made it beyond his studio wall. It survives because fellow designer Usher rescued it from the trash, not knowing (then or now) what the pattern might have been intended for.[6] ¶ **UPA LOGO, 1946.** The United Productions of America logo, the first of two that Lustig designed for the Los Angeles–based animation studio, has the look of much of the modern furniture that Lustig and others in Southern California were creating from materials at hand—in this case, iron rods and balls.

SUNBAKED MODERNISM

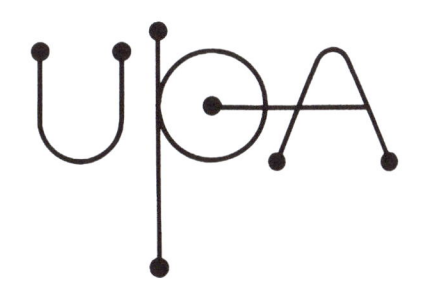

Alvin Lustig. NEW DIRECTIONS BOOK COVERS: FLOWERS OF EVIL, 1946; THREE LIVES, 1945; THE WANDERER, 1946; THE DAY OF THE LOCUST, 1950. NEW DIRECTIONS MODERN READER BOOK COVER: CAMINO REAL, 1953. EACH 5 x 7¼ IN. In 1940, Lustig began designing for the publisher New Directions, where he produced a body of work that significantly influenced book cover design for decades to come. Rather than resorting to the conventional depiction of a scene or character from the story, Lustig employed a more symbolic, abstract language that, as he put it, "could quickly summarize the spirit of each book.... Sometimes the symbols are quite obvious and taken from the subject itself. Others are more evasive, and attempt to characterize the emotional content of the book." Despite this experimental approach, Lustig did not shy away from the commercial purpose of design, declaring that his aim was to "catch the roving eye of the potential buyer."[7]

SUNBAKED MODERNISM

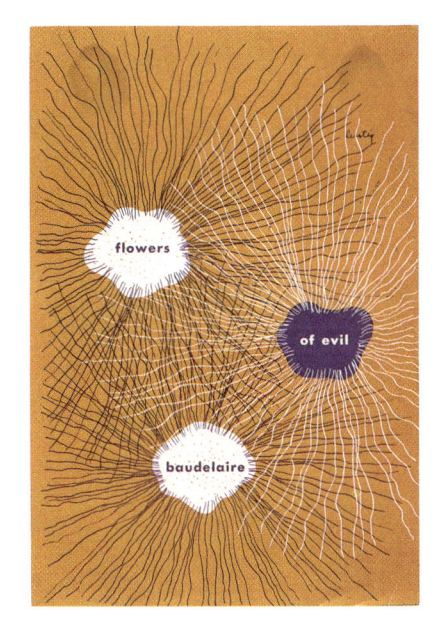

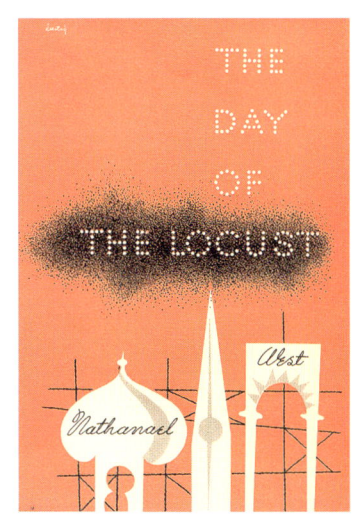

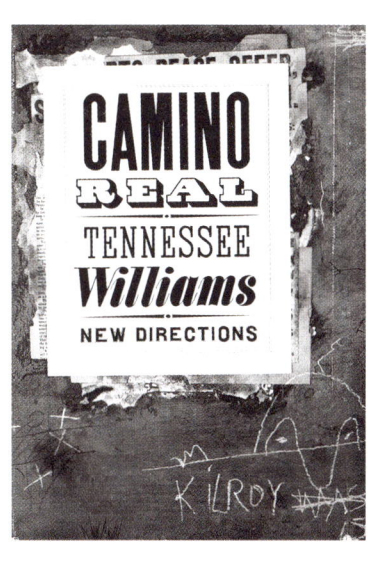

Herbert Matter [1907–1984]. **ARTS & ARCHITECTURE COVERS, JULY 1945 AND MAY 1948, EACH 10 x 12 ¾ IN.** Matter immigrated to Los Angeles in 1943 to work as a photographer and graphic designer for the Eames Office, where he remained until 1946.[8] Yet he was possibly influenced more by his native Switzerland than California: he brought with him a modern graphic sensibility distinct from what was going on in Los Angeles at the time. Working at Arts & Architecture along with Alvin Lustig (who designed the magazine's logo in 1942) and John Follis, Matter contributed to the magazine's layout and typography and designed the two covers depicted here. While the peppermint-candy swirls for July 1945 seem in keeping with visual abstractions typical of Matter's European design training, the cactuslike graphic for May 1948 suggests that the forms and shapes of California's natural environment had entered his visual vocabulary. ¶ Arts & Architecture played a central role in cultivating a culture of modern design and taste in Southern California, while putting local architects and architecture on the international map. It also increased consumer demand for products with a modern aesthetic, such as lighting and furniture, and therefore was crucial in establishing a market that would sustain local graphic designers with modern sensibilities and approaches.[9]

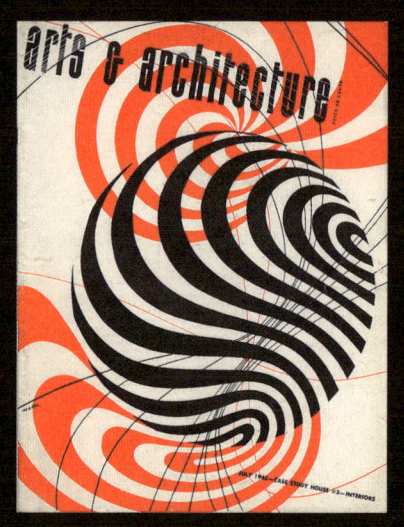

arts & architecture

PRICE 50 CENTS

MAY 1948

Bjorn Aronson [dates unknown]. **POSTERS FOR DISNEYLAND HOTEL, 1956; SKYWAY, 1956; AND AUTOPIA, 1955, EACH 36 x 54 IN.** Advertising the Disneyland Hotel and Tomorrowland theme-park attractions, these large, colorful, silk-screen posters suggest a design mash-up—modernist traditions churned through the Disney machine of nostalgia and futuristic utopianism. Inspirations included the aesthetics of Works Progress Administration murals and world's fair promotional materials, as well as Aronson's work as a travel-poster designer. ¶ The Tomorrowland posters reflect Walt Disney's vision of a place that celebrated the "constructive things to come."[10] In the case of Autopia, the idealized driving experience seemed to include congestion-free highways that anyone—even children—could joyfully navigate. (Incidentally, architectural historian and critic Reyner Banham gave highway culture the name "Autopia" in laying out the four types of environments, or ecologies, that define L.A.'s built environment.[11]) ¶ The distinctive visual oomph of these modern-ish delicacies was not lost on the local design community. Deborah Sussman said that even her former employer Charles Eames paid attention to Disney's graphics, because they were so well done. As she puts it: "You could laugh with it, rather than at it."[12]

STAY AT Disneyland Hotel

THE CONVENIENT-LEISURELY WAY TO VISIT WALT DISNEY'S MAGIC KINGDOM

RESTAURANT * SHOPS * SWIMMING POOL * PLAYGROUND
OPEN 7 DAYS A WEEK

© WALT DISNEY PRODUCTIONS

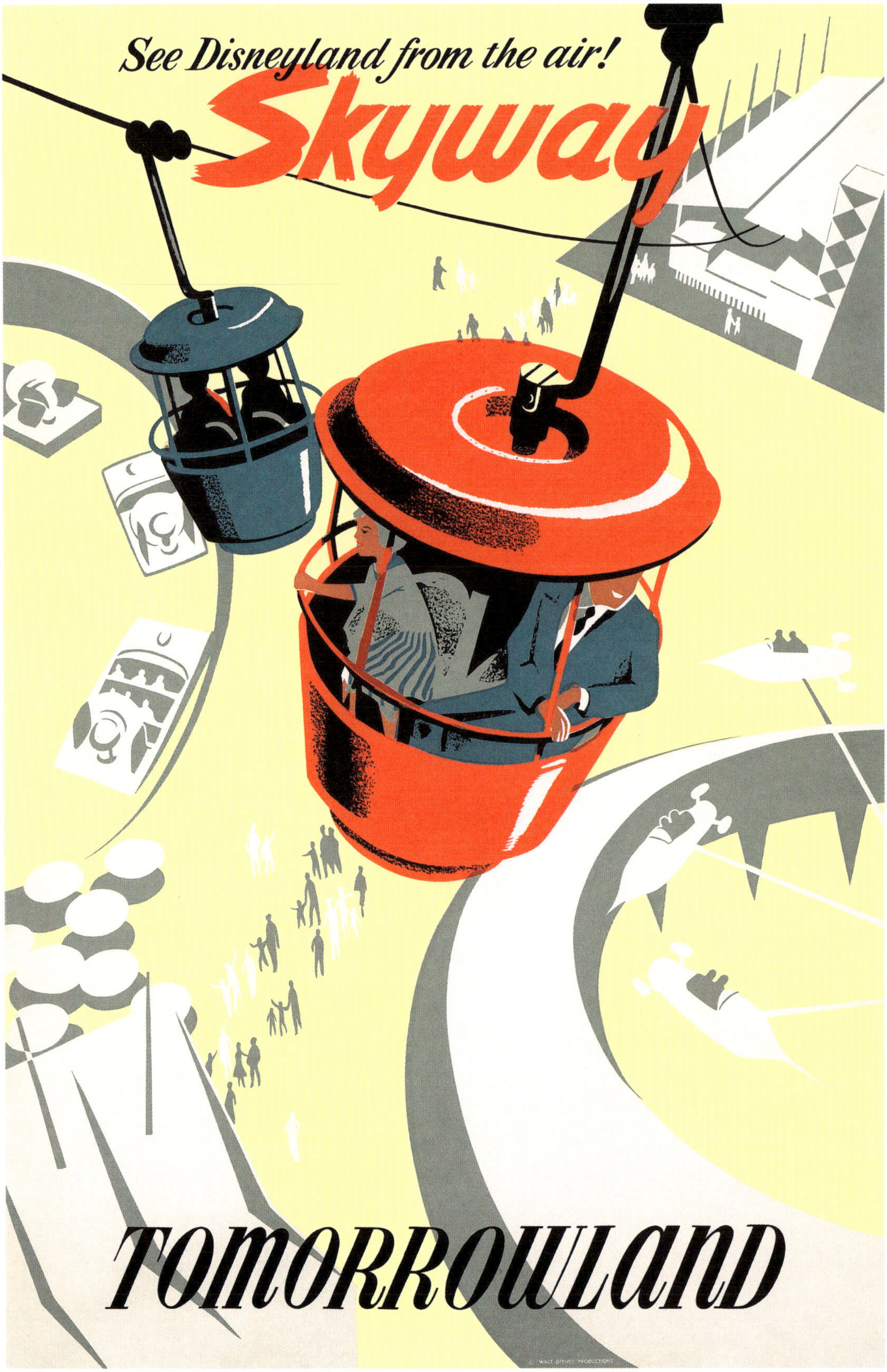
See Disneyland from the air!
Skyway
TOMORROWLAND

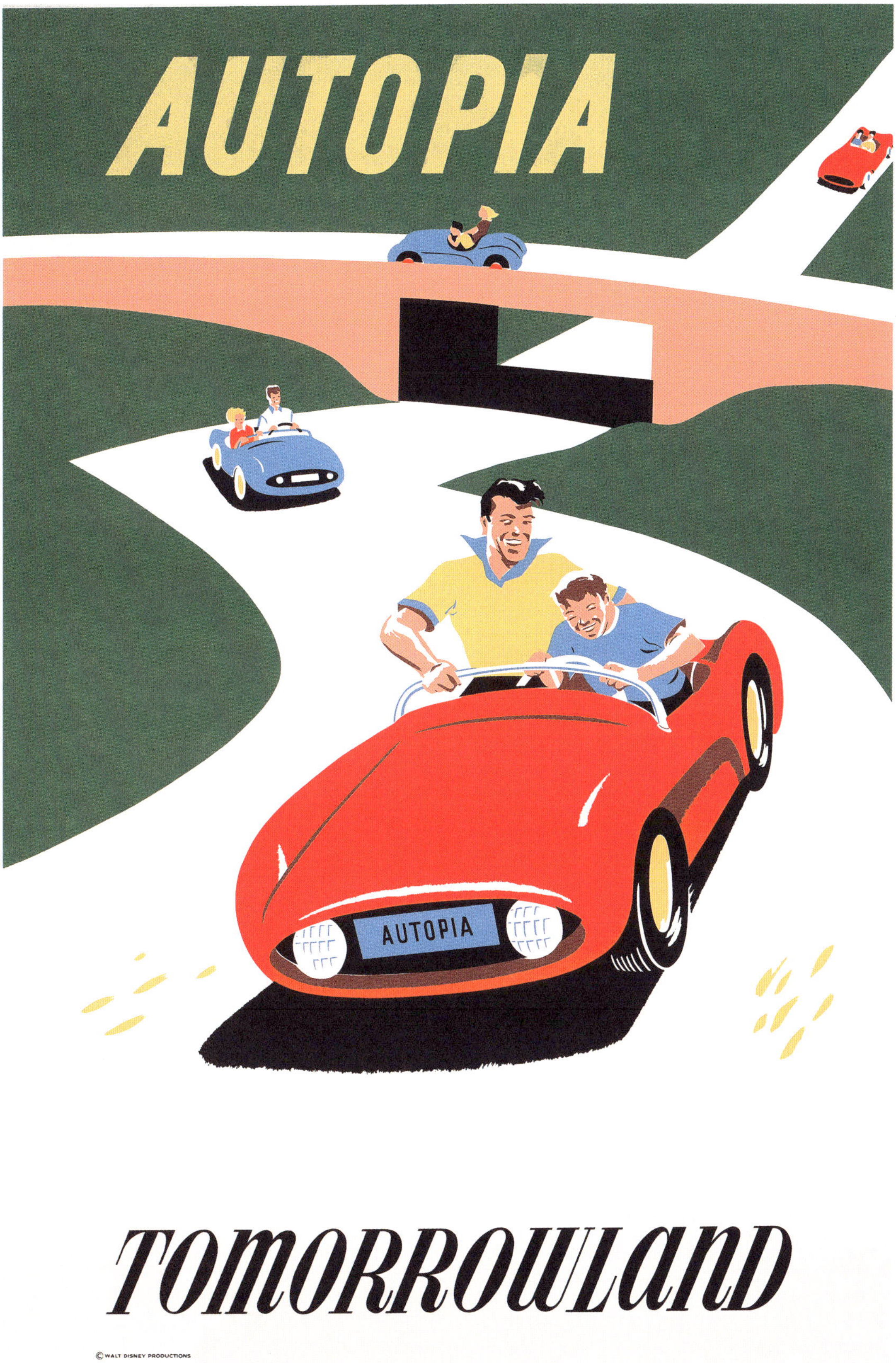
AUTOPIA
AUTOPIA
TOMORROWLAND
© WALT DISNEY PRODUCTIONS

John Follis [1923–1994]. **ARTS & ARCHITECTURE COVERS, 1950–57, EACH 10 x 12¾ IN.** Follis designed and illustrated many covers for this publication, first, from 1942 to 1944, for art director Alvin Lustig, and then as art director himself. Follis's covers display his bold yet refined sense of composition and his great sensitivity to form and color. The same sensibility marks the planters he created for Architectural Pottery, the operation he cofounded in 1950 and whose elegant modern forms became icons of California's outdoor leisure lifestyle. Like his modernist colleagues, he believed good design could improve the world.[13] ¶ Follis was one of Lustig's many former students who went on to shape the L.A. design scene, and these magazine covers only hint at the wide range of his talents and the types of projects to which he applied his gifts. Follis is credited as among the first to merge graphic-design principles with large-scale architecture, making him a pioneer in the establishment of the field of environmental graphics.[14] ¶ Along with other creators of A&A covers, Follis founded the Society of Contemporary Designers, an organization both ironic and serious that created a community of designers before the establishment of local professional organizations such as the Art Directors Club and the L.A. chapter of the American Institute of Graphic Arts (AIGA).[15]

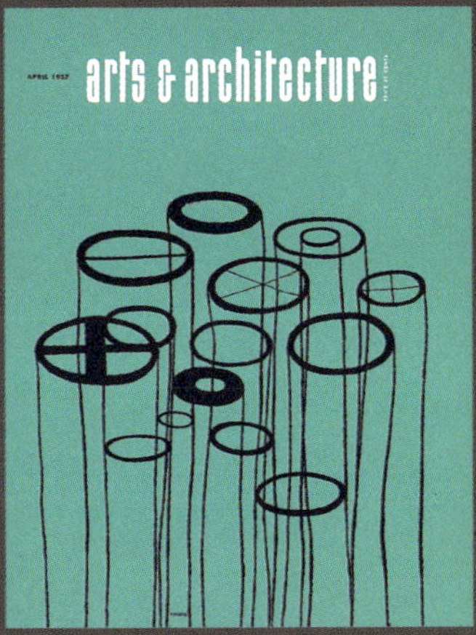
APRIL 1957
arts & architecture

arts & architecture
FEBRUARY 1957

MAY 1955
arts & architecture

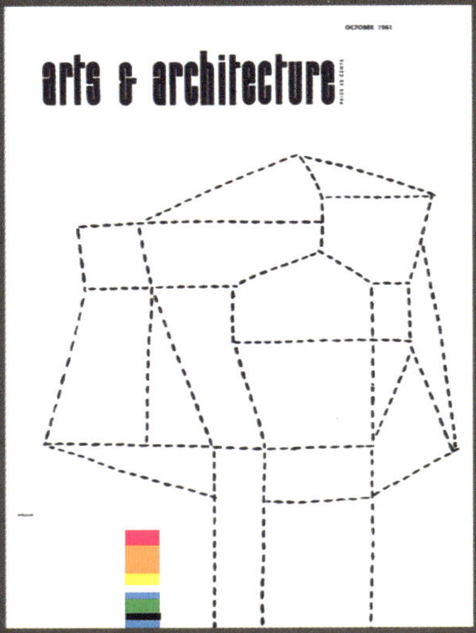
OCTOBER 1961
arts & architecture

arts & architecture

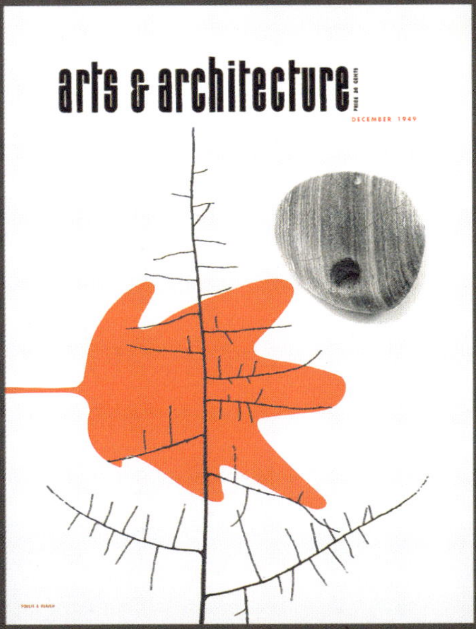
arts & architecture
DECEMBER 1949

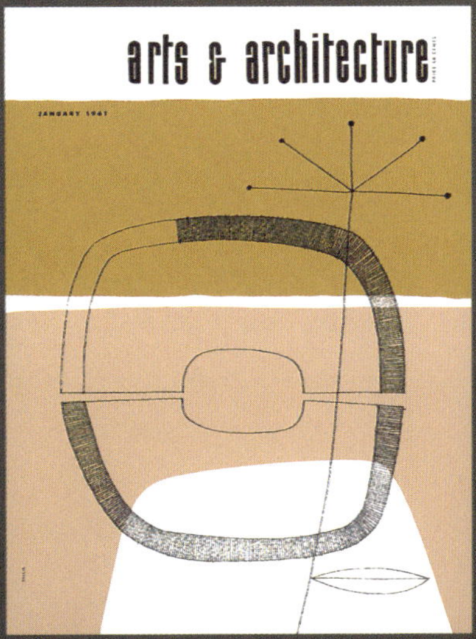
arts & architecture
JANUARY 1961

Frederick Usher [1923–2009]. In reflecting on what distinguished California design from that of the East Coast, Usher commented that California embraced a "polymorphic society—one that acknowledged that everybody is unique or different." He found the same quality of openness in terms of design when he came to Los Angeles as a teenager and then launched his career.[16] ¶ Initially self-taught, Usher enrolled at Art Center College of Design in 1946, after his military service, to "become a polished and credentialed designer." In his words, he had a "nagging feeling that a new world was building." He was wary at first of instructor Alvin Lustig's position on the potential for design to have broad social impact but eventually became a convert; later on, he furthered Lustig's ideas in articles for the AIGA newsletter and Arts & Architecture magazine.[17] ¶ **FELIX CANDELA: SHELL FORMS EXHIBITION CATALOGUE, 1957, 9 x 5 ½ IN.** This publication accompanied an exhibition of the revolutionary work of Spanish architect Felix Candela, known for developing a method for engineering parabolic forms from thin concrete. ¶ **MONTEREY BAY AQUARIUM LOGO, 1950.** This elegant two-color graphic rendering of "the growing tip of a giant kelp frond" was a particular favorite of Usher's; however, the aquarium ended up using a one-color version. ¶ **ARTS & ARCHITECTURE COVER SKETCH, 1950, APPROX. 10 x 12 IN.** Usher did quite a few covers for Arts & Architecture, although this particular proposal was rejected. According to David Travers, who took over the magazine from founder John Entenza in 1962, the cover designs weren't intended so much to echo the content of a given issue as to "stimulate newsstand sales." And as Entenza explained, the publication's ambition was to "present good contemporary design… to a largely lay audience and nudge its professional and architectural student subscribers toward a truer path." Why this compelling design didn't fit the bill remains a mystery.[18]

FELIX CANDELA: SHELL FORMS

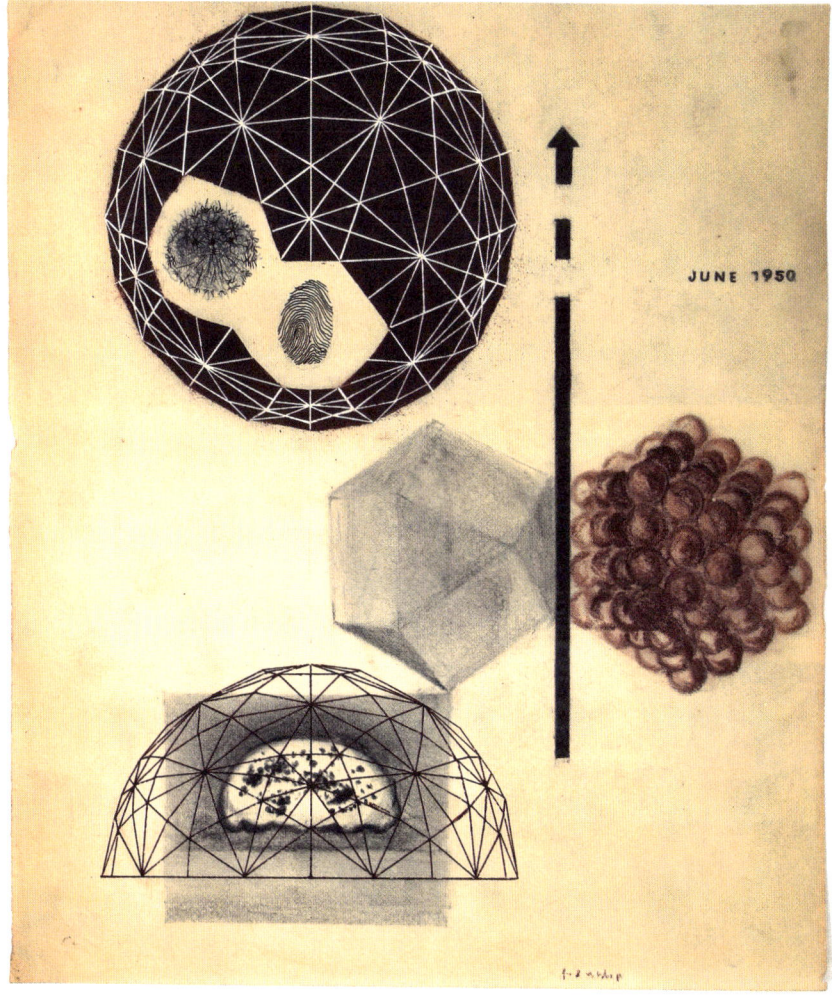

JUNE 1950

SUNBAKED MODERNISM

Louis Danziger [b. 1923]. **GENERAL LIGHTING AD, DECEMBER 1949. Allen Porter** [b. 1926]. **GRUEN LIGHTING AD, OCTOBER 1952. EACH 8¼ x 5½ IN.** The photographic experiments for these and other ads that appeared in Arts & Architecture between 1949 and 1953 represent collaborations between Danziger and Porter with architectural photographer Marvin Rand. Danziger devised a technique of using multiple images as an undergraduate at Art Center College of Design. ¶ "In 1947, when I was studying with Alvin Lustig… he had us design a magazine opening spread for [an imaginary article about] James Joyce's The Dubliners," he recalled. "We were teamed with an Art Center photo student, and it was then that I developed this way of working. Herbert Matter's tourist brochures with the multiple images of skiers probably inspired it. We photographed some small boys running toward us, a church, and photocopies of old engravings of cathedral windows. I think there were five negatives in all, which we then combined in the darkroom. It was wonderful. Alvin, loath to ever give fulsome praise to anything, said in the class critique, 'You get A+ for what is on paper but those are not Irish boys.' I wanted to kill!" ¶ For these ads, Rand photographed the lighting fixtures, then he and Danziger enlarged and combined negatives using 10 or more exposures to achieve an image. Danziger later turned the account over to Allen Porter, with whom he shared a studio.[19] Porter had studied at the New Bauhaus in Chicago (now the IIT Institute of Design) and came to Los Angeles in the 1950s in hopes of seeing more modern design. He found it not only in the work of Danziger but also in the furniture displayed in the storefronts of West Hollywood.[20]

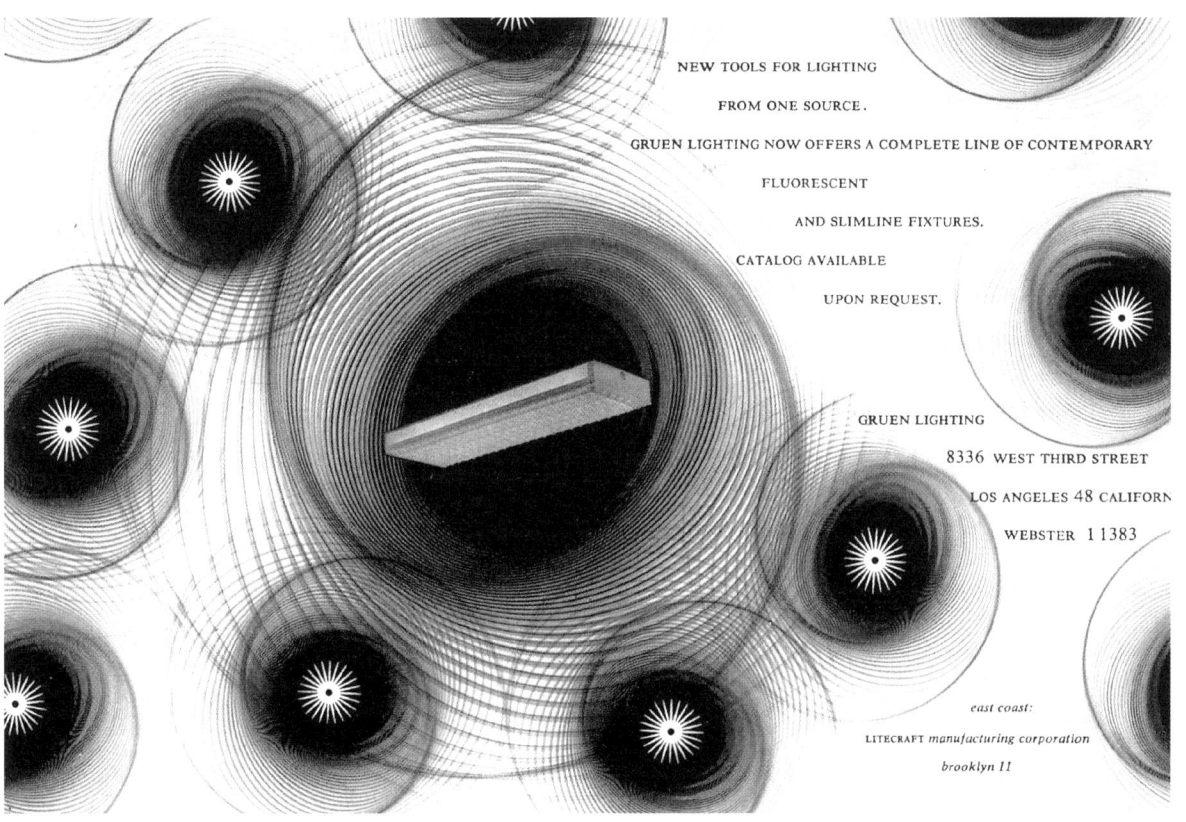

GENERAL LIGHTING COMPANY · CONTEMPORARY LIGHTING FIXTURES

WESTERN DIV. OF LITECRAFT MFG. CO., N.J.
8336 W. 3RD ST., L.A. 48, WY. 2275

NEW TOOLS FOR LIGHTING
FROM ONE SOURCE.
GRUEN LIGHTING NOW OFFERS A COMPLETE LINE OF CONTEMPORARY
FLUORESCENT
AND SLIMLINE FIXTURES.
CATALOG AVAILABLE
UPON REQUEST.

GRUEN LIGHTING
8336 WEST THIRD STREET
LOS ANGELES 48 CALIFORN
WEBSTER 1 1383

east coast:
LITECRAFT *manufacturing corporation*
brooklyn 11

Eames Office. GIANT HOUSE OF CARDS, 1953, 7 x 11 IN. This colorful 20-card deck, designed by Charles Kratka with Deborah Sussman, was a follow-up to the smaller House of Cards, which Charles and Ray Eames produced with John and Marilyn Neuhart in 1952. The package describes the cards as "Colorful Panels to Build With," each printed with "a Graphic Design Taken from the Arts * The Sciences * The World Around Us."[21] The mention of California modernist design usually brings the Eameses to mind, at least in the popular consciousness. Having met at Cranbrook Academy, in Michigan, the Missouri-born Charles and California native Ray married and moved to Los Angeles in 1941. Like their design contemporaries, the Eameses disliked L.A.'s commercial glitz and faddishness, and yet the Giant House of Cards, while in line with modernist tastes, exudes the playful spirit of pop culture.[22]

Giant House of Cards displayed in the social room at Immaculate Heart College, mid- to late 1960s

SUNBAKED MODERNISM

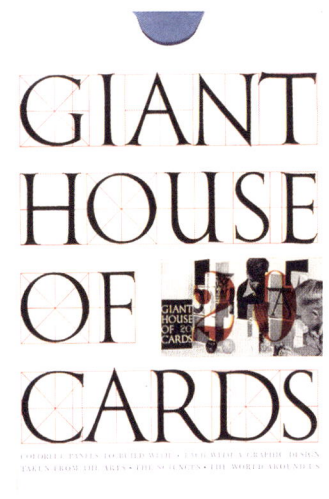

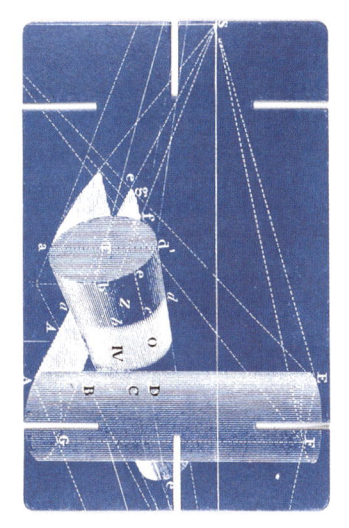

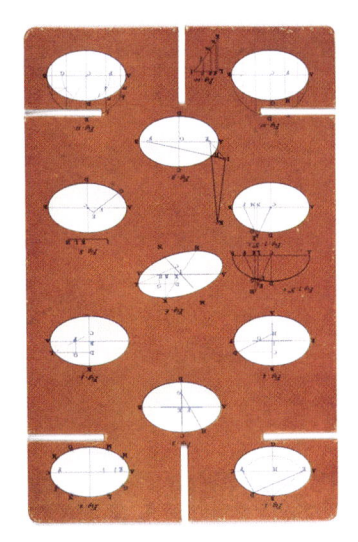

Louis Danziger. GELVATEX PAINT AD, 1956, 8½ x 11 IN. This colorful ad uses text listing the addresses of the company's 300 dealerships to create images of a tree, a house, and a fence. It also includes the Gelvatex logo, which Danziger designed as well. ¶ Originally from New York, Danziger studied with Alvin Lustig at Art Center but acquired much of his design education through his own initiative, driven by his many interests and expansive curiosity. Designer Deborah Sussman remembers him as a "hot number and a guru to everyone." Danziger belonged to a circle of California graphic designers—including Lustig, Ray and Charles Eames, and Saul Bass—that achieved national recognition. Like Lustig, Danziger was an influential educator. With his CalArts colleague Keith Godard, he developed what many in the field say was the first class on graphic design history to be offered in the United States. ¶ This ad for Sunset magazine was commissioned by the Dreyfus Agency, which, fittingly, had an office in architect Rudolph Schindler's legendary residence on King's Road, in West Hollywood. Small advertising agencies played a significant role in the history of graphic design in California. Large firms like McCann Erickson handled their design needs in-house, often with little inclination toward modernist ideas. But agencies such as Dreyfus and Hal Stebbins appreciated modern design and hired those, like Danziger, able to produce it.[23]

Louis Danziger

There's more to Gelvatex than meets the eye! Look sharply and you may find the name of your neighborhood independent paint dealer in the house above. If you're planning on painting, he's the man to see. He's an expert on paint, and because he's an independent paint dealer he isn't restricted to the paints of just *one* manufacturer, but can suggest any paint he thinks is best for your job. We're proud of the fact that independent paint dealers recommend Gelvatex as the finest paint for stucco and masonry surfaces . . . and that more architects in California specify Gelvatex for stucco and masonry than any other paint. Follow the advice of the experts, paint your house with Gelvatex, first and finest vinyl emulsion paint. **Gelvatex** Coatings Corporation, Anaheim, California.

Don Birrell [1922–2005]. **NUT TREE GRAPHICS AND ENVIRONMENTAL DESIGN, VACAVILLE, CALIFORNIA.** BELOW: **MID-1960s**; RIGHT: **MID- TO LATE 1950s.** A World War II vet, the California-born Birrell attended L.A.'s Chouinard Art Institute thanks to the G.I. Bill and graduated in 1949. From 1953 to 1990, he served as Nut Tree's design director with a mandate to modernize the image of the western-themed roadside attraction and local produce vendor. Working closely with Nut Tree co-owner Bob Powers, Jr., Birrell developed a playful extravaganza for the small Northern California town of Vacaville that featured three themed dining rooms, a gift shop that sold curios from around the globe, and children's activities including a train. Among the modern design delights were graphics by Birrell, furnishings by the Eames Office, and a wall hanging composed of dolls Marilyn Neuhart had produced for Alexander Girard's Textiles & Objects shop in New York. One local booster credited Birrell with putting Vacaville "on the map of artistic endeavor."[24]

SUNBAKED MODERNISM

Advertising Designers (Louis Frimkess [1912–1979], Ken Parkhurst [b. 1925], and Edd Smith [dates unknown].) <u>A DICTIONARY FOR MODERNS</u>, 1956, 4½ x 7 IN. Frimkess, an advertising art director, and Smith, a typographer, founded the aptly named Advertising Designers in the early 1950s, later bringing on Parkhurst, who had worked for Alvin Lustig.[25] Together, they created a collective of designers, illustrators, and typographers that raised the bar for the industry. Lou Danziger recalls Advertising Designers as "the best art studio around in the 1950s and onward. Frimkess was an early advocate of modern design in this area."[26] ¶ Advertising Designers spearheaded a revolution in annual-report design, transforming bland legal documents into flashy PR vehicles that required close collaborations among designers, writers, accountants, and printers. From that point on, the annual report become a major source of creative production and revenue for design studios across the country. Parkhurst very likely first introduced this new approach while he worked for Lustig: Danziger remembers that "prior to Ken, almost all annual reports were designed in-house by printers, and were pretty dry, traditional, and bad. I don't remember ever seeing a 'designed' annual report prior to Parkhurst's."[27] ¶ <u>A Dictionary for Moderns</u>, an intimately scaled 40-page booklet, was written by Hal Stebbins, who often hired Advertising Designers, and printed at Ward Ritchie Press. A letterpress project, edition of 50, it was likely created as a holiday gift for Stebbins's self-named agency. The booklet presents a cynic's worldview, with charming but wry slogans such as "Advertising: Free speech—except that you pay for it," "Ears: Through these portals pass the most beautiful lies in the world," "Eyes: A Technicolor camera that never needs reloading," and "Hollywood: A place where people actually believe what they write about themselves."

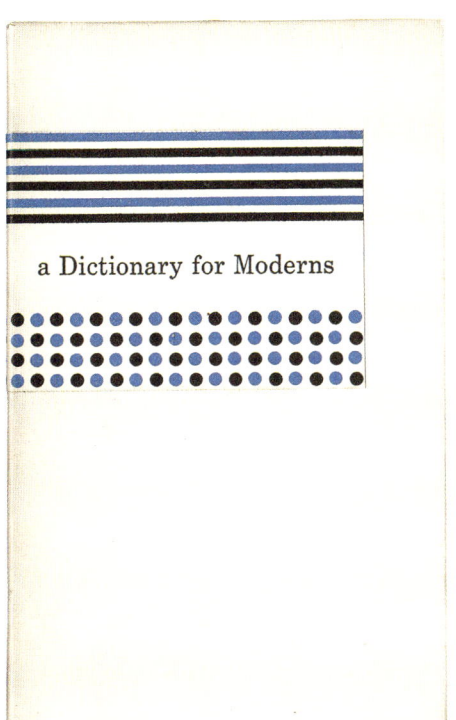

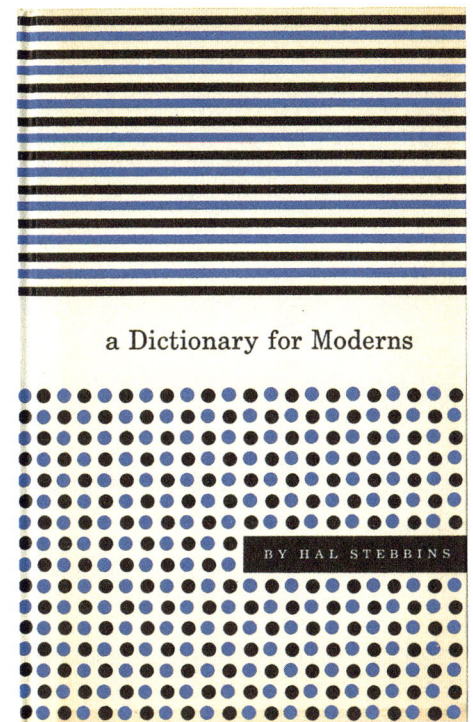

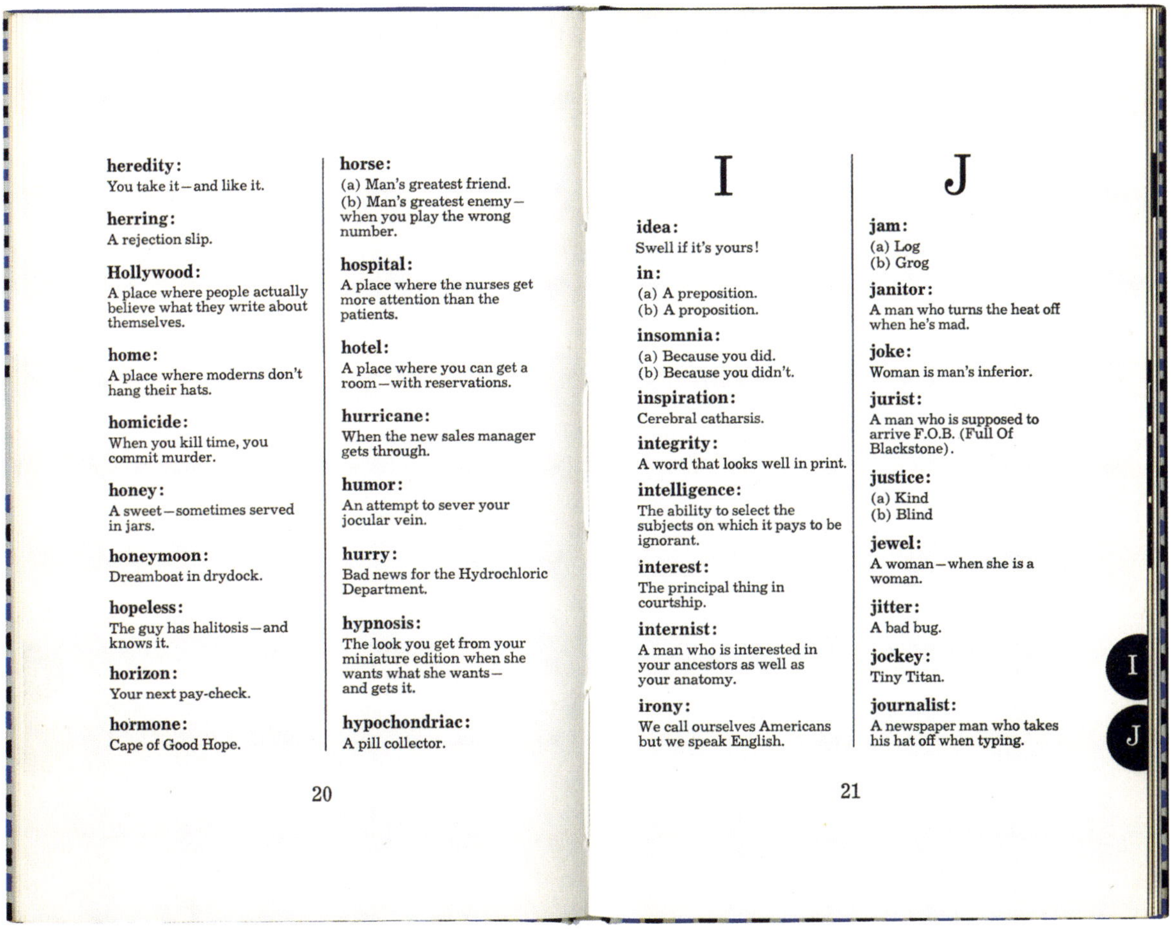

heredity: You take it—and like it.	**horse:** (a) Man's greatest friend. (b) Man's greatest enemy—when you play the wrong number.
herring: A rejection slip.	
Hollywood: A place where people actually believe what they write about themselves.	**hospital:** A place where the nurses get more attention than the patients.
home: A place where moderns don't hang their hats.	**hotel:** A place where you can get a room—with reservations.
homicide: When you kill time, you commit murder.	**hurricane:** When the new sales manager gets through.
honey: A sweet—sometimes served in jars.	**humor:** An attempt to sever your jocular vein.
honeymoon: Dreamboat in drydock.	**hurry:** Bad news for the Hydrochloric Department.
hopeless: The guy has halitosis—and knows it.	**hypnosis:** The look you get from your miniature edition when she wants what she wants—and gets it.
horizon: Your next pay-check.	
hormone: Cape of Good Hope.	**hypochondriac:** A pill collector.

I

idea:
Swell if it's yours!

in:
(a) A preposition.
(b) A proposition.

insomnia:
(a) Because you did.
(b) Because you didn't.

inspiration:
Cerebral catharsis.

integrity:
A word that looks well in print.

intelligence:
The ability to select the subjects on which it pays to be ignorant.

interest:
The principal thing in courtship.

internist:
A man who is interested in your ancestors as well as your anatomy.

irony:
We call ourselves Americans but we speak English.

J

jam:
(a) Log
(b) Grog

janitor:
A man who turns the heat off when he's mad.

joke:
Woman is man's inferior.

jurist:
A man who is supposed to arrive F.O.B. (Full Of Blackstone).

justice:
(a) Kind
(b) Blind

jewel:
A woman—when she is a woman.

jitter:
A bad bug.

jockey:
Tiny Titan.

journalist:
A newspaper man who takes his hat off when typing.

Cal Anderson [dates unknown]. **INVITATION, 1956, DIMENSIONS UNKNOWN.** Best known for his design of posters, stage sets, and costumes for the San Francisco Ballet, Anderson studied at California College of Arts and Crafts and, in 1948, at Art Center College of Design with Alvin Lustig. ¶ This invitation was a call for entries for the experimental section of the 8th Annual Exhibition of Advertising Art, in San Francisco. The competition sought examples of advertising art, design, and photography "carried out without restraint." ¶ Anderson's scratched letterforms and translucency have the hallmarks of Lustig's encouragement toward visual invention. The white lettering and black copy were printed on one side of a translucent sheet that was then folded to complete the letterforms. According to graphic design historian Steve Reoutt, "Cal did this project in '56, and in '59 [the legendary designer Robert] Brownjohn [of Brownjohn], Chermayeff & Geismar did a similar thing. I don't think Brownjohn copied Cal's idea, but at least it shows that in some cases the west was ahead of the east."[28]

SUNBAKED MODERNISM

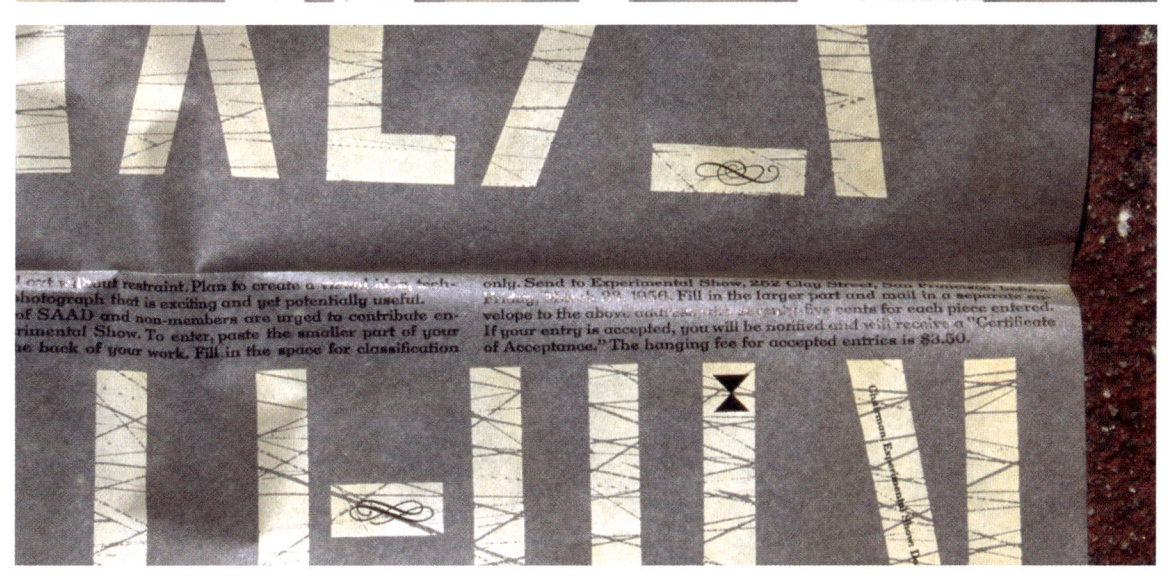

Robert Tyler Lee [1910–1987] and Georg Olden [1920–1975]. LASSIE AND THE GALE STORM SHOW INTERSTITIAL CARDS, 1958. In the late 1950s, the financial incentives for relocating TV production to California enticed westward movement within the industry.[29] Presciently, in 1952, CBS had realized its Television City in West Hollywood—the first studio to put TV production and broadcast facilities under one roof. In-house graphic design was part of the setup. Yet title design in California was handled by Georg Olden, the art director back in New York in charge of on-air graphics, an arrangement that would explain why Olden shared art direction credit with California designer Robert Tyler Lee.[30] Among interstitial cards, a standard way to let viewers know what programming was "coming up next," these examples stand out for their particular charm and sophisticated modern idiom in a time when many local TV stations where cobbling together more "low brow" versions of their own.[31]

THE GALE STORM SHOW

LASSIE

SUNBAKED MODERNISM

Eames Office. DAY OF THE DEAD TITLE CARD, 1957. One of many films made by the Eames Office, Day of the Dead was produced at the prompting of renowned designer Alexander Girard, close friend, inspiration, and occasional collaborator of Ray and Charles Eames, and sponsored by the Museum of International Folk Art, in Santa Fe. Girard, a folk-art junkie, wanted to identify "the fantastic stuff" made for the annual Mexican celebration of All Souls' Day. The film documented the various handmade objects used in the Day of the Dead ritual. ¶ For the film titles, the camera moved around a single card, designed by Eames employee Deborah Sussman, that had nine different sections featuring credits and other information. Typography and letterpress ornaments, which Sussman acquired in Mexico, flavored the design with the sensibility of the printers located in Mexico City's Santo Domingo Plaza.[32] In 1530, this locale was home to the first printing press in the Americas and to this day remains a center of small-press activity. The overall effect of the card, suggesting a broadside printed with traditional letterpress border ornaments interspersed with wooden type, reflects Sussman's graphic sense of play, Charles Eames's proclivity for uppercase fonts, and the design firm's overall knack for marrying folk and modern sensibilities.

THE MUSEUM OF INTERNATIONAL FOLK ART
SANTA FE, NEW MEXICO

PRESENTS

A Festival in Mexico

MUSIC
COMPOSED AND PLAYED BY
LAURINDO ALMEIDA

MADE BY
CHARLES AND RAY EAMES
1957

DAY OF THE DEAD
NOVEMBER 2

2 NOVIEMBRE
DÍA DE LOS MUERTOS
TECHNICOLOR

ASSISTANCE IN MEXICO
GATHERING MATERIAL AND TAKING PHOTOGRAPHS
SUSAN AND ALEXANDER GIRARD
DEBORAH SUSSMAN

FIELD ANTHROPOLOGIST, VICTOR J. SEGOVIA
OF MEXICO, D.F.

NARRATION READ BY
EDGAR KAUFMANN JR.

PRODUCTION CREW
PARKE MEEK
JOHN WHITNEY

ACKNOWLEDGEMENTS TO
MUSEO NACIONAL DE ARTES E INDUSTRIAS POPULARES
DR. DANIEL F. RUBÍN DE LA BORBOLLA, DIRECTOR
MUSEO NACIONAL DE ANTROPOLOGÍA
MEXICO, D.F.
ALMA USHER
COOK LABORATORIES, INC.
FOR
MARIACHI MUSIC RECORDED IN MEXICO

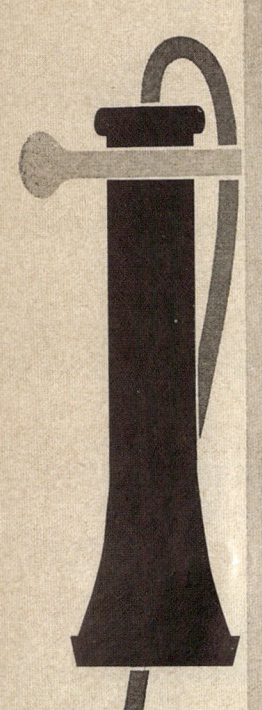

Advertising Designers. HAL STEBBINS INC. AD, 1959, APPROX. 11¼ x 16½ IN. This promo for Hal Stebbins's agency appeared in Portfolio of Western Advertising Art, a special issue of the trade publication Western Advertising. It was likely aimed at persuading reluctant clients to try the modern approach—the selling point being that a more visual strategy would grab the attention of the hurried consumer with no time to read lengthy ad messages.

EVERY
MAN, WOMAN and CHILD
SHOULD CAREFULLY EXAMINE THE WORKINGS OF
PROF. BELL'S
Speaking and Singing Telephone,
In its practical work of conveying
INSTANTANEOUS COMMUNICATION BY DIRECT SOUND,
Giving the tones of the voice so that the person speaking can be recognized by the sound at the other end of the line.

The Sunday School of the
Old John Street M. E. Church,
Having secured a large number of Prof. A. G. Bell's **TELEPHONES**, will give an **EXHIBITION** at the **CHURCH, 44 & 46 JOHN ST. N. Y.** where all visitors desiring can make for themselves a practical investigation of the **Telephone**, by asking questions, hearing the answers to their questions, and listening to the singing conveyed through the Telephones from the other end of the line.

On Tuesday and Wednesday Afternoons
November 20th & 21st, 1877,
From 11½ A. M. until 7 P. M.
Admission to either Afternoon Exhibition 15 Cents.

AN ENTERTAINMENT
OF THE
Sunday School of Old John St. M.E.Church
WILL BE HELD
IN THE CHURCH,
TUESDAY EVENING, Nov. 20th, 1877, at 7.30 P. M.
CONSISTING OF
RECITATIONS by PROF'S SHANNON and McMULLEN,
SINGING by LITTLE NELLIE TERRY and others.
Concluding with the **TELEPHONE EXHIBITION.**
ADMISSION TO EVENING ENTERTAINMENT 25 Cents.
COME AND SEE THE TELEPHONE.

This rare photocopy is used through the courtesy of the Museum of the City of New York

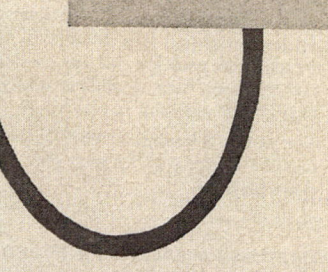

DEDICATED TO ADVERTISING W

THE ART OF "INSTANTANEOUS COMMUNICATION"

Even Prof. Bell would say it has come
a long way in 82 years. But we still
have much to learn about the mass
communication of ideas. Advertising, for
the most part, is using the same
approaches; the same commonplaces; the same
weary words and time-tattered phrases.
There is too little imagery and ingenuity;
too much talking and too little saying.
At a time when there is so much clamor
for the eye and ear of the consumer—
when there is so much competition for
the same segment of the same dollar—
we must raise our creative sights.
We must learn to say more with less.
For, if Advertising is to achieve its
destiny in an ever-burgeoning America,
we ourselves must become adept in the
Art of "Instantaneous Communication."

HAL STEBBINS INC. Advertising
714 West Olympic Blvd., Los Angeles 15

ADVERTISING AGENCY THAT PRACTICES WHAT IT PREACHES: *Advertising*

Dean Smith [1933–1987]. **AHWAHNEE RESORT ADS, 1959, DIMENSIONS UNKNOWN.** These Ahwahnee ads were probably among Smith's first projects once he established his own design office in San Francisco. His previous employer, McCann Erickson, had likely passed the job on, finding it too small.[33] Educated at Pratt Institute, in New York, and Art Center College of Design, in Pasadena, Smith was known for employing a classic Swiss style of bold compositions with sans serif typography and photographic, as opposed to illustrated, imagery. He was among a handful of designers who introduced an uncompromising modern aesthetic to a city slow to embrace it. In less than a decade, however, San Francisco's influence on American graphic design would be profound, for both its acceptance <u>and</u> rejection of the modern idiom. ¶ Recognized for his experimentation with photography, according to his obituary in the <u>Los Angeles Times</u>, Smith probably produced the images in these ads. The high-contrast aesthetic stunningly forecasts a dominant motif in San Francisco graphics of the 1960s, what design historian Lorraine Wild calls "hippie modernism"—the stylistic "baby" born when the societal idealism of postwar European modernism, which aimed to develop a universal visual language, met the societal idealism of the West Coast counterculture and its desire to quickly publicize events with at-hand production methods that called for imagery without gray tones, only black and white.[34] Smith later moved to Los Angeles to work for Saul Bass.[35]

On a summer day at The Ahwahnee you can hike, fish, swim, stroll or relax beside cascading falls with magic names, in the shadow of mighty cliffs. Or you can take it all in from your table-by-the-window in the dining room. The air does wonders for your appetite—and so do our chefs. Set aside some Summer days, and we'll reserve your room at The Ahwahnee...as splendid a hotel as the valley it's in.
THE AHWAHNEE IN YOSEMITE

In autumn you will find The Ahwahnee as restful and friendly as Yosemite Valley itself. Breakfast in baronial style while the sun warms the air outside. Then drive as far as the Big Trees, or walk to Indian Cave. The chef will pack lunch to sustain you. Scuff the leaves and pine needles underfoot. Meditate, if you will. But come back to The Ahwahnee...as splendid a hotel as the valley it's in.
THE AHWAHNEE IN YOSEMITE

John Neuhart [1928–2011] **and Marilyn Neuhart** [b. 1930]. **HAND PRESS LOGO, 1957.** The Neuharts, a design power couple overshadowed in their field only by the looming popularity of Ray and Charles Eames, established their own operation, the Hand Press, in 1956, when John was working for the Eames Office. The press's logo hinted at the Neuharts' self-declared love affair with printers' "sorts"—modular geometric and pictorial elements that could be assembled in countless ways—and their willingness to tackle tricky, delicate handwork on press and off. Many of their projects were intensive labors of love for which they accepted small gifts in lieu of money. Their flexible logo, Marilyn Neuhart remembers, "left the center space, where the heart is, open so that we could insert other symbols depending on the particular occasion."[36] ¶ While many important Los Angeles designers were introduced to modern design through the teachings of Alvin Lustig at Art Center College of Design, the Neuharts met it—and each other—at Long Beach City College. They transferred to UCLA, where design professor Kenneth Kingrey became an important mentor. The Eameses and designer Alexander Girard influenced the couple's aesthetic development as well.[37] ¶ **OPENING ANNOUNCEMENT FOR TEXTILES & OBJECTS STORE, 1961, 20 x 26 IN.** The Neuharts' relationship with Girard began when Deborah Sussman asked John to take over freelance work she was doing for Girard; she was heading off to travel on a Fulbright. Marilyn ended up sharing in the work, and through this professional relationship the Neuharts met Girard's wife, Susan. The couples became lifelong friends and collaborators—kindred spirits in their love of handmade objects from foreign cultures. This announcement recognized the opening of the Herman Miller store Textiles & Objects, in New York, which featured Girard's designs along with dolls he commissioned Marilyn to produce.[38] ¶ The Neuharts were prolific in their graphic output. But

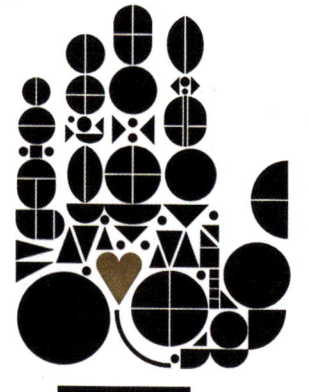

HERMAN MILLER INC.

announces the opening

OF

Textiles & Objects

AT

8 EAST 53RD. STREET NEW YORK CITY

a wholesale and retail shop

OFFERING

THE HERMAN MILLER COLLECTION

OF

FABRICS & TEXTILE ITEMS

Designed by Alexander Girard

& UNUSUAL & SYMPATHETIC

DECORATIVE OBJECTS

Selected by Alexander Girard

OPEN FOR BUSINESS · MAY · 22ND, 1961

PLAZA 3-5106

because they chose not to enter design competitions, much of their work is largely unknown, aside from Marilyn Neuhart's modernist take on the rag doll. The Neuharts spent months documenting the Eameses' production in preparation for the show Connections, organized and curated by John Neuhart, which opened at UCLA's Wight Gallery in December 1976.[39] Another Neuhart legacy is the book Eames Design: The Work of the Office of Charles and Ray Eames, which was published in 1989. ¶ **ABOVE: BIRTH ANNOUNCEMENT FOR LISA FERREIRA, 1960, 5¾ x 5¾ IN.** The handmade "flowers" in this image were created with small stickers and letterpress ornaments. Each flower stem slides in and out to reveal and hide bits of printed text. ¶ **RIGHT: JUNIOR ART COUNCIL NEWSLETTER COVERS, EARLY 1960s, 8½ x 11 IN.** During this period, the Neuharts produced stationery, announcements, and several posters for the Los Angeles County Museum of Art and its volunteer group, the Junior Art Council. Many of the Art Council pieces, including its newsletter, were printed in small runs; this allowed the Neuharts to experiment with type, color, and paper. ¶ **BOTTOM RIGHT: WEDDING ANNOUNCEMENT FOR MARILYN MARQUA AND JOHN NEUHART, 1957, 3¾ x 2¼ IN. (CLOSED), 3¾ x 4½ IN. (OPEN)** ¶ **FAR RIGHT: BIRTH ANNOUNCEMENT FOR PETER FERBER, 1958, 11½ x 1¾ IN.** This unusually long card is pictured with the front flap closed (farthest right) and open to reveal the baby's name printed with the Neuharts' eclectic collection of wood type.

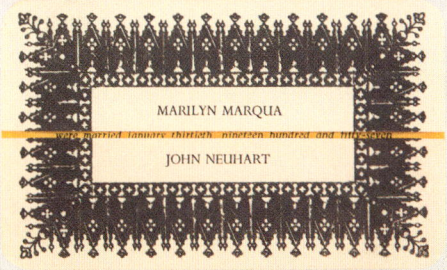

Junior Art Council

JUNIOR ART COUNCIL — NEWSLETTER 2
JUNIOR ART COUNCIL — NEWSLETTER 3
JUNIOR ART COUNCIL — NEWSLETTER 4
JUNIOR ART COUNCIL — NEWSLETTER 5
JUNIOR ART COUNCIL — NEWSLETTER 6
JUNIOR ART COUNCIL — NEWSLETTER 7
JUNIOR ART COUNCIL — NEWSLETTER 8
JUNIOR ART COUNCIL — NEWSLETTER 9

MARILYN MARQUA
were married January thirtieth, nineteen hundred and fifty-seven
JOHN NEUHART

PETER MORDECAI COE FERBER

A BOY

BORN TO MARK & VANN FERBER   APRIL 21, 1958

A BOY

SUNBAKED MODERNISM

ABOVE: "GREETINGS, GREETINGS, GREETINGS," MID-1960s, 6 x 8¾ IN. This technically challenging holiday card reflects the Neuharts' infatuation with the modular geometric and pictorial letterpress elements known as "sorts." **RIGHT: "A FOURTH GREETING," 1957, 6¾ x 16 IN.** An articulated puppet card made for the Fourth of July.[40]

SUNBAKED MODERNISM

Charles Kratka [1922–2007]. MURALS FOR THE LOS ANGELES INTERNATIONAL AIRPORT, 1961. Like so many other designers of his generation, Kratka studied with Alvin Lustig at Art Center in 1947–48. He took a job with the Eames Office in 1947 but left six years later, frustrated by Charles Eames's failure to acknowledge his contributions.[41] ¶Stories conflict about the meaning and purpose of the mosaic murals Kratka designed for the LAX tunnels, one of several large interior projects he completed during a diverse career.[42] Ethel Pattison, an airport information specialist for the City of Los Angeles who has been cataloging the LAX archives, says that "the mosaics were designed to make the approximately 300-foot tunnels seem shorter… and [Kratka's] approach gave passengers something of interest to look at."[43] Ann Proctor, director of volunteers at the LAX Flight Path Learning Center and Museum, remembers tour guides for school field trips comparing a walk alongside the mosaics to a trip eastward across the United States: the blue tiles at the entrance represent the Pacific, followed by browns, yellows, and oranges to evoke the heartland. "There was one line of red tile in the middle, and we'd say, 'We're halfway across now, in the Midwest.' The blue on the other end, that was the Atlantic Ocean."[44] For his part, Kratka offered a different explanation, telling his daughter that the geometric compositions that lined the seven tunnels (only two of which remain) depicted the changing seasons.[45]

SUNBAKED MODERNISM

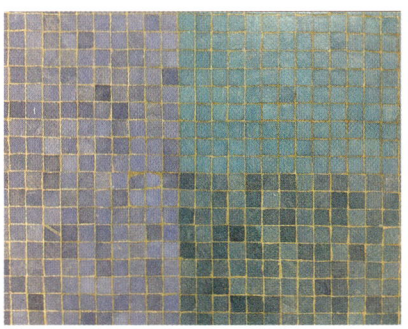

95

Doyald Young [1927–2011]. **TELETYPE MONOCASE FONT, 1965.** This typeface, which Young designed for the Teletype machine, originated with Henry Dreyfuss and Associates—the industrial design office in South Pasadena renowned for such legendary American products as the standard black dial telephone, the Big Ben alarm clock, and various models of the John Deere tractor and Polaroid camera. ¶ Teletype was an early digital means of transmitting text via telephone lines, allowing a message typed into the system at one end to be received as typed output at the other. Engineers creating the machine were challenged in their efforts, however, to devise a system capable of handling upper- and lowercase letters. To get around the problem, they proposed to "fake it" with a custom font. Dreyfuss was instructed to create a typeface that looked "like lower-case but would not offend people by having proper names uncapitalized." In the end, the "monocase" font was never used: it "was hard to read and didn't fool anybody," according to one of the engineers.[46] ¶ Born in Texas, Young moved to Los Angeles as a young man in search of new adventures. He learned technical illustration at Frank Wiggins Trade School and went to work for the Lockheed Corporation. His job demanded exact renderings of curves to illustrate performance charts, and it was there that Young honed the skills needed to draw letterforms. Eventually recognizing that Lockheed as a creative path was a dead end, Young returned to school to study lettering for advertising and then set up his own practice.[47] He produced numerous lettering projects, logotypes, custom typefaces, and commercial fonts and wrote, designed, and published three books about his work. His practice was thriving until his death, in 2011.[48]

these paragraphs are set in monocase. we were requested to design this special typeface for the teletypewriter to satisfy the needs of upper and lower case without sacrificing the legibility of either. like all things that replace the traditional, it takes getting used to. space is left around the letters, which makes for comfortable reading.

these paragraphs are set in monocase. we were requested to design this special typeface for the teletypewriter to satisfy the needs of upper and lower case without sacrificing the legibility of either. like all things that replace the traditional, it takes getting used to.

Saul Bass [1920–1996]. **INSTALLATION FOR XIV MILAN TRIENNALE, 1968.** One of the world's most widely recognized graphic designers, Bass studied, worked with, and, like many postwar American designers, was greatly influenced by the European modernist and educator György Kepes and his book Language of Vision. Bass helped spread a love of the modern aesthetic to American designers and audiences and played a vital role in the development of a more playful approach to modernist design. He moved to Los Angeles from New York in 1946 to work on film-studio accounts for his Manhattan employer, and opened his own studio in 1952, one of the first in which designers worked directly with clients rather than through an agency. ¶ Launched in 1923, the Milan Triennale had long been a showcase for modern decorative and industrial arts with a goal to "stimulate relations" between those who design and those who produce the work.[49] In 1968, the Triennale abandoned its customary format and invited participants, including Bass, to "respond to the issue of quantification and urban life." Bass's concept looked at "compartmentalization." Working with architect and exhibition designer Herb Rosenthal, Bass created a "skyscraper city from stacked file cabinet/boxes... A number of the boxes could be opened to reveal objects and sounds reflecting a sense of mass accumulation of things 'that threatens the quality of contemporary life.'" Included in the exhibition was Bass's film Why Man Creates, originally produced for Kaiser Aluminum, which celebrated "the importance of a creative vision in contemporary life" and of redirecting energy to "that which is most deeply human in us."[50] It was a year of social protest and upheaval, and this spirit spilled over to the Triennale when rebellious Italian students closed down the event but left the Bass piece intact. Writes forecasting expert James Woudhuysen, "They put his maze of 6,000 stacked filing-cabinet drawers to use, admired the trays full of mannequins, flowers, and butterflies, and played his Oscar-winning short film, Why Man Creates, again and again."[51]

SUNBAKED MODERNISM

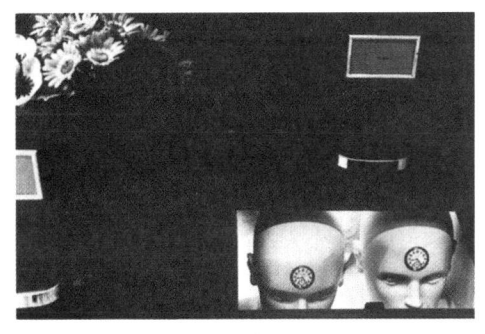

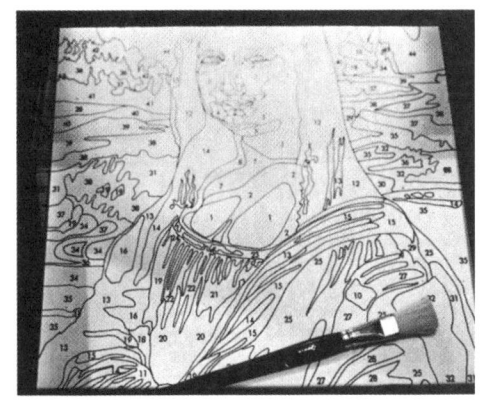

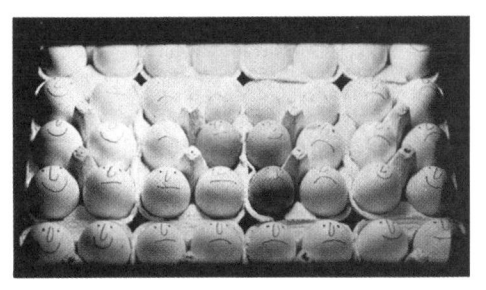

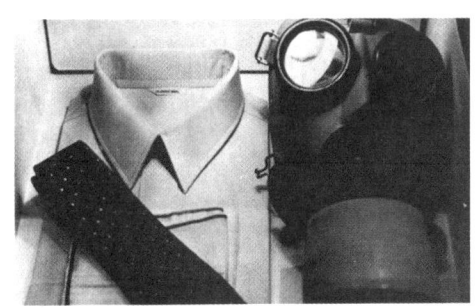

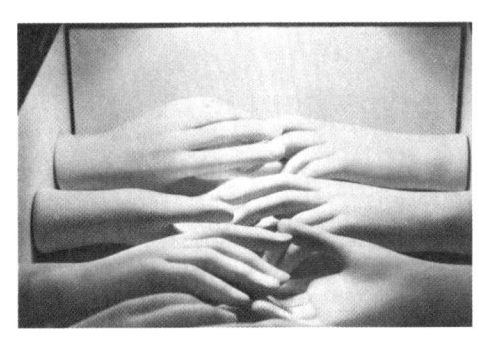

Alexander Girard [1907–1993]. **MAIN ENTRANCE DOORS FOR SCOREN HOUSE, WOODSIDE, CALIFORNIA, 1969.** Although technically not a California graphic designer, Girard wielded a considerable cross-pollinating influence via his collaborations with many Left Coast designers including the Eameses and the Neuharts. Their common bond was a love of folk art, a passion shared by many others, including Northern California dentist Robert Scoren. Scoren approached Girard about doing some work to enliven his dental office and then commissioned him to collaborate with architect Don Knorr on his home. ¶ Girard's gleeful designs added character throughout the house. A colorful grid of 96 cupboards stretched for 55 feet along the wall from the dining room through the kitchen, each with a fiberboard front sporting a different Girard textile in a mix of brights, neutrals, solids, and patterns. Girard also repurposed handbags from Crete as upholstery for a pair of benches. An early supergraphic, the design for the front door flips and repeats "RSCOREN" to create a gridlike pattern, and its glossy surface contains another, more subtle reference to the client's identity in that it is made of "pulverized glass sprayed onto ferrous steel panels and then fired. It's like dental veneers," Scoren explained.[52]

SUNBAKED MODERNISM

Jack Stauffacher [b. 1920]. A self-taught fine printer and book designer, Northern California–native Stauffacher learned about avant-garde art, film, and literature from his filmmaker brother Frank Stauffacher.[53] His introduction to printing came from less elevated sources, namely, an ad in the back of Popular Mechanics asking, "You want to be a printer?"[54] San Francisco had a tradition of fine book printing, so Stauffacher was following in established graphic-design footprints, in any case. ¶ In contrast to his early and quite conventional book production, these typographic experiments created with wooden type reveal a traditionalist whose passions and interests nonetheless generated a modern aesthetic rooted in avant-garde influences. ¶ **BELOW: THE REBEL ALBERT CAMUS: TWENTY-FIVE TYPOGRAPHIC MEDITATIONS, 1969, 10 x 14 IN.** Stauffacher used wooden letterpress type for this suite of statements, edition of 10, from Camus' essay The Rebel. ¶ **RIGHT: G2, 1969, 10 x 14 IN.** Although Stauffacher describes himself as conservative in his practice, a gift of late-ninteenth-century wooden type that he received in the late 1960s prompted him to create what he calls "typographic meditations." These boldly abstract monoprints celebrate the various characteristics of the letterforms and their wood substrate—from the graceful lines and curves to the pocks and scratches of the aged wood captured in the inked impression.

SUNBAKED MODERNISM

Keith Godard [b. 1942]. **PROPOSED COMMEMORATIVE POSTER FOR OPENING OF CALIFORNIA INSTITUTE OF THE ARTS, 1972, 34 x 40 x 7 IN.**

English-born, with an MFA from Yale, Godard headed west in 1970 to join the faculty at CalArts, recently established by Walt Disney. The invitation came from Craig Hodgetts, Godard's partner in the New York–based architecture, planning, and design group Works (and then, associate dean of the CalArts School of Design). Once Godard arrived in Los Angeles, he and Hodgetts quickly re-formed their studio as Works West.[55] The group, which included other Yale classmates, created original and imaginative projects such as Punch-Out Furniture—flat, colorful constructions of Tri-Wall, a corrugated cardboard, that could be assembled into seating—and UniverCity Now, a utopian reenvisioning of academia.[56] ¶ Godard also worked on some promotional materials for CalArts, including this poster commemorating the opening of the institute's permanent home in Valenica, 30 miles north of Los Angeles. The poster exemplifies Godard's interest in "experimental 3-D media and other technologies [that were of] great excitement to me at CalArts." This literal yet intelligent and witty solution involved a plaster topographic relief model that would be employed to create a holographic poster. The school's deans rejected the design, likely because of ongoing disputes over the direction of the curriculum and, thus, uncertainty over what message the announcement should convey.[57]

California Institute of the Arts is open in Valencia 1972

SUNBAKED MODERNISM

Louis Danziger. **EARTH QUAKE ALBUM COVER, 1971, 12⅜ x 12⅜ IN.** For the rock group Earth Quake, Danziger created this fragmented typographic treatment by photographing hand-lettered type through a prism. He amped up the visual tension by using blue and red of equal value for the background—an op-art treatment that causes the image to vibrate as the color wavelengths hit the eye simultaneously. ¶ **XYBION LOGO, 1975.** This computer-generated logotype for a high-tech developer of underwater sonics was created at the California Institute of Technology, in Pasadena. It was a daring enterprise at the time, one that Danziger believes was probably the first professionally designed logo created on a computer—an effort that required the support of a programmer and time-shared computer.[58] ¶ With formal guidance from Danziger, the programmer would have plotted the geometric letterforms on graph paper and then translated this drawing into vectors—thus, the gridded look of the letterforms. The angle was then achieved by exploring variations; this was a particularly complicated process, given that it was too expensive to print out different iterations. In order to choose the best option, Danziger had to capture the different angle options by photographing them directly off the computer screen as the programmer changed coordinates. Once the angle was chosen from the crude photos, and tweaks were applied, the final logo was printed out on a plotter. ¶ The use of computers to create animated graphics was pioneered by John Whitney, in the 1960s in California, to create his own work as well as work for the Eameses and Saul Bass. Danziger, who had an early interest in the potential applications of computers in graphics, collaborated with Whitney to design an opening sequence for a television program that, sadly, was never realized.[59]

SUNBAKED MODERNISM

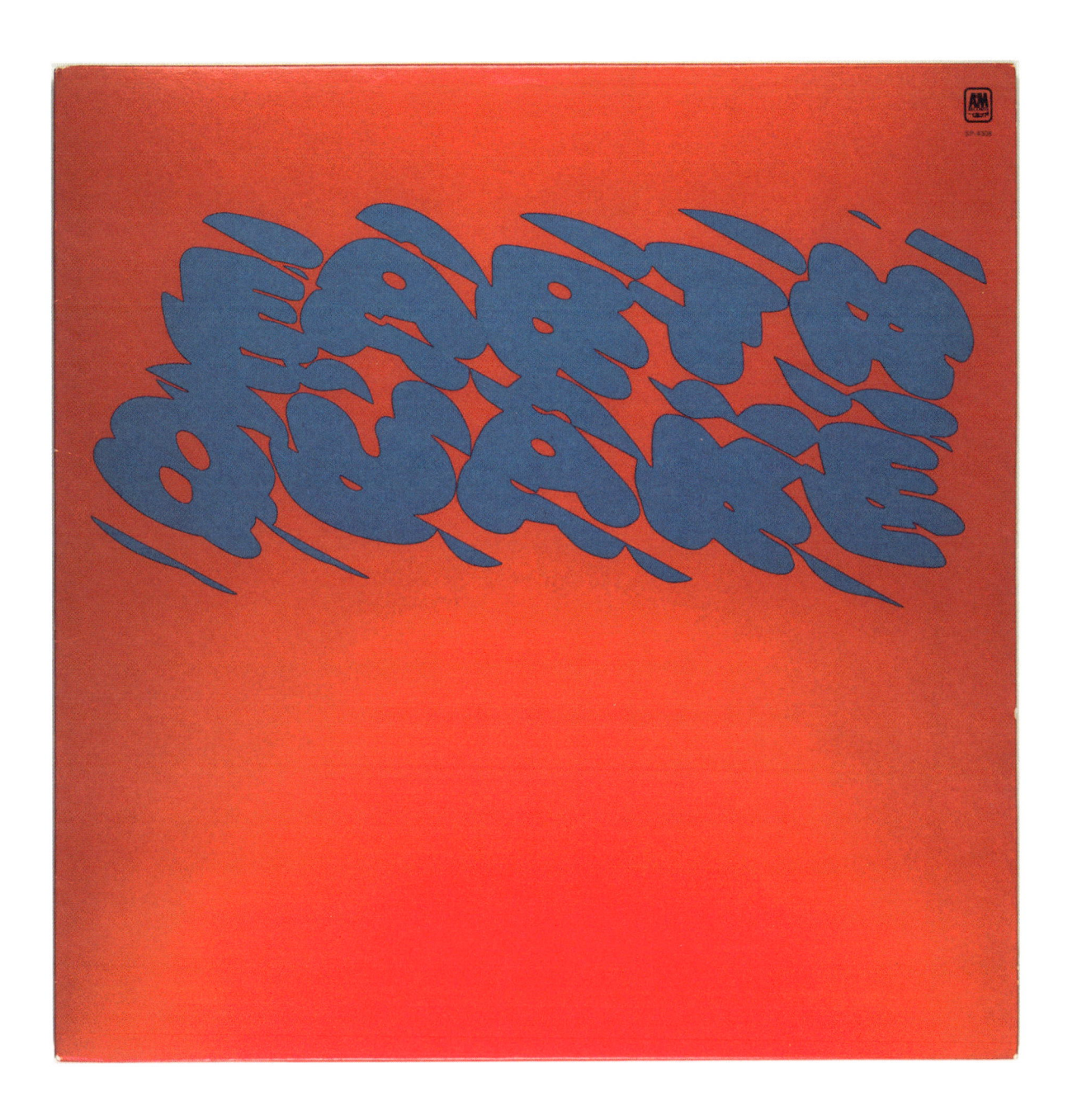

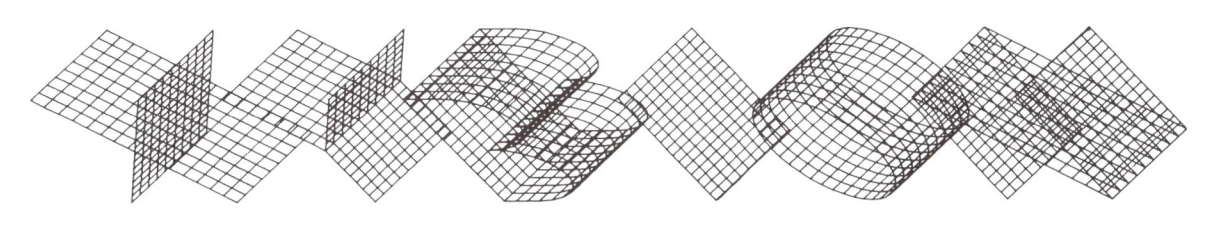

Notes

1 Alvin Lustig, "California Modern," in Holland R. Melson, Jr., ed., <u>The Collected Writings of Alvin Lustig</u> (New Haven: Holland R. Melson, Jr., 1958), 79–84. **2** Steven Heller and Elaine Lustig Cohen, <u>Born Modern: The Life and Design of Alvin Lustig</u> (San Francisco: Chronicle, 2010), 40. **3** Ward Ritchie, <u>A Tale of Two Books</u> (Los Angeles: The Book Collectors, 1985), 24. **4** <u>Monthly Letter of The Limited Editions Club</u> 134, June 1941, 4. **5** From Alvin Lustig's 1947 essay "California Modern Design," in Heller and Lustig Cohen, <u>Born Modern</u>, 138. **6** Frederick Usher, interview with the author, Santa Barbara, Calif., September 1, 2008. **7** Alvin Lustig, preface, from <u>Book Jackets by Alvin Lustig for New Directions Books</u> (New York: Gotham Bookmart, 1947), www.alvinlustig.com, accessed March 12, 2013. **8** See Bobbye Tigerman, ed., <u>A Handbook of California Design, 1930–1965: Craftspeople, Designers, Manufacturers</u> (Cambridge, Mass.: MIT Press, 2013). **9** Louis Danziger, interview with the author, Pasadena, Calif., 2008. **10** Daniel Handke and Vanessa Hunt, <u>Poster Art of the Disney Parks</u> (New York: Disney, 2012), 91. **11** See Reyner Banham, <u>Los Angeles: The Architecture of Four Ecologies</u> (New York: Harper and Row, 1971). **12** Deborah Sussman, interview with the author, Los Angeles, April 2008. **13** Wayne Hunt and Grant Follis (John Follis's son), interview with the author, Glendale, Calif., April 10, 2008. **14** Wayne Hunt, <u>SEGD Messages</u>, winter 1995. **15** Joe Molloy, interview with the author, Los Angeles, 2004. **16** Usher interview. **17** Frederick A. Usher, "A Tribute to Alvin Lustig," <u>AIGA LA Newsletter</u>, summer 1987, no 3. **18** David Travers, ed., <u>Arts & Architecture 1945–1967: The Complete Reprint</u>, vol. 1 (Cologne: Taschen, 2008), 7. **19** Louis Danziger, e-mail correspondence with the author, July 29, 2008. **20** Allen Porter, phone interview with the author, 2008. **21** John Neuhart, Marilyn Neuhart, and Ray Eames, <u>Eames Design: The Work of the Office of Charles and Ray Eames</u> (New York: Abrams, 1989), 181. **22** Pat Kirkham, <u>Charles and Ray Eames: Designers of the Twentieth Century</u> (Cambridge, Mass.: MIT Press, 1995), 52. **23** Louis Danziger, e-mail correspondence with the author, July 10, 2013. **24** Quote by Kathryn Schwartz, former president of the Saturday Club of Vacaville, in Richard Bammer, "Don Birrell 1922–2006: He Was a Local Icon and Artistic Genius," www.thereporter.com, posted July 1, 2006, downloaded July 2, 2013. **25** Ken Parkhurst, e-mail correspondence with the author, June 15, 2013. **26** Louis Danziger, e-mail correspondence with the author, June 2013. **27** Ibid. **28** Steve Reoutt, e-mail correspondence with the author, March 15, 2008. **29** Lynn Spigel, <u>TV by Design: Modern Art and the Rise of Network Television</u> (Chicago and London: University of Chicago Press, 2009), 127. **30** Lynn Spigel, e-mail correspondence with the author, June 14–17, 2013. Spigel clarifies the relationship between Olden and work done outside the New York offices. **31** Interstitial cards were recognized in 1959 by the trade publication <u>Western Advertising</u> in its 14th Annual Exhibition of Western Advertising. Lee, who was art department head, art director, and set director at Television City from 1953 to 1974, likely hired fellow employee Jane Sai. While the exhibition gives Sai credit for the art, the visual style strongly resembles Lee's. For other examples of his work, see announcements for <u>Robert Tyler Lee: Casein Painting and Drawings</u> and <u>Robert Tyler Lee</u>, Setay Gallery, March 7–31, 1966. **32** Neuhart et al., <u>Eames Design</u>, 213. **33** Reoutt e-mail correspondence. **34** See also "G. Dean Smith," <u>Communication Arts Magazine</u> 12, no. 3, 1970. **35** For acknowledgement of Smith's contributions at Bass's office, see Jennifer Bass and Pat Kirkham, <u>Saul Bass: A Life in Film & Design</u> (London: Laurence King, 2011), 394, n. 96. **36** Marilyn Neuhart, e-mail correspondence with the author, December 17, 2012. **37** Marilyn Neuhart, interview with the author, Hermosa Beach, Calif., September 28, 2012. **38** This announcement has been attributed elsewhere to Alexander Girard, but the Neuharts very likely had a strong hand in its production. The style closely resembles their other work, and the couple's reticence about publicity may have resulted in Girard's receiving credit. **39** Neuhart interview, September 28, 2012. **40** Ibid; Marilyn Neuhart, interview with the author, Hermosa Beach, Calif., December 12, 2012; and Marilyn Neuhart, e-mail correspondence with the author, July 18, 2013. **41** Peggy Kratka (Charles Kratka's daughter), phone interview with the author, May 20, 2013. **42** Tigerman, Handbook of California Design, 150. **43** Ethel Pattison biography, TEDx Manhattan Beach, www.tedxmanhattanbeach.com, accessed March 12, 2014. **44** Valerie J. Nelson, "Charles D. Kratka, 85; Designer, Artist Created Tunnel Walls at LAX," Los Angeles Times, November 25, 2007, www.latimes.com, accessed June 30, 2012. **45** Ibid. **46** Jim Haynes, "First-Hand: Chad Is Our Most Important Product: An Engineer's Memory of Teletype Corporation," IEEE Global History Network, www.ieeeghn.org, accessed January 18, 2014. **47** Doyald Young, interview with the author, Sherman Oaks, Calif., April 9, 2008. **48** Marian Bantjes, "Doyald Young," biography for AIGA Medal, www.aiga.org, accessed March 15, 2014. **49** Triennale di Milano website, www.triennale.it/en/institution, accessed January 18, 2014. **50** Bass and Kirkham, Saul Bass, 92. **51** James Woudhuysen, "Bass Profundo," Design Week, September 22, 1989, www.woudhuysen.com, accessed January 18, 2014. **52** See Edie Cohen, "Welcome to 1969 Pix: That's When Alexander Girard Put His Upbeat Modernist Imprimatur on a Northern California House by Don Knorr," Interior Design, March 1, 2007, www.interiordesign.net, accessed January 18, 2014. **53** Frank Stauffacher, with Jack and Richard Foster, founded the influential avant-garde film series Art in Cinema, presented by the San Francisco Museum of Modern Art from 1946 to 1953. **54** "SFMOMA 75th Anniversary: Jack Stauffacher," interview with Lisa Rubens, 2006, Regional Oral History Office, Bancroft Library, University of California, Berkeley, copyright San Francisco Museum of Modern Art, 2008, transcript, 2. **55** Martin Fox and Janet Vrchota, "Can a British-born Yale-trained Designer Find Happiness and Fulfillment in Southern California?" Print, March/April 1972, 57–59. **56** See Sylvia Lavin and Kimberli Meyer, Everything Loose Will Land: 1970s Art and Architecture in Los Angeles (Nürnberg: Verlag für Moderne Kunst, 2014), 269. **57** Keith Godard, e-mail correspondence with the author, June 25–July 17, 2013. **58** Louis Danziger, e-mail correspondence with the author, June 18, 2013. Danziger's claim is based on the fact that 1975 was almost a decade before the Macintosh was introduced and therefore very early for designers to be working with computers in any capacity. **59** Ibid. Other conclusions about computer graphics in 1975 are based on information on the Computer History Museum website showing similarities between the Xybion logo and the vector-drawn wire-frame model of the Utah Teapot, www.computerhistory.org, accessed June 17, 2013. Also see Wayne Carlson, "A Critical History of Computer Graphics and Animation, Section 3: The Computer Graphics Industry Evolves," at design.osu.edu.

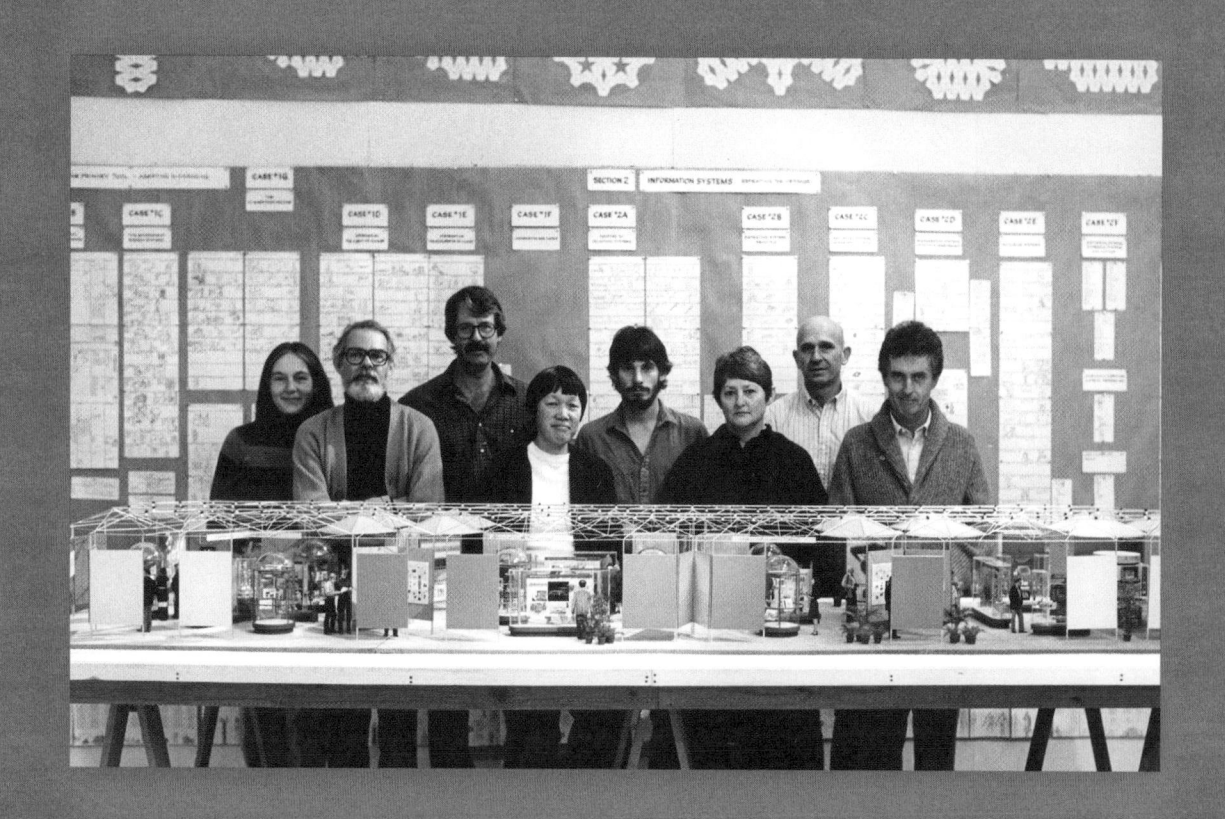

↑ Neuhart Donges Neuhart, 1982. John is second from left; Marilyn third from right.
→ "Spring in the Gold Country," from Beautiful California, 1971

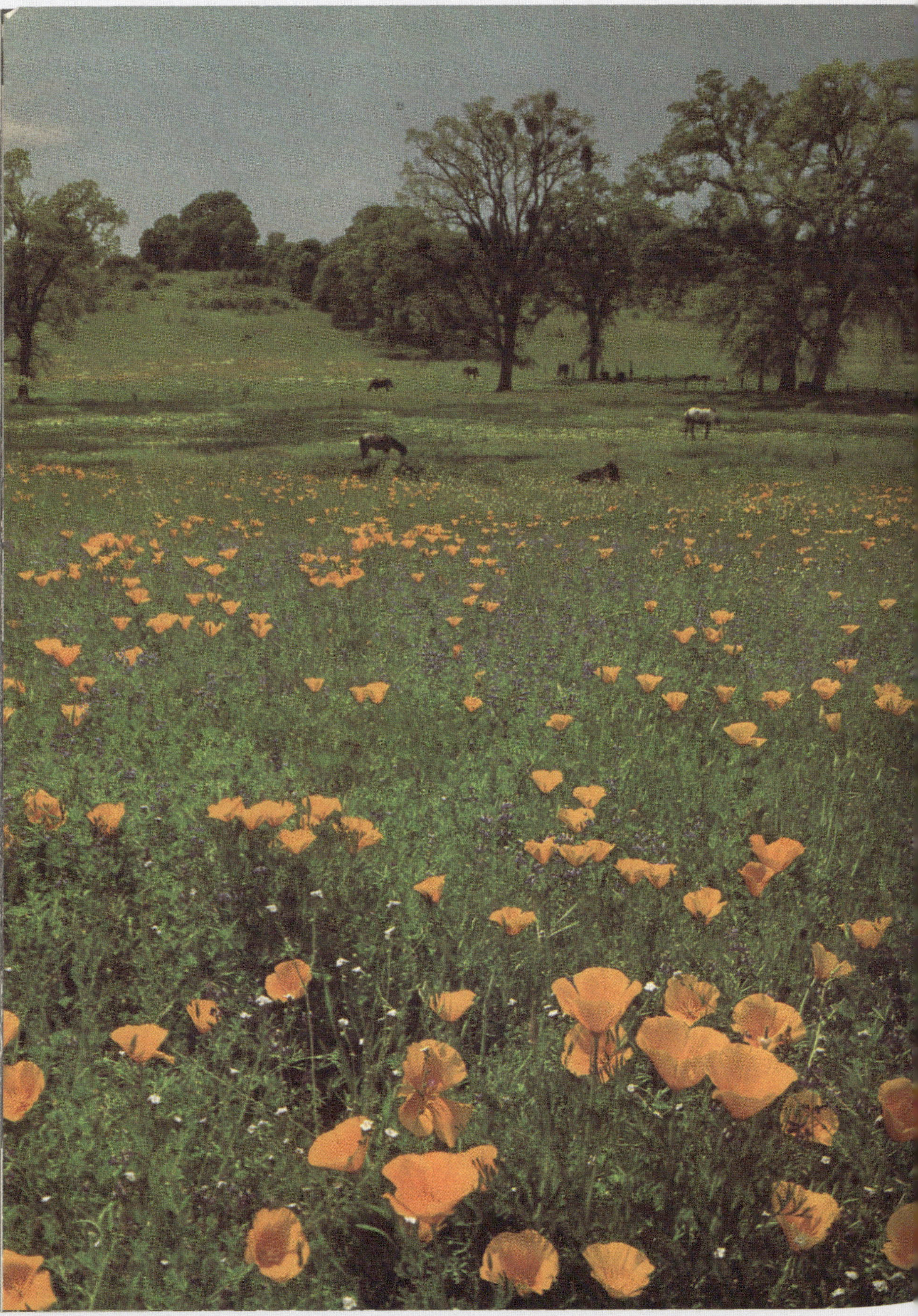

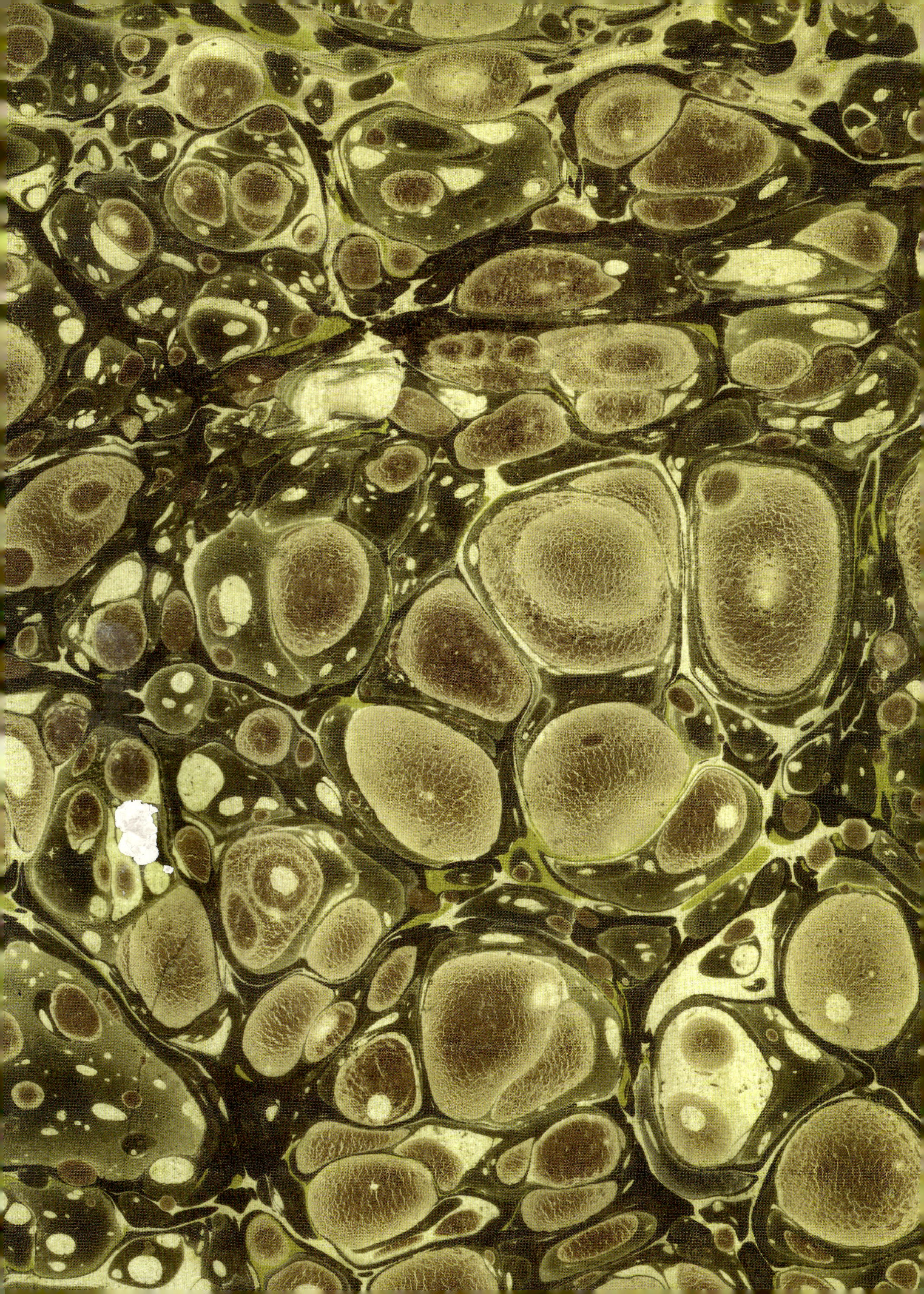

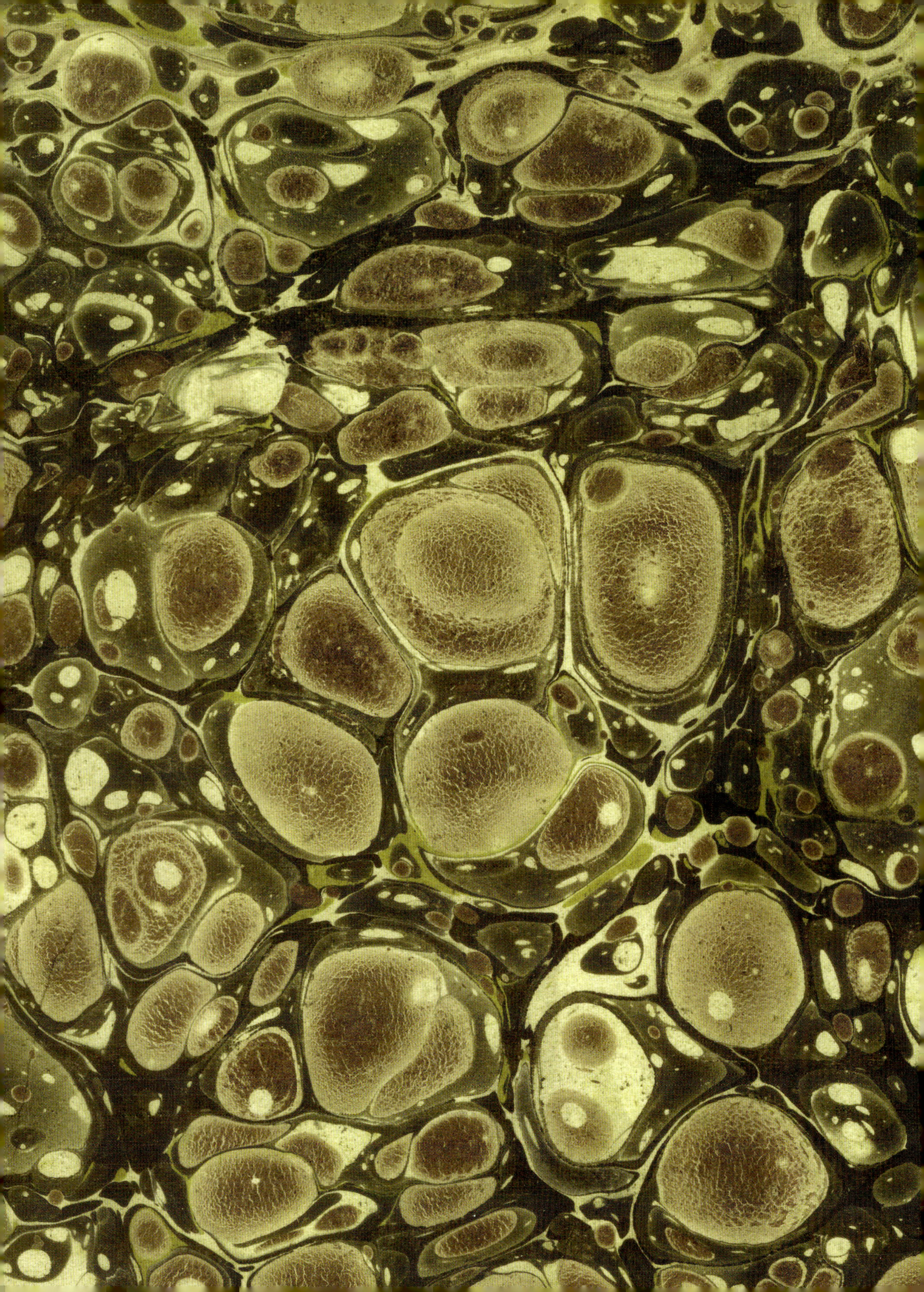

" SAID CALIFORNIA GOVERNOR ARNOLD SCHWARZENEGGER:

'THESE EARTHQUAKES ARE FANTASTIC! I PROMISED YOU MORE ACTION AND EXCITEMENT. WE'VE GOT WILDFIRES. SOON WE'RE GOING TO HAVE A SUPERMEGA TORNADO, GIANT SINKHOLES, LOCUSTS ARE GOING TO BE THERE—WE'RE GOING TO MAKE CALIFORNIA THE NUMBER ONE ACTION STATE IN THE COUNTRY!' "

TINA FEY
"WEEKEND UPDATE," SATURDAY NIGHT LIVE
NOVEMBER 1, 2003

INDUSTRY ☞ & THE ☜ INDIES

INTRODUCTION: FOR YOUR VIEWING PLEASURE

Among types of design native to California, motion graphics is right at home. As a concept, motion graphics emerged in the 1950s as a way to identify the practice of creating movie titles and animated TV commercials—much of which were being produced in Hollywood. And it was Los Angeles–based artist, inventor, and designer John Whitney who first distinguished the difference between regular ol' static graphic design and graphics that moved. Whitney, at the Catalina Design Conference in 1962, argued that while a designer might make excellent graphic design—a book cover or an image sequence for a storyboard—it took imaginative design applied to the articulation of kinetic graphic elements to achieve what he christened "motion graphics."[1] I like to think of it as "graphic design on wheels."

Yet a history of motion graphics is tricky to pinpoint, in part because the practice taps hand- and brainfuls of skills in a spectrum of fields. Was this a branch of graphic design or a new genre altogether? Where and how did motion graphics develop? What talents and practices were at play? The work combined typography, animation, still photography, filmmaking, and sometimes performance, all mostly set to sound. And the possible applications for this interdisciplinary work ranged from television and movie titles to network branding and product commercials to "sponsored" and independent films.

Further, when we talk about graphics for screens, what kind of "screens" might those be? The options extend beyond films and TV to arcade games, projected light shows at rock concerts, and even screens as immersive spaces or alternative experiences. There also is the more metaphorical notion of California as a screen in itself—an image factory and state of mind, a place that watches the world while the world watches it.

Another complication is that the evolutionary path of motion graphics includes contributions from talent outside the traditional zones of graphic design. As animation historian Amid Amidi characterized the circumstances, "There was a great deal of cross-pollination between cartoonists, illustrators, graphic designers, and animators—far more than is typically acknowledged in neatly compartmentalized design histories."[2] I would emphatically add visual and special-effects artists to Amidi's list. The diverse backgrounds of these makers should not in any way disqualify their efforts from the context of design: their time-based works are roses that smell just as sweet. Yet this early mix of unorthodox producers meant that significant achievements sometimes flew under the establishment radar.[3] Mostly print oriented, graphic design organizations were slow to acknowledge the full scope of this work, however groundbreaking, from contributors they perceived as outside the field. Lacking a clear identity, graphics for screens received attention mostly in dribs and drabs.

It was Saul Bass who helped realize motion graphics as we understand it today with his titles for Otto Preminger's 1955 Man with the Golden Arm, the first film whose introductory credits integrated visual plot elements at a level attaining that of high-concept design. This innovation marked another first in earning a mark of "official" respect for motion graphics within the design profession. Yet many preceded Bass, and this would be a pretty skimpy volume if it included only the bona fide. Motion graphics is only now garnering the accolades it deserves within the graphic design canon. And the role of California-based artists and designers, in terms of their towering contributions to the genre, deserves particular recognition.

A helpful place to start filling out the record is the complicated relationship between what we commonly think of as "the industry"—i.e., Hollywood—and "the indies"—that is, the independent artists who produced experimental films. The source of this intersection—the godfather, as it were, of the avant-garde filmmaking that led to motion graphics—is émigré designer Oskar Fischinger, who came to California in 1936 to work for Paramount and to escape the rising political tensions in his native Germany. Fischinger sought to express ideas and emotions with a language of bright, popping colors and moving abstract shapes, achieved through stop-motion animation of painted elements and geometric objects. His engaging creations and abstract visual vocabulary influenced generations of artists, including Whitney, another important bridge figure between the worlds of avant-garde filmmaking and the industry. Whitney and his brother, James, developed technical advances that led to the creation of highly original animated imagery (as did Fischinger, who invented a wax-cutting device to speed the animation process). This mode of working—one that conflates technical and artistic development—served as both muse and model for future practitioners whose cinematic endeavors involved mechanical and, later, digital innovation.

John Whitney looms especially large for introducing the slit-scan technique, which he witnessed in a college astronomy class and applied to artistic ends in his titles for MGM's 1966 film The Glass Bottom Boat. Adopted by the following generations, the slit scan is just one example of how exchanges between the avant-garde and the commercial drive the history of motion graphics: Special-effects artist Doug Trumbull further developed the slit scan to create the legendary "Star Gate" interdimensional travel sequence for Stanley Kubrick's 2001: A Space Odyssey (1968). Trumbull then collaborated with Harry Marks in designing the ABC Movie of the Week promo (1969), which applies the abstract visuals of the time-space continuum to the network's logo. This extravagant gesture radically transformed the look of television graphics—and represents a prescient twinkle-in-the-eye in terms of future uses of the computer.

Equally instrumental in the development of "California" motion graphics during the 1950s were designers Charles and Ray Eames. The Eameses worked on a parallel trajectory alongside those artists who straddled the worlds of "indie" and "industry." The Eames Office (which employed John Whitney for a few years) produced its celebrated independent and educational films in service of its clients as well as its own interests. Two prime examples: Glimpses of the U.S.A., produced in 1959 for the American National Exhibition in Moscow, was a commercial project for the U.S. State Department, while Kaleidoscope Jazz Chair, of 1960, was a playful experiment born of Charles Eames's need to give a public lecture. At the same time, artists making abstract films were receiving commissions for corporate-sponsored projects that offered considerable creative freedom while providing a paycheck.

Of course, this was the sixties, and counterculture experimentation was in the air. California, in particular, was no longer a mere state but a state of mind, offering the allure of manifest destiny in the territory of consciousness itself. People hungered for new sensations and modalities—other ways of "being"—and with that desire came advances in screen-based experiences, which media theorist Gene Youngblood famously identified in his book Expanded Cinema. There were new types of screens, new ideas about what could be considered a screen, new forms and aesthetics for existing screens, and new kinds of graphic and artistic practices. Light shows that accompanied rock or psychedelic music performances were immersive, multiprojector extravaganzas of swirling, pulsing colors and images, which viewers often enhanced by taking perception-altering substances. These and other types of "happenings" inspired thinkers such as the artists and engineers of the collaborative group E.A.T. (Experiments in Art and Technology), who, working with the architectural renegades of Envirolab, created a giant dome filled with fog, mirrors, and holograms for the Pepsi Pavilion at Expo '70, in Osaka, Japan, giving visitors a new kind of inhabitable "screen."

Counterculture "indie" effects erupted on the TV screen with Robert Abel and Associates' 1975 7UP ad "Bubbles," which forever transformed expectations—including my own—of the kind of design thrills possible in a commercial. The spot covers the historical transformation of the 7UP logo: the original red-and-green motif of a girl tossing bubbles evolves into a chorus line of bubble-wielding nymphs, and the bubbles transmogrify into a shimmering butterfly that vanishes but reemerges in neon from the colored shapes of a radiating sun. Wow. With eyeball-dazzling work like this, motion graphics at last gained its place as a specialized genre rooted in graphic design. Abel and Associates was also among the several studios that contributed to TRON, the 1982 science-fiction Disney film that popularized computer-generated imagery. Although not pictured in this volume, Kenny Mirman's "mandala" sequence from TRON, which depicts the transition from the "real" world to the "computer" world, recalls the arcade video games of the time, as well as John Whitney's earlier abstract computer-generated artistic works. And so the cycle of design evolution continues.

An additional dimension to this story comes from graphic designer and founder of the motion graphics MFA program at California Institute of the Arts, Michael Worthington. In his whimsical essay "Out of Time: How to Make Motion Graphics in Southern California," he time-travels through the genre from the perspective of shifting technical changes. Complementing this fictive journey are three historical texts: Gene Youngblood's "The Artist as Design Scientist" (1970), John Whitney's "Animation Mechanisms" (1971), and an excerpt from Jeffrey Altshuler's "Robert Abel: Video Surrealist" (1975). A final note: The illustrations included here offer just a glimpse of the spirit of these artists and designers at work. Attempting to translate to print form the complexity, luminosity, and titillation of this imagery when it operates in tandem with sound is a losing proposition. I encourage the reader to see the films—some of which are available on YouTube (via yet another kind of screen)—in order to fully understand a school of creative genius of which too many people are still unaware.

[1] Michael Betancourt, The History of Motion Graphics: From Avant-Garde to Industry in the United States (Rockville, Md.: Wildside, 2013), 129. [2] Amid Amidi, e-mail correspondence with the author, September 4, 2013. [3] Notable exceptions are several books, including Roy Laughton, TV Graphics (London: Reinhold, 1966); John Halas and Walter Herdeg, eds., Film & TV Graphics: An International Survey of Film and Television Graphics (Zurich: Graphis Press, 1967); Walter Herdeg, ed., Film & TV Graphics 2: An International Survey of the Art of Film Animation (Zurich: Graphis Press, 1976). In the 1950s and '60s, Ralph K. Potter regularly wrote about developments in television commercials for the advertising trade journal Art Direction. By the 1970s, the graphic design trade journal Print ran the bimonthly report "New Developments in Print/TV Film," and the American Institute of Graphic Arts in 1970 began to issue its collection "Fifty TV Commercials of the Year."

INFLUENCES & INTERSECTIONS
The Indies & the Industry

- EMPLOYER → DESIGNER
- INFLUENCER → DESIGNER
- COLLABORATOR ⊢⊣ COLLABORATOR
- DESIGNER/ARTIST ┄┄→ FIELD INFLUENCED

RAY & CHARLES EAMES

PHILL NORMAN

ALVIN LUSTIG

ANIMATION

UPA

OSKAR FISCHINGER

AVANT-GARDE CINEMA

HARRY SMITH

JOHN WHITNEY

ELIAS ROMERO

EXPANDED CINEMA

SINGLE WING TURQUOISE BIRD

ENVIROLAB

BILL HAM

E.A.T. (EXPERIMENTS IN ART & TECHNOLOGY)

LIGHT SHOW

Saul Bass Network Diagram

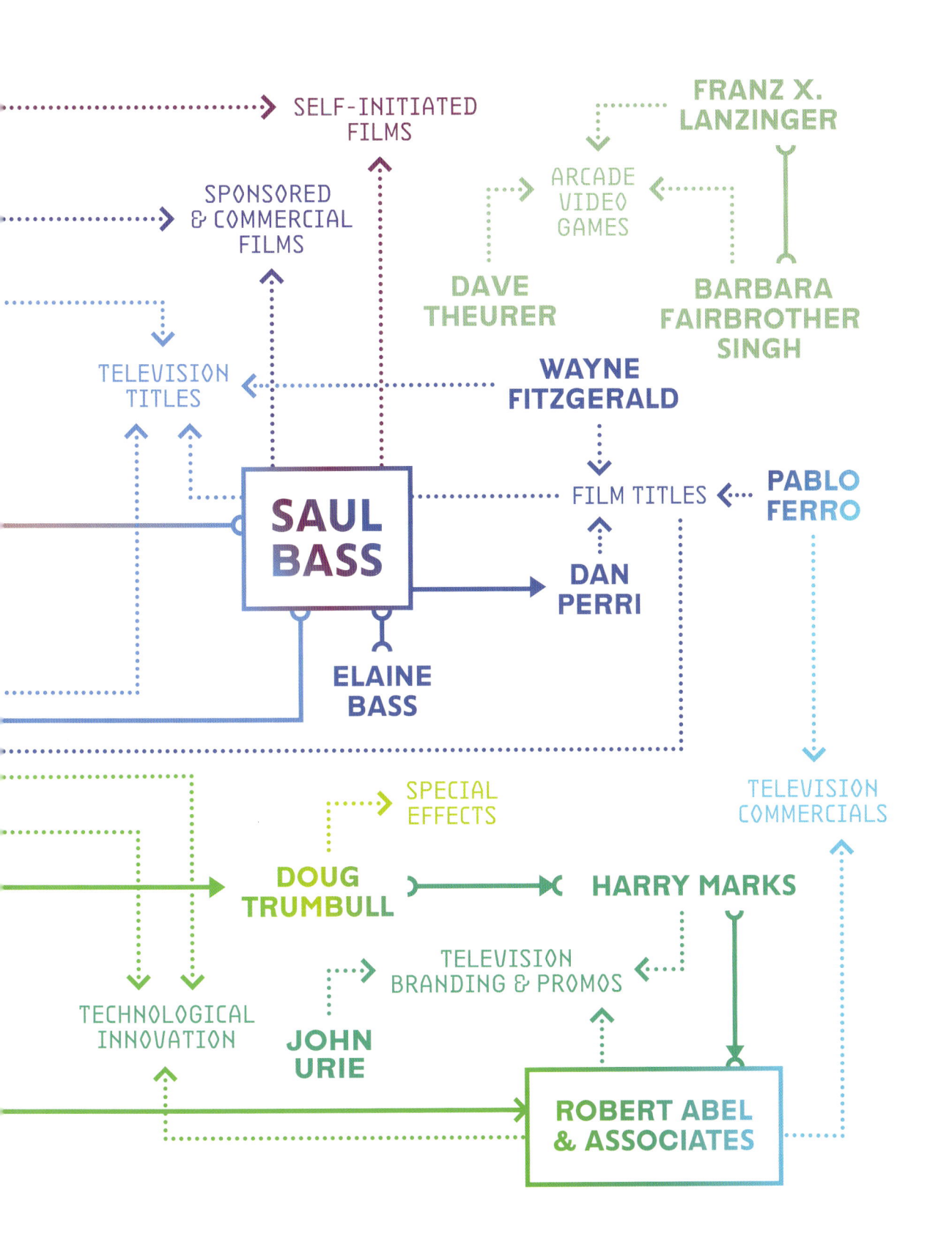

- **SELF-INITIATED FILMS**
- **SPONSORED & COMMERCIAL FILMS**
- **TELEVISION TITLES**
- **FRANZ X. LANZINGER** → ARCADE VIDEO GAMES ← **DAVE THEURER**
- **BARBARA FAIRBROTHER SINGH** — ARCADE VIDEO GAMES
- **WAYNE FITZGERALD** → FILM TITLES ← **PABLO FERRO**
- **SAUL BASS** → **DAN PERRI**
- **ELAINE BASS**
- SPECIAL EFFECTS
- **DOUG TRUMBULL** → **HARRY MARKS**
- TELEVISION BRANDING & PROMOS
- **JOHN URIE**
- TECHNOLOGICAL INNOVATION
- **ROBERT ABEL & ASSOCIATES**
- TELEVISION COMMERCIALS

MICHAEL WORTHINGTON

OUT OF TIME: HOW TO MAKE MOTION GRAPHICS IN SOUTHERN CALIFORNIA

If you want to make motion graphics, there's no better place to be than Southern California. An abundance of space, beautiful light and weather, and a host of movie studios, production companies, TV stations, and advertising agencies make it the top choice for anyone moving from the East Coast or even Europe. There's the added bonus of having budding actors available—if you should need them—in every restaurant and retail store in Hollywood, and should you desire a cool soundtrack, just pop into any Silver Lake coffee shop and you'll be sure to find a hipster who can help.

You probably already have a computer, a digital video camera, and a heap of assorted software. You'll also need a drive large enough to store all your files, and it's probably a good idea to keep a second backup as well, just in case your mum knocks over your giant can of super-strength coffee-infused energy drink—the third one you've consumed today—and your computer gets fried and you try to grab your backup drive before the syrupy energy drink destroys that, but in your over-caffeinated state you forget to unplug it, and the power cable snaps tight and pulls the drive from your hands, and it falls to the floor, smashing the casing and scattering bits of plastic and metal across your bedroom. You might want to shout at your mum at this point; it won't get you your lost files back, but it might make you realize you should probably get some sleep.

If it's the 1970s, you won't have to worry about this. The computer won't be yours, and it won't be in your house. It'll belong to a giant tech company, say, IBM, and if you're lucky they might be letting you play on it to create some experimental films, using a "light pen" to mark coordinates on a screen. The creative options might be more limited than you are used to and production will certainly be more laborious. You'll have to output your work to single pieces of microfilm, which you'll need to reshoot onto 35mm negative film before making a 35mm positive print for screening. Remember, while there will be scientists in long white coats there to help you operate the multimillion-dollar machinery, there won't be any energy drinks to see you through the long hours.

If you are working in a time before computers have been invented, you should probably think about investing in a film camera—or at least knowing someone who will lend you one. You're going to need some film stock as well, and something to animate. Geometric shapes cut out of cardboard will do, or perhaps some paint or sand that you can shape and scrape. Whatever material you choose to animate, you're probably going to have to build some kind of contraption to hold the objects in place while you film them, moving them small distances and shooting them frame by frame. You'll need lights as well, and an assistant or two. Don't be discouraged if you have a few failures and this labor-intensive process frustrates you. And don't forget, you won't really be able to see what you've made until you've shot it, so be prepared to shoot, animate, view, and reshoot. Give yourself plenty of time: it can take a year to make a six-minute film, and there's nothing worse than meticulously animating 24 frames a second for a six-minute film (that's 8,640 shots, folks) only to find you left the lens cap on! Just get straight back on the horse and start all over again; after all, it's not easy to paint with light. It's going to take a long time, but that's the price of being a pioneer. You might want to let that friend who lent you the camera know she's not getting it back for a while. Don't forget to store your film stock somewhere cold and dry, somewhere it won't spontaneously combust, with the added bonus that once safely stored your mum can't spill any drinks on it.

If you don't have a camera, or can't afford film stock, don't despair! As long as you have a few months to spare, and better than average eyesight, you can draw directly on clear 35mm film, frame by frame. And if you can't afford color paint, you can always use black ink and add the color in processing when you make a print—and you'll have to make a print at some point—so you will still need to shell out some cash, but think of all the money you've saved so far, and it should be fine, as long as the doctor's bills for carpal tunnel syndrome don't bankrupt you. You can also scratch into the film, and if you have film with synchronized sound, you can scratch into the magnetic sound coating to make your own music. No more frumpy orchestras! You can be your own one-man avant-garde band.

If you have a client, especially if it's the '80s, money should be less of a concern. Make sure you are billing the client as much as possible to cover the costs of renting a Henry or a Harry, and also an operator to navigate the complicated software. If your client works in TV, or even better is a TV station, you are in luck, since you'll be able to make the most of the limited effects options available. You'll be able to spin pictures, add drop shadows, solarize images, and, most important, make logotypes neon and/or 3-D. It'll take a while to render, and the operator is going to give you some back talk, but when you have that three-second interstitial of your 3-D logo spinning meaninglessly through space, you'll know it was worth it. Now all you need to do is transfer it to handy, compact, and ever so stable one-inch tape and you are home and dry.

If you have a client in the 2010s, you may be in less luck. You'll probably be doing the work of five or six people, from ideation to storyboards to animation to post-production, but only being paid the salary of one of them. Some friendly advice: get as many interns as possible. You can find them at design schools, and a good one will probably last about two years at full speed, before he burns out and needs to be replaced. Remember, today's intern is tomorrow's competition! So try to pay him so little that he can't set up his own company. You'll also be able to save money on books and space. Your office can be tiny and all your research done online. You won't need a meeting room since you won't meet your clients in person, and if you are really smart everything will be built digitally in 3-D, so you won't even need sets or actors.

If it's the early '90s, and you are still set on being a motion designer, consider going to work in film titles. You might think this is bad advice, that every facet of entertainment is heading toward the computer scene, but believe me, a renaissance is coming. If you can make your work fast-cut, close-up, distressed, and with an emphasis on typographic experimentation, you should be fine. You'll be the surfer riding the wave of a new generation. If you're making motion and it's prior to 1997, you don't have to worry so much about knowing all the programs, or even having a reel. Just make sure you have a good design education and are a strong image-maker, or a skilled typographer. As long as you've got exciting ideas and a strong sense of design, you'll be able to hire anyone else you need to help you with all the detailed stuff like operating cameras, creating sound, editing, and post-production. You'll just need a client with enough money—but hey, you'll be getting paid pretty well, so it all balances out. And in this "post-Seven" moment, everyone is going to want to have a cool title sequence, even if it costs as much as the film itself.

If you can get through the titles boom and you still want to work in motion, you might want to think about making the switch to broadcast around 1998. By then, the software you need will be running on any consumer computer, all the programs will be right at hand, and most of the time you'll only be making a few seconds of end tag or some brief interstitials. Top tip: keep your render farm away from the California sun! You might need your own small wind farm to stop it from overheating... For the cooling ocean breezes, you'll almost certainly want to base your studio in Santa Monica, or Marina Del Rey, or Venice. Real estate is expensive and traffic terrible, not to mention the swaths of Brit tourists, but at least you won't have to worry about thermonuclear server meltdown.

Interest in typography will come and go, and so will interest in different graphic styles. If it's prior to 2000, it's best to pick one or two and try to own them, create your own look that you are known for. Make sure you are aware of who already owns what though: Saul Bass owns the flat paper cutout, the close-up eye, and the spinning spiral; Pablo Ferro owns the skinny hand written over live footage and the endless zoom; and Kyle Cooper owns the classically distressed and the fragmented fast cut. Try not to step on toes, even if the client asks you to. If it's after 2000, you are going to have to be a lot more flexible! Even if you are really successful, you'll need to be much more content/context specific, and you might want to think about having a style based on conceptual or strategic continuity rather than formalistic similarity.

If things work out and you start to turn a profit, don't let it go to your head. Stay a motion designer, don't try to be a director. It hardly ever works, even for the best title designers of any decade. The grass may look greener on the other side of the fence, but I'm fairly sure the hue and saturation have been pumped up in post.

If you exist in the future and you want to make motion graphics, I'm guessing things are going to be a little tougher for you. Everyone will have access to all the software needed to make anything instantaneously, all the footage that has ever existed, all the music and sounds there ever were, and a worldwide audience available at the press of a button. Your camera will be embedded in your pupil, the audio implanted in your ears. Your design moves will all be spoken, and your orders carried out by software algorithms that do exactly what you say (unlike those pesky interns). You will be able to immediately make anything, absolutely anything. Anything within the range of the software, that is. So if you want to stand out at this stage in the game, you might want to think about stepping out into the California sun, cutting some shapes out of paper, or clay, or sand, and making something frame by frame, move by move, step by step.

The Artist as Design Scientist

Our discussion obviously has excluded many important works of art that function completely within the genres of drama, plot, and story. *Citizen Kane, L'Avventura, Pierrot le Fou,* and *8½* are dramatic, plot films, yet no one denies their greatness. We know also that most of the truly significant films such as *Beauty and the Beast* or *Pather Panchali* operate entirely within parameters of the human condition as generally recognized. Moreover, common sense tells us that the artist *must* work with what exists, with the given, the human condition; he could produce no art at all if he relied exclusively on information that is totally new.

Yet the undeniable aesthetic value of these works does not contradict what I have said about art and entertainment. These films transcend their genres. They are not important for their plots or stories but rather for their design. Susan Sontag: "If there is any 'knowledge' to be gained through art, it is the experience of the form or style of knowing the subject, rather than a knowledge of the subject itself."[38]

To perceive that the artist functions as design scientist we must first understand that in their broadest implications art and science are the same. Eddington's classic definition of science, "The earnest attempt to set in order the facts of experience," corresponds with Bronowski's view of science as "The organization of knowledge in such a way that it commands more of the hidden potential in nature . . . all science is the search for unity in hidden likenesses."[39] It's the same in art: to set in order the facts of experience is to reveal the relation between man and his circumambient universe with all its hidden potential.

Herbert Read: "Only in so far as the artist establishes symbols for the representation of reality can mind, as a structure of thought, take shape. The artist establishes these symbols by becoming con-

[38] Susan Sontag, "On Style," *Against Interpretation* (New York: Delta Books), p. 22.
[39] J. Bronowski, *Science and Human Values* (New York: Harper & Brothers, 1965), pp. 3, 13.

scious of new aspects of reality and by representing his consciousness in plastic or poetic form . . . it follows that any extension of awareness of reality, any groping beyond the threshold of present knowledge, must first establish its sensuous imagery."[40]

Our word "design" is composed of "de" and "sign," indicating that it means "to remove the symbol of." In this context "symbol" signifies ideas distinct from experiences. As design scientist the artist discovers and perfects language that corresponds more directly to experience; he develops hardware that embodies its own software as a conceptual tool for coping with reality. He separates the image from its official symbolic meaning and reveals its hidden potential, its process, its actual reality, the experience of the thing. (A. N. Whitehead: "Process and existence pre-suppose each other.") He establishes certain parameters that define a discrete "special case" phenomenon, principle, or concept known as the subject. The work, in effect, poses this "problem" of perception and we as viewers must draw from this special case all the "general case" metaphysical relationships that are encoded within the language of the piece.

This language is the experiential information of aesthetic conceptual design; it is addressed to what Wittgenstein termed the "inarticulate conscious," the domain between the subconscious and the conscious that can't be expressed in words but of which we constantly are aware. The artist does not point out new facts so much as he creates a new language of conceptual design information with which we arrive at a new and more complete understanding of old facts, thus expanding our control over the interior and exterior environments.

The *auteur* theory of personal cinema indicates those instances when the filmmaker's design science transcends the parameters of his genre; our comprehension of that genre, that human condition, is thus expanded. But cybernetics has demonstrated that the structure of a system is an index of the performance which may be expected from it.[41] That is, the conceptual design of a movie determines the variety and amount of information we're likely to obtain from it. And since we've seen that the amount of information is

[40] Herbert Read, *Icon and Idea* (New York: Schocken Books, 1965), p. 53.
[41] Wiener, *op. cit.*, p. 79.

directly proportional to the degree of available choices we can see that drama, story, and plot, which restrict choice, also restrict information. So the auteur is limited to developing new designs for old information, which we all know can be immensely enjoyable and instructive. There are no "new" ideas in *L'Avventura*, for example, but Antonioni voiced the inarticulate conscious of an entire generation through the conceptual and structural integrity of his transcendental design science, merging sense and symbol, form and content.

Rudolph Arnheim: "Perceiving achieves at the sensory level what in the realm of reasoning is known as understanding . . . eyesight is insight."[42] If we realize that insight means to see intuitively, we acknowledge that Arnheim's assertion is true only when ordinary vision—conditioned and encultured by the most vulgar of environments—is liberated through aesthetic conceptual design information. Film is a way of seeing. We see through the filmmaker's eyes. If he's an artist we become artists along with him. If he's not, information tends toward misinformation.

The artist's intuitive sense of proportion corresponds to the phenomenon of absolute pitch in musicians and answers a fundamental need in comprehending what we apprehend. In the final analysis our aptitudes and our psychological balance are a result of our relation to images. The image precedes the idea in the development of consciousness: an infant doesn't think "green" when it looks at a blade of grass. It follows that the more "beautiful" the image the more beautiful our consciousness.

The design of commercial entertainment is neither a science nor an art; it answers only to the common taste, the accepted vision, for fear of disturbing the viewer's reaction to the formula. The viewer's taste is conditioned by a profit-motivated architecture, which has forgotten that a house is a machine to live in, a service environment. He leaves the theatre after three hours of redundancy and returns home to a symbol, not a natural environment in which beauty and functionality are one. Little wonder that praise is heaped on films whose imagery is on the level of calendar art. Global man stands on the moon casually regarding the entire spaceship earth in a glance,

---

[42] Rudolph Arnheim, *Art and Visual Perception* (Los Angeles, Calif.: University of California Press, 1954), p. 37.

yet humanity still is impressed that a rich Hollywood studio can lug its Panavision cameras over the Alps and come back with pretty pictures. "Surpassing visual majesty!" gasp the critics over *A Man and a Woman* or *Dr. Zhivago*. But with today's technology and unlimited wealth who couldn't compile a picturesque movie? In fact it's a disgrace when a film is not of surpassing visual majesty because there's a lot of that in our world. The new cinema, however, takes us to another world entirely. John Cage: "Where beauty ends is where the artist begins."

John Whitney

Animation Mechanisms

The October, 1969 issue of American Cinematographer contained an article on filming the Star Gate sequences for "2001: A SPACE ODYSSEY". Reference was made to my animation mechanisms and I have been invited to describe these.

As early as 1957 I had begun to construct mechanical drawing machines, reasoning simply that since the motion picture phenomenon is a precise incremental stepping process, a drawing tool capable of incremental variation would be useful. It is important to explain that I was not motivated to create representational images with these machines but, instead, wanted to create abstract pattern in motion. Since 1940, I had found myself devoted to the concept of an abstract visual art of motion structured in time, having for some years reflected over and over again upon the extraordinary power of music to evoke the most explicit emotions directly by its simple patterned configurations of tones in time and motion. The tendencies of much art of this century toward abstraction and kinetics served to reinforce these views during many moments of serious doubts of the validity of my own concepts.

My first machine, 1957, was immediately put to use in an unexpected way when Saul Bass included a few short sequences, drawn upon hundreds of animation cells with the machine's stylus, for the title to Alfred Hitchcock's film "VERTIGO". For one with such visions as mine centered in the fine arts, (an art so "fine", incidentally, as to be quite invisible), such applications as titles to a not very significant movie were scant reward.

Also, I soon saw the absurdity of a drawing machine producing countless animation cells which had to be photographed in turn onto motion picture film. So my next machine replaced the drawing stylus with a light which optically exposed the image sequences directly onto motion picture film by the simple dynamic process of holding the camera shutter open while the light itself completed one excursion for each frame.

There were plentiful absurdities in this procedure, it soon became clear since, in effect, I found I had labored long and hard only to produce hardly more than a mechanical equivalent of the cathode ray tube oscilloscope.

The mechanical motion which first moved the drawing pen over animation cells and, later, the light to and fro over the objective field of an ordinary animation stand assembly was merely a set of crank and lever arrangements similar to the ubiquitous child's circle pattern drawing toy or the more elaborate drawing or etching mill used in the bank-note printing industry.

By this time, however, I became aware of two areas of possibility, the coincidence of which had considerable effect upon the following developments.

I began to comprehend how camera advance, art work, orbital and rotational motion, and illumination, could all be knit into a comprehensive automated functioning system. Simultaneously I acquired, (not exactly overnight) a highly specialized skill in adapting the almost worthless mechanical junk excreted from army depots across the country as the Army, Navy, Air Force, and Marines unloaded materiel on the surplus market. Junk such as brand new thirty-thousand-dollar anti-aircraft specialized analog ballistic problem-solver computers dating back to World War II.

My next machine employed hardware from war surplus. Selsyn motors to interlock camera functions with artwork motions. Ball integraters to preset rate programming of some motions. And differential assemblies to control the incremental advance of the motions as each frame advanced.

Instead of a point source of light capable of drawing only lines, the camera was fixed above a light field about twelve inches wide. Artwork consisting usually of film negatives of typography or rudimentary abstract patterns (clear images on an overall black field) could be orbited, rotated or moved in a great variety of compound sine function excursions within the twelve-inch light field.

LAYOUT DESIGN BY *STEPHEN NOWLIN*

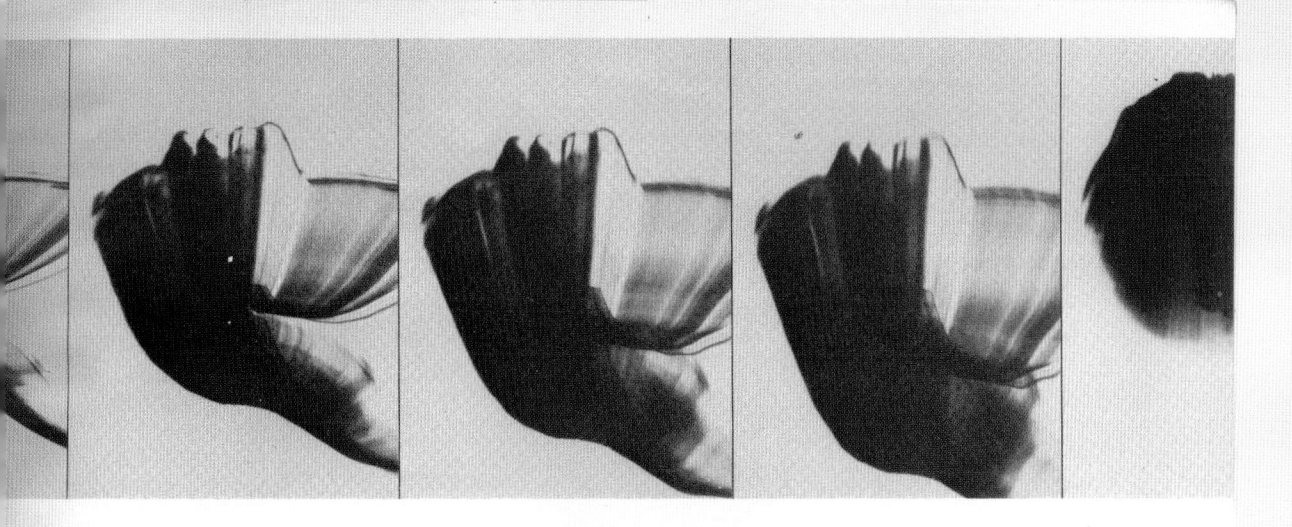

The camera above was motorized to advance one frame automatically at the instant of the completion of one cycle of the artwork motion. Driven through a clutch-brake and continuously running motor, camera advance was made as rapid as practical to minimize that blind segment of the artwork cycle required for pulldown for the next frame to be exposed. Thus, throughout the major portion of the artwork excursions the camera shutter would be in open position.

In order to clarify the simple principles involved here we may take as an example a sequence from my film "CATALOG"*. A film negative having

---

*Byjina Flores, 1964, produced by John Whitney Jr., age 18. See Expanded Cinema, Gene Youngblood, E. P. Dutton, New York, 1970.

"1961" (clear type face on a black field) is mounted on the artwork holder. This artwork is attached so that "1961" is located at dead center in the camera field when viewed through the rack-over viewfinder of the 35mm Mitchell camera (crank and lever mechanisms had been replaced by a more elaborate variable amplitude compound cam assembly by this time).

The art, "1961", so positioned in center field, can be articulated by the cam system which, for the moment, is set at "0" amplitude. The light field below the artwork is turned on, then the entire system is turned on. Art Work "1961" sits there throughout several complete "0" amplitude cycles while the camera advances at the completion of each cycle, exposing on each frame the image "1961", immobile at dead center field. Now the amplitude controls, through

differential gears, begin a minute orbiting which moves the art on an orbit with an increasing radius whose center is still camera field center. The simple image, "1961" now begins to be transformed into a progressively less readable pattern. The pattern that is produced, moving as it does, smoothly, and expanding outwardly, will continue to hold visual interest if only as a simple attractive abstract pattern. (see illustration, FIGURE 1)

If, instead of a continuously operating filament-type light source, a strobe light is used, the continuous pattern on the film can be broken into individual distinct overlaying images such as those illustrated. (FIGURE 2)

I have selected both of these simple actions to suggest some of the possibilities of which the machine is capable. My

AMERICAN CINEMATOGRAPHER, JANUARY, 1971

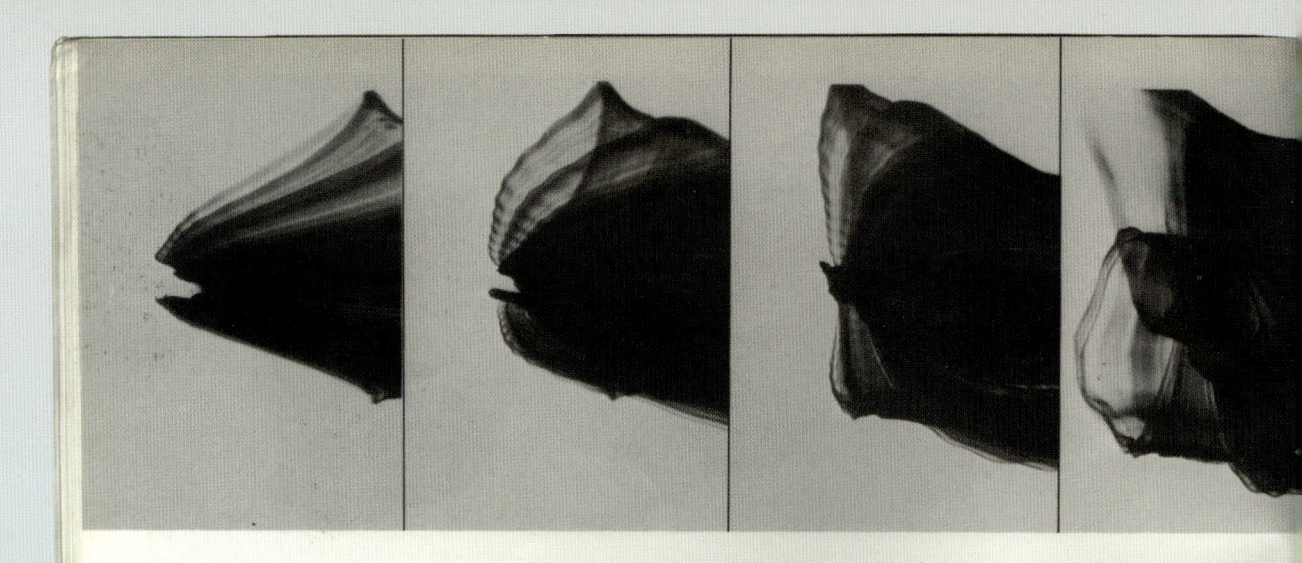

film "CATALOG" (see cover illustration) is a more diverse demonstration of the versatility of the machine. This film, used as a sample reel, was to be very productive of commercial assignments in the following years. The titles to the Chrysler, Bob Hope Television Show and portions of *To the Moon and Beyond* of the New York World's Fair, Alcoa commercials and titles to the Dinah Shore Show were typical. Of all the productions of this period, however, the one film which will probably endure was produced with my second version of this machine and made by my brother James. The film I refer to is titled "LAPIS". It has received many awards and continues to be a very popular film.

The following is a description of the effects seen throughout "LAPIS". Most of the patterns are center-oriented, constantly moving dots of color which continuously reform into new concentric arrays. They were achieved by a strobed rotary action of the artwork which combined an orbit, whose diameter was constantly changing, with drifting rotation. The artwork consisted usually of nothing more than a simple random dot pattern which was hand-drawn.

My brother and I were much intrigued by the results achieved by these simple random dot inputs. It was astonishing to discover the variety of orderly patterns generated by as random a source as these dot patterns. The original artwork contains no hint of the patterns that were produced. (FIGURE 3)

The above descriptions, however, still represent but the simplest of countless transformations that can be achieved with essentially the same mechanical system. For example, the shape of the orbital motion can be varied into back-and-forth motion on any angular axis with the X and Y controls of the compound cam assembly. A straight back-and-forth motion along a line at right angles to a line of type for example produces an effect such as that illustrated. (FIGURE 4)

Countless further variations can be produced by altering cycle phasing relative to camera advance or exposing only some fraction of each cycle or by changing the timing of the illumination, its frequency and/or its on-and-off duration.

These possibilities are greatly expanded by inclusion in this fully integrated system of a servo-motorized zoom lens. The zoom cycle is phased and operated

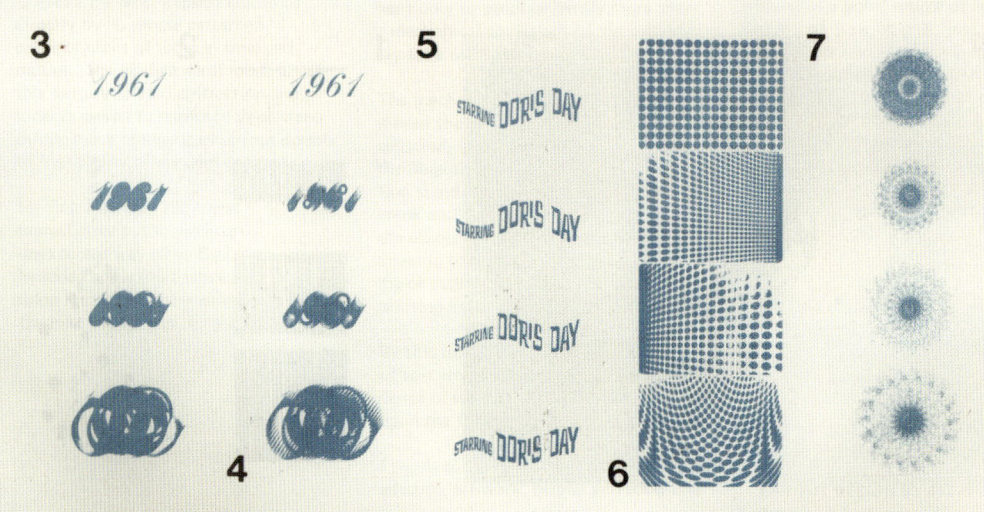

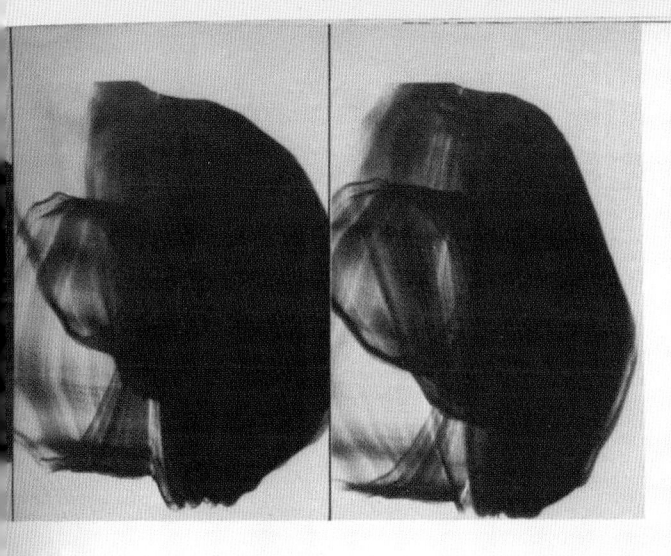

Selected frames from a new film by John Whitney, Jr., "TERMINAL SELF", sponsored by Universal Education and Visual Arts.

through all or part of its full magnification range in cycles that coincide with the various excursion cycles of the artwork. The illustration (FIGURE 5) is from a commercial for a milk product made in 1964 and was generated from artwork consisting of a careful hand-rendering of a single droplet of milk. In this case the orbit of the artwork began with the zoom lens at about mid-point of its magnification range. Then the zoom was operated through progressively greater magnification amplitudes per cycle as the elliptical orbits of the artwork were modified. The drawing was strobed nine times per cycle, producing a ring of nine orbiting spheres.

Finally, since my earliest casual interest with motion picture photography had been in a college astronomy department, I was familiar with various applications of optical slit-scanning connected with solar spectroscopy. It was, therefore, logical to apply these principles to my motion picture system. The titles for MGM's "GLASS BOTTOM BOAT", and many other commercial assignments, were done with a slit attached to one element of the compound cam assembly. The typography was attached to the other cam. The slit was set to move one full excursion across the full width of the type, while the type moved north and south one or more times per half-cycle of the slit. The return phase of the slit-scan cycle was accomplished while the camera shutter remained advanced, one half cycle, in closed position. Since there was a preset differential drift of the north and south movement of the typography the lettering on the screen appeared to undulate smoothly as if in water. (FIGURE 6)

The combination of this slit-scan technique with zoom produces very pronounced spatial motion in depth. This is specifically the slit-scan effect used to produce the Star Gate sequence of "SPACE ODYSSEY". My son's film, "BYJINA FLORES"* was produced by this slit-scan zoom combination. The artwork consisted merely of a standard Benday process overall dot pattern with a slit-scan and zoom cycle in differentially drifting interlock. (FIGURE 7)

The existing machine is grossly overdesigned. As a prototype, many experimental sub assemblies have been installed and removed or permanently established over the recent years. In fact, like some machine tools, each new film assignment involves some hardware assembly or knock-down. The machine practically fills the room into which it was built. The machine was featured on a CBS 21st Century Television segment in 1968. Two overhead wood beams, 4" x 12", span the room and carry the camera on a transverse dolly hanger assembly whose movement is free and independent of the artwork manipulating mechanism and illumination table below. This camera hanger assembly permits 360° continuous rotation of the camera, and back-and-forth straight-line travel over about twenty-four inches. The assembly connects all the camera's electrical leads; selsyn, film advance, zoom functions and phase shift through slip ring contacts to permit the continuous around-and-around camera rotation. These camera motions, of course, can be phased and synchronized precisely with the artwork motions below.

The artwork table below can be rotated 360° as a total unit, but cannot be operated continuously around because of its electrical connections. Since some of the cam functions have been covered already I will skip any further description except to say that at present the machine possesses four complete cam assemblies, any one of which can be set up to manipulate artwork or scanning slits or color filter patterns, etc. These units can be compounded in various ways to produce sum and difference effects.

It is somewhat idle information to count components but as an index of the complexity to which this kind of design system can be extended, the following statistics are suggestive:
    17 Bodine Motors
    8 Selsyns
    9 differential gear units
    5 Ball integrators

This present machine is now serving to test out a vastly simplified and rationalized system operated by servo drives and controls which, with a designed interface, will permit direct digital computer control. The new machine will be marketed under a patent granted in 1963 and others in development.
Continued overleaf

*Catalog—7 min., and other films by the Whitney family are available from the Museum of Modern Art, New York or Pyramid Films, Box 1048, Santa Monica, California 90406.

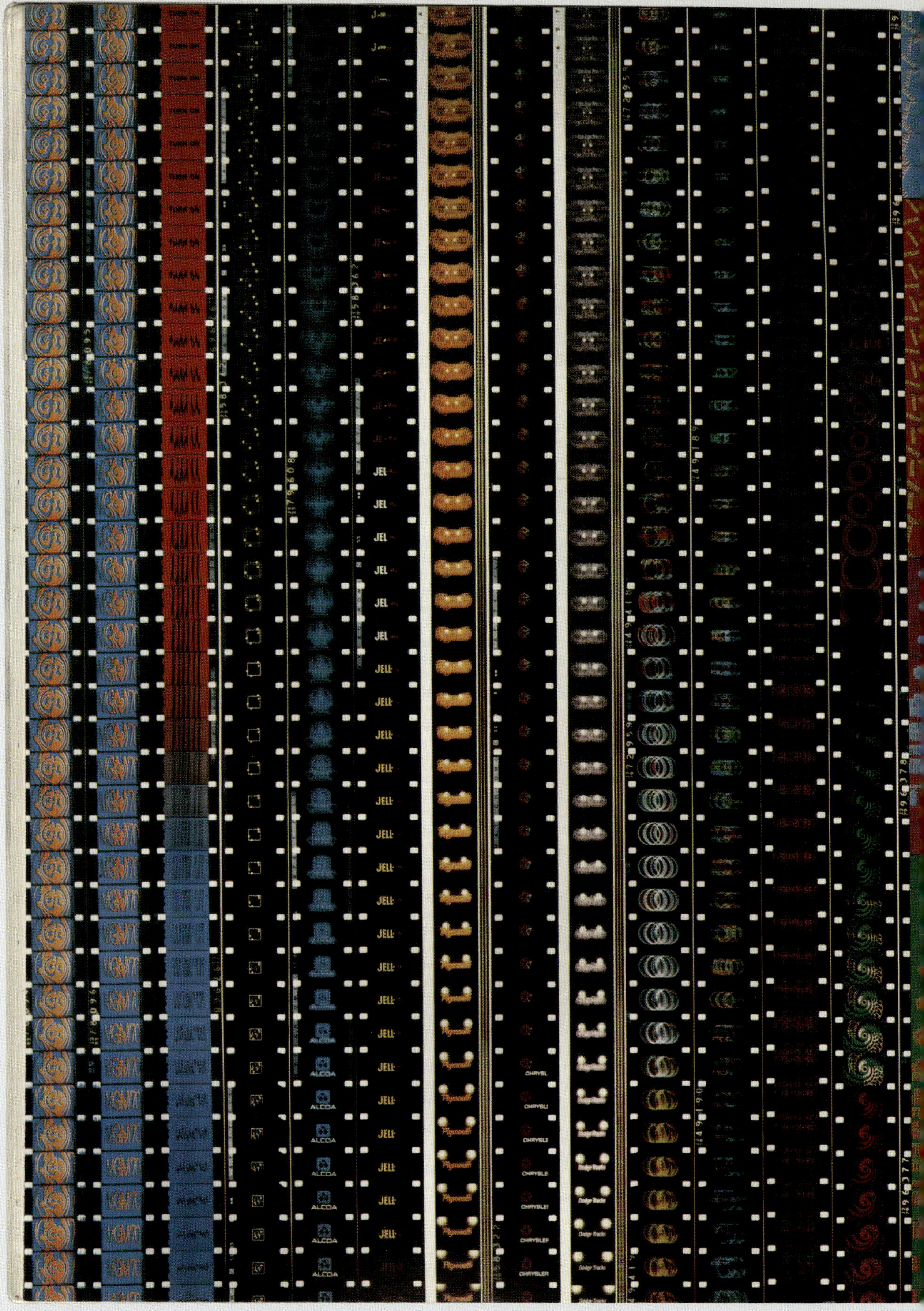
JELL
ALCOA
CHRYSLER

OPPOSITE PAGE: A selection of strips from commercials and titles dated at random throughout the 1960's.

(RIGHT) a recent photo of the analog cam machine. The overhead camera hanger is rotating and, therefore, appears blurred in this photograph.

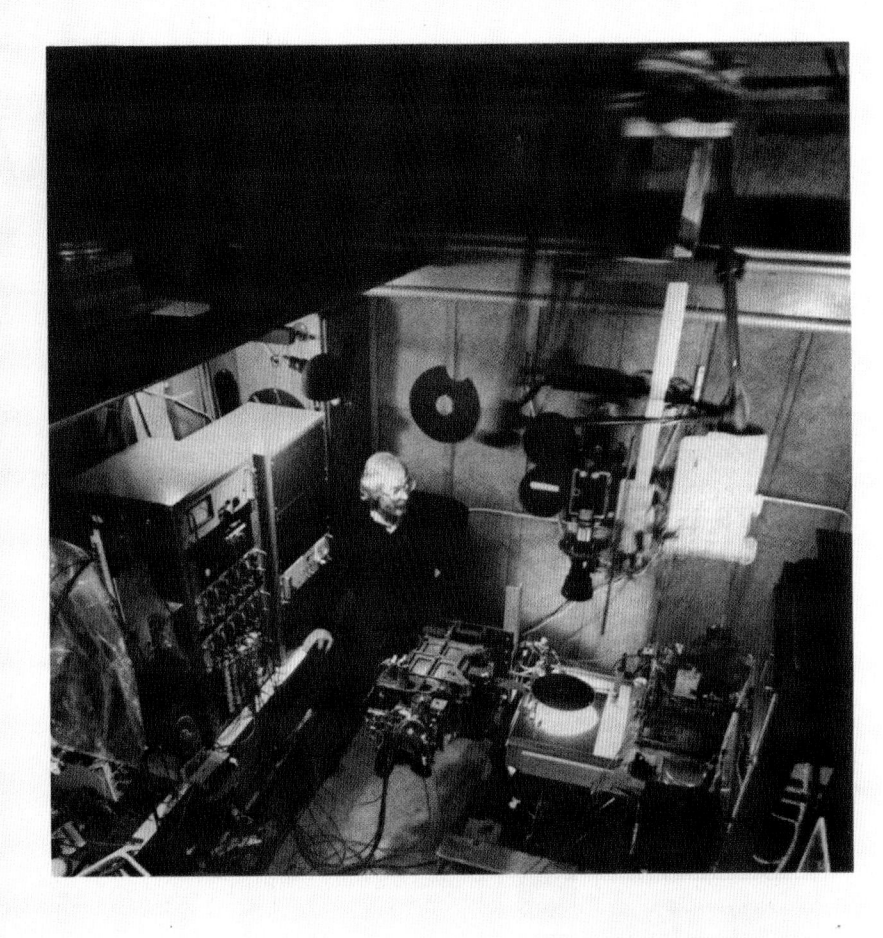

A refinement of the slit-scan process involving compound rotation.

In conclusion, may I be permitted a comment from a very specialized point of view:

My optimisms are more secure today than in 1940 regarding the arrival of altogether new forms of art for television and the newer home library cassette systems. I foresee new forms of abstract design and typography, which will bring unfamiliar delights of music for the eye to enjoy and a language of information that would mean the ascendancy of a new way with words, images and ideas.

Any casual viewer of television throughout the year 1970 may have noted that graphics, especially typography, have found a new dynamics that is quite happily suited to the television medium. For example, three major networks, in 1970, sponsored promotional interludes that anyone with an eye for design could respond to with unreserved pleasure. Yet, television in the United States, which is sometimes a thing of national pride, is, also, far too frequently, a matter of national disgrace. Aside from bad taste, bad design, establishmentarianism and commercial imprudence, the problems of television still have much to do with a medium that seeks to find its own "right way to fly". Traditions, especially from the theatre, are still a dead weight against flying new video ideas. My work has always been with new kinds of "flying machines". ■

AMERICAN CINEMATOGRAPHER, JANUARY, 1971

ROBERT ABEL: VIDEO SURREALIST

By Jeffrey Altshuler

He and his team create dazzling imagery of a kind that is new to TV commercials.

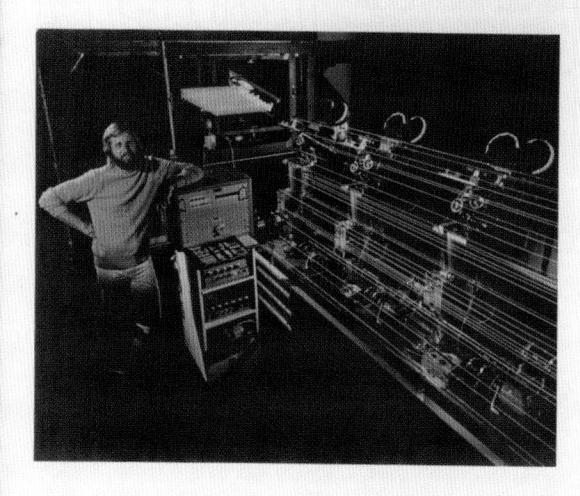

1. Robert Abel with animation camera system. This photograph was made by exposing the film six separate times — once for each camera position, twice for the Whirlpool logo, and once for Abel himself.
2. Abel '75 logo — introduction to sample reel using "Candy Apple Neon" technique. Art director: Robert Abel; designer: Richard Taylor; animator: Con Pederson.

Robert Abel is still just a little surprised that he has found a way to do exactly what he wants and get paid for it. And that he does it in a medium known for its restrictive preconditions and limitations of time and finance — TV commercials. What Abel wants to do is conjure up visual fantasies and put them on film, to imagine things as no one else has and then make those images exist in a kind of "artificial reality." This combination of Busby Berkeley, Magritte, and Earl Scheib may be the TV commercial industry's first Video Surrealist.

With the introduction last year of the now-famous Seven-Up "Bubbles" commercial — produced for EUE/Screen Gems, who represent Abel for commercials — Abel broke new ground in exploring images and techniques not normally associated with commercial design. But, while "Bubbles" may have been the first of a new genre of commercials, Abel's eclectic graphic sense has also proved successful in network promos for ABC and in logos for such companies as Kodak, Whirlpool, and RCA. Abel's graphics are uniquely suited to the elements of motion, time, and space inherent to the medium. Too often, designers working in film or television use two-dimensional images and simply move them around on the surface of the screen. But Abel utilizes his techniques to create the illusion of depth and perspective, covering the infinite number of planes in the mind's eye, designing in the total context of the visual medium he is working in.

Abel's work reflects a combination of influences: a fine arts education, extensive experience in live-action film production, and the Pop culture of Southern California, where he grew up. Attracted by the ability of motion pictures to turn fantasy into reality (at least vicariously), he discovered the perfect outlet for his imagination. The lush imagery of "Bubbles" borrows from extravaganzas of the Busby Berkeley era as well as the surrealist school of painting. It also displays more contemporary influences, such as the idea of weightlessness and electric light imagery, both visual themes of the space age technology which surrounds us.

The "Candy Apple Neon" which Abel and his design associates, Wayne Kimbell and Richard Taylor, developed for the ABC network promos this year resulted from a combination of Southern California influences — the neon and plastic of Los Angeles at night and the "Candy Apple" paint jobs typical of the Hot Rod era of the late fifties and early sixties. Abel had always admired airbrush illustration like that of Charles White III and wanted to achieve a similar look in film. It was with this in mind that the techniques for "Candy Apple Neon" were developed.

Abel's highly original film style is the result of his ability to work with several methods of production while maintaining a consistent and cohesive overall look. He has chosen to ignore barriers which have traditionally separated, or at least restrained, the thorough integration of live-action, animation and special-effects photography, particularly in commercial production. In the Seven-up "Bubbles" spot, for example, live-action, rear projection, streak photography, and slit-scan animation were combined in the "sea of bubbles" scene alone.

The principal tool in the execution of Abel's concepts is a computer-operated, horizontal animation camera similar to the one used to create the special-effects photography for *2001: A Space Odyssey*. The operation of this camera allows Abel to combine

35 Print

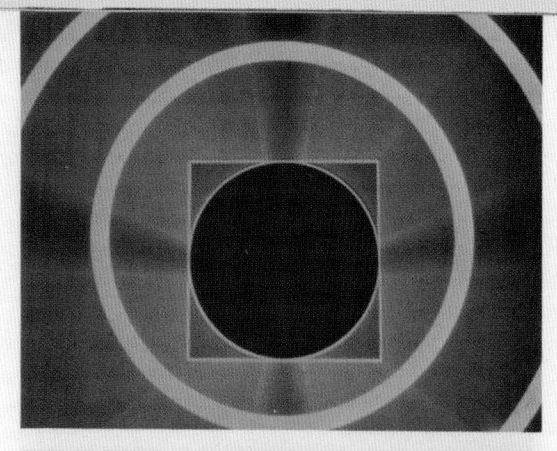

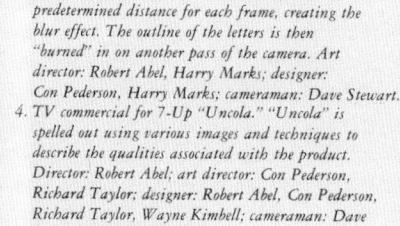

3. ID for ABC News Closeup. Words are given dimension and motion using streak-photography technique. The shutter is kept open as the artwork is moved a predetermined distance for each frame, creating the blur effect. The outline of the letters is then "burned" in on another pass of the camera. Art director: Robert Abel, Harry Marks; designer: Con Pederson, Harry Marks; cameraman: Dave Stewart.

4. TV commercial for 7-Up "Uncola." "Uncola" is spelled out using various images and techniques to describe the qualities associated with the product. Director: Robert Abel; art director: Con Pederson, Richard Taylor; designer: Robert Abel, Con Pederson, Richard Taylor, Wayne Kimbell; cameraman: Dave Stewart, Don Miskowich.

elements with perfect accuracy and to repeat moves, control exposures, and execute shots precisely, frame for frame. Since each scene is shot one frame at a time, the computer is an invaluable aid for keeping track of the enormous amount of information that goes into every shot.

In conventional animation, three basic moves are used — pan, tilt, and zoom. However, by mounting the artwork on a specially designed stand which is also controlled by the computer, Abel has added three new movements — pitch, roll, and yaw — allowing the artwork to rotate both vertically and horizontally and to spin in its own plane. It is this facility which gives his work its dimensional perspective.

Color is a critical element in Abel's work, and again he has developed special processes to generate the full, rich tones which characterize his design. Most often in conventional, animation-stand photography, light is reflected from artwork already inked with the desired colors. Abel, however, uses transparent or translucent artwork and projects light through it from behind. He controls his colors by introducing gels at various points between the light source and the film plane. In effect, he draws directly on the film with light.

Abel tries to utilize the visual devices at his disposal without getting bogged down in technique at the expense of design. Yet he and his staff are constantly trying to develop new processes to execute their concepts. In fact, Robert Abel is really more than one person. While Abel himself functions as the chief conceptualizer, there are several other key people, each with a specific area of responsibility, without whom the work could not be realized.

Working very closely with Abel is Con Pederson, whose background includes animation for Disney and work on the special effects for *2001*. Pederson's main area of responsibility is in planning the relationships of images in motion and figuring the proper timings. Abel and Pederson have worked together for 11 years, and it is their close personal interaction which ensures successful results. Richard Taylor and Wayne Kimbell are both graphic designers, each working in specific elements of a production. When all the design and timing has been thought out, it is Dave Stewart who

3. executes the project on film. The Robert Abel staff also includes

computer operators, engineers, and other related artists, and Abel is the first to admit that it is their unified creative attitude that makes the highly complex design system work so effectively.

Since there is very little for the client to see other than design sketches or mattes before filming has been completed and dailies are ready (everything is shot on original negative to maintain the quality of first-generation film), a relationship of mutual trust and understanding between Abel, his staff, and the client is essential. Abel spends a great deal of time determining what qualities his client is looking for in a specific project. However, since there is an element of experimentation in all his work, Abel finds the most gratification and success when the client approaches the job with an open mind, allowing him freedom to exercise his imagination.

Bob Abel's work is complex, time-consuming, and requires a great deal of creative precision. But he is content as long as he can continue to exercise his imagination. And, in doing so, he is at the same time bringing an entirely new look to the visual imagery we respond to on television.

5. *Opening for CBS Bicentennial programs. Tunnel effect is created by a perspective-building device, slit-scan photography. The artwork is shot through a circular slit (1/64") in an all-black field, in this case corresponding to the circumference of the CBS Eye. For each frame the camera zooms in on the slit with its shutter open, making a constant exposure and causing what is first photographed in the center of the frame to move to the outer edges and ultimately out of the frame entirely. The artwork behind the slit also moves at a coordinated rate of speed. The slit itself acts like a shutter, keeping the artwork from blurring. The artwork is then partially cranked back and the process is repeated for the next frame. The effect can also be done with a rectangular slit. The three-dimensional model of the CBS Eye was matted in later. Art director: Robert Abel; designer: Robert Abel, Richard Taylor, Richard Edlund; cameraman: Dave Stewart, Richard Edlund.*
6. *ABC-TV fall '75 titles. Here, Abel uses the neon techniques to illustrate theme, "It's a bright new day on ABC." Art director: Robert Abel, Harry Marks; designer: Richard Taylor; animator: Dave Augsburger.*
7. *Titles for ABC-TV series, "Kung Fu." Art director: Harry Marks, Robert Abel; designer: Con Pederson; cameraman: Dave Stewart.*
8. *7-Up billboard — lifted from 35mm "Bubbles" commercial.*

8.

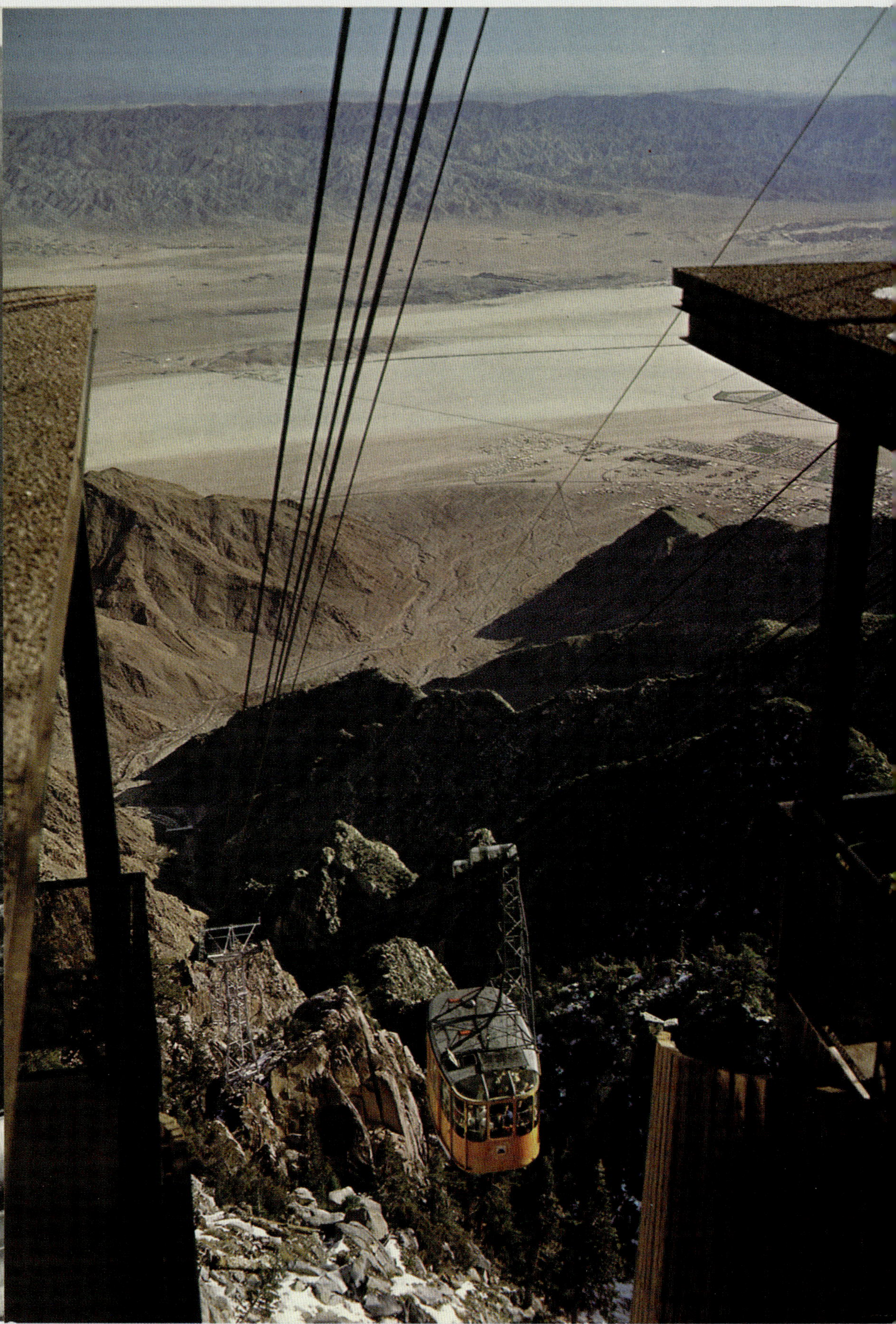

↑ Oskar Fischinger in his Hollywood studio, 1942
← "Aerial tramway from the heat of the desert and the sun-drenched resort of the Palm Springs," from Beautiful California, 1971

Oskar Fischinger [1900–1967]. **ALLEGRETTO, 1936–43, 2:30 MIN.**
Originally from Germany, Fischinger combined a love of music and graphic arts with an ability to design and build his own equipment for creating some of the most influential avant-garde films of the early twentieth century. These films represent a "collision between high art abstraction and mass commercial culture" that was to play a vital role in the development of the movie industry.[1] ¶ Fischinger began his experiments with animated abstraction seeking to realize his theory that messages could be expressed without words or literal depictions. It was this visual language that eventually allowed Hollywood productions to express more abstract ideas and spaces. ¶ Fischinger came to Los Angeles in 1936 after fleeing his Nazi-controlled homeland. He was lucky enough to have German émigré director Ernst Lubitsch witness an audience's delighted response to a Hollywood screening of two of his films; as a result, Lubitsch invited Fischinger to work for Paramount. Allegretto was intended as animation for the opening musical number of the feature film Big Broadcast (1937), but Fischinger withdrew it when he realized his colorful work would appear in black-and-white. A second version, also never used, included abstract patterns and nonanimated images. The final version, depicted here, was realized through a private grant that allowed Fischinger to purchase his original work back from the studio and continue its development. In this iteration, wrote film historian William Moritz, "the colors are more diverse, California colors—the pinks and turquoise and browns of the desert sky and sand, the orange of poppies and the green of avocados."[2]

INDUSTRY & THE INDIES

Harry Smith [1923–1991]. FILM #5: CIRCULAR TENSIONS (HOMAGE TO OSKAR FISCHINGER), 1947, 10 MIN.

Smith, a known eccentric who considered himself an anthropologist rather than an artist, began making films after moving from Washington to the Bay Area in 1945.[3] It was at Art in Cinema—a series of avant-garde film screenings presented by the San Francisco Museum of Modern Art from 1946 to 1953—that Smith gained exposure to abstract experimental films, including those of Oskar Fischinger. This influential series, organized by brothers Frank and Jack Stauffacher, and Richard Foster, screened abstract and nonnarrative films from New York, Europe, and California. Inspired, Smith sought training and equipment from his friend Hy Hirsh, a generous photographer, cinematographer, and avant-garde filmmaker. Smith's early experiments utilized a batik-like process applied directly to the film, with results that graphically and organizationally reference the complex structures and improvisations of the artist's beloved bebop jazz. The colorful, madly exuberant, prepsychedelic Circular Tensions represents a departure from the cruder techniques of Smith's early work and paved the way for the playful pictorial collages of his later films. He recollected that through watching Fischinger work he learned the discipline and concentration required to make the leap to more sophisticated productions.[4] ¶ Smith's and Fischinger's independent avant-garde creations set the stage for a generation of filmmakers whose artistic gifts would be embraced by a mainstream industry.[5]

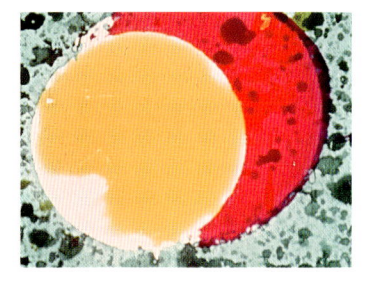

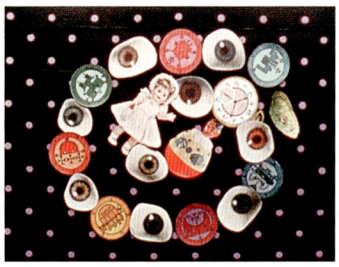

TOP: Harry Smith, still from Film #2: Message from the Sun, ca. 1946–48; ABOVE: Still from Film #10, ca. 1957

INDUSTRY & THE INDIES

Alvin Lustig [1915–1955]. **MISTER MAGOO TITLES, CA. 1950.** These titles for the cartoon series Mister Magoo, a box-office hit produced by legendary animation studio United Productions of America (UPA) for Columbia Pictures, depict the visually challenged Magoo entering the frame from the right, then peering through the double o's of the title.[6] UPA had hired Lustig to design its original logo in 1946 and a revised logo in 1950. The studio then invited him to try his hand at animation and wound up using Lustig's Mister Magoo graphics for several years, beginning with the cartoon's third installment, "Trouble Indemnity," produced in September 1950.[7]

Columbia Pictures presents
THE NEARSIGHTED
MISTER
MAGOO

Columbia Pictures presents
THE NEARSIGHTED
MISTER
MAGOO

Columbia Pictures presents
THE NEARSIGHTED
MISTER
MAGOO

United Productions of America's
TROUBLE
INDEMNITY
COLOR BY TECHNICOLOR
COPYRIGHT MCML COLUMBIA PICTURES CORPORATION
INTERNATIONAL COPYRIGHT SECURED, ALL RIGHTS
RESERVED • CODE CERTIFICATE NO. 14309
SOUND RCA SYSTEM

Saul Bass. THE FRANK SINATRA SHOW TITLES, 1957. ABC contracted Sinatra for a weekly half-hour drama and variety program. Bass's title design for the show—a variety of icons emanating from a top hat—suggests the hybrid format. Bass first gained recognition for his title designs for the 1955 film The Man with the Golden Arm (another Sinatra vehicle). But while the big screen clearly had begun to embrace modernist graphics, 1957 was early in ABC's creative evolution. By contrast, competitor CBS, under the guidance of its advertising and promotional creative director, William Golden, had already established a streamlined design brand for the network, reflected in its advertising and ubiquitous use of the now-classic "eye" logo. In 1964, ABC hired renowned graphic designer Paul Rand to make it a new trademark of simple geometric letters based on circles and lines—a move in step with the times. Graphic art had become so important to the networks in the 1960s that the trade magazine Print declared that TV promotional graphics "often outshine the shows being promoted!"[8]

INDUSTRY & THE INDIES

Eames Office. <u>**GLIMPSES OF THE U.S.A.**</u>**, 1959, STILL AND MOVING IMAGES PROJECTED ONTO SEVEN SCREENS, EACH 30 x 20 IN., 10 MIN.** This project began when the U.S. State Department commissioned George Nelson to design the 1959 American National Exhibition of art and products in Moscow, part of the first "cultural exchange" between the United States and the Soviet Union since the Russian Revolution. Nelson enlisted Charles and Ray Eames to create a film about "a day in the life of the United States" to introduce the show. Working with Hollywood director Billy Wilder and the U.S. Information Agency's coordinator of design and construction, Jack Masey, Nelson and the Eameses settled on some basic parameters. From there, the Eameses proceeded with a free hand to create the multiscreen <u>Glimpses of the U.S.A.</u> Working with a team that included John Neuhart and John Whitney, they selected 2,200 images from everyday life—how Americans work, play, dine, travel, and dress—to be projected in simultaneous juxtapositions. The sequence of images came from sources ranging from Eames staff and friends to photo archives. Determining the ending was a particular challenge that Ray resolved by suggesting that it close with views of people saying goodnight. The final image was a bowl of forget-me-nots, which represented "remembrance, constancy, and simplicity" in America and "love, friendship, and remembrance" in Russia, according to Eames biographer Pat Kirkham. ¶ On the night before the premier, Charles and Ray arrived dressed like a Boy Scout and a Girl Scout with the films in hand. The 16 daily showings, accompanied with music by Elmer Bernstein, took place in one of Buckminster Fuller's geodesic domes.[9]

INDUSTRY & THE INDIES

155

Eames Office. **KALEIDOSCOPE JAZZ CHAIR**, 1960, 6:28 MIN. One of 80 film projects produced by the Eames Office, Kaleidoscope Jazz Chair was an outgrowth of an earlier work shown at the Royal College of Art. To produce a film about chairs and furniture for a talk Charles Eames was giving in England, he attached mirrors to a camera and thus produced a fragmented effect. According to scholar Pat Kirkham, "He had been asked to bring some illustrations of the Eames Office so that students might see how the famous workshop functioned. Charles thought this too boring and decided [instead] to make a short film that would capture the experimental nature and excitement of the work. Former Royal College students recall that the event felt more like the beginning of the Swinging Sixties than a lecture by one of the world's most 'serious' designers."[10]

INDUSTRY & THE INDIES

John Whitney [1917–1995]. **CATALOG, 1961, 7 MIN.** Many consider Whitney to be the father of motion graphics. Although commercial work was not his ambition (he was a highly accomplished artist), its graphic and typographic possibilities resonated nonetheless, and he was instrumental in giving birth to a new design field. ¶ In 1957, Whitney began building drawing machines from outmoded analogue military computers, seeking to create a correspondence between animated imagery and music. He produced hundreds of animation cells with the device, some of which Saul Bass repurposed to create the spiraling effects in his titles for the 1958 Alfred Hitchcock film Vertigo.[11] ¶ Whitney's other commercial work included projects during the 1950s at UPA, the animation studio known for cartoons including Mister Magoo. In 1956, he joined the Eames Office, where he was part of the team that created the multiscreen presentation Glimpses of the U.S.A. ¶ In 1960, Whitney formed Motion Graphics, and his new company's promotional reel, Catalog, demonstrated the versatility of his animation machine and led to commercial assignments ranging from titles for TV programs such as the The Dinah Shore Show and the Chrysler-sponsored Bob Hope Show to portions of the film To the Moon and Beyond, presented at the New York World's Fair of 1964–65. The overall trippy-ness of Catalog made it a classic of the psychedelia subculture of the 1960s.[12]

INDUSTRY & THE INDIES   159

Phill Norman [1935–2009]. **VARIOUS TITLE GRAPHICS FOR UPA, LATE 1950s–EARLY 1960s.** Title design wasn't Norman's goal, but it turned out to be his fate. On vacation in California, he had lunch with a high school friend who was working at UPA. It happened that the studio was slammed with Mister Magoo and Dick Tracy shorts and needed help with lettering and title cards. Norman's lack of experience (or the fact that he had no formal education in design, although he did attend art school in Indiana for three years) didn't discourage UPA, and Norman wasn't fazed by the long hours the studio demanded. During his three years at UPA, he handled all the studio's title sequences, credits, and lettering, and occasionally contributed backgrounds. ¶ The playful hand-lettered type that appears in these titles, a staple of midcentury American advertising, was inspired by the expressive typographic language used in comics and newspaper cartoons of the 1920s and 1930s. As design historian Steve Heller puts it (and any doodler can attest), "Once you let your hand do the work, quirky things are bound to happen."[13] Animation historian Amid Amidi commented further that this kind of chunky, cartoonish lettering was "treated then as an organic part of the entire composition [in print cartoons], whereas [title] designers isolated the funny type and gave it renewed prominence as a design element."[14] John Van Hamersveld, creator of the legendary poster for the surfing film The Endless Summer, cites this cartoonish lettering style as the source for much of surf graphics' letterforms as well.

INSOMNIAC MAGOO

MAGOO'S GNU

lady in black

FOOD FEUD

FISH 'N TRICKS

NIGHT FRIGHT

Elias Romero [1925–2009]. **STEPPING STONES, 1968, 34 MIN.** Projected imagery can be traced back to the seventeenth-century Dutch astronomer and mathematician Christiaan Huygens and his innovations with glass slides, but the originator of live "painting with light" set to music was Seymour Locks, a professor at San Francisco State College. In 1952, Locks was looking to wow a group of art educators convening in San Francisco by reviving "the European experiments of the twenties and thirties in projected scenery, and have dancers running in and out of scrim projected with designs," recalls '60s historian Charles Perry.[15] He ended up using an overhead projector to cast images on the wall of swirling colored liquids in a dish while a jazz group improvised.[16] It was a mutant, hybrid artistic enterprise born of the convergence of two trajectories: Abstract Expressionist painting and avant-garde filmmaking of the sort being produced by Oskar Fischinger and others seeking to create a correlation between abstract visuals and music. ¶ Originally a painter, Romero was introduced to light shows when he saw a "painting" performed by two of Locks's former students in Los Angeles. By 1958, he had created his own approach and performed his visual compositions in Beat hangouts in L.A., accompanied by a friend on drums. ¶ Romero relocated to San Francisco and by 1962 was presenting his colorful, luminous experiments at parties, galleries, coffeehouses, and other spaces; one performance group inspired by Romero explored projecting images onto the bodies of nude performers.[17] Stepping Stones translates a liquid-light performance onto film, capturing the composition and movement of these glowing expressions. Today, many recognize Romero as paving the way for the undulating, hypnotic graphic imagery of 1960s rock shows.

INDUSTRY & THE INDIES

Saul Bass. APPLES AND ORANGES, 1962, 14 MIN. Bass arrived in Los Angeles in 1947 to discover a lush culture of avant-garde filmmaking. The situation resonated with the graphic designer, who while studying with György Kepes at Brooklyn College had ingested the legendary modernist's idea that "graphic design and motion pictures could play a major role in changing the world because they were less hidebound by tradition."[18] Apples and Oranges afforded a new opportunity for Bass to try his inspired hand. ¶ Commercial filmmaking—aka "sponsored films" or "business films"—was a ripe industry at the time, offering creative opportunities, and potentially a financial livelihood, for both avant-garde filmmakers and adventurous graphic designers. These commissions gave artists more experimental leeway than conventional Hollywood feature films did, and in return, corporate clients gained the imprimatur of being patrons of the arts, along with vehicles with which to "soft sell" their products. ¶ Desiring a creative foray with a new type of client, Bass used his considerable charm to persuade Lou Dorfsman, art director at CBS Television, to hire him. The resulting "sponsored film" translates a weighty research document into a compelling and playful narrative that pits apples (television commercials) against oranges (magazine ads) to demonstrate the superiority of broadcast advertising. ¶ The film, as described by Bass's biographers Jennifer Bass and Pat Kirkham, "combines animation with live action, contrasts black and white with vibrant colors, and lets the statistical data of graphs and flowcharts run riot in delightfully sophisticated arrays of numbers and type." A cartoon private eye represents the 6,000 researchers who gathered the data—a conceit Bass said reflected his sense that such surveys were "a socially approved kind of spying."[19] ¶ The color shown in these frames at best hints at the original color, which is now lost to time. Knowing that Bass tended to use rich, saturated hues, we can assume these images must have featured bright colors where dull, faded ones now appear.

INDUSTRY & THE INDIES

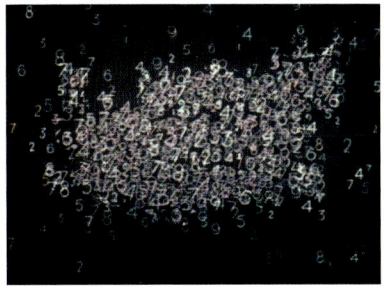

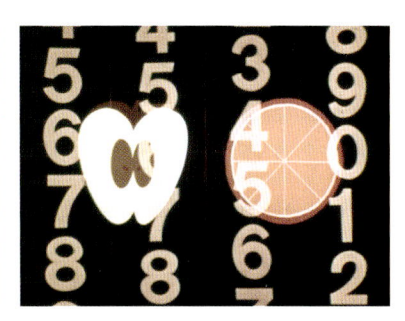

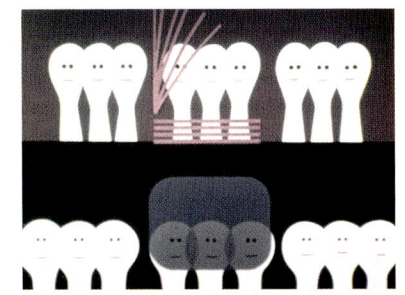

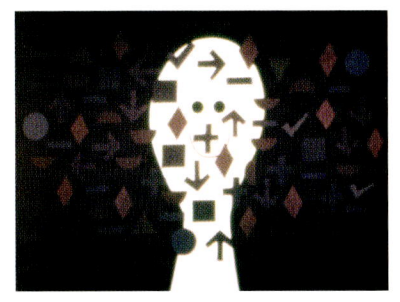

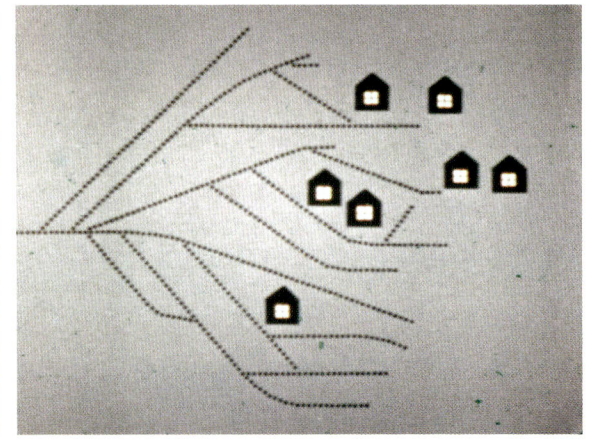

165

John Urie and Associates. **ABC 1964–65 FALL SEASON PROMO, 1964.** This charming one-hour black-and-white promo show featured all sorts of zippy camera moves—quick cuts, zooms, and pans of an image array that included sharply cropped photographs of jazz performers, vintage graphics, celebrity head shots, circus graphics, and a spinning tower built from stacked wooden letters that spelled the days of the week. Also in the mix, of course, was Paul Rand's 1962 ABC logo design. According to iconoclastic broadcast designer Harry Marks, ABC was willing to work with smaller, more adventurous job agencies, which is why John Urie—"one of the most renowned and expensive"—got the job.[20] Urie produced commercials for UPA during the 1950s before opening his own shop, and is remembered today for creating the animated character Hawaiian Punch to sell the eponymous juice drink.[21]

INDUSTRY & THE INDIES

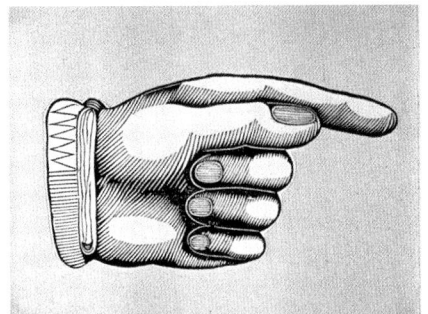

Elaine Bass [b. 1927] **and Saul Bass.** <u>SECONDS</u> TITLE SEQUENCE, **1966.** This dark science-fiction film directed by John Frankenheimer concerns a man who is unhappy and bored with middle age. Through plastic surgery and psychiatric intervention, he receives a new, younger identity and a hip Malibu lifestyle. But all does not turn out well, and the Basses' distorting, disfigured title imagery presages the jarring cinematography of James Wong Howe as well as the terrifying fate of the film's protagonist.[22] Elaine first tested this title-sequence concept with the game cooperation of longtime collaborator and fellow graphic designer Art Goodman. Reflections of his face were projected onto thin aluminum sheets; these were manipulated to create distortions, which were then photographed.[23] The tests demonstrated for Saul how this "distorted and reconstituted" face could successfully suggest the psychological terror that the film evokes.

film editors FERRIS WEBSTER · DAVID NEWHOUSE

ROCK HUDSON

key grip RICHARD BORLAND
property master FRANK AGNONE
costumers JACK MARTEL
PETE SALDUTTI
make-up artist JACK PETTY
MARK REEDALL
dialogue coach THOM CONROY
sound mixer STEWART LINDER
sound effects editor HOWARD BEALS

SECONDS

directed by JOHN FRANKENHEIMER

Bill Ham [b. 1932]. **SPONTANEOUS PAINTING OF PROJECTED IMAGERY, 1966–69.** An Abstract Expressionist painter and true "indie," Ham began developing a method for what he called "spontaneous painting of projected imagery" after witnessing Elias Romero's liquid-light projections for rock shows. (As luck or fate would have it, Romero, the originator of the improvisational light show, was living in a building that Ham managed.[24]) Romero's work inspired Ham to take his creative practice from labor-intensive oil on canvas to more immediate experiences made using overhead projectors—an idea first introduced by Hungarian artist and former Bauhaus professor László Moholy-Nagy. ¶ The luscious and vibrant graphic experiences Ham created from illuminated swirls of ink and oil were often presented at concerts produced by the Family Dog for the Avalon Ballroom and became a central part of the San Francisco rock scene of the '60s. Musicians and spectators alike were bathed in the psychedelic projected imagery, allowing graphics on a grand scale to function as a form of total immersion in which audiences participated through dance. Unique to Ham's work was its incorporation of playful montages of slides, films, and strobes, along with the manipulation of colorful liquids. Ham was also ambitious in terms of the architectural scale of his projections, which often covered several walls.[25] ¶ For Ham, these live experiences were "happenings" driven by an impulse toward expanded consciousness—they were art experiences rather than entertainment.[26]

Bill Ham's projection set-up for live video performance for Marin County Public Access TV, 1977

INDUSTRY & THE INDIES

171

Harry Marks [b. 1931] **and Douglas Trumbull** [b. 1942]. <u>ABC MOVIE OF THE WEEK PROMO</u>, 1969. Sophisticated graphics for television may have originated at CBS in New York under Lou Dorfsman and in L.A. with Saul Bass, but Harry Marks took their ideas and ran with them. ¶ A love of typography struck when he was a 15-year-old apprentice at Oxford University Press; Marks then became interested in music and film. This vibrant young gun with an expansive vision of what graphics for the screen could be made his way to Los Angeles and, in 1966, landed a job at ABC just as its ratings skyrocketed and its graphics started earning national attention.¶ Only a couple of years later, when Trumbull shared his special-effects outtakes from Kubrick's <u>2001: A Space Odyssey</u>, Marks's imaginative prowess really took flight. His mind blown by the possibilities of how he might translate this "graphic madness into something legible," Marks joined with Trumbull to use experimental techniques to create abstracted yet legible dimensional typography and a new sense of space and dynamic movement for the small screen.[27] These efforts led to the legendary graphics for ABC's <u>Movie of the Week</u>. But that was only the beginning. ¶ Marks's work was duly credited to a host of collaborators who along the way established the technical and artistic base from which his ideas sprang. This recognition of the combined talents of musicians, artists, scientists, and engineers led Marks to conceive of a conference to gather all the diverse, exceptional, inventive people who often worked on the same projects but didn't know each other. In 1984, in Monterey, California, Marks and partner Richard Saul Wurman organized the first Technology Entertainment and Design conference, now a regular event known the world over as TED.[28]

INDUSTRY & THE INDIES

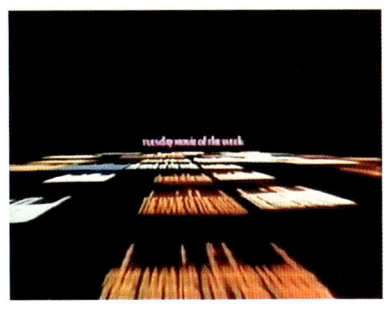

Robert Abel [1937–2001] and Harry Marks. THE ABC FRIDAY NIGHT MOVIE PROMO, 1970. Following Marks's and Doug Trumbull's groundbreaking ABC Movie of the Week promo, Trumbull turned toward film projects and Marks returned to collaborator Abel, who had recently acquired some of Trumbull's equipment and was setting up his studio, Robert Abel and Associates, soon to become known for its radically innovative work. While Marks and Abel couldn't equal the technical wizardry of the ABC Movie of the Week graphics, the team nonetheless created dynamic and colorful imagery for The ABC Friday Night Movie, evoking a cinema marquee of multiple rows of small lights that appeared to zoom beyond the space of the screen and the viewer.[29] According to designer Richard Taylor, who joined Abel's firm in 1973, a similar title treatment for The ABC Saturday Night Movie sparked the concept for "Bubbles," the psychedelic-chorus-girl-neon-butterfly fantasia the team concocted to advertise 7UP.[30]

INDUSTRY & THE INDIES

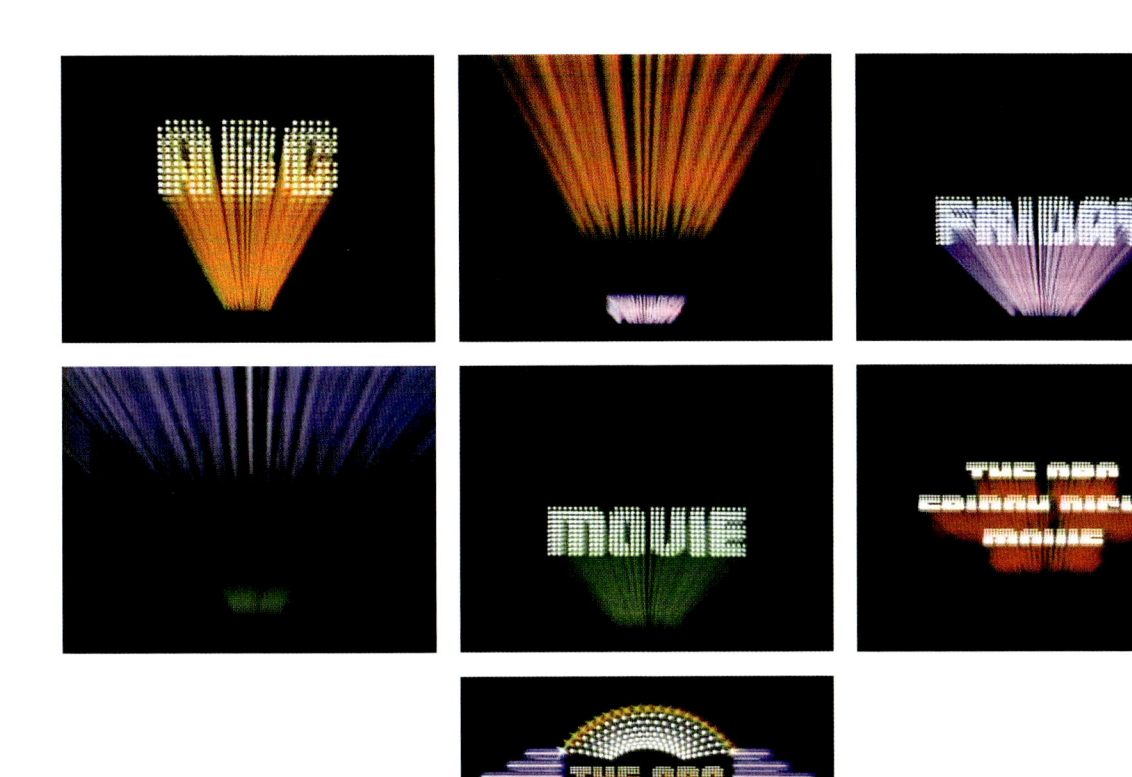

Single Wing Turquoise Bird. RE-CREATION OF PERFORMANCE, CA. 1969. The collective Single Wing Turquoise Bird (Larry Janss, David Lebrun, Peter Mays, Jeffrey Perkins, and Michael Scroggins) came together at the prompting of graphic designer John Van Hamersveld, whose production company, Pinnacle, organized rock concerts at L.A.'s Shrine Auditorium and wanted to establish a group of artists to produce dynamic light shows.[31] SWTB attracted creative people from various communities, including young filmmakers from UCLA, a commune resident who'd learned chemical procedures from light-show elder statesmen Bill Ham and Elias Romero, and a surfer interested in abstract animation. The group made its mark with complex visual orchestrations, merging a spectrum of original and appropriated imagery with abstract liquid-light painting and then montaging the combinations through high-powered projection machines. Their productions created graphic immersions joining big-name rock bands and throbbing, chemically liberated audiences. ¶ In 1968, after Pinnacle's demise, SWTB began to move away from the rock scene. A few members left the collective and those who remained began working, with rigorous practice, to transform projections that had been spontaneous and supplementary to the music into a disciplined artistic endeavor with its own integrity; the results came to be regarded as an example of what film scholar Gene Youngblood dubbed "expanded cinema." ¶ The utopian idealists behind this genre envisioned a grand, global collective artwork realized through computers and satellites. Yet avant-garde efforts with these new technologies lost out to electronic advertising and mass-media entertainment, such as Hollywood, television, and the pop- and rock-concert market, a significant trajectory within the field of motion graphics.[32] ¶ There is little documentation of SWTB's work; the images here are re-created based on their techniques and footage.

INDUSTRY & THE INDIES

Envirolab (Chris Dawson, Denny Lord, and Alan Stanton) **and E.A.T. (Experiments in Art and Technology)** (David McDermott and Ardison Phillips). **PEPSI PAVILION AT EXPO '70, OSAKA, JAPAN, 1970.** Southern California played a vital role in this global convergence of art-meets-engineering graphic productions for the screen—or, in this case, the reflective surface. The project was also a convergence of East and West, left and right brain, environment and image, and it all started in the rebellious and experimental UCLA urban design program of the 1960s. Grad students Dawson, Lord, and Stanton began developing multimedia events that eschewed standard practices of urban-design studies. Their experiments began with the creation of an inflatable black tube, which delighted campus denizens, including some film school students. It was these filmmakers (who were also part of the original Single Wing Turquoise Bird group) who suggested to the members of Envirolab that they talk to the L.A. chapter of E.A.T., an international group founded in 1966 to facilitate collaborations between artists and engineers. One of E.A.T.'s most significant projects was the Pepsi Pavilion at Expo '70, in Osaka. Envirolab worked with E.A.T. members McDermott and Phillips to realize an inflatable geodesic structure that housed an immersive holographic experience combining real and virtual imagery with light and sound. The project concept included the idea of a reflective experience inside a mirrored dome space, and E.A.T.'s "Alice-through-the-looking-glass" dream became a reality thanks to Envirolab's ingenuity with their early inflatable productions.[33]

INDUSTRY & THE INDIES

Designer unknown. SMOTHERS BROTHERS SUMMER SHOW PROMO, 1970. The art-house film culture of the 1950s spawned a yen for more sophisticated television commercials as well as commercial television. As a result, the political and social upheaval of the 1960s included a burst of creativity and a revolution within broadcasting. A new crop of viewers who were visually literate expected more from the small screen, and The Smothers Brothers Comedy Hour, which premiered on CBS in 1967, epitomized this new attitude.[34] ¶ There was a trend toward socially relevant programming at a point when countercultural resistance was being commodified, but the Smothers Brothers weren't just along for the commercial ride: because of their antiwar stance they often found themselves in conflict with the network and its advertisers. This led to the show's cancellation in 1969. Tom and Dick Smothers had a trendsetting following of anticonsumerist consumerists, however, so ABC gave them a shot the following year with the Smothers Brothers Summer Show. In this promo, upon being prompted by a voiceover announcer to "say a few words about television," the brothers respond by demonstrating a litany of new TV special effects, which they identify. These include solarization, keyhole matte, and spin, but finally escalate into more fantastical made-up effects, such as "psychedelic," "flames," and "earthquake." The piece was perfectly pitched to the savvy audience that the renegade brother act attracted.[35]

INDUSTRY & THE INDIES 181

Wayne Fitzgerald [b. 1930]. **MCMILLAN & WIFE TITLES, 1971.** After graduating from high school in 1948, Fitzgerald could see the writing on the wall: television was going to be big and he wanted to be part of it! He studied advertising design and illustration at Art Center College of Design but realized that "motion" was something he'd have to learn on his own. Having earned his degree in 1951, he landed a job at Pacific Title and Art Studio, a Hollywood company that had been creating title cards for "the industry" since 1919.
¶ Fitzgerald was the first Pacific employee with a background in design, and initially his creativity was lost on a business bogged down by convention and lack of vision—in short, the title industry had no interest in making things move. It wasn't until 1955, when Saul Bass broke the mold with his opening sequence for The Man with the Golden Arm, that new ideas began to get a foothold. Fitzgerald became possibly the most prolific title designer in the business, creating hundreds of sequences for films and television. He also was one of the first motion-graphics designers in the entertainment industry to be credited on screen for his work—although he'd been working for years before receiving this acknowledgment.[36] ¶ For this NBC crime drama centered on a San Francisco police commissioner aided by his kooky wife, Fitzgerald superimposed a static type treatment over photographic assemblages composed of iconic Bay Area imagery and signifiers of "police" and "crime." Vaguely reminiscent of the static-type-over-a-background title style Fitzgerald worked so hard to move past, the masterful montages in these titles have a distinctive flair that was in tune with the show's hip sophistication.

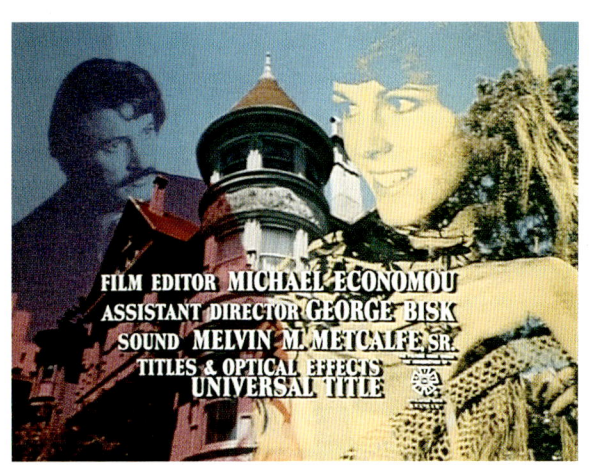

INDUSTRY & THE INDIES

Robert Abel and Richard Taylor [b. 1944]. **7UP "BUBBLES" COMMERCIAL, 1975, 1 MIN.** "Bubbles" broke the mold for television commercials, ending the Madison Avenue era of Big Idea live-action spots and ushering in extravaganzas inspired by pop graphics and psychedelia. ¶ After graduating from UCLA with a dual degree in film and design, Abel first worked for James and John Whitney and then made documentary films. In 1971, he launched Robert Abel and Associates in Los Angeles, further developing an approach to graphic work for the screen that combined technological and artistic invention.[37] Abel and his team took this experimental pas de deux between left and right brain—the legacy of avant-garde pioneers including Oskar Fischinger, the Whitney brothers, and Doug Trumbull—into the computer era. "Bubbles," along with Abel's work for Harry Marks at ABC, heralded the arrival of a new graphic age for television that necessitated close creative collaborations among multiple talents, skills, and disciplines.[38] ¶ Richard Taylor, the first graphic designer hired at Abel's firm, had worked on light shows during the rock 'n' roll heyday. This experience informed his provocative visual contributions to the manipulations of color and light in the "Bubbles" spot, a psychedelic morphing of 7UP's original red-and-green bubble-tossing girl into a chorus line and a neon butterfly. This extravaganza of technique, including the complex integration of rotoscoped live-action dancers and hand-drawn animation, evolved into the much-lauded "candy-apple neon" effect—a chromelike glowing aura surrounding a graphic image or type—for which the studio became widely known.[39]

INDUSTRY & THE INDIES 185

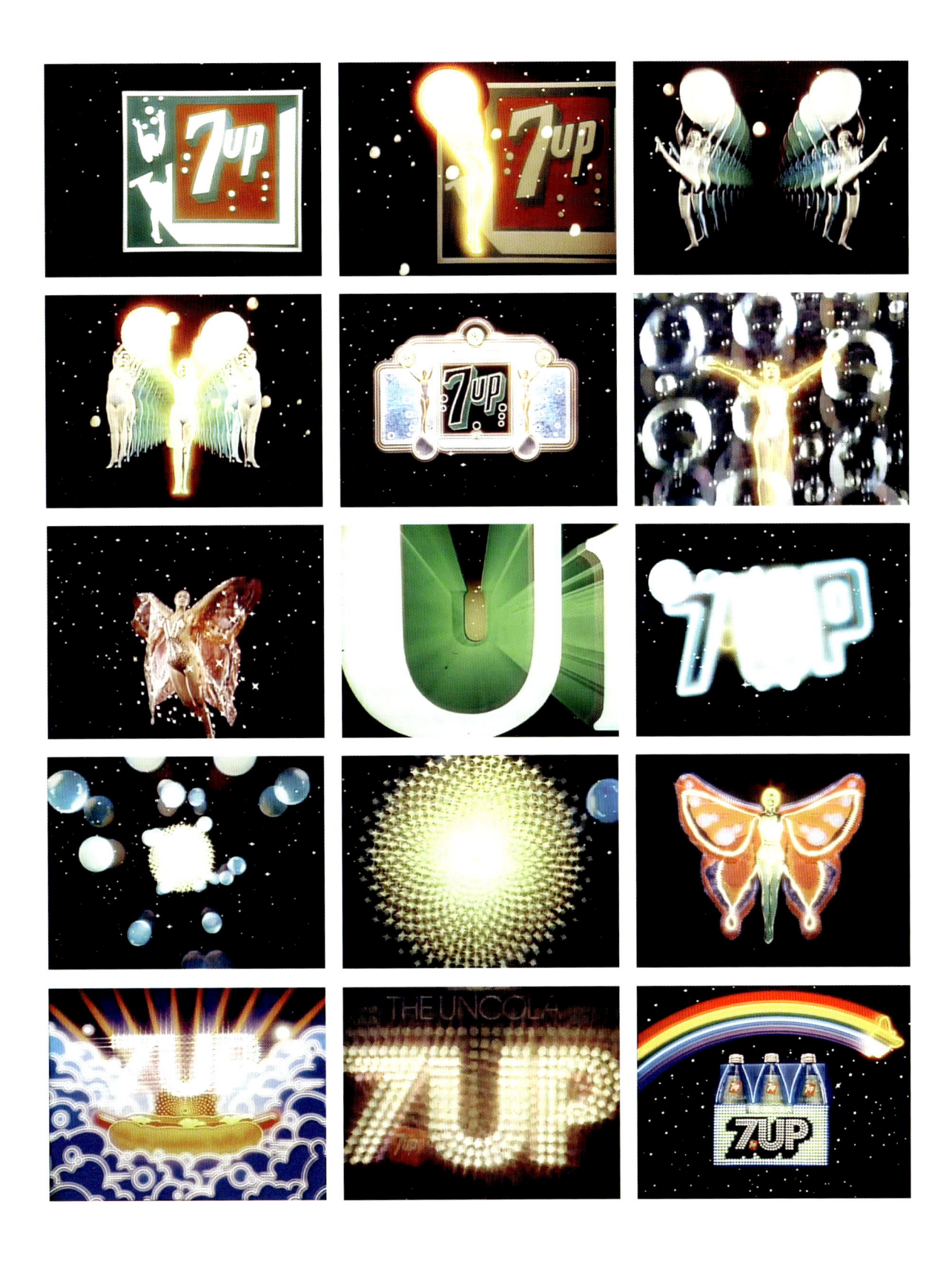

Chris Blum [b. 1944] **and Heidi Endemann** [b. 1941]. **LEVI'S "EVOLUTION" COMMERCIAL, CA. 1975, 1 MIN.** The concept for this mind-bending and, at the time, controversial, ad originated with creative director Blum, of the San Francisco agency Honig, Cooper, and Harrington, who worked closely with copywriter Mike Koelker. (Blum and Koelker often worked with Robert Abel and Associates on the design and production of many of Levi's most acclaimed commercials.) It was Endemann, however, a young commercial artist with a studio around the corner, who got the call to propose and illustrate a number of characters based on a question: if man had turned out differently, where and how would he wear his pants?[40] Endemann let her fantasies run amok and came up with such witty concoctions as Buck Man, who had Levis for antlers. (Sadly, many of these characters got left on the proverbial cutting-room floor.) After the selection of key images for animation, Endemann went down to Los Angeles to supervise the cel drawings at Spungbuggy, one of the "hot" animation studios.[41]

INDUSTRY & THE INDIES

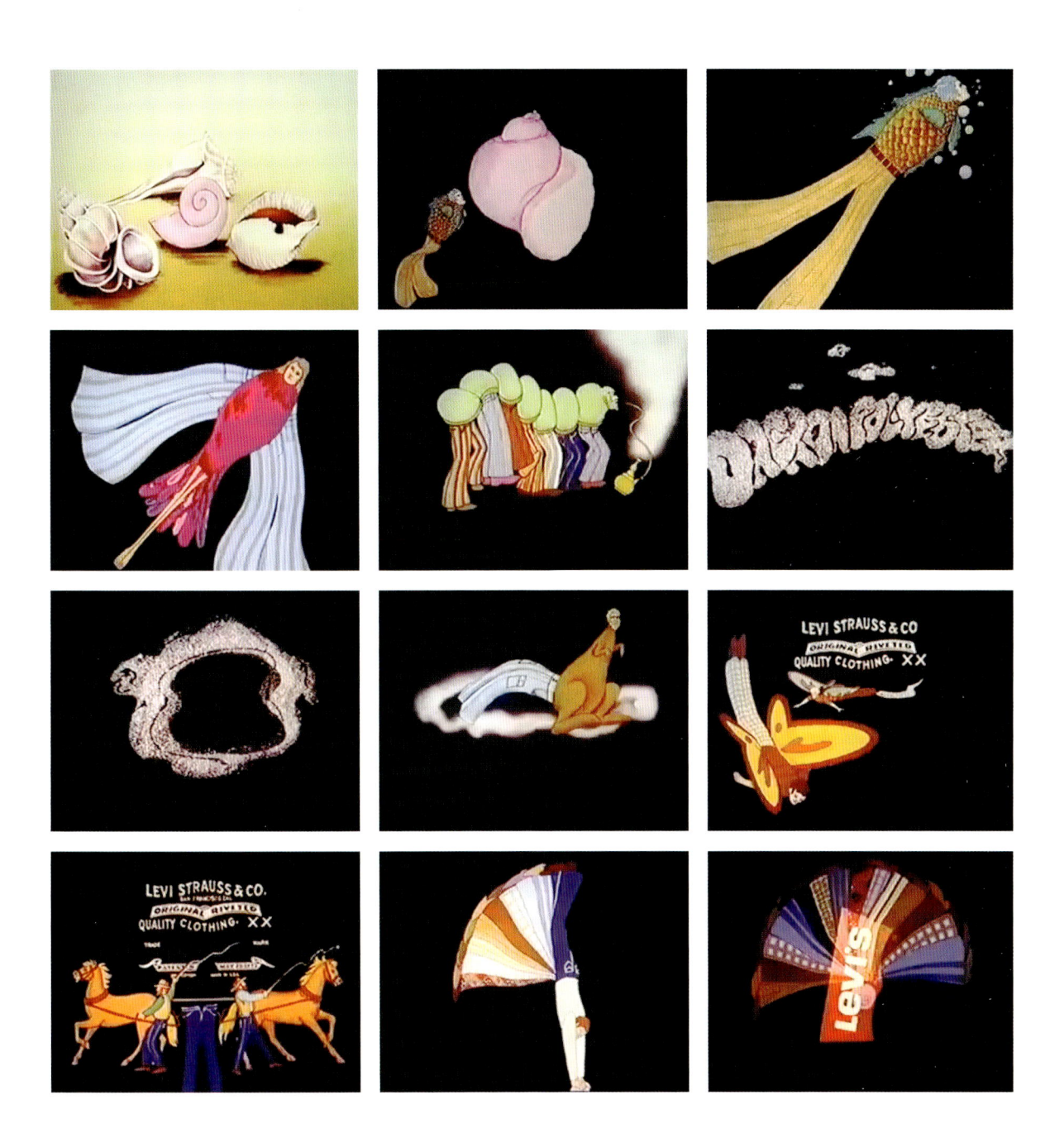

Phill Norman. WONDER WOMAN TITLES, SEASON ONE, 1976, 1:40 MIN. After designing titles for the animation studio UPA, Norman worked for Pacific Title, an entity responsible for many of the anonymously produced movie and television titles of the day. In 1965, he went out on his own. As luck would have it, he befriended a neighbor named Quinn Martin, who happened to be the producer of the popular series <u>The Fugitive</u> and <u>The FBI</u>; Norman wound up doing the main titles for all of Martin's shows, including <u>I Dream of Jeannie</u>, <u>Charlie's Angels</u>, and <u>Dynasty</u>.[42] He also designed titles for feature films—among them, <u>Out of Africa</u>, <u>On Golden Pond</u>, and <u>Ordinary People</u>—and other TV series, including season one of <u>Wonder Woman</u>. Unusually long, these titles combine animation and live action to present a pop culture backstory of Wonder Woman the comic character transitioning into Wonder Woman the oh-so-alive female, played by Lynda Carter. The show's title zooms up from the corner in a cartoonish script font, followed by a comic-book-style sequence of frames showing Wonder Woman performing astounding feats, including rescuing her romantic foil, Major Steve Trevor. The show's theme song—with lines such as "in your satin tights, fighting for your rights" and "now the world is ready for you"—appealed to the feminist leanings of 1970s TV viewers. Animated starbursts propel the narrative, providing scene transitions and showcasing the names of talent (the actors, the producer, etc.) in the center of larger, individual stars. The Wonder Woman story forms a nice parallel with California's own mythical narrative, dating from the sixteenth century, which imagines a land ruled by Amazons—brave and youthful warrior women of super strength. Wonder Woman, as her legend has it, hails from an Amazonian island.

INDUSTRY & THE INDIES

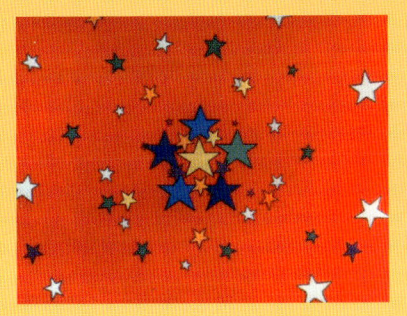

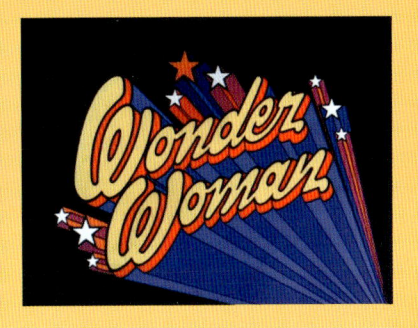

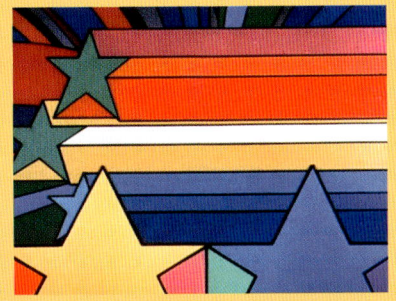

Dan Perri [b. 1945]. **TAXI DRIVER TITLES, 1976.** Among Perri's many film-title credits is the iconic text crawl that narrated the backstory in Star Wars as well as THE emblem of the era, the Star Wars franchise logo. The year before that, he designed titles for another cinematic landmark, Taxi Driver. Along with Wayne Fitzgerald, Perri represented a generation that, following in the footsteps of Saul Bass, perpetuated the art of title design and helped establish solid footing for this new graphic-design genre. ¶ Perri first encountered the specialized practice as a high school student in the Van Nuys neighborhood of L.A.: his art teacher was a New York transplant and former Mad Man. Perri went on to Art Center and cultivated his craft with the ultimate goal of working for Bass himself. When the offer finally came, Perri, realizing that the grail had been attained, turned down the job and launched his own studio instead. ¶ For the Taxi Driver titles, he wanted to create something that would establish the dark urban experience that mirrored protagonist Travis Bickle's bleak inner life. Using cinematographer Michael Chapman's footage, Perri saturated the colors and upped the contrast to evoke the surreal environment that the character inhabited mentally. Halfway through the sequence, we see Perri incorporate a particularly complex application of slit-scan technique (à la Whitney and Trumbull) to create the blurry, weird, drifting vantage of Bickle. Completing the tableau were the designer's urban-inflected typographic choices, bleeding and swelling over, glowing and glowering from within the imagery.[43]

INDUSTRY & THE INDIES

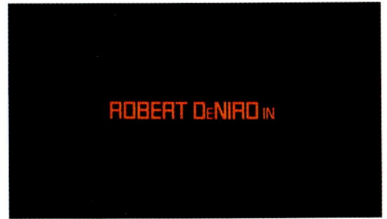

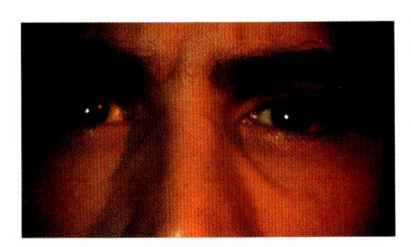

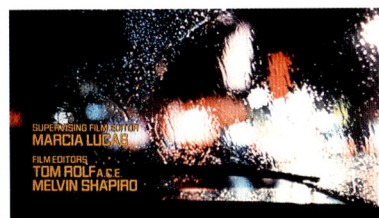

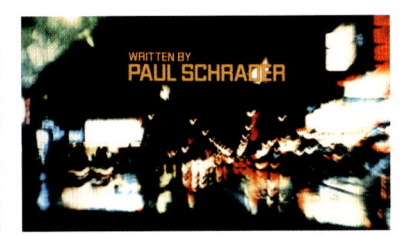

Robert Abel and Con Pederson [b. 1934]. **BERGER PAINT TV COMMERCIAL, 1977, 30 SEC.** This complex sequence by Robert Abel and Associates was a 180-degree departure from the live-action footage of satisfied customers that was standard fare at the time. The first TV spot for this European firm, the Berger ad had almost no dialogue or narration but instead used gymnastic, movement-generating techniques including rear-projection, animation, slit-scan, and streak photography. As Abel described the piece, the "background is a surrealist plain formed of the [Berger] system's color chips. A 'sun' is transformed into a globe and then a multicolored ball. And a rotating cube has sides which constantly 'repaint' themselves to show various wall treatments." Despite the abstract approach, the message of color and the transformative potential of paint was very clear. The ad, which ran in England, Wales, and Northern Ireland during 1977, achieved "streaking" photography through Luminetics, a multiple-exposure process that captures changes in form, direction, or speed onto a single piece of film.

INDUSTRY & THE INDIES

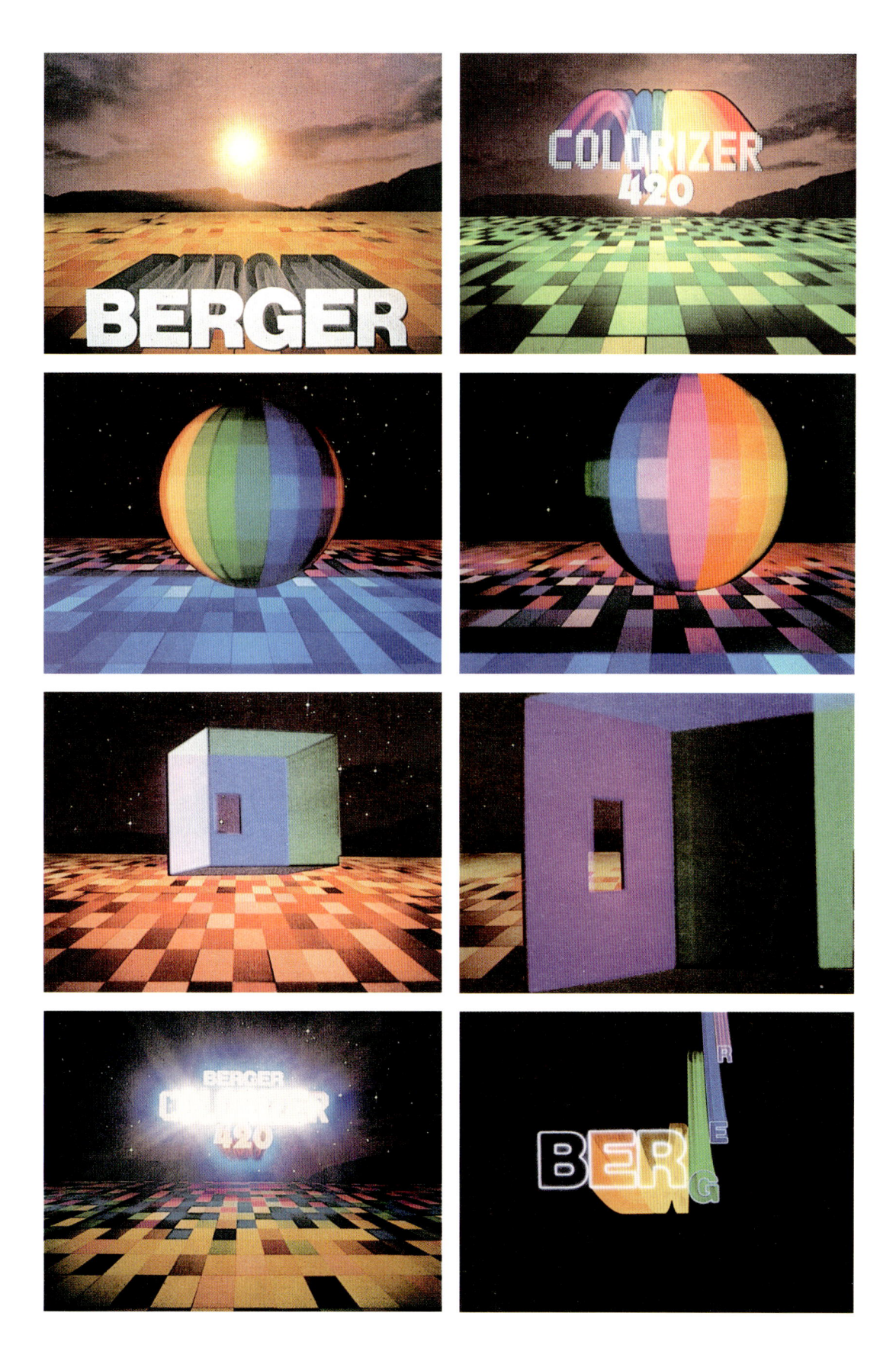

Pablo Ferro [b. 1935]. **CITIZENS BAND** TITLES, 1977. The fourth feature film directed by Jonathan Demme, Citizens Band struggled at the box office when first released but went on to be selected as a New York Times Critics' Pick of the best thousand films. The narrative revolves around the citizen's band, or CB, radio, an important method for communication primarily used by big-rig drivers during the 1970s, when the fuel crisis threatened their livelihoods. The colorful, subversive language the medium fostered became a popular fascination and inspired songs and films, including Demme's. ¶ Ferro's title design for Citizens Band echoes the glare and flash of roadside lights and electronic communications, including the mazelike guts of the radios. Set to the buzzing, hissing, and fragmenting sounds of CB-radio connections and conversations, the titles look "inside of the CB radios, all the electronic connectors and all that stuff," according to Ferro. "I pulled them apart to stage them for a stop-motion shoot. I photographed them, using special lenses, and animated them on a stand" using an animation camera."[44] ¶ A young Cuban émigré in New York, Ferro started out drawing comics for Stan Lee (co-creator of Spiderman and Iron Man) and working in a foreign-film cinema but soon became a vital part of the heyday of auteur commercial productions. His career as a film-title designer developed thanks to director Stanley Kubrick, who, in 1963, engaged him to do the opening sequence for Dr. Strangelove. Ferro moved west in the late '70s and continued his film work for Hollywood. His aesthetic—fast-paced "quick-cut" editing (which he is known for pioneering) merged with stop-motion animation—reflected his era and has endured as a modus operandi for the media age.[45] A vast talent with a notoriously flamboyant personality, Ferro became a film-title-design darling who helped define the genre.

INDUSTRY & THE INDIES

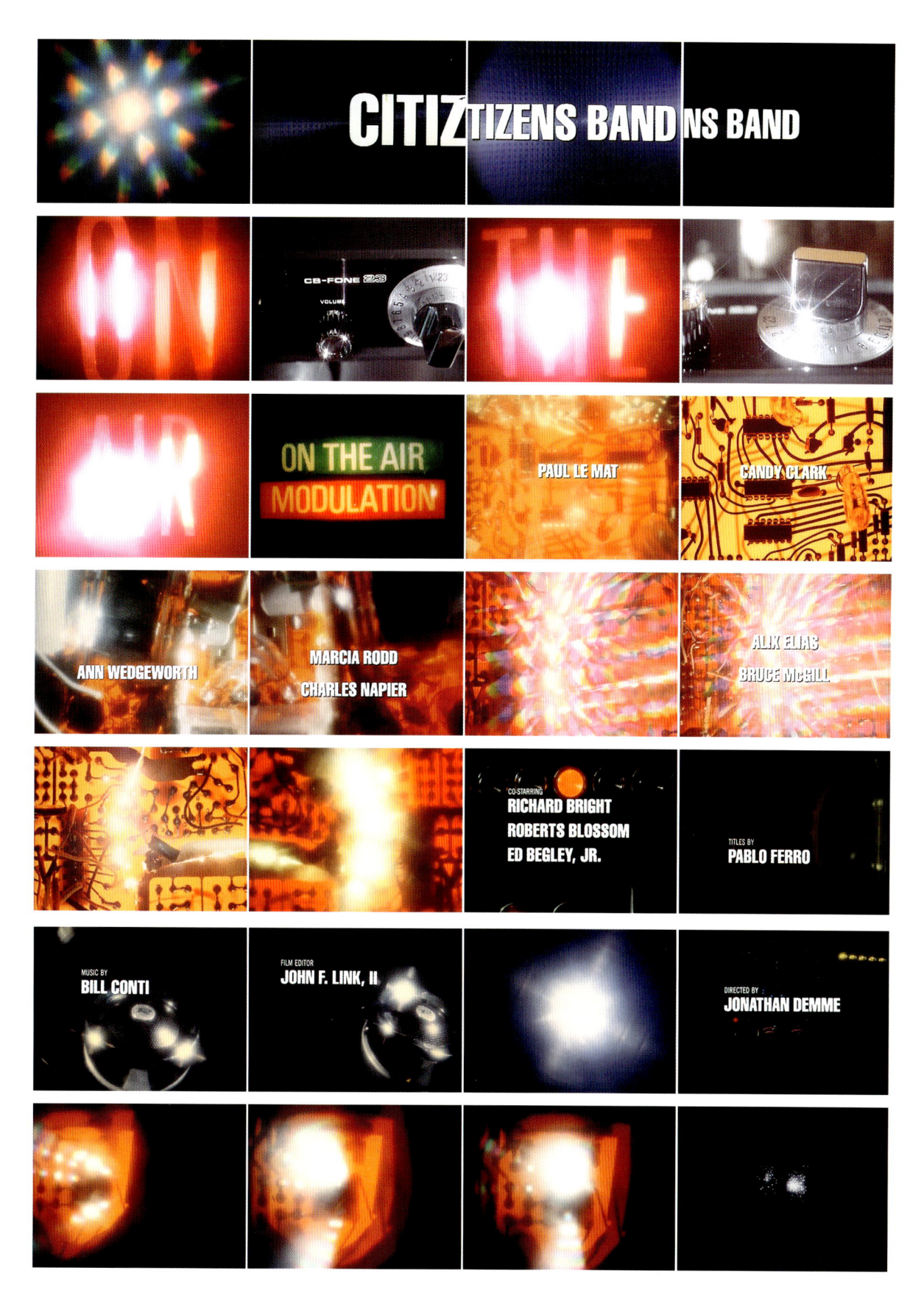

195

David Theurer [b. 1950]. **TEMPEST, ATARI ARCADE VIDEO GAME, 1980.** Held in the collection of the Museum of Modern Art as an example of game design, Tempest was the first arcade video game produced using color vector drawing. Known more colloquially as "wireframes," these graphics were created from jagged line segments, resulting in fairly crude drawings of characters and objects. Yet Theurer managed to inventively exploit these limitations—conceptually and visually—to produce what hardcore gamers reverently consider "one of the most innovative and beautiful video games ever made." As related by video-game writer Paul Drury, players encountered "multicolored Fuseballs dancing skittishly inside the abyss [and] deadly Pulsars crackling with electricity."[46] The game's captivating and beautiful abstract aesthetics echo earlier decades of technical experimentation: think Fischinger, Whitney, Trumbull. ¶ Equally remarkable are the game's title graphics.[47] A minor extravaganza, they serve to introduce not only the game but also its new technological features, its capacity to convey a sense of movement as well as a colorful electronic experience overall. Tempest reveals Theurer as possessing a visual prowess equal to his programming genius, and an ability to conceive a game with a compelling theme.

INDUSTRY & THE INDIES

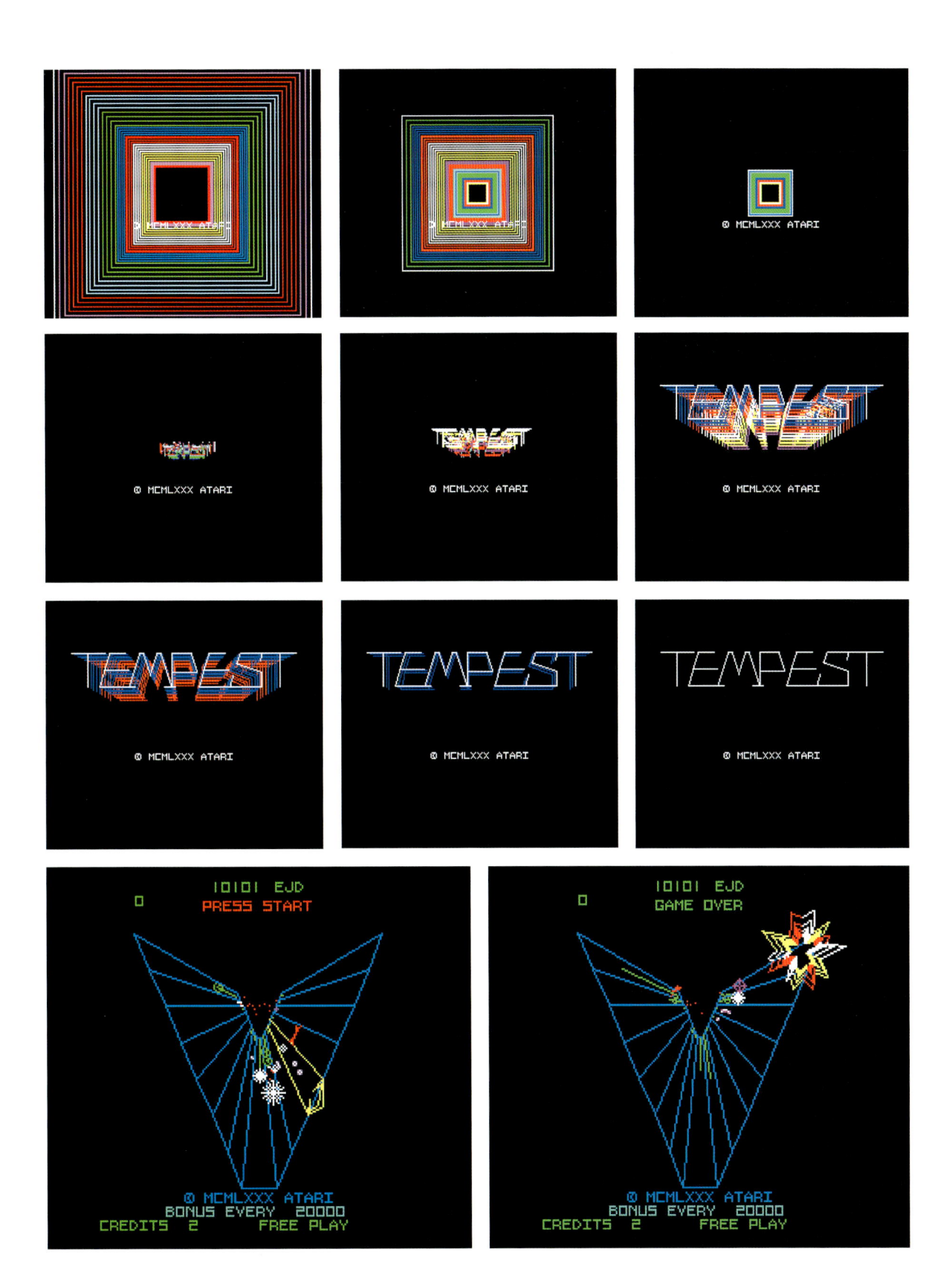

Robert Abel, Syd Mead [b. 1933]**, Kenneth Mirman** [b. date unknown]**, and Richard Taylor.** TRON**, 1982, 1:36 HR.** A product of writer/director Steve Lisberger's vibrant imagination, TRON is a masterful exploitation of cutting-edge computer technology and a convergence of animation; cinematography; music; visual effects; and graphic, costume, product, interface, and sound design. The images featured here highlight the contributions of Mead, Taylor, Robert Abel and Associates team member Mirman, as well as Abel himself. Executed within the vocabulary of 2-D design, and combining photography with colorful illustrative techniques (such as the glowing effect that was added to the live-action figures), their work exemplifies the murky boundaries between disciplines that characterized early visual creativity in the computer age. ¶ The film tapped the skills of far-reaching artistic talent and reflects the many historical tangents that combined to build the field of motion graphics. Moments of visual abstraction in TRON seem to have been transported through the decades from the hands of visual-music pioneer Oskar Fischinger, with echoes of John Whitney and Doug Trumbull. And TRON's vector graphics readily recall Dave Theurer's arcade game designs. ¶ The narrative follows a software-engineering maverick named Flynn, whose authorship of the video game Space Paranoids has been poached by a power-hungry colleague. Seeking to right this wrong, Flynn is transported into the virtual world of digital gaming, where he battles programs and the game system's master controller to gain the evidence to prove his ownership. He triumphs in a cityscape resembling San Francisco—a mirror of which had been featured in the electronic circuit-world of Flynn's program.

INDUSTRY & THE INDIES

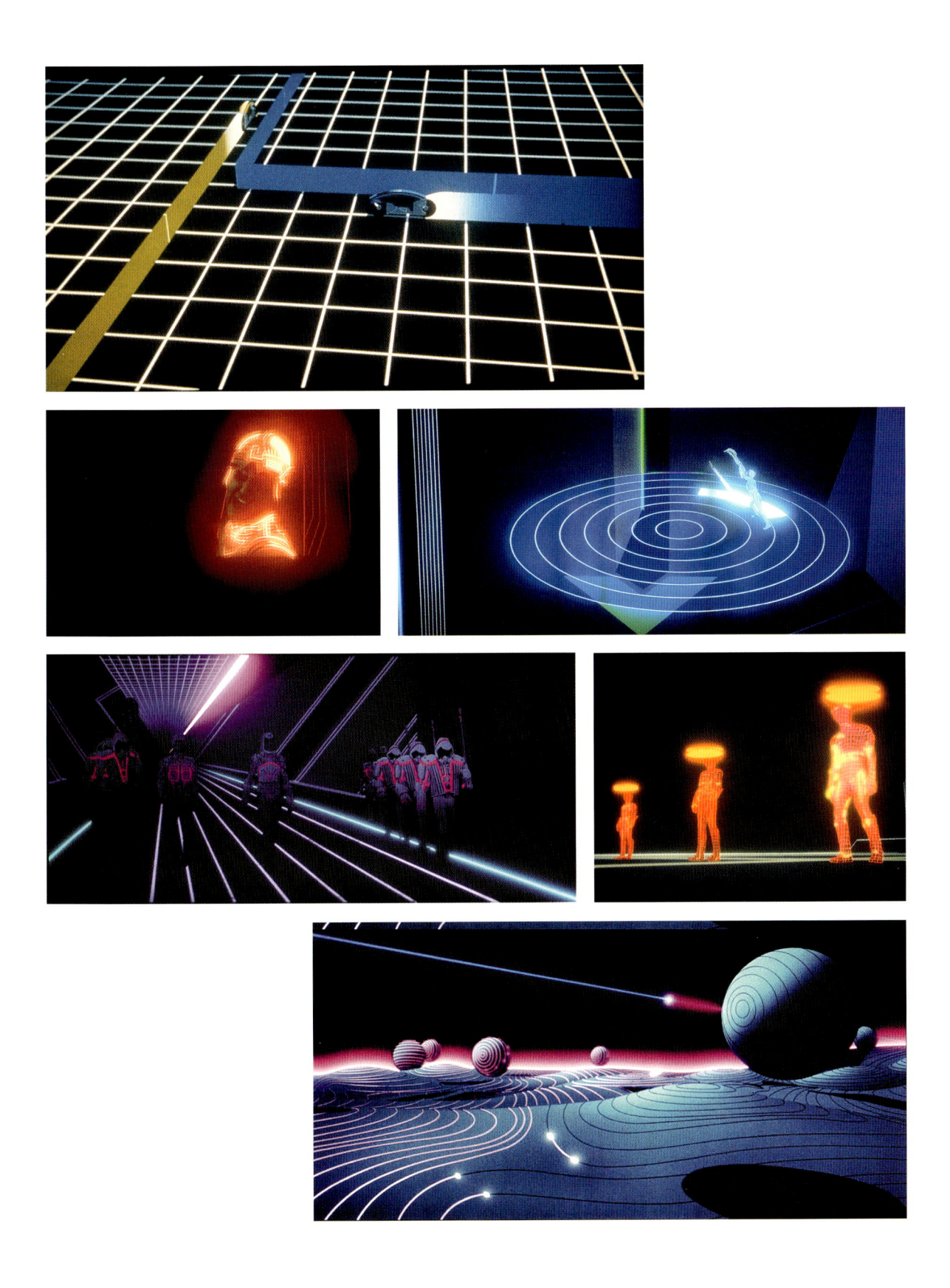

Barbara Fairbrother Singh [b. 1954] **and Franz X. Lanzinger** [b. 1955]. <u>**CRYSTAL CASTLES**</u>, ATARI ARCADE VIDEO GAME, 1983. A breakthrough in game-design narrative, <u>Crystal Castles</u> features protagonist Bentley Bear, who navigates axonometrically rendered castles collecting gems while avoiding enemies such as Nasty Trees and Gem Eaters. It was the first arcade video game considered to have a conclusion—and the first to have a graphic designer involved in its creation. Until then, programmers were also engineers and artists: they produced a game's concept, programming, and art. For <u>Crystal Castles</u>, designer Barbara Fairbrother (now Barbara Singh) assisted with the game's aesthetic, characters, and action, and her contributions represent yet another branch in the genealogy of motion graphics. Singh had studied sculpture and knew nothing about computers, but she learned to draw for the screen using graph paper to create the "bitmapped" objects and characters. Her art school background gave her the know-how to conceive in 3-D, which allowed her to create animated figures viewed from different directions as they moved. Lanzinger, the game's mastermind and programmer, instructed Singh about <u>Crystal Castles</u>' overall objectives and gave her plot suggestions such as "create something to test the bear." The rest was hers to run with. ¶ Lanzinger had become fascinated with games while working in the defense industry. In 1982, he moved to Atari, where he transitioned from addressing more consequential real threats to the perils of imaginary characters.[48]

INDUSTRY & THE INDIES

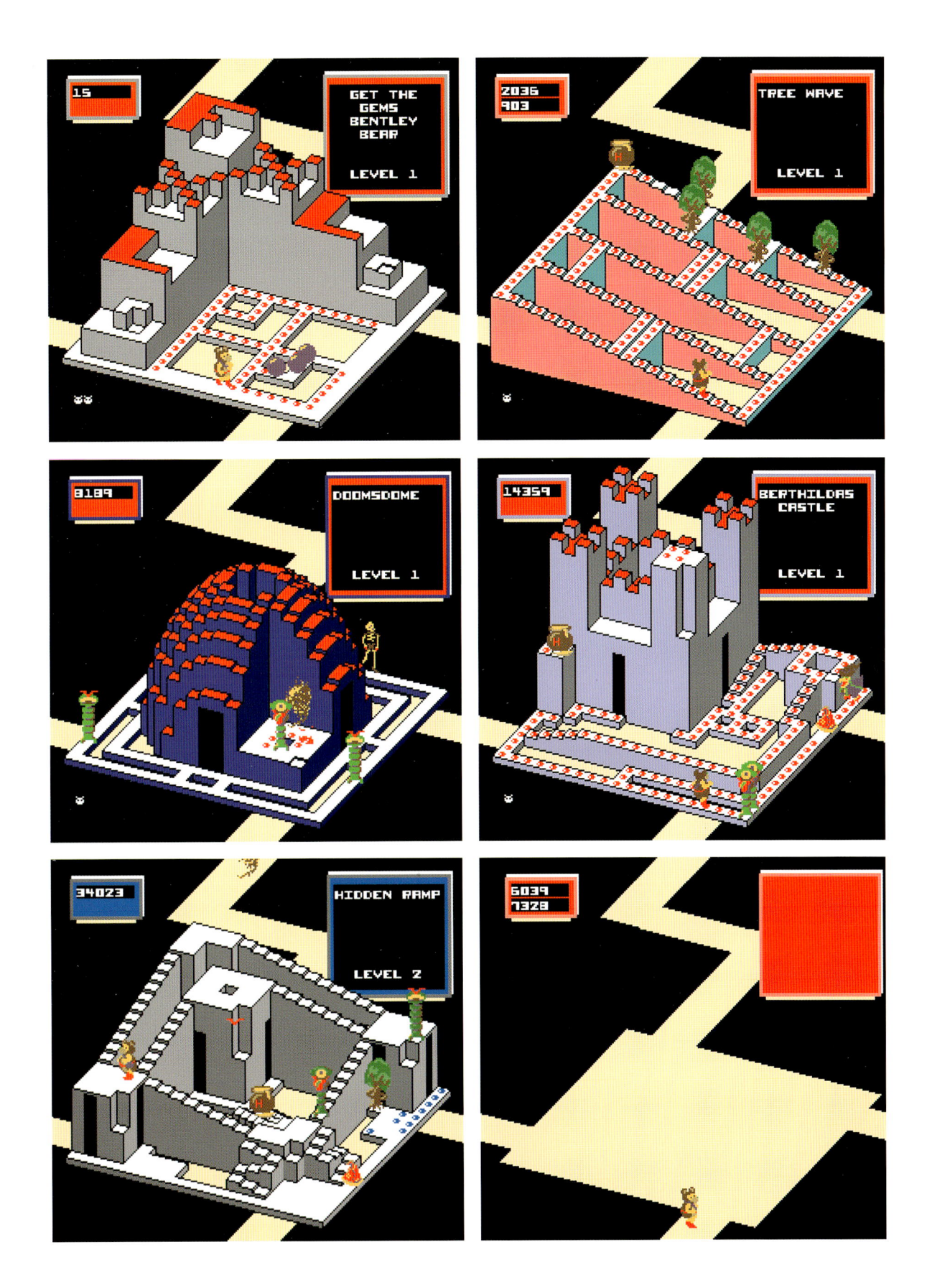

David Theurer. I, ROBOT, ATARI ARCADE VIDEO GAME, 1983.
With I, Robot, Theurer introduced yet another milestone within arcade-game graphics. The shift from vectors to pixels meant that characters, objects, and backdrops could appear as more detailed shapes rather than as the stunted, wireframe drawings of previous games. A dynamic camera system allowed gamers to scale and rotate their views in real time, which, combined with I, Robot's more sophisticated graphics, meant for a more immersive visual experience. The game's protagonist is "a self-aware robot known only as Unhappy Interface Robot #1984" who decides to rebel against Big Brother, represented by a massive eye hovering above the maze in which the action takes place."[49] The goal of the game is to navigate the maze at increasing levels of difficulty in order to exit and thus gain the ability to destroy Big Brother. ¶ When released, I, Robot was so innovative and different from the standard fare that most gamers were unable to make the leap it demanded; this, combined with hardware problems, resulted in its failure. Rumor has it that half of the manufactured games wound up at the bottom of the sea.[50]

INDUSTRY & THE INDIES

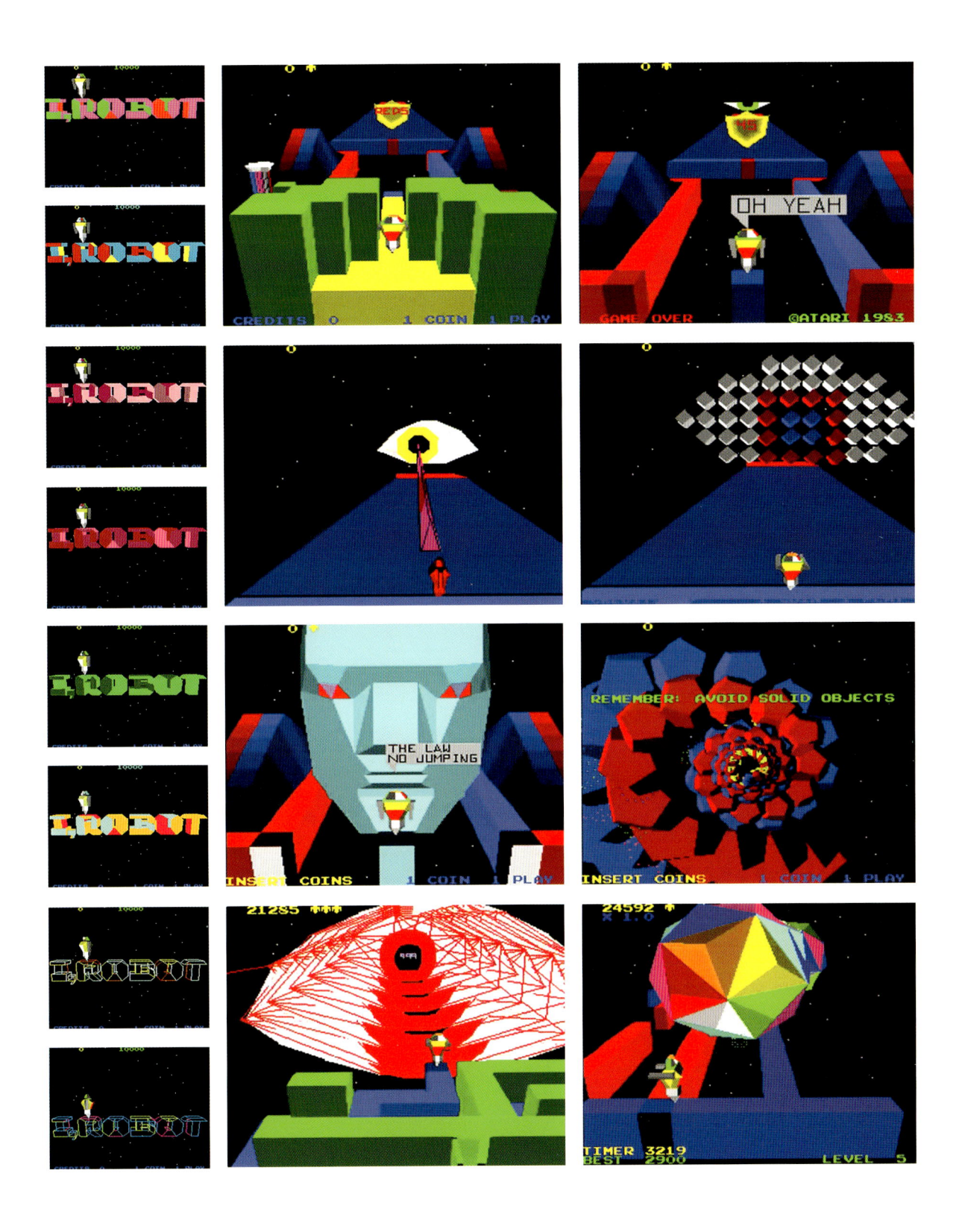

Notes

1 Esther Leslie, "Wassily Kandinsky: Where Abstraction and Comics Collide," in Cindy Keefer and Jaap Guldemond, eds., *Oskar Fischinger 1900–1967: Experiments in Cinematic Abstraction* (Amsterdam: EYE Filmmuseum/Los Angeles: Center for Visual Music, 2012), 89. **2** See William Moritz, *Optical Poetry: The Life and Work of Oskar Fischinger* (Bloomington and Indianapolis: Indiana University Press, 2004). **3** Andrew Perchuck, "Struggle and Structure," in Perchuk and Rani Singh, eds., *Harry Smith: The Avant-Garde in the American Vernacular* (Los Angeles: Getty, 2010), 6. **4** See Rani Singh, "Harry Smith, An Ethnographic Modernist in America," in Perchuk and Singh, *Harry Smith*; and William Moritz, "Harry Smith, Mythologist," paper presented at the Getty Research Institute's Harry Smith Symposium, 2001, www.centerforvisualmusic.org. **5** See Michael Betancourt, *The History of Motion Graphics: From Avant-Garde to Industry in the United States* (Rockville, Md.: Wildside, 2013), 129. "The Whitney Brothers, like Harry Smith, are transitional figures between the earlier avant-garde and films of the first experimental period and the consolidation characteristic of the second period." Betancourt refers to the postwar moment when opportunities for experimental filmmakers emerged for commercial work, thanks to a wider embrace of a modernist aesthetic in America. Lynn Spigel elaborates on this history in her book *TV by Design: Modern Art and the Rise of Network Television* (Chicago and London: University of Chicago Press, 2009). **6** Steven Heller and Elaine Lustig Cohen, *Born Modern: The Life and Design of Alvin Lustig* (San Francisco: Chronicle, 2010), 36. **7** Amid Amidi and Jerry Beck, e-mail correspondence with the author, December 4–5, 2013. **8** Spigel, *TV by Design*, 106. **9** Pat Kirkham, *Charles and Ray Eames: Designers of the Twentieth Century* (Cambridge, Mass.: MIT Press, 1996), 320–24. **10** Ibid., 338. **11** John Whitney, "Animation Mechanisms," *American Cinematographer*, January 1971. **12** William Moritz, "Digital Harmony: The Life of John Whitney, Computer Animation Pioneer," *Animation World Magazine*, August 1997. **13** Steve Heller, e-mail correspondence with the author, September 4, 2013. **14** Amid Amidi, e-mail correspondence with the author, September 4, 2013. **15** Charles Perry, *The Haight-Ashbury: A History* (New York: Wenner, 1985), 64. **16** Kerry Brougher, "Visual-Music Culture," in Brougher and Jeremy Strick, eds., *Visual Music: Synaesthesia in Art and Music Since 1900* (New York: Thames and Hudson, 2005), 159, n. 69. **17** Perry, *Haight-Ashbury*, 65. **18** Jennifer Bass and Pat Kirkham, *Saul Bass: A Life in Film and Design* (London: Laurence King, 2011), 9. **19** Ibid., 232–33. **20** Harry Marks, e-mail correspondence with the author, October 20, 2013. **21** Adam Abraham, *When Magoo Flew: The Rise and Fall of Animation Studio UPA* (Middletown, Conn.: Wesleyan University Press, 2012), 238. **22** Bass and Kirkham, *Saul Bass*, 217. **23** Ibid., n. 124. **24** Perry, *Haight-Ashbury*, 65. **25** Gregory Zinman, Handmade Cinema, www.handmadecinema.com, accessed May 31, 2014. **26** Bill Ham website, www.billhamlights.com, accessed May 31, 2014. **27** Harry Marks is quoted from the documentary *Harry Marks, Broadcast Designer*, Creative Inspirations series, produced by www.lynda.com, accessed May 31, 2014. **28** Harry Marks, interview with the author, Carmel, Calif., October 11, 2012; and e-mail correspondence with the author, October 22, 2012–January 2, 2014. **29** Marks e-mail correspondence. **30** Richard Taylor, interview with the author, Los Angeles, November 28, 2012. **31** The group found its name when one of its members stabbed his finger in a book of Vedic hymns while en route to a meeting with John Van Hamersveld. **32** David James, "Expanded Cinema in Los Angeles: The Single Wing Turquoise Bird," *Millennium Film Journal* 43/44, summer 2005, 9–31. **33** Chris Dawson, Skype interview with the author, November 8, 2013; and e-mail correspondence, November 18, 2013. **34** Spigel, *TV by Design*, 225.

35 David Bianculli, *Dangerously Funny: The Uncensored Story of "The Smothers Brothers Comedy Hour"* (New York: Touchstone, 2009), 189. **36** Wayne Fitzgerald, Skype interview with the author, March 13, 2013. **37** UCLA Film and TV Archive, "Collection Profile: Robert Abel & Associates," www.cinema.ucla.edu, accessed January 12, 2014. **38** Full credit for "Bubbles" goes to Robert Abel and Associates (art directors: Wayne Kimbell, Con Pederson, Richard Taylor; animation director: Con Pederson; animation camera: Richard Edlund, Dave Stewart; camera design: Dick Alexander) and J. Walter Thompson, Chicago (creative director: Bob Taylor). **39** Richard Taylor, interview with the author, Los Angeles, November 28, 2012. The "candy apple" effect reflected a combination of Southern California influences—the neon and plastic of nighttime Los Angeles and the hot-rod paint jobs typical of the fifties and early sixties. Abel had always admired airbrush illustration like that of Charles White III and wanted to achieve a similar look in film. See Jeffrey Altshuler, "Robert Abel: Video Surrealist," *Print*, November/December 1975. **40** Chris Blum, e-mail correspondence with the author, January 9, 2014. **41** Heidi Endemann, e-mail correspondence with the author, January 4, 2014. Although Endemann recalls the animation bein done at Disney, Spungbuggy parnter Frank Terry recalls working on this project in detail. **42** Darrell Van Citters, "Phill Norman, Titles," from the blog Mr. Magoo's Christmas Carol, www.mrmagooschristmascarol.blogspot.com, accessed January 1, 2013. **43** Dan Perri, e-mail correspondence with the author, November 7, 2013. **44** Pablo Ferro, phone conversation with the author, July 22, 2012; and "Interview: Pablo Ferro, Title Sequence Director," from the website We Love Your Names: The Art of Titles, www.weloveyournames.com. **45** Betancourt, *History of Motion Graphics*, 221. **46** Paul Drury, "The Making of Tempest," *Retro Gamer*, issue 105, 2012. **47** For more information about video-game titles, see Betancourt, *History of Motion Graphics*, 257. **48** Franz Lanzinger, Skype interview with the author, February 6, 2012; and e-mail correspondence, February 20, 2012. **49** Levi Buchanan, "The Revolution of I, Robot: This 1983 Landmark Is the Origin of Polygons," www.ign.com, posted August 28, 2008. **50** Ibid.

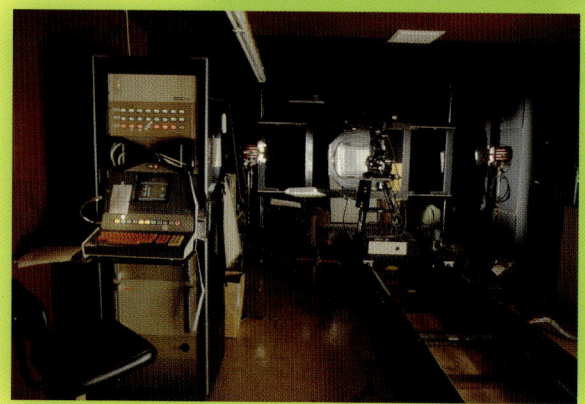

↑ Robert Abel and Associates offices. TOP: Richard Taylor at his desk, 1978; LEFT: Camera room with motion control camera system and a custom motion control computer, 1977; RIGHT: On the set of a Levi's commercial. Seated: Robert Abel, Richard Taylor; back row, middle, creative directors Chris Blum and Mike Koelker, of Levi's advertising agency
→ "In Elysian Park [Los Angeles], California native palms," from Beautiful California, 1971

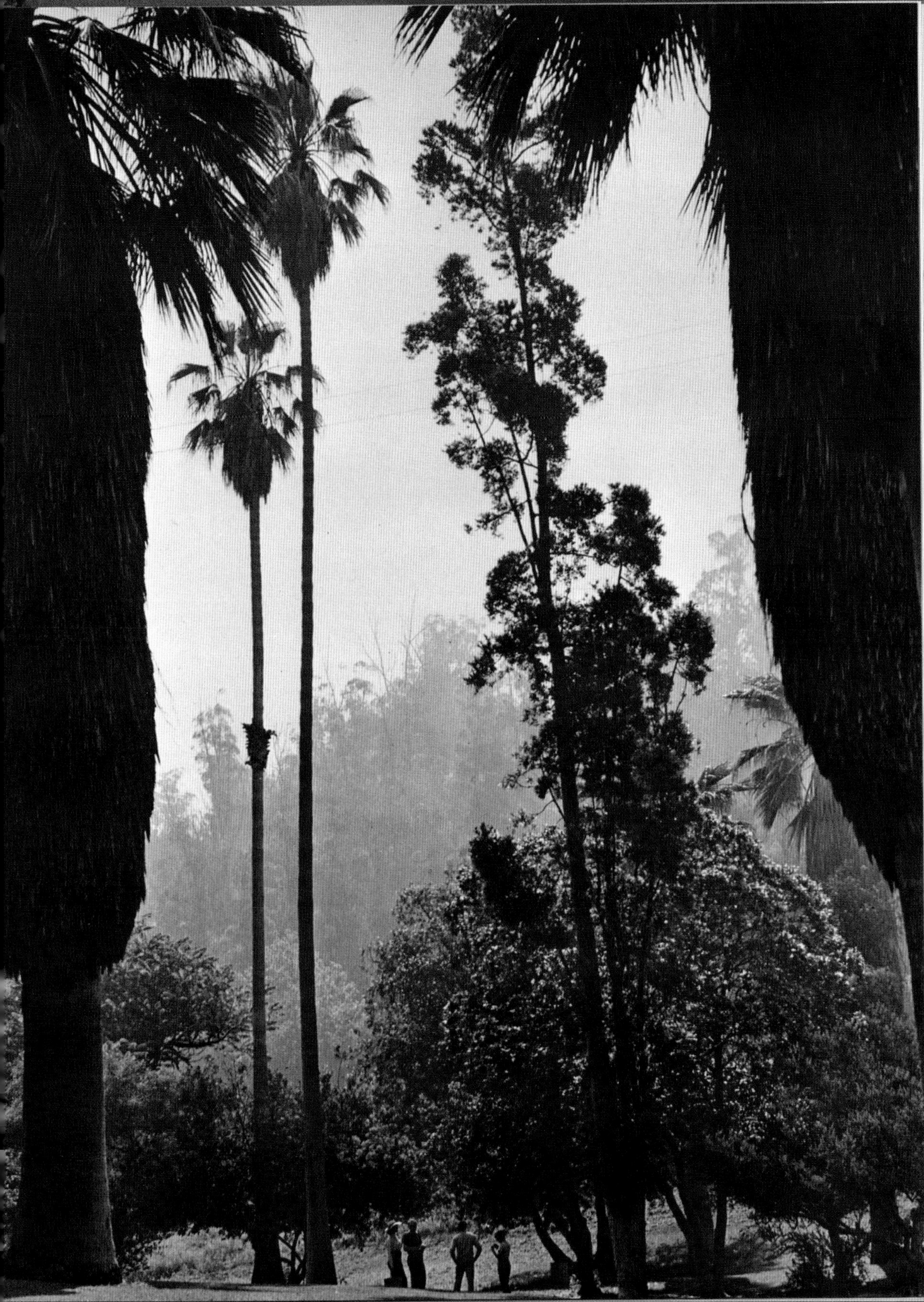

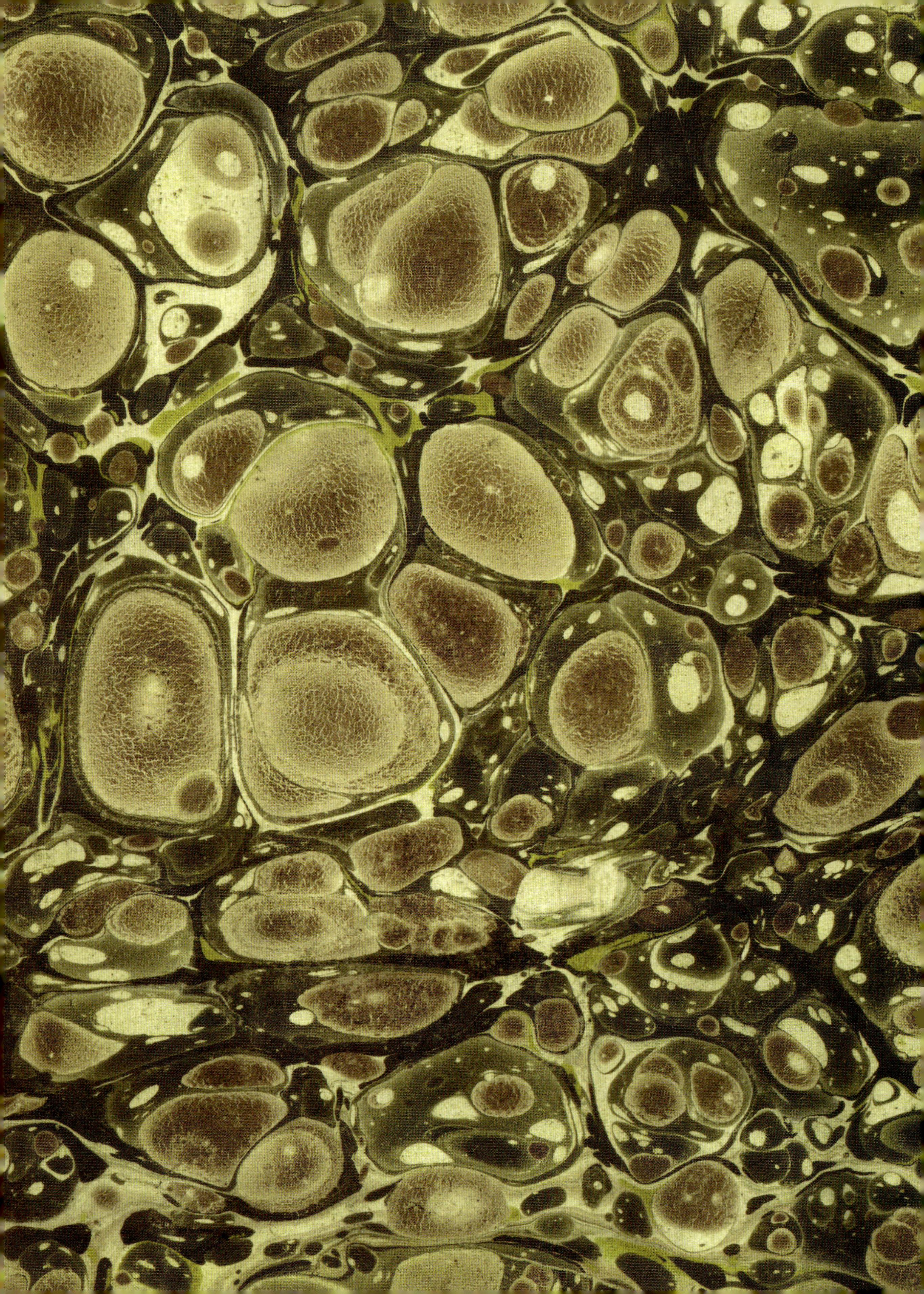

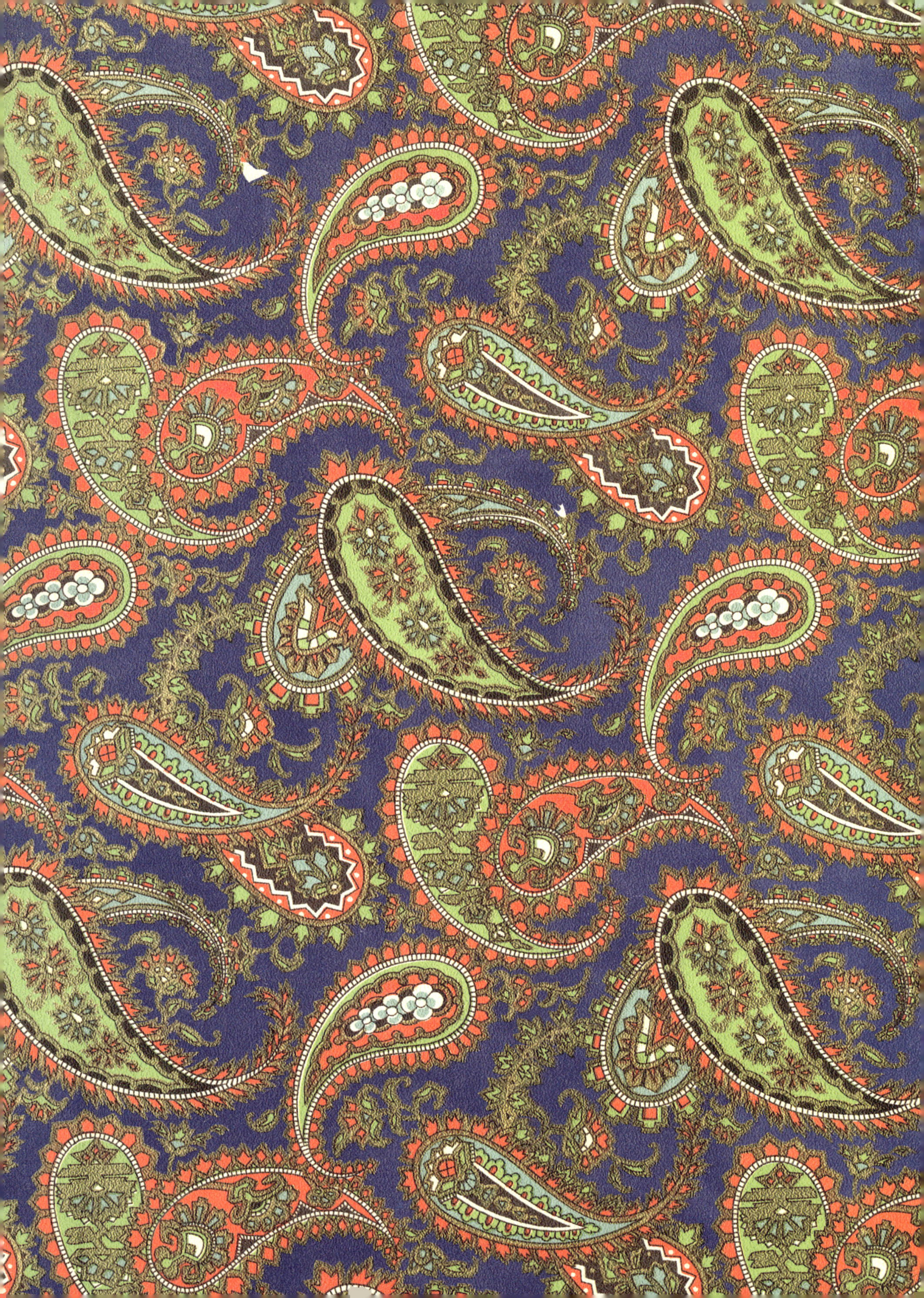

> **"California can and does furnish the best bad things that are obtainable in America."**

HINTON R. HELPER
"LAND OF GOLD: REALITY VERSUS FICTION"
1855

SIXTIES ALT SIXTIES

INTRODUCTION: THE COUNTERCULTURE WAS NEVER WHAT IT USED TO BE

In the popular imagination, California graphic design of the sixties tends to conjure visions of posters, and posters of a very specific kind: those with Art Nouveau–inspired lettering and undulating colors that would come alive when viewed under the influence of marijuana, acid, or 'shrooms. And yet this type of psychedelic image, however much local and global attention it drew to Left Coast graphic production, was only a fraction of what was going on within 1960s poster design, not to mention graphic design overall during this period. To take a metaphor from music—since music and visual culture went hand-in-hand in defining the decade—the archetypal trippy poster represents about four bars of a 12-bar riff within the tuneful melody of an extremely complex song.

"Variety" would be the defining word for sixties California graphics, which exhibited a vast of array of colors, flavors, and voices—from Beats to hippies to political and social activists. If there was a common theme, be it conscious, subconscious, or unconscious, it lies someplace within the desire and commitment to remake the look of the world. Even so-called mainstream work was as vibrant and experimental as the production of those just "doing their thing." How can we measure the charming, Victorian-inspired math-game graphics the Eames Office created for IBM against the exuberant, colorful circus-themed poster Dave Hodges conjured for the anticapitalist "free" commune known as the Diggers? How to compare Archie Boston's in-your-face race-themed promotional ads for his design studio, seeking clients unafraid of daring work, to Emory Douglas's posters for the Black Panthers, aiming to unite factions within the movement and radicalize the wider black community? Graphic design by those with elite training and aesthetics sits quite comfortably beside the more homegrown variety. And it wasn't only those with revolutionary agendas for reform, aesthetic or social, who made an impact. The Pate/Francis and Garrett-Howard team (later to become Group Five) had no particular interest in setting the graphic-design world afire, yet the sheer verve of its productivity during the 1950s and early '60s had undeniable influence: creating hundreds of album covers, the group established visual vernaculars including surfer cool and Rat Pack ring-a-ding-ding.

Sixties design innovation also blazed vigorously outside the industry-sanctioned confines of the mainstream design studio, heating up in the streets and the underground. Many of the most exciting California makers were anonymous or, at least, little known and underrecognized, thanks to relatively inexpensive, easy-to-use technology and counterculture agendas that valued the collective over the individual: this was not the era of the singular design hero. Armed with X-ACTO knives, cameras, and varying degrees of ability, these committed artists made up for any lack of formal skill with an abundance of get-out-the-message enthusiasm. Some had a bit of design training, and not necessarily just from art class: poster-design collaborators Alton Kelley and Stanley Mouse studied at the college of hot-rod culture, of pinstriped cars and airbrushed t-shirts. In terms of sheer visual thrills, though, the quick-and-dirty product of the counterculture stands shoulder-to-shoulder with the bona fide.

Lines blurred between art and design. Ed Ruscha both inspired and was inspired by commercial typography and, fascinated by the Los Angeles urban landscape, moved from behind the camera and canvas toward mass production and the multiple. A year before his first and groundbreaking artist's book, Twentysix Gasoline Stations, Ruscha teamed up with the street-savvy Majestic Poster Press to create a poster for the Pop Art exhibition New Painting of Common Objects. Artist Wallace Berman also straddled commissioned and independent work, designing book covers or event flyers while at the same producing works of art using methods and modes closely aligned with graphic design. Sister Corita Kent is yet another example of a producer whose visual works defy easy categorization: are the colorful, food-packaging-and-marketing–influenced banners she created for her Mary's Day events, the once-routine Catholic festivals she transformed into counterculture-style happenings, works of art or graphic design?

We see uncanny convergences and transitions in the 1960s, leaps from one practice to another and alliances among key players. John Van Hamersveld embodies this sort of mobility, starting with the iconic surf graphics he created early in the decade that whetted and fed a national craving for Southern California cool. His surfer-artist buddy Rick Griffin headed north to the Haight-Ashbury scene and became one of the legendary "Big Five" designers of psychedelic posters. Van Hamersveld would visit Griffin in San Francisco and there he met Victor Moscoso, another of the "Big Five," with whom he collaborated on a poster advertising a Who and Fleetwood Mac concert arranged by Van Hamersveld's new, L.A.-based company, Pinnacle Productions. In another tangent, Van Hamersveld initiated the creation of the light-show production team Single Wing Turquoise Bird. And as if that weren't enough, he collaborated with Warner Brothers art director Ed Thrasher to design projects including an album cover for the West Coast Pop Art Experimental Band.

On the pages that follow, an array of texts bears witness to the period's vivacious and divergent strands of production. A new essay by Lorraine Wild entitled "Orange" examines the evocative California color palette—a loud and proud signifier against the staid and demure hues of Europe and the East Coast. This vibrancy of thought continues through a selection of historical writing, including works that, like the graphic design of the time, break with conventional forms in their concern with not only the meaning of words but also their visual representations. Take, for example, the "Immaculate Heart College Art Department Rules," created by one of Sister Corita's classes in 1965 and set to visual form by another student in 1968. This text inspired not just a local college art department but also reverberated across a nation made aware of the visual culture of the everyday through growing mainstream attention to Pop Art. In juxtaposition to the "Rules," I've included two examples from a 1967 issue of the more conventionally formatted graphic-design trade magazine CA (Communication Arts): the cover, which features a "message of messages" that seems to sum up the sensibility of the era; and from the pages inside, Dugald Stemer's article "Rock Posters," which introduced this counterculture genre to the "legitimate" design community. A sampling of pages from the "Communications" section of a 1970 issue of the Whole Earth Catalog recommends how-to sources for budding DIY graphic communicators, including texts on subjects such as geometry, drawing, and calligraphy. Finally, a spread from an issue of Arts in Society co-edited and designed by Sheila Levarant de Bretteville pairs texts by CalArts founder Walt Disney and the art school's first president, Robert Corrigan, demonstrating two differing perspectives on the best way to train new generations of graphic designers.

    The bottom line: California graphic design of the sixties leaped and surged across all sort of divides. It was produced by everyone and for everyone, during a decade of revolution and revelation, and its influence continues to reverberate across the visual landscape.

INFLUENCES & INTERSECTIONS

The Alternative Sixties

EMPLOYER → DESIGNER
INFLUENCER ⇒ DESIGNER
COLLABORATOR ⊢⊣ COLLABORATOR
DESIGNER/ARTIST ┄▸ CULTURE INFLUENCED

ART MUSEUM/ ART GALLERY CULTURE ← ED RUSCHA

JOHN VAN HAMERSVELD ⊢⊣ ED THRASHER

MUSIC INDUSTRY

NICOLAS SIDJAKOV → OFFICIAL DESIGN CULTURE

SURF CULTURE

PATE/ FRANCIS

R. CRUMB ┄▸ COMIX CULTURE ← RICK GRIFFIN

BILL HAM

PSYCHEDELICS

VICTOR MOSCOSO ┄▸ PSYCHEDELIA/ DANCE AND ROCK CONCERT CULTURE

STANLEY MOUSE

WES WILSON

HOT ROD/ CAR CULTURE ← ALTON KELLEY

SÄTTY

LEMONADO DE SICA

FAMILY DOG COLLECTIVE

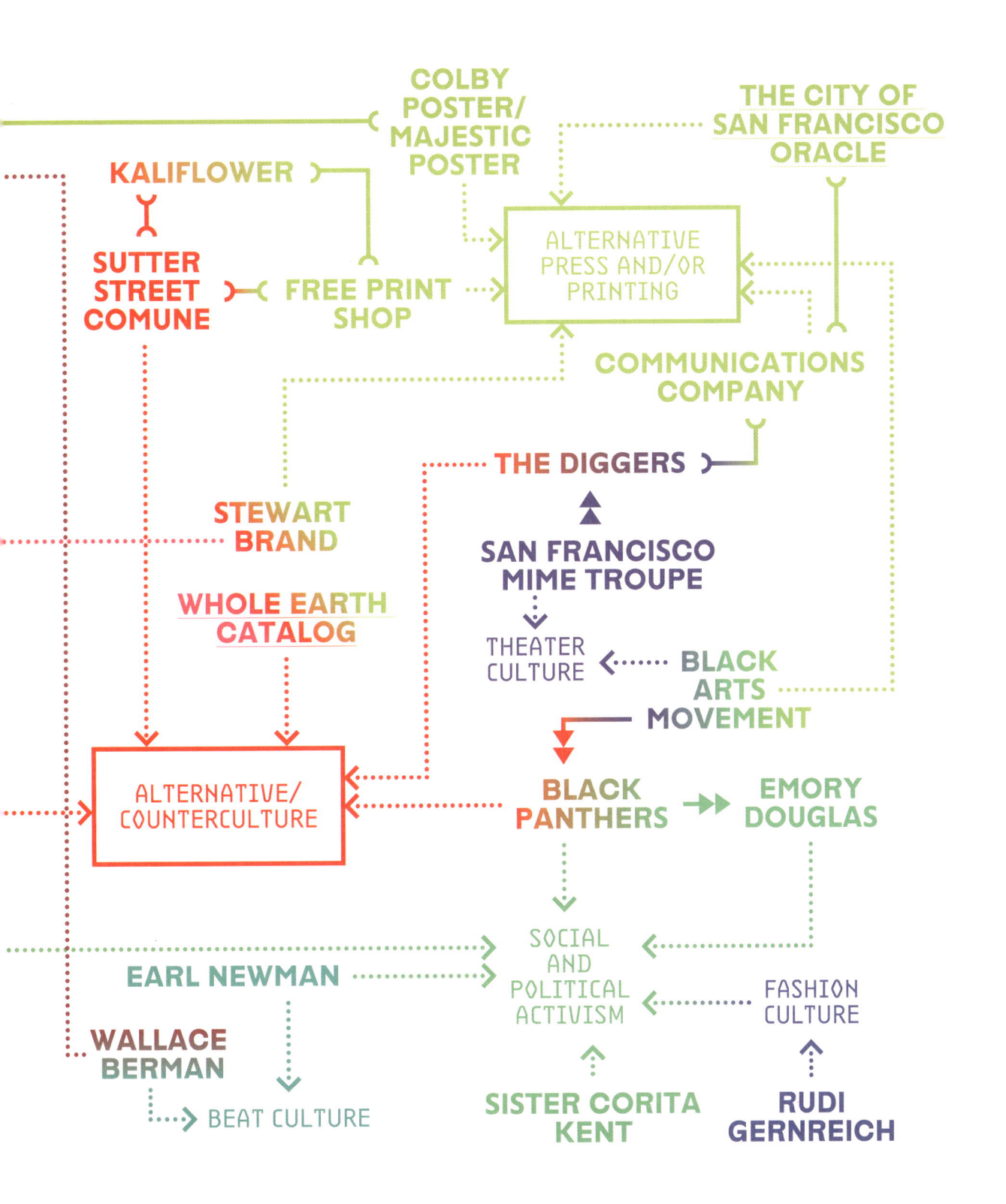

```
                                    COLBY                          THE CITY OF
                                    POSTER/                        SAN FRANCISCO
                                    MAJESTIC                       ORACLE
                                    POSTER

         KALIFLOWER
                                                   ALTERNATIVE
                                                   PRESS AND/OR
         SUTTER                                    PRINTING
         STREET              FREE PRINT
         COMUNE              SHOP

                                                   COMMUNICATIONS
                                                   COMPANY

                              THE DIGGERS

                  STEWART
                  BRAND       SAN FRANCISCO
                              MIME TROUPE
                  WHOLE EARTH
                  CATALOG          THEATER        BLACK
                                   CULTURE        ARTS
                                                  MOVEMENT

                   ALTERNATIVE/          BLACK           EMORY
                   COUNTERCULTURE        PANTHERS        DOUGLAS


                                           SOCIAL
                                           AND
                   EARL NEWMAN             POLITICAL       FASHION
                                           ACTIVISM        CULTURE
         WALLACE
         BERMAN
                                           SISTER CORITA   RUDI
                       BEAT CULTURE        KENT            GERNREICH
```

LORRAINE WILD

ORANGE.

How strange to look back to 40 years ago or so and observe that the color orange was rarely utilized by serious graphic designers east of the Rockies! Pantone 185 was fine, and the near-orange of PMS Warm Red (what was in that stuff, anyway?) was delectable, and 376 was great for green (though 384, grown in California, made its appearance on all sorts of printed matter and even appliances). And 286 was good to wrap up the primary spectrum. High, clear, uncomplicated color, but not orange. Orange provided some sort of dividing line between the Euro-modernists of the East Coast and their (perceived) less-serious West Coast relations. At the beginning of my career in New York City in the late 1970s, I swear I witnessed designers there laughing about all that orange in posters and ads and whatnot designed in California.

Maybe Pantone just loaded vats of 165 onto giant semis bound for the Golden State? For it could be seen all over graphic design produced in California, from the vibrating chroma of Bay Area psychdelia to the more commercially domesticated album covers assembled in Burbank, to the supergraphics and the exploding inevitable of work produced by people more familiar with sunlight and not so constipated by notions of correctness (scratch that, not encumbered by any notions of correctness). In the work of the counterculture, and the work of the marketing of the counterculture, and the work of designers working in the context of all that—who could not help but be affected by that context, if their eyes were open at all—there is a formal freedom in direct proportion to the degree that the designers identified themselves as part of their own audience. Pleasure and freedom are big issues operating in the culture at large, and in those years local interpretations were shaped intuitively in ways that could only be envied by designers elsewhere (or certainly emulated by those who identified with all that those sunny colors stood for).

So while it must be acknowledged that the postwar "A list" designers on the West Coast (OK, some names: Saul Bass or Deborah Sussman or Lou Danziger) were hardly unaware of New York or Europe, in fact, Sussman and Danziger had both made short-term escapes from Los Angeles to go work in Europe, where their innovative production was appreciated. The difference was that designers in California were not bound to New York or Europe in quite the same way. Many miles and time zones, but most of all a sensibility, separated designers who worked on the West Coast from those on the East. For one thing, the linkages between West Coast schools and educators from Europe were attenuated (at best). After the war, Art Center in Los Angeles was perhaps the most active school training young designers attuned to the modern style, yet the teachers there were not really connected to the postwar International Style (which started to affect graphic design, particularly corporate work on the East Coast, by the early '60s) as closely as some of the people teaching graphic design on the other side of the country. For instance, Alvin Lustig, who taught at Art Center in the late 1940s, belonged to that first generation of American designers who self-consciously allied themselves to the modern movement, and yet he was probably the least didactic or programmatic of them all. He declared that the essence of modern practice was to develop flexibility in one's visual response to a given situation or problem, to work without preconceptions or rote visual solutions. Lustig was interested in an aesthetic that reflected the wider contemporary culture of modern art and architecture, but he refused to formalize a set of visual responses as the correct response to any situation. This is in stark contrast to some of the American modernist designers back East who, like their Swiss counterparts, would approach their work with somewhat more preconcieved sets of typographic and visual syntaxes. In that work (produced largely for corporate clients), which we now refer to as the International Style, form is intended to be interpreted as "objective"—delivering the message without editorializing through design—yet it is simultaneously meant to signal to the cognoscenti that the designer <u>and client</u> are sophisticated enough to be able to assume this detached tone, and that whatever is being designed is enhanced by that discipline. The much more open and informal modernism of West Coast design seems not to impose an order on the world so much as embody that which is perhaps already happening. And that may have had something to do with it not being taken as seriously. Also, the International Style was connected to the newly developed, postwar, multinational, globalized world, whereas the more intimate California Style was definitely marked as more regional, which of course could be regarded as charming, or parochial, or... both.

That California had its own robust design culture (across architecture, interiors, furniture, fashion, and craft production, along with graphic design) by the '40s has been well documented, particularly in the series of exhibitions sponsored by the Getty Center's Pacific Standard Time project. **And while the scholarly work that has excavated the diversity and strength of design in California is of relatively recent vintage, the visual evidence has been there all along, in that the work simply looks different: and color is an important, contributing factor to that.** As Lawrence Wechsler (among others) has pointed out, the light is different out here (though San Francisco "light" is quite different from what is right across the East Bay—that is, a bright, flat light similar to Los Angeles and Southern California light). Sunlight on the beaches of Southern California can be particularly strong since it reflects off the surface of the ocean. Intense colors look exaggerated in that light but not out of place; and the spatial experience of vivid hues in the wide-frame landscape (or framed by a windshield) feels of a piece with the place, particularly in the slanted light of early morning or late afternoon. The desert also has a particular palette, with an overall dusty landscape punctuated by extremely bright (but tiny) flowering plants, which the blaring sun accentuates even further. So the liberal use of strong colors in paint, in clothing, in architecture and interiors, and in all sorts of other designed projects is echoed in the use of those colors in graphic design. While one can attribute a taste for color to the specifics of how a palette appears in local light (or the speed by which intense colors fade and buffer into something else, due to sunlight or seawater or both), one cannot say that light alone offers the complete explanation. The association of those colors with a place that, in both the local and national imagination, stood for an easy climate, a fresh start, and the promise of the future only bolstered their continual use, and finally they just became part of the vernacular of a place and its culture.

The bright palette refers not only to sunlight and reflections and flora, then, but to the local culture(s) and an extreme degree of social diversity, too. The futurism evident in California graphic design is not necessarily referencing only technology but also sociology: the vast and varied populations (particularly in Southern California, where the demographic mix exploded in the 1950s), with their cultures and subcultures and the visual expression of that incredible florescence.

So the psychedelic poster designers of San Francisco were hardly the first Californians to use the neon bright colors in their work (and let's set aside the one degree of separation between Victor Moscosco, the deftest of the psychedelic colorists, and the Bauhaus via Joseph Albers, with whom he had studied at Yale before ending up in the Haight pulling all-nighters making Fillmore Ballroom announcements, up to his elbows in Rubylith and weed).

Looking at graphic design in Los Angeles after World War II, one can see Bass utilize extremely high-contrast color as part of his integrated "identity systems" for movies (such as <u>The Man with the Golden Arm</u> or <u>Vertigo</u>), where a symbolic rendering of the idea of the film replaces the usual movie-star portraits. **The bold, simple color relations (with vivid reds and oranges) are not related to specific colors in the films themselves but more in sync—and competitive—with the (increasingly) colorful visual environment of advertising in magazines and newspapers and street posters and billboards.** Black and white makes its appearance in California design in the numerous high contrast (and low budget/mostly typographic) ads that can be seen in <u>Arts & Architecture</u> (many designed by a young crew that sometimes included Lou Danziger or Fred Usher), layouts that are designed entirely for black-only printing; or via the use of documentary (or documentary-like photography, in the work of Danziger for several pharmaceutical clients). However, one does not often get the feeling that black is being used out of puritanical or minimalist impulses, since the bias toward high-keyed color is so established. **And it is this free use**

of color by designers working on the high end of the graphic design spectrum that is so interesting, in that there is no desire to signal a higher level of taste (or expense) via the denial of color. Monotone does not signal class (at least in Southern California). Elite California fashion eccentrics such as James Galanos or Tony Duquette were masters of weird and unexpected color combinations, but the same intense hues could be seen in new bathing suits on the beach: it all looked good in the sunlight, and the use of color (or lack of it) as signifier or polemic just would not work here.

❋

Thinking of the visual environment of brash commercial color—and very bright sunlight—as the context that all designers were a part of makes sense of the strong use of color by those who were communicating in that context even if their work was not commercial. Sister Corita Kent starts, in the early '60s, by appropriating shards of common print advertising slogans from large consumer corporations (General Mills, Hunt's) and composing completely new-looking posters with messages that address spirituality in the context of the everyday. Her sly repurposing of common advertising language sets aside any cynicism about where it might come from in favor of embracing its value as a familiar and seductive vernacular. Corita employed the existing color in the advertising without altering or aestheticizing it, and even when she produced pieces that were not based on the reuse of slogans (such as her Circus Alphabet series of screenprints, made in 1968), she continued to use high-contrast and even Day-Glo inks to retain the power of pop street-side advertising. Corita acknowledged that seeing Andy Warhol's first exhibition of the Campbell's soup can paintings at Ferus Gallery in Los Angeles in 1962 had set her thinking about the ubiquitousness of advertising, and that opened her eyes to the idea of using the brightness and scale and power of the commercial for her revolutionary work.

The garishness of Day-Glo and the eye-straining use of complimentary colors (red/green, blue/orange) were visual strategies used by the Bay Area psychedelic designers of concert posters for the Fillmore Ballroom (and other venues) to create images that would speak to their own community. The posters are marvels of imagination <u>and</u> limited production, yet even within the narrow stylistic range and tight budgets, different designers produced recognizably personal languages. Wes Wilson made particular use of the buzz of complimentary color to make posters that appear to move as you stare at them; Moscoso used Day-Glo to pick out compositions that would look best in eerie black-lighting. No one was ever too high to steal the first run of these announcements off the street poles, and it took only about five minutes for this very local style to morph into the rainbow hues of hippie culture and rock music and the counterculture in general. (Not to mention the "alternative" appropriation of Indian and other Asian images and decorative motifs, with all their bright colors, in the psychedelic/hippie style, as well.) And while the true counterculture of the underground press was generally produced with so little money that color was a luxury, it is noticeable that the most radical West Coast publications—the Black Panther newspapers, the gay Kaliflower tabloid, and broadsides published by the Diggers—all used color in a more aggressive way than many of their sister publications in the East. The psychedelia of Haight-Ashbury had turned into a symbol of youth and resistance, laced with anarchy and pleasure.

A few years later, when Swiss-trained graphic designer April Greiman started creating her shockingly new-looking work in Los Angeles, the first thing that distinguished it as new was the integration of hyper-California color (and motifs from Asian and Latin American decoration). Her typography read as a logical extension of the International Style continuum (which it came out of, given her training at the Kunstgewerbeschule in Basel), but her use of color and ornament in projects of the late 1970s and early '80s—such as the Spacemat products; her covers for Wet magazine; and her promotional work for CalArts, where she taught—announced a radical creative independence from the tradition that had governed her education. However, Greiman's use of color is less of a critique of where she came from and more of an intuitive, positive, and energizing response to her new context, of living and working on the West Coast.

A different source for high-keyed California color can be found in the design coming out of the Eames Office, where seemingly nothing was produced in monotone, ever. Like Corita, Charles and Ray Eames looked to the vernacular—specifically, when they were faced with producing a graphic design project. The obsessive shooting of 35mm slides for the studio's visual library provided inspiration for their aesthetic, attaching a global sensibility to their West Coast work. The couple traveled frequently, and their project of visual research (which was not always assignment-driven) never stopped; when they could not leave the office, they sent their assistants out with the same order to build documentation. Their association with the designer Alexander Girard, who was particularly inspired by "outsider" design, also prompted the Eameses to incorporate the lively and clashing palettes of global vernaculars. The contrast of the unschooled (and loud) folk art artifacts or style served to both enliven and soften the challenge of the Eameses' modernist furniture and environments. It is hard to imagine a more iconic Californian interior than the living room of their own home, the Case Study House No. 8 (1949), with its tough steel frame punched to life by hundreds of books, art, plants, and piles of pink-and-orange-striped-and-embroidered pillows and throws. Clichés of modernity might require austerity; the Eameses' domestic melange of intellectuality and sensuality smilingly contradicts all of that.

A fairly straight line connects the decor of the Eames living room to the giant striped Sono Tube temporary signage and space constructions for the 1984 Los Angeles Olympics, art directed by Deborah Sussman (longtime associate of the Eameses') and Paul Prezja. The Olympic Committee demanded a solution to creating an image for the Summer Games that would be inexpensive and create an impact in the sprawled out and sunbaked spaces of Los Angeles for both the participants on-site and the audience watching at home, on television. The ingenious modules in pink, orange, turquoise, and purple were seen as playful and informal, and even though they were not that monumental they created a lot of visual impact: the bright constructions worked as excellent TV backdrops, and the color palette itself became a critical part of the identity of the games. **While the term Pacific Rim was only starting to be used in 1984, the embedded references to Asian** (quoting Diana Vreeland, "Pink is the navy blue of India"), Mexican, and Central and South American color palettes through the familiarity with the Girardian/Eamesian folk-arts/modernist mind-meld then combined again with the countercultural Day-Glo to become something Californian with a capital C.

It must be noted that West Coast retailers embraced a very modern, eclectic, and strongly hued approach to the design of store interiors and graphics. Earlier examples of this would include work that Victor Gruen's Los Angeles–based office did for Barton's Bonbonniere (which looks like a bizarre cross between a circus interior and a Calder mobile exhibition) not long after World War II, and the rebelliously vivid designs for Joseph Magnin department stores by Marget Larsen and Rudi Baumfeld with Gruen Associates in the 1960s. In both cases, the combination of a striking (and, again, very strong) color palette used with other graphic standards across advertising, packaging, and interiors created a "proto-brand identity" approach to the enticement of customers that retained its novelty even through the work of Tamotso Yagi for Susie Tompkins's Bay Area clothing company, Esprit, which used color in clothing and graphics in a visually aggressive way that practically defined the American pop-culture look of the 1980s.

When <u>Wired</u> magazine (which, in turn, became the pop-culture voice of the Silicon Valley elite, at least in its early years) started publishing, in 1993, one of the remarkable decisions by the founding designers, John Plunkett and Barbara Kuhr, was to incorporate an expensive extra plate of ink in the printing of this new magazine dedicated to a technological revolution largely designed and marketed in California. And the extra plate, used to print the stencil font masthead and the headlines inside, was dedicated to (what else?): fluorescent orange. This choice of color is an important aspect of what we now would regard as an aesthetic of high tech, seen today across electronics, digital technology, "high performance" sportswear, and a gazillion other products, each one bearing a tattoo, a nod to the DNA of an idea of California, once quite specific to a place and time but now made the world over: a globalized style.

IMMACULATE HEART COLLEGE ART DEPARTMENT RULES

Rule 1 FIND A PLACE YOU TRUST AND THEN TRY TRUSTING IT FOR A WHILE.

Rule 2 GENERAL DUTIES OF A STUDENT: PULL EVERYTHING OUT OF YOUR TEACHER. PULL EVERYTHING OUT OF YOUR FELLOW STUDENTS.

Rule 3 GENERAL DUTIES OF A TEACHER: PULL EVERYTHING OUT OF YOUR STUDENTS.

Rule 4 CONSIDER EVERYTHING AN EXPERIMENT.

Rule 5 BE SELF DISCIPLINED. THIS MEANS FINDING SOMEONE WISE OR SMART AND CHOOSING TO FOLLOW THEM. TO BE DISCIPLINED IS TO FOLLOW IN A GOOD WAY. TO BE SELF DISCIPLINED IS TO FOLLOW IN A BETTER WAY.

Rule 6 NOTHING IS A MISTAKE. THERE'S NO WIN AND NO FAIL. THERE'S ONLY MAKE.

Rule 7 The only rule is work. IF YOU WORK IT WILL LEAD TO SOMETHING. IT'S THE PEOPLE WHO DO ALL OF THE WORK ALL THE TIME WHO EVENTUALLY CATCH ON TO THINGS.

Rule 8 DON'T TRY TO CREATE AND ANALYSE AT THE SAME TIME. THEY'RE DIFFERENT PROCESSES.

Rule 9 BE HAPPY WHENEVER YOU CAN MANAGE IT. ENJOY YOURSELF. IT'S LIGHTER THAN YOU THINK.

Rule 10 "WE'RE BREAKING ALL OF THE RULES. EVEN OUR OWN RULES. AND HOW DO WE DO THAT? BY LEAVING PLENTY OF ROOM FOR X QUANTITIES." JOHN CAGE

HELPFUL HINTS: ALWAYS BE AROUND. COME OR GO TO EVERYTHING. ALWAYS GO TO CLASSES. READ ANYTHING YOU CAN GET YOUR HANDS ON. LOOK AT MOVIES CAREFULLY, OFTEN. SAVE EVERYTHING—IT MIGHT COME IN HANDY LATER. THERE SHOULD BE NEW RULES NEXT WEEK.

"Immaculate Heart College Art Department Rules," created by a class of Sister Corita Kent's, 1965, calligraphy by David Mekelburg, 1968

ARCHIVE

CAL ARTS LIBRARY PERIODICALS

CA MAGAZINE • VOLUME 9, NUMBER 1, 1967 • $2.50

CALIFORNIA INSTITUTE OF THE ARTS L
0 02201 0308839

- comnunicate
- OUTLAW CHURCH GAMBLING
- EAT FAT
- STAMP OUT MENTAL HEALTH
- COME BACK TRUMAN ALL IS FORGIVEN
- INVESTIGATE GOD *
- SOME OF MY BEST FRIENDS ARE
- 1ST ANNUAL END OF THE World DAY JUNE 12, 1967
- MUZZLE MUZAK
- RED POWER
- TAKE A HIPPY TO LUNCH
- UP
- RONALD REAGAN EATS PEANUT BUTTER
- WAR IS GOOD BUSINESS $ INVEST YOUR SON
- "LEVITATE"
- FRODO LIVES
- PEANUT BUTTER IS BETTER THAN POT
- I'LL NEVER FORGET WHAT'S HER NAME
- I'm number 3 I don't try at all
- I AM ANONYMOUS HELP ME
- MARY POPPINS IS A JUNKIE
- LOVE IS GOD
- CHARLES EDWARD WHITE III RULES THE WORLD
- CA
- TURN ON TUNE IN DROP OUT GET WELL
- DON'T READ THIS BUTTON
- IF YOU CAN READ THIS YOU'RE TOO CLOSE
- come alive!
- GREAT SOCIETY
- curse you RED BARON
- Piglet Lives
- LEMMINGS ARE SILLY. DINOSAURS ARE EXTINCT. S.P.U.
- KISS DON'T KILL
- ROOMMATE WANTED
- OLD ENOUGH TO FIGHT, OLD ENOUGH TO VOTE
- SPU
- I HATE EVERYBODY
- JESUS SAVES GREEN STAMPS
- LOVE IS LOVELY WAR IS UGLY
- REPEAL INHIBITION
- POP ART STINKS

COVER OF CA, vol. 9, no. 1, 1967

SIXTIES ALT SIXTIES

229

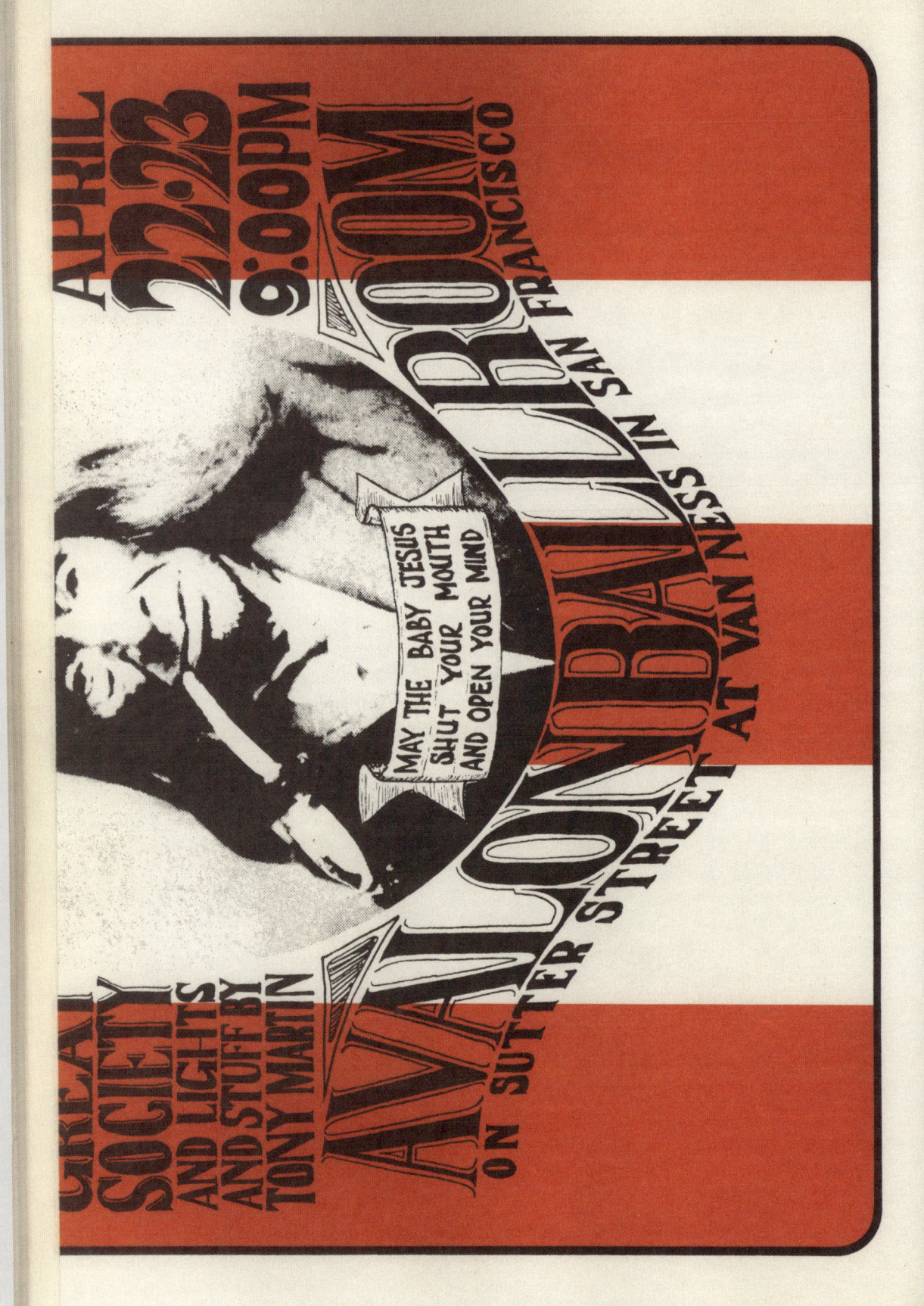

EXCERPT FROM Dugald Stermer, "Rock Posters," CA, vol. 9, no. 1, 1967

ROCK POSTERS

by Dugald Stermer

What may well be one of the more important new directions in art in this country has occured, surprisingly, in postermaking. This has never been one of America's graphic strong points; just a glance at the posters in front of our motion picture theatres, campaign headquarters, or Selective Service offices should convince anyone of that.

Before we go any further I feel that I ought to clarify my definition of posters, so as to exclude those of the 24-sheet variety. I refuse to endow anything designed to be viewed from an automobile window at speeds upwards of 55 m.p.h. with any redeeming aesthetic or social values whatsoever. (I will admit that there is some scenery lining the highways of our land, such as junkyards, high-rise apartments and Kansas, that is only improved by the installation of some selected billboards. But that is another argument.)

For the sake of this review, I am only covering posters in the European sense; that is, posters for pedestrian consumption. And that is just the point. By the time we got around to discovering what the Europeans were doing in this area—so that we would know where to begin—we were no longer pedestrian except in the figurative sense; and posters just have no value in a motorized society.

So it would seem appropriate that the only significant movement in American poster making should spring up in that last hotbed of peripatetics: San Francisco.

Although the examples shown do borrow a great deal from Art Nouveau techniques, the artists distort those techniques to their own ends—and add to them—in the traditions of all art movements. To argue with this in terms of integrity is like censuring Isaac Stern for rendering *Variations on a Theme by Paganini*.

In marketing talk, these posters are a kind of "institutional" advertising. They are designed primarily to sell the general atmosphere surrounding the Fillmore Auditorium, the Avalon Ballroom, or the Matrix, and the dance/happenings held therein. The specific rock group playing on a specific date is of secondary importance. The lettering meanders all over the place with complete disregard for our Gutenberg training, so that it takes considerable time and visual acrobatics to find out what the words say. This illegibility is no disadvantage; on the contrary it is essential. It comes right out of the same bag that requires one to hear the same song by The Rolling Stones quite a few times before the words become clear.

Wes Wilson

Kelly / Mouse

To describe these dances to one who had never been there (loud, insistent, all-encompassing sounds; liquid, writhing lighting; populated by silent, expressionless young gypsies) is as impossible as describing red to a blind person. It simply cannot be done except by some kind of imaginative association of general terms.

These posters are unquestionably successful in doing just that. The choice of symbols, flowing words, names of the various groups, colors, all contribute to communicating the essence of a unique sub-culture: the San Francisco Hippie scene.

The two artists primarily responsible for this movement are all somewhat in this scene. Wes Wilson, the originator of the basic style, and still its most prolific purveyor, studies a little philosophy, no art, and began his career as a printer's apprentice. He is just now beginning to pursue painting and other artistic endeavors such as making money from the distribution of reprints.

Kelly/Mouse Studios: represents the collaboration of one of the founders of The Family Dog (the producer of the dances at the Avalon) with an ex-T-shirt "monster" artist/cartoonist, in the same idiom with Ed "Big Daddy" Roth of Los Angeles. With flowing locks, burning incense, their vestments dripping with beaded necklaces, iron crosses and peace buttons. They are prototypes of the Haight/Ashbury Hippie. (The small enclave of San Francisco hippiedom, near Golden Gate Park, gets its name from two of the streets in the district, Haight and Ashbury.)

Victor Moscoso is the last to enter the poster field, and of the four he is the only one to have a real art background. He has exhibited his paintings, teaches at the San Francisco Art Institute, and works as an illustrator and cartoonist.

As a final word: These posters have already gained status as an art form, in that local and national galleries are currently collecting and exhibiting complete sets. While this is certainly no final judgment as to their intrinsic artistic merit, it does mark the first time in this country that works designed specifically for advertising have been generally accepted as art.

Whether the McLuhanists would argue that this acceptance is simply a recognition of our age as "instant-on, electric, non-specialized" and a return to a "tribal" community (the latter has made Mr. McLuhan somewhat of a folk-hero in tribalized Hippie circles), or whether it is a case of complete boredom with pop/opism, coupled with well-timed legitimate thievery of techniques, its very success does pose a danger.

We have a way of smothering independence by absorbing it. It is no accident that these posters grew up in the midst of anti-establishment rebellion, "acid" and raids by the "Fuzz", and that the artists have little or no formal training in art. The value of these posters lies in an independent, ingenuous crudeness and honesty that just could not survive in an institutionalized environment.

Dugald Stermer

Right: commercial application of the poster style for Levi Straus & Co., Wes Wilson designer.
Far right: posters by Mouse.

Victor Moscoso

Photographs by Bob Seideman

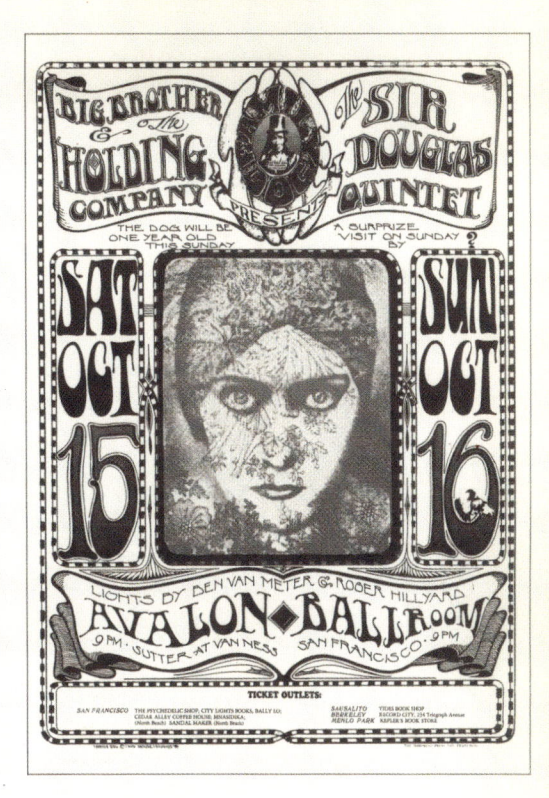

67

Communications

The Japanese Abacus

Hey all you businessmen out there here's your chance to save some more money while you count your money. A little honey of an abacus and a clear concise one night (maybe two it took me three) lesson in how to add, subtract, multiply and divide on this simple, cheap, lightning fast device.

[Reviewed by D. Smith]

The abacus, or *soroban* as it is called in Japan, is one of the first objects that strongly attract the attention of the foreigner in Japan. When he buys a few trifling articles at some store, he soon notices that the tradesman does not perplex himself with mental arithmetic, but instead seizes his *soroban*, prepares it by a tilt and a rattling sweep of his hand, and after a deft manipulation of rapid clicks, reads off the price. It is true that the Japanese tradesman often uses his board and beads even when the problem is simple enough to be done in one's head, but this is only because the use of the abacus has become a habit with him. If he tried, he could no doubt easily add 84 and 48 in his head. But such is the force of habit that he does not try to recognize the simplicity of any problem; instead, following the line of least resistance, he adjusts his *soroban* for manipulation, and begins clicking the beads, thus escaping any need of mental effort.

The Japanese Abacus,
It's Use and Theory
1965; 102pp.

$1.50 (book alone) postpaid

$4.25 (book plus abacus) postpaid

from:
Charles E. Tuttle Company
28 South Main
Rutland, Vermont 05701

Regular Polytopes

shel kaphan,
mathematician,
boy wizard,
bookkeeper,
bicyclist,
alpinist,
shel kaphan recommended this,
as an old standard for mathematical model builders.

—jd

Regular Polytopes
H.S.M. Coxeter
1948; 63; 321pp.

$4.95 postpaid

from:
Crowell Collier and MacMillan
866 Third Avenue
New York, New York 10022

or WHOLE EARTH CATALOG

A honeycomb is said to be quasi-regular if its cells are regular while its vertex figures are quasi-regular. This definition (cf. #2-3) implies that the vertex figures are all alike, and that the cells are of two kinds, arranged alternately. To find what varieties are possible, we have the same two alternative methods as in #4-6. Either we seek (as cells) two different regular polyhedra whose respective dihedral angles have a submultiple of 2π for their sum; these can only be a tetrahedron and an octahedron, where the sum is π. Or we look at the possible vertex figures, admitting the cuboctahedron, whose edge is equal to its circum-radius, and discarding the icosidodecahedron (for which the ratio of edge to circum-radius is dodecahedron (for which the ratio of edge to circum-radius is $2 \sin \pi/h = 2 \sin \pi/10 = 2 \cos 2\pi/5$). From either point of view, we conclude that there is only one quasi-regular honeycomb. Each vertex is surrounded by eight tetrahedra and six octahedra (corresponding to the triangles and squares of the cuboctahedron).

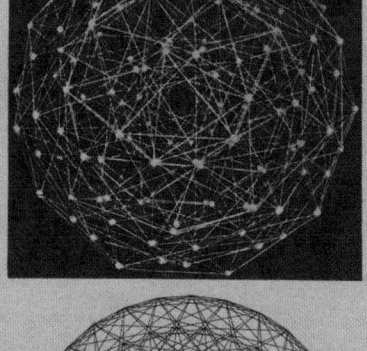

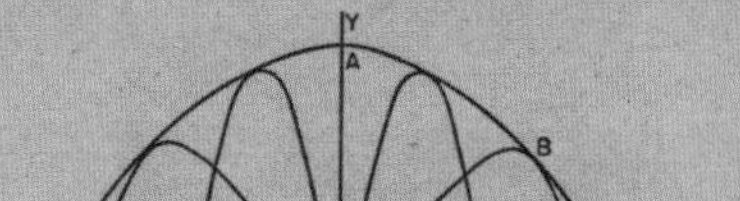

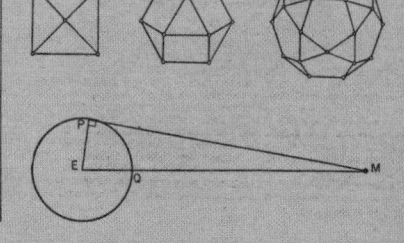

communication,
wow,
communication,
a few thoughts.
that its not how you do it but what you do,
although,
what you say has a lot to do with how you say it.
that its harder to listen than to talk,
although but,
you don't get quite as much said.
that arrows and words are seperate but equal,
and
that action, times say, speaks louder than words.

—jd

AAA Adding Machine Company

I wish we'd known about this outfit when we started business. They carry used and reconditioned calculators, adding machines and cash registers at good prices.

—SB

Catalog
FREE

from:
AAA Adding Machine Company
26-09 Jackson Avenue
Long Island City, New York 11101

MARCHANT $99.00
Automatic carriage return • Carriage tabulation; preset decimal as well as multiplication • No repeat or non-repeat keys • Automatic elimination of 1 in division • Complete carriage carry-over • Exclusive keyboard check dial • Complete in line 3 figure proof.

Mathematics and the Physical World

i'm no mathematician.
in the woods,
between dodging timber,
and dripping sweat,
ken hoffman tried to explain
how, mathematically,
you can put a handle on a basketball,
make a donut out of the earth.
this book doesn't go into either of those problems,
but it does try to tie things together,
using numbers as the language.

—jd

Mathematics and the Physical World
Morris Kline
1959; 482pp.

$2.95 postpaid

from:
Thomas Y. Crowell Company
788 Bloomfield Avenue
Clifton, New Jersey 07012

or WHOLE EARTH CATALOG

Mathematics is commonly regarded as highly abstract and remote from the real world. It is true that as mathematics developed it built more abstract and more complex ideas. An equation involving unknowns is more a abstract and perhaps more complicated notion than that of number, and the reasoning about equations is less immediately subject to the physical interpretation than the manipulations of arithmetic, but every abstraction that even the greatest mathematician has introduced is ultimately derived from objects or phenomena. The mind does play its part in the creation of mathematical concepts and in determining the direction that the reasoning shall pursue, but the mind does not function independently of the world outside. Indeed, the mathematician who advances concepts that have no physically real or intuitive origins is almost surely talking nonsense. The intimate connection between mathematics and events in the physical world is reassuring, for it means that not only can we hope to understand the mathematics proper but also expect physically meaningful conclusions. From dust thou art to dust returneth may perhaps not be spoken of the soul but it is well spoken of earthborn mathematics.

Edlie's Flyer

Beginners in electronics who don't want to be stuck with very beautiful but very unusable gadgets (and also experts who know what's-used-for-what) can get a lot of value from industrial (civilian) surplus electronics, these days.

For the "consumer" uses of electronics—music, p.a., TV, repair parts and instruments, experimenting—Edlie Electronics has the best selection and the lowest prices of any mail-order dealer I have found.

They handle everything from hi-fi components (e.g. an FM tuner from a discontinued console) to single resistors. Some of it is new, and some of it is sold "as is" (e.g. small radios and tape recorders returned to the store under a warranty.)

If you don't feel safe about repair work or experiments, though, better concentrate on getting electronic stuff with a dependable guarantee, maybe by buying from a repair shop.

[Suggested and Reviewed by John Huntley]

Edlie's Flyer Catalog
free

from:
Edlie Electronics, Inc.
2700 Hempstead Turnpike
Levittown, Long Island,
New York 11756

CT628 CLAIRE STEPPING RELAYS MODEL 26 (removed from brand new chassis -- similar to picture). 26 positions, 10 poles. 24-36 volts.
Price only $8.95

CT629 CLAIRE STEPPING RELAYS TYPE 211. 11 positions, 6 poles. 24-36 volts.
Price $3.95

CT630 TELEPHONE RELAY. 24-36V. 2500 ohms. No. 37 E.C. 2 sets of contacts: one set 2P, 3T, second set 2P, 4 T.
Price 65¢

CT631 WESTERN UNION TEL. CO. CHASSIS. Consists of 1 - No. 26 Relay (as listed above); 3 - No. 211 Relays (as listed above); 1 - No. 37 E.C. Relay (as listed above.) Comes mounted on a brand new chassis.
Bargain Price for Complete Chassis (including 5 relays)
only $18.95

CT281 WESTON MODEL NO. 1 Precision Mirror Backed Meters.
A) D.C. Voltmeter, dual scale, fan type 0-75, 0-150 D.C. Volts.
Price $37.50
B) D. C. Voltmeter, Triple Scale, 0-150, 0-300, 0-750 Volts D.C.
Price $41.50

CT548 TRANSDUCER 200 K.C. Made by Brush. Brand new. For use with Marine Depth Finder Equipment or experimental purposes.
Price only $2.95

Communication Arts

a slicky for graphics freeks,
and ad men,
people who cut things out of magazines,
to paste them on walls,
christmas cards,
kleenex boxes,
and catalogs.
expensive but pretty.

—jd

Communication Arts
Richard Coyne, editor.

$15.00 per year (bimonthly)

from:
Communication Arts
P.O. Box 10300
200 California Avenue
Palo Alto, California 94303

Electronics

For technical freaks. If you are a double e ENGINEER, the articles may be of interest. Otherwise, spend your time with the ads. Learn about all the new hardware and bits and pieces. Reader service card whereby all of the advertisers will send you piles of shit on their products. By far the best part is the Electronics Buyers Guide, a three-inch thick directory that comes once a year and lists all manufacturers (and their sales reps) that have anything to do with electronics.

Don't forget your title and company name. Get a subscription blank from one at the library and have no trouble.

[Reviewed by Fred Richardson]

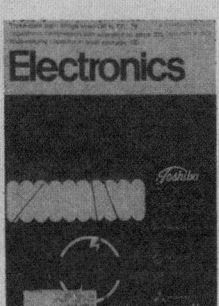

Electronics
$8.00 a year, biweekly

from:
Electronics
P.O. Box 514
Hightstown, N.J. 08520
Subscription department

Subscriptions limited to persons with active, professional, functional responsibility in electronics technology. Publisher reserves the right to reject non-qualified requests. No subscriptions accepted without complete identification of subscriber name, title or job function, company or organization, including product manufactured or services performed. Subscription rates: qualified subscribers in the United States and possessions and Canada, $8.00 one year; $12.00 two years. $16.00 three years; all other countries $25.00 two years. Limited quota of subscriptions available at higher-than-basic rate for persons outside of field served, as follows: U.S. and possessions and Canada, $25.00 one year; all other countries $50.00. Air frieght service to Japan, $60.00 one year, including prepaid postage. Single copies: United States and possessions in Canada, $1.00; all other countries, $1.75.

October 5, 1970

Mr. Megan Raymond
WHOLE EARTH TRUCK STORE & CATALOG
558 Santa Cruz Avenue
Menlo Park, CA

Dear Mr. Raymond:

As you will undoubtedly recall, back in June I'd written to you expressing our apologies over the unfortunate misunderstanding that occurred when we originally received your request for approval to list Heathkit products in the WHOLE EARTH CATALOG.

I assume our recognition of the "error of our ways", plus the letter sent to you at that time, have rectified the situation. I must add that "I surely hope so" . . . as your readers have really made believers out of us! Although it has been quite embarrassing for us, it certainly points to the fact that the WHOLE EARTH CATALOG is carefully read by large numbers of highly intelligent, perceptive and articulate people. We're impressed!

Aside from the above, I'm taking this opportunity to write for two reasons. First, I'd like you to enter my subscription to the WHOLE EARTH CATALOG and bill same to me here at the office. Secondly, I'm enclosing three copies of our new 1971 Heathkit catalog . . . just off the press.

In summary, and at the risk of redundancy, you may be assured that we're "for you" . . . not "against you"!

Yours very truly,
SCHLUMBERGER PRODUCTS
CORPORATION
William E. Johnson
Vice President

Heathkit catalog
free

from:
Heath Company
Benton Harbor, Michigan 49022

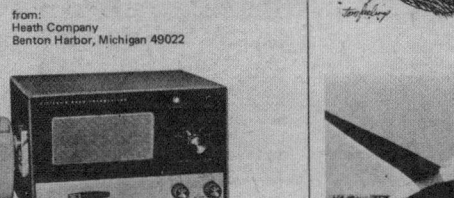

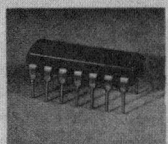

Integrated Circuit Multiplex

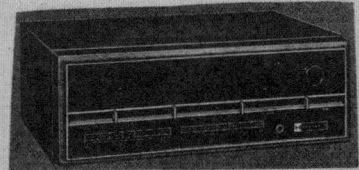

The Way of Chinese Painting

chinese painters do more with brush, ink, inkstone and paper than western gadgeteers accomplish with their complicated mixing formulas, apprenticeship programs, and didactic traditions.

has a lot to do with thinking simply.

this book can provide you with good access to the tools and ideas of eastern brush painting,

things you can carry around in your hip pocket as you move; you provide the practice.

—jd

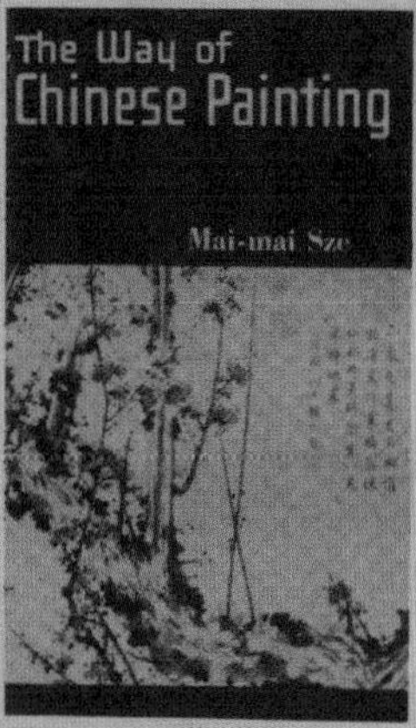

The materials of Chinese painting—brush, ink, inkstone, paper—are the same as the simple equipment on the table in a scholar's study. Always held in deep respect, they have long been called the Four Treasures of the Abodes of Culture. Each is dependent on the others, and all are highly prized. Each has a long history of development amounting to a pedigree. Each is also endowed with symbolic significance that has enveloped it in elaborate layers of meaning. Besides paper, silk has also been used for paintings, and, besides ink, colors; so that silk and colors should be included in discussing the materials of painting.

•

Lu Ch'ai says:
Among those who study painting some strive for an elaborate effect and others prefer the simple. Neither complexity in itself nor simplicity is enough. Some aim to be deft, others to be laboriously careful. Neither dexterity nor conscientiousness is enough. Some set great value on method; others pride themselves on dispensing with method. To be without method is deplorable, but to depend entirely on method is worse.

You must learn first to observe the rules faithfully; afterwards, modify them according to your intelligence and capacity. The end of all method is to seem to have no method.

•

Choose an umber that is hard and of a beautiful hue. These are the two points to keep in mind in picking the best. There are kinds that are hard as iron, others soft as mud; they are not all desirable.

Use a small earthen bowl in which to grind the color, with a little water, to the consistency of mud. Then add a lot of clear glue and water and stir well. Skim off the upper layer for use. Drain off the bottom layer, which is coarse and dull in color, and throw it out.

•

PURIFYING WHITE
In paintings, the areas where white is used often darken. Chew the heart of a bitter apricot seed, and with the juice wash these spots once or twice. The dark spots will then disappear.

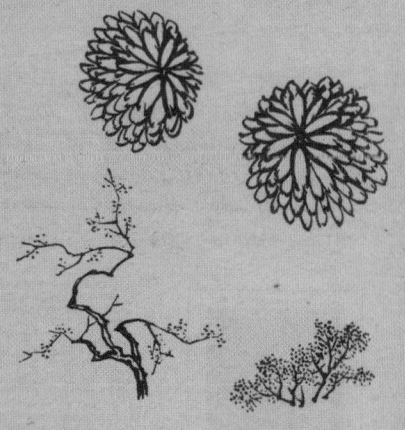

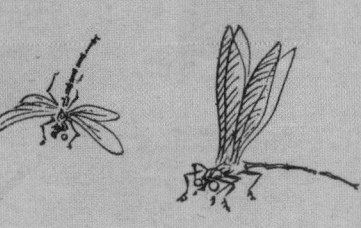

The Way of Chinese Painting
Mai-mai Sze
1956, 59; 456pp.

$1.65 postpaid

from:
Random House, Inc.
Random House Building
201 East 50th Street
New York, New York 10022

or WHOLE EARTH CATALOG

The Natural Way to Draw

Drawing is a deeper and wider kind of writing. It's better communication in many ways than writing, and it's much closer to your mind. (The same goes for music and speech.)

This classic work by an outstanding art teacher is not only the best how-to book on drawing, it is the best how-to book we've seen on any subject.

—SB

[Suggested by Roy Sebern]

TWO TYPES OF STUDY. The way to learn to draw is by drawing. People who make art must not merely know about it. For an artist, the important thing is not how much he knows, but how much he can do. A scientist may know all about aeronautics without being able to handle an airplane. It is only by flying that he can develop the sense for flying. If I were asked what one thing more than any other would teach a student how to draw, I should answer, "Drawing—incessantly, furiously, painstakingly drawing."

Probably you realize already that contour drawing is of the type which is to be done "painstakingly". On the other hand, gesture drawing, which you will begin today, is to be done "furiously". In order to concentrate, one can act furiously over a short space of time, or one can work with calm determination, quietly, over a long-extended period. In learning to draw, both kinds of effort are necessary and the one makes a precise balance for the other. In long studies you will develop an understanding of the structure of the model, how it is made—by which I mean something more fundamental than anatomy alone. In quick studies you will consider the function of action, life, or expression—I call it *gesture*.

The Natural Way to Draw
Kimon Nicolaides
1941; 221 pp.

$6.00 postpaid

from:
Houghton Mifflin Company
Wayside Road
Burlington, Massachusetts 01803

or WHOLE EARTH CATALOG

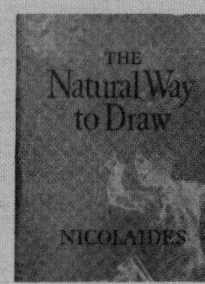

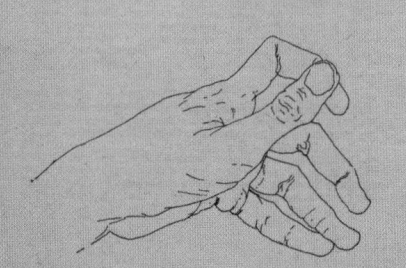

Calligraphic Lettering with wide pen and brush

calligraphic lettering, by ralph douglass, presents a lot of different forms of lettering; italic, chancery cursive, english roundhand, spanish gothic, etc., but it's up to you to do them right. he just shows you what the letters should look like.

[Suggested by Cappy McClure
Reviewed by Ruth Wyant]

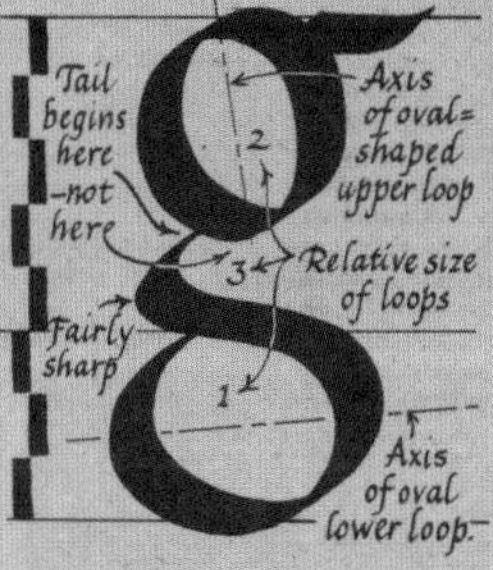

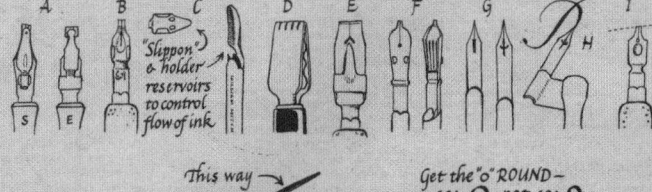

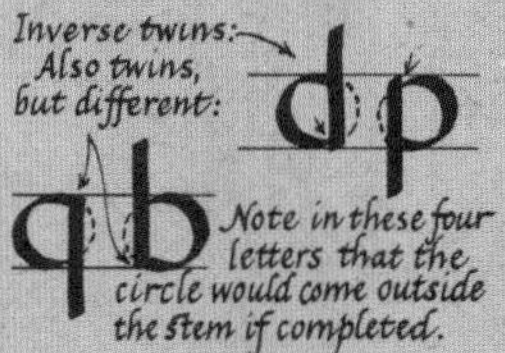

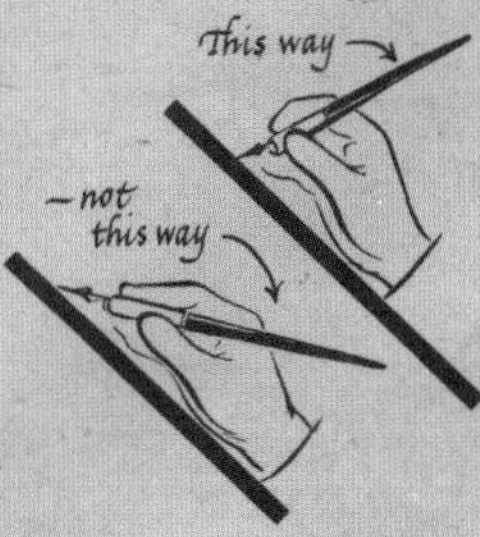

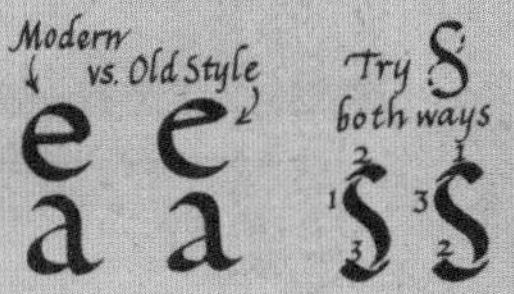

**Calligraphic Lettering
with wide pen and brush**
Ralph Douglass
1949, 68; 111 p.

$5.95 postpaid

from:
Watson-Guptil Publications
165 West 46th Street
New York, New York 10036

or WHOLE EARTH CATALOG

Printers' Supply Book

A look at the Whole Earth Catalogue or any other piece of printing (especially "Movement" stuff) confirms that the items sold by the Kelsey Co. are obsolete—today good, cheap quick printing is done offset. And Kelsey sells only letterpress equipment. But they have a full line—everything. Good and reasonably priced.

For the holdout who still prints letterpress and wants to make some cash from stationary, business cards, billheads, invitations and announcements or just fiddle in the basement, Kelsey has the supplies. I wouldn't suggest buying a hand press from them. They are costly, especially since good used Chandler and Price or other motor-driven hand fed presses can be gotten cheaply. But they do sell all sizes of paper and will custom cut. This is a help to the person who is not employed at a printing office where he can get off-cuts or paper at cost. And they have the whole range of equipment—bodkins, line gages, composing sticks, type cases and stands, galleys, quoins, furniture, reglets—the works. A nice range of inks is listed, and they are ready to answer your letter about inking problems.

Their types cover a wide range. The job printing standbys are all there—Copperplate and Bond Gothics; Caslon, Goudy, Caramond; Egyptians; and the whole mess of ugly cursives you need to do social stationery for your aunt. Several are worthy of note. Steelplate Shaded is one. There isn't much use for this, but it is well-designed and fine-looking. A rather mundane range of sans-serif wood type is listed. Two lines of type are sold—New England and Connecticut. With the Connecticut faces (more expensive) spaces and quads are included. Fonts are sold in regular, large or all cap.

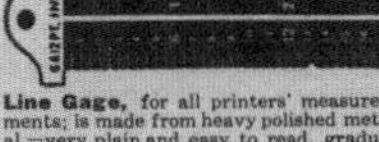

Service reputed to be good to East Coast. Can't say about other areas.

Will Powers
RFD 2
Lancaster, New Hampshire
03584

Printers' Supply Book

$.35 (refunded with first order)

from:
The Kelsey Company
Meriden, Connecticut 06450

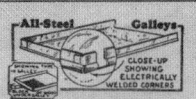

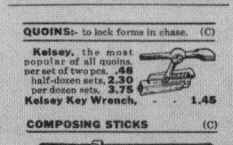

NAZ-DAR

complete catalog of paraphenalia for screen printing, in case you need a few posters or bumperstickers.

—jd

Problems Answered.

The film refuses to adhere to the silk.
The silk was not washed with both solvent and water before use. Insufficient solvent is used during adhering operation.

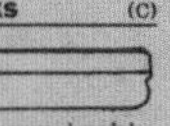

The film buckles while cutting.
There is an excessive humidity, hence the work must be handled rapidly and not allowed to stand around too long before adhering.

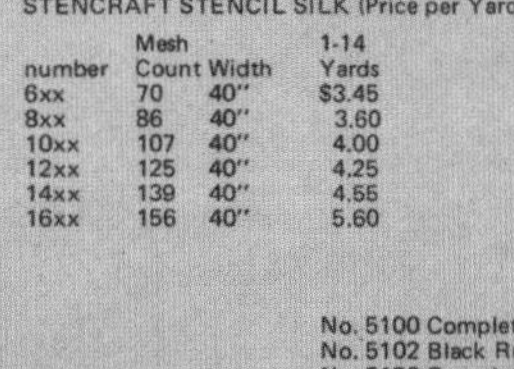

Spots appear on the print.
Pieces of dirt or lint get on the under surface of the screen and must be picked off. Fine skins from the ink have been ground into the meshes of the silk by the squeegee action, necessitating washing up of the job.

Colors on a several color job fail to register.
The film is allowed to lie around after cutting and expands on a very humid day. The guides moved during printing of early colors. The frame is loose or sprung from constant, hard use. The first colors were not printed with all sheets fed carefully to guide.

Catalog

free

from:
The NAZ-DAR Company
1087 N. North Branch Street
Chicago, Illinois 60622

STENCRAFT STENCIL SILK (Price per Yard)

number	Mesh Count	Width	1-14 Yards	15-29 Yards	30 Yards
6xx	70	40"	$3.45	$3.20	$3.00
8xx	86	40"	3.60	3.35	3.10
10xx	107	40"	4.00	3.70	3.45
12xx	125	40"	4.25	3.95	3.65
14xx	139	40"	4.55	4.20	3.90
16xx	156	40"	5.60	5.20	4.85

	Per Inch
No. 5100 Complete Squeegee, Black Rubber, Medium Grade	$.20
No. 5102 Black Rubber only	.15
No. 5150 Complete Squeegee, Gray Rubber, Hard Grade	.20
No. 5151 Gray Rubber only	.15
No. 5200 Complete Squeegee, Amber Rubber, Soft Grade	.20
No. 5202 Amber Rubber only	.15
No. 5420 Complete Squeegee, Extra Hard Grade	.20
No. 5421 Rubber only	.15

66

The remarkable thing that's taking place in almost every field of endeavor is an accelerating rate of dynamic growth and change. The arts, which have historically symbolized the advance of human progress, must match this growth if they are going to maintain their value in, and influence on, society.

The talents of musicians, the self expression of the actor, and the techniques and applications of fine and commercial artists are being used more and more in today's business, industry, entertainment and communications – not by themselves, but rather, in close association with each other. What we must have, then, is a completely new approach to training in the arts – an entirely new educational concept which will properly prepare artists and give them the vital tools so necessary for working in, and drawing from, every field of creativity and performance. There is an urgent need for a professional school which will not only give its students thorough training in a specific field, but will also allow the widest possible range of artistic growth and expression. To meet this need is exactly why California Institute of the Arts has been created, and why we all believe so strongly in its importance.

—Walt Disney

In all candor, the market process seems to underlie almost every discussion of the problems of the arts. Over and over again, we hear the phrase "the collecting of audiences," and such a phrase reflects a limited concept of what the arts actually are. It implies that the arts are something to which people go, but today the truth of the matter is that all of the major problems of our society are not dealt with through market processes, but increasingly, if anything, through political processes. Urban redevelopment, the poverty program, the Appalachia program and others like it are political and not market processes, and their revolutionary character – and they really *are* revolutionary – resides precisely in the fact that they are essentially political, no matter what their aims and goals; and in a highly industrialized society, we must think of public and social problems this way, and we must begin to think of the public and social dimension of the arts in this way too. We are dealing with the community and the needs of people and until we first concern ourselves with what people want (not necessarily what people think they want), and how the arts meet these wants, we will not be able to develop scholarship and criticism of the arts which is vital, meaningful, and relevant.

-Robert W. Corrigan

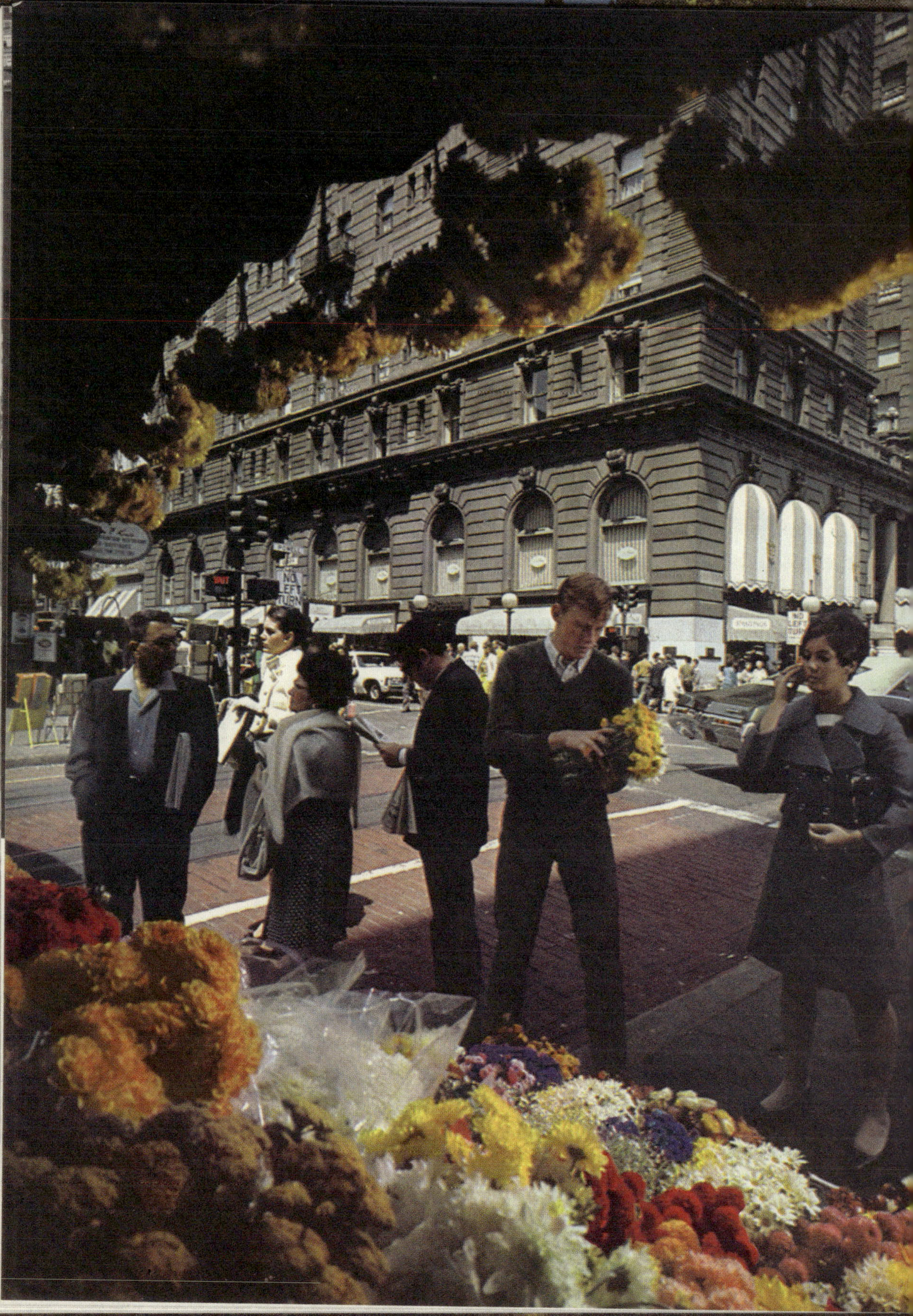

↑ Business partners and brothers Brad, David, and Archie Boston, in front of their Newport Beach office, Boston and Boston, 1968
← "Bright splashes of color contribute a cheery note in the midst of downtown [San Francisco] bustle," from <u>Beautiful California</u>, 1971

Bill Pate [dates unknown] **and Gene Howard** [1920–1973]. <u>THE SWINGIN' EYE!!!!!!!!</u> **ALBUM COVER, 1960, 12⅜ x 12⅜ IN.** In the 1950s, one of the most prolific teams producing LP record covers (such as this one, for Si Zentner and His Orchestra) was the design group Pate/Francis and photography studio Garrett-Howard. Murray Garrett snapped many of Hollywood's stars and star-studded events; his partner, Gene Howard, had been a crooner for Big Band greats Stan Kenton and Gene Krupa before becoming a Hollywood publicity portraitist. Pate/Francis comprised art director Bill Pate and production manager Ed Francis. In the early '60s, the foursome added designer and art director Leo Monahan to form Group Five, though Pate and Francis left shortly afterward. ¶ Reminiscing recently, Garrett and Monahan engaged in lively banter, suggesting that a working atmosphere of fun and adventure formed the core of the firm's success. With this instinctive, just-go-for-it creative process, Group Five in its heyday produced as many as 350 album covers a year.[1] As Art Chantry, designer and design-critic provocateur, puts it: "It was either THESE GUYS do your cover, or it was NOT a record cover." He says the team produced albums for the Rat Pack (Frank Sinatra, Dean Martin, Sammy Davis, Jr., Peter Lawford, and Joey Bishop) and affiliated acts such as Nancy Sinatra and Dino, Desi & Billy (Dean Paul Martin, Desi Arnaz Jr., and Billy Hinsche) as well as Latin groups and the Beach Boys. "They invented so many style genres that they may be the single greatest pop culture innovators of all time."[2]

SI ZENTNER
AND HIS ORCHESTRA

LIBERTY

LRP 3166

THE SWINGIN' EYE!!!!!!!!

PRINTED IN U.S.A.

Eames Office. MATH GAME AND MULTIPLICATION CUBE FOR MATHEMATICA: A WORLD OF NUMBERS AND BEYOND, 1961.
The Eameses had already made films for IBM when the technology giant commissioned their firm to create a display about mathematical concepts and phenomena for the new wing of the California Museum of Science and Industry. The resulting 3,000-square-foot project included a comprehensive history wall (the first timeline to appear in an exhibition), mechanical interactive demonstrations, and short animated films.[3] The idea was "to present mathematical concepts in a pleasurable way," according to Charles Eames, and one example of this strategy was a game that explained logistical thinking. ¶ Eames employee Deborah Sussman designed the game using a Victorian and post-Victorian aesthetic, a stylistic vocabulary whose whimsy and color made the concepts seem approachable.[4] The display paired a board game with a cube of 512 lightbulbs, which lit up to demonstrate aspects of multiplication, for example, that three times five is the same as five times three: 15.

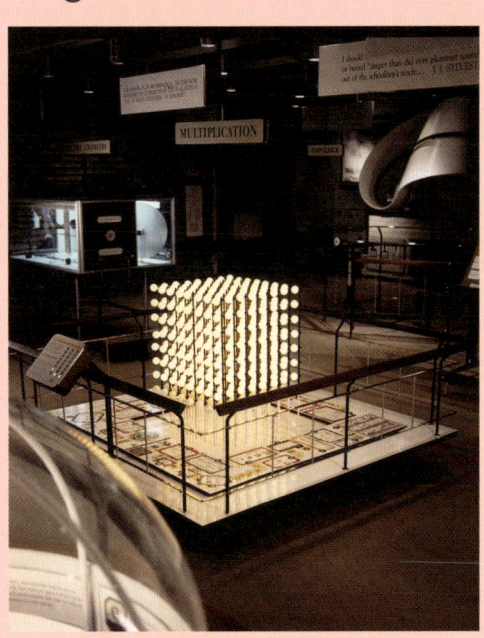

SIXTIES ALT SIXTIES

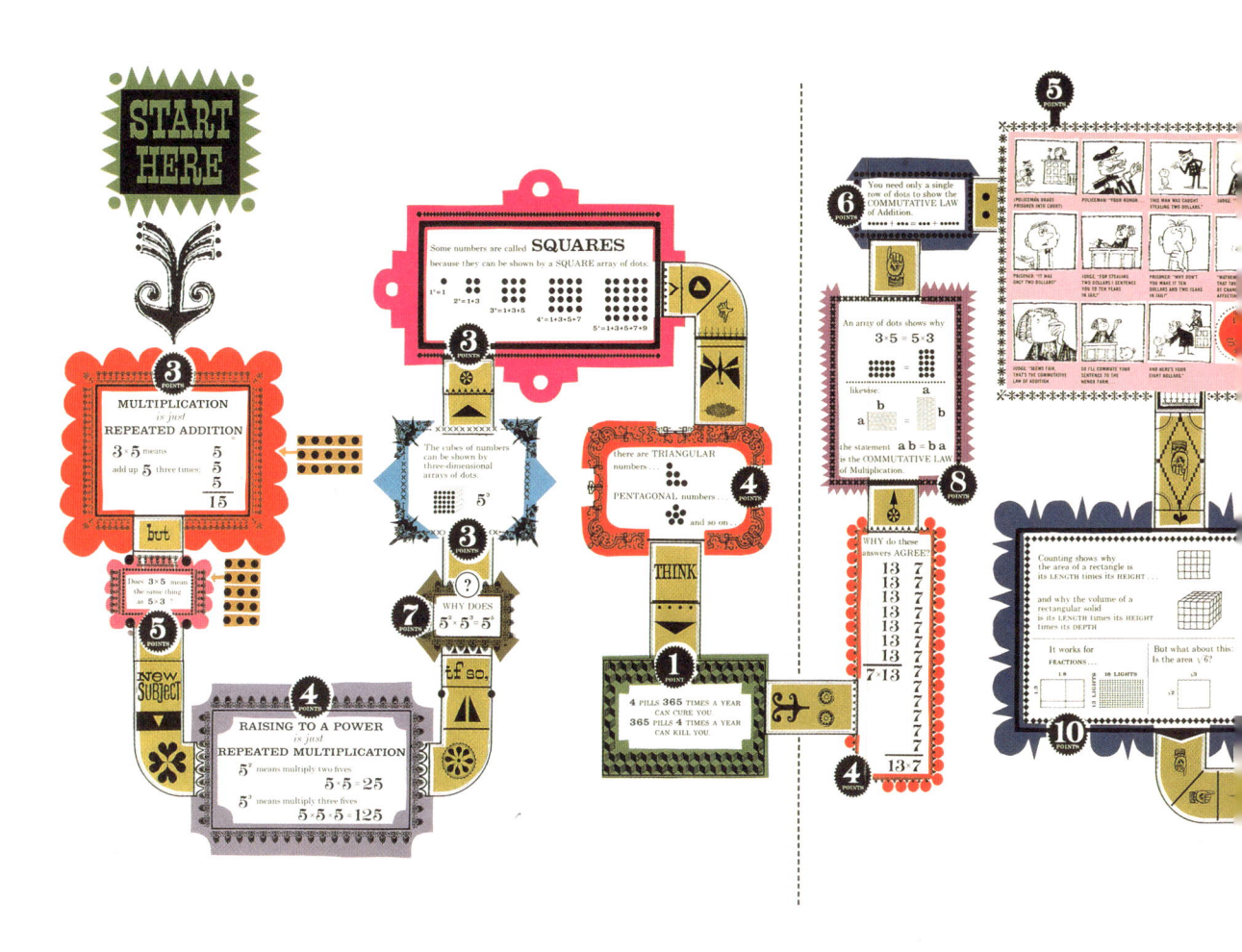

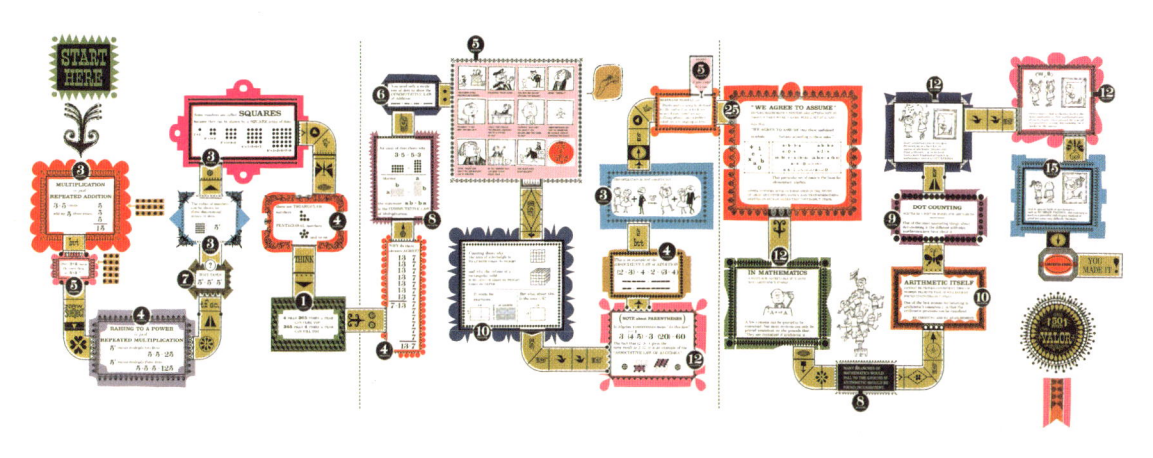

Ed Ruscha [b. 1937] **and Majestic Poster Press. NEW PAINTING OF COMMON OBJECTS EXHIBITION POSTER, PASADENA ART MUSEUM, 1962, 28 x 42 IN.** Artist Ruscha had a fascination with everyday language and its visual manifestations. Majestic, along with its competitor, Colby Poster Printing Company, were Los Angeles–based print shops that took banal advertising messages and transformed them into bold, bright neon signage, which was pasted up on telephone poles and fences throughout the city. To produce this advertisement for New Painting of Common Objects, the first museum survey of American Pop Art, curator Walter Hopps approached Ruscha. The artist turned to Majestic, drawn to their unassuming aesthetic. As for the poster's design, Ruscha gave them only scant instructions over the phone.[5] ¶ Before (and even after) the psychedelia that had its moment in the sun of street graphics in 1967, posters advertising performances—on the stage, in the boxing ring, or under the big top—employed seemingly every graphic tool in the box to boldly and brashly attract attention. Majestic, acquired by Colby in the mid-1970s, was among a handful of printers in the United States known for producing the quick-and-colorful graphics that adorned many a city. The shop's typesetters translated clients' handwritten messages into sans-serif wood- or metal-type layouts. Then, employing their trademark design voodoo, the pressmen showcased the texts against neon, fluorescent, or rainbow backdrops. Although Majestic's and Colby's lowbrow aesthetic evaded notice within the official design industry, at least a few people were paying attention. Designer John Van Hamersveld was among those inspired by the neon backdrops: his iconic Endless Summer film poster has the same glow.

PASADENA ART MUSEUM
46 N. LOS ROBLES
NEW PAINTING
OF
COMMON OBJECTS
DINE - DOWD - GOODE
HEFFERTON - LICHTENSTEIN
RUSCHA - THIEBAUD
WARHOL
SEPT. 25 - OCT. 19, 1962
Majestic Poster Press, 1209 W. Washington Blvd.

Wallace Berman [1926–1976]. **SECOND LOS ANGELES FILM-MAKER'S FESTIVAL POSTER, 1963, 16 x 20 IN.** Berman was a fine artist interested in graphics; and graphics-associated production forms—handwriting, typography, photography, appropriated imagery, offset lithography, and letterpress—figured in both his own work and his designs for event posters and book covers. Rather than imitating the refined visual languages sanctioned by the graphic- and advertising-design canons, Berman preferred the simple, direct images and just-the-facts-ma'am lettering he saw on the streets. He had particular affection for boxing posters, especially those from Los Angeles in the 1940s, 1950s, and 1960s.[6] ¶ Berman's efforts at ephemera that seem to cross the line between art and graphic design are probably best represented by Semina, the zinelike publication (in fact, predating zines!) that he lovingly assembled and printed between 1955 and 1964 in Los Angeles and San Francisco.

485

Earl Newman [b. 1930]. INSOMNIAC POSTER, CA. 1965, 23 x 35 IN.

Newman moved from Massachusetts to Berkeley in the early sixties to teach public school. Disappointed in the job and wanting to try to make it as an artist, he and his young family headed south to Los Angeles. Things were tough, and in the local coffeehouses and jazz clubs he saw a moneymaking opportunity for his graphic-design and silk-screening skills. His first poster, for a beachfront beatnik headquarters called the Gashouse, was sold at local shops as well as the club itself. ¶ The Insomniac was yet another Southern California venue for the Beat and jazz crowd, a dusk-to-dawn, all-night party house in Hermosa Beach. Newman got the job by showing the Insomniac people his Gashouse poster, and he became, for a time, one of the city's most popular designers. "He was really the poster maker before the whole psychedelic thing came around in '67," says Earl Pearl, owner of the seminal L.A. folk-and-blues club Ash Grove.[7] For his distinctive hand-drawn lettering, Newman blended the quirky-crude look that already dominated coffeehouse and jazz-club signage with what he called "German style"—the edgy, anxious look of the Weimar-era Expressionists.

The Hollywood nightclub Shelly's Manne-Hole, captured in 1970 by the renowned L.A. street photographer William Reagh, featured the kind of signs and lettering that influenced Newman.

PAGE 252: HIROSHIMA, 1966, 23 x 35 IN. Influenced by anti-Vietnam sentiments, Newman reflected on an earlier wartime horror—the dropping of the atomic bomb on the Japanese city of Hiroshima. Here, the split-fountain rainbow so associated with sixties graphics suggests radiation and forms a backdrop for flowers, a primary symbol of the peace movement. The combination makes the poster an appealing yet tense recollection of the consequences of politically sanctioned violence.

Coffee House
ENTERTAINMENT
Art Gallery
BOOK STORE
THE Insomniac
53 PIER AVE * HERMOSA BEACH * CALIFORNIA

HIROSHIMA

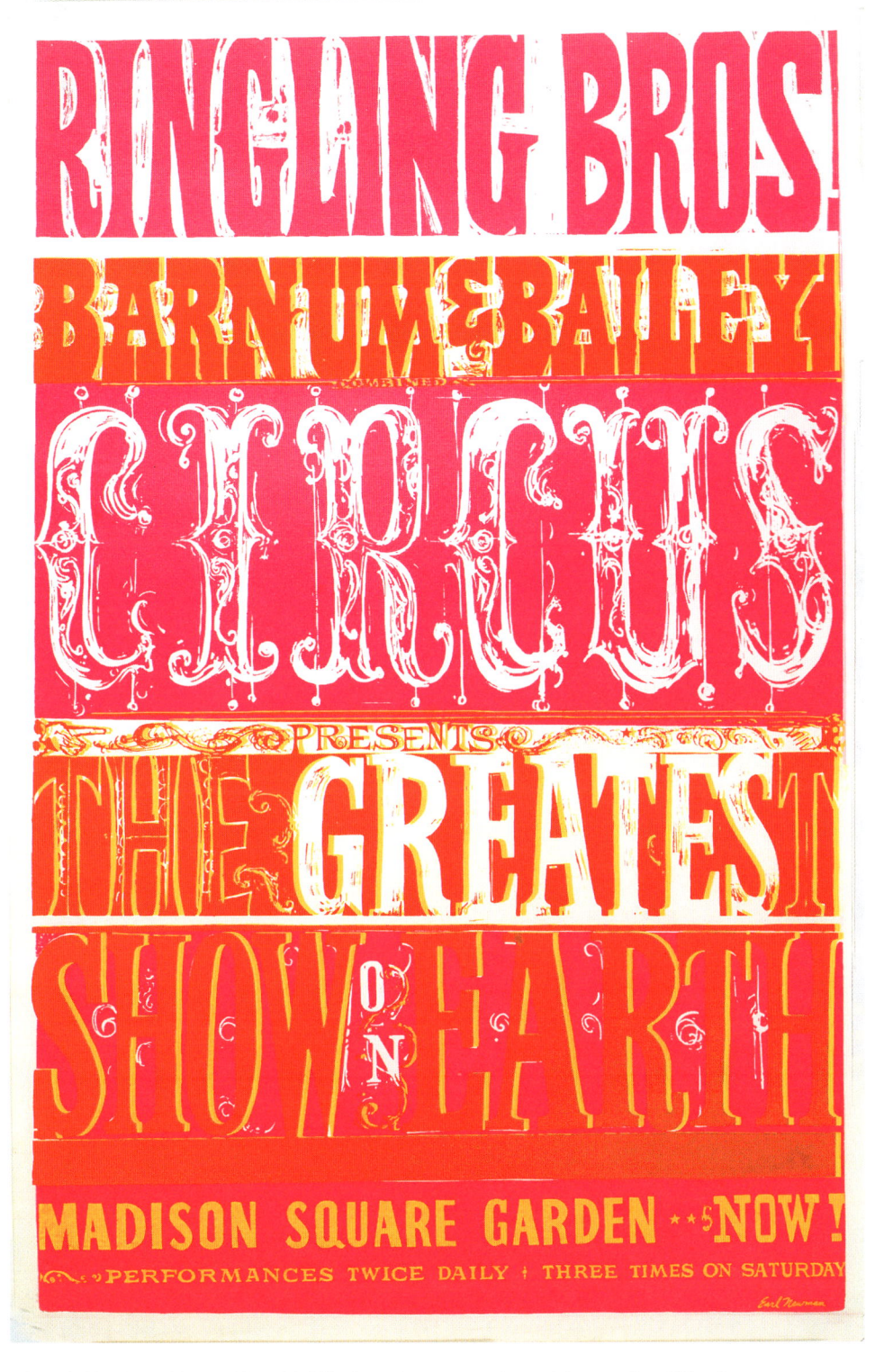

CIRCUS, CA. 1965, 23 x 35 IN. In a departure from his usual political and commercial work, Newman made this poster just for fun.

John Van Hamersveld [b. 1941]. **THE ENDLESS SUMMER POSTER, 1964, 18 x 24 IN.** If there is a single popular image of California graphic design, this must be it. Van Hamersveld started surfing in the 1950s, after his family moved from the East Coast to the West. Among other roles in a long and versatile career, he was art director of Surfer magazine and at Capitol Records, and a significant figure in rock-concert poster design. But he was still a student when he made the original Endless Summer poster, pictured here, the result of a $150 commission from friend and filmmaker Bruce Brown to make a promo image for his 1964 surfing documentary. Brown and his team provided the concept of silhouetted surfers on the beach, and Van Hamersveld did the rest. He directed the photo shoot and, using silk-screen, printed the stark black-and-white images and hand-lettered type on a Day-Glo background—techniques he learned in an advertising class at Art Center College of Design.[8] The poster became a sensation, capturing the imaginations of both sides of the postwar youth divide, the "straight" shaggy-haired surfer blonds as well as the drug-using hippie "long hairs." And this was just the beginning of its fame. ¶ As Lili Anolik recounts in her extensive Vanity Fair article honoring the original poster's fiftieth anniversary, this emblem of the sixties lives on within the echo chamber of pop culture—and the collection of New York's Museum of Modern Art. The original was followed up in 1964 by an 11-by-14-inch version printed in offset lithography for distribution at movie screenings. In 1965, it was reprinted as a 48-by-72-inch theatrical poster, with text describing the film. In 1966, a 30-by-40-inch silk-screen version quickly became a college dorm-room staple, available at head shops and record stores. Additional printings followed in 1986, 1996, and 2014 (the golden-anniversary edition).

The Endless Summer

Sister Corita Kent [1918–1986]. <u>DAISY</u>, 1966, 35 x 28½ IN. In the 1960s, Immaculate Heart College in Los Angeles was a hotbed of activism, driven by its own humanistic impulses as well as the 1962 reforms of Vatican II, which sought to modernize Catholic doctrine and encouraged churches to become more relevant to their communities. For Corita, activism fed her passions for printmaking and teaching her craft. The deep affection the college inspired among its students and within the wider design community was due, in large part, to her. Like other social-reform-minded avant-gardists, Corita sought to change the way the world looked, which, to her, meant reimagining its representations. She took everyday consumer logos and slogans and transformed them—literally and figuratively bent and folded them—into striking and straightforward messages of hope and affirmation. <u>Daisy</u> is just one example of the warped letterform work for which she is best known. She discovered the technique while photographing a student poster mounted on a curved wall. Noting how the type morphed in the resulting image, she traced and otherwise redrew it, resulting in a curvaceous text that seems to swirl and move.[9]

Yes. Yes. Yes. Yes. Yes. Yes. Yes. Yes. Yes. Yes. Yes. Yes.

two heads really are better than one.

Rudi Gernreich [1922–1985] **and Layne Nielson** [b. 1938]. CREAM, BROWN, AND ORANGE TRIANGLE PRINT SCARF AND ASTROLOGY PRINT SCARF, BOTH MID-1960s, 30 × 30 IN. Austrian native Gernreich was among the European émigrés in Los Angeles whose sophisticated visions produced radical results. He is best known for his 1964 "topless bathing suit" (actually, a bottom with slender, suspender-like straps), a design associated both with women's politics and flamboyant fashion. Gernreich was interested in clothing that reflected the complexities and multidimensionality of life. "Fashion will go out of fashion," he mused in a

LIFE magazine interview. "The utility principle will allow us to take our minds off how we look and concentrate on what really matters."[10] In 1965, costume and graphic designer Nielson, already a longtime associate, began executing accessories for the Gernreich line. Remembers Gernreich model and muse Peggy Moffatt, "Layne produced the delicious icing on Rudi's cake."[11] Among the scarves he conceived are several that include enigmatic graphic symbols. These reflect trends of the day, namely, the infiltration of mystic, counterculture impulses into the more mainstream culture.

Archie Boston [b. 1943] **and Brad Boston** [b. 1939]. **SELF-PROMOTIONAL POSTERS, 1966–67, EACH 11 x 17 IN.** Soft-spoken but not afraid of controversy, Archie Boston, with his partner and brother, Brad, created these posters to draw new business to their design office, Boston and Boston. "We wanted to work with clients that were interested in working with designers that were daring and courageous enough to speak their mind," Archie says of the tactic, which continued until 1982 and produced about 10 of these promotional pieces.[12] In many, the brothers featured themselves as models for the photography, shot by Jerry Trafficanda. The point was to declare that race was irrelevant to the ability to produce great design, and that clients who assumed only a white agency could do strong work could go elsewhere. Boston described the poster series in his autobiography, Fly in the Buttermilk, by saying, "I like to use black humor. (Excuse the pun.)"[13]

For a discriminating design organization specializing in Annual Reports,
Brochures, Package Design, Direct Mail, Trademarks and completCorporate
Identity Programs, call the BOSTON KLAN at either one of our Klaverns.
In Los Angeles: 931-8751 or 931-8163. In Newport Beach: 540-4110.

BOSTON & BOSTON: EQUAL OPPORTUNITY DESIGNERS

Doyle Phillips (pseudonym, Lemonado de Sica) [dates unknown]. **FLATT AND SCRUGGS AVALON BALLROOM CONCERT POSTER, 1967, 20 X 14 IN.** In 1965, the San Francisco rock scene started to explode, accompanied by a culture of hallucinogenic drugs. Dancing and light shows were equal to music in terms of the concert experience, and all these elements combined to ignite in 1966, when Stewart Brand (later of Whole Earth Catalog fame) and Ken Kesey's Merry Pranksters manifested the Trips Festival, a two-night extravaganza of rock, pulsing multicolored lights, dancing, and acid dropping. After that, nothing was the same. Psychedelia—as a term encompassing posters, light shows, music, drugs, and hippies—became synonymous with San Francisco. At the time, the city had two main concert-promotion entities, Bill Graham and the Family Dog Collective, and they shared the Fillmore as a concert venue and Wes Wilson as a poster designer. Wilson is credited with introducing letterforms that seemed to bend and bloat to fill shapely spaces and surround voluptuous, turn-of-the-century female figures. He and other San Francisco designers embraced this nostalgic sensibility, partly inspired by an exhibition of Jugendstil and German Expressionist posters at the University Art Gallery in Berkeley in 1965.[14] ¶ But psychedelia—with its lush, distorted typography and electric colors—wasn't the only style in town. This poster for a Flatt and Scruggs concert at the Avalon Ballroom speaks a different language, a sophisticated modernist grammar tinged with a psychedelic accent. Commissioned by Family Dog (itself the offshoot of a commune), it has an old-timey feel that reflects a counterculture interest in authenticity and, in the case of these bluegrass innovators, the kind of musical virtuosity that influenced rock 'n' roll.

FAMILY DOG
dance
PRESENTS
concert
FLATT & SCRUGGS
THE LEWIS and CLARKE EXPEDITION
THE LEWIS and CLARKE EXPEDITION
AVALON
Ballroom
9 p.m.
Sutter & Van Ness
San Francisco
GOODHOUSEKEEPING SEAL OF APPROVAL
Nov. 30 - Dec. 1 & 2
thursday, friday & saturday $3.
lights by
diogenes
lantern works
TO THE GRASS ROOTS OF AMERICA
The Free Enterprise System-Lemonade de Sica D.-Frisco Gazette
TICKET OUTLETS – SAN FRANCISCO: MNASIDIKA (HAIGHT-ASHBURY), CITY LIGHTS BOOKS (NORTH BEACH), THE TOWN SQUIRE (1318 POLK). BERKELEY: DISCOUNT RECORDS. SAUSALITO: TIDE'S BOOKSTORE. REDWOOD CITY: REDWOOD HOUSE OF MUSIC (700 WINSLOW). SAN MATEO: TOWN & COUNTRY MUSIC CENTER (4TH & EL CAMINO). LA MER CAMERAS & MUSIC (HILLSDALE AT 19TH). MENLO PARK: KEPLER'S BOOKS & MAGAZINES (825 EL CAMINO). SAN JOSE: DISCORAMA (235 SO. FIRST ST).
No94-1
1967 © FAMILY DOG PRODUCTIONS 639 GOUGH ST., San Francisco, Calif. 94102

Stanley George Miller (aka Stanley Mouse) [b. 1940] **and Alton Kelley** [1940–2008]. **CELESTIAL MOONCHILD, 1967, 14 X 20 IN.** This poster, for a concert with Canned Heat and Allmen Joy, was commissioned by the Family Dog Collective, described in the New York Times as "a loose confederation of artists, poets, musicians and other free spirits who put on the some of the earliest psychedelic dance concerts."[15] Just as foundational to the era was Mouse Studios, a collaboration of California native Stanley Mouse, or "Mouse," and Kelley that helped define the psychedelic visual style. ¶ Mouse studied at the Detroit Society of Arts and Crafts but since his early teens had earned a living pinstriping cars and traveling the country airbrushing t-shirts at hot-rod shows. Kelley, who also had some art-school training, shared Mouse's passions, yet the two met not via the world of hot-rod art but through Family Dog founder and Texas transplant Chet Helms. Helms, who hired and supported numerous poster artists, had graphics and promotion in his blood. His father and uncles were printers, and they produced materials that their fundamentalist-preacher father deployed to spread the gospel. So Helms understood the power of both the press and the DIY strategy of pasting up flyers around town. Psychedelic posters like this one, titled Celestial Moonchild, became highly prized collectables and would often disappear from the streets almost as soon as they appeared.

OCT. 20
OCT. 27
CANNED
LIGHTS ✶ DIOGENES
LANTERN WORKS
1601 W. EVANS
DENVER ✶ COLORADO
Kelley
TICKET OUTLETS

Victor Moscoso [b. 1936]. **NEON ROSE #12, 1967, 13¾ x 20 IN.** The psychedelic poster artist with the most formal training, Moscoso studied art at Yale with legendary colorist Josef Albers. After earning his bachelor's degree in 1959, he headed to San Francisco, inspired by Jack Kerouac's <u>On the Road</u> and the poet Gregory Corso.[16] Moscoso's formal education turned into his calling card when he started making posters for Family Dog. Though there were certain rules he had to unlearn—typographic legibility being a key one—Albers's theory of color relationships, how juxtaposing equal values creates optical vibrations, allowed him to achieve electric effects without fluorescent inks. His posters became instantly coveted. ¶ At the end of 1966, Moscoso formed his own company, Neon Rose. Working independently, he could commission, design, produce, and distribute his own pieces, and offer clubs that otherwise could not afford him a deal: he would produce a poster, give the venue 200 copies, and sell the rest. Neon Rose #12—titled with a number like all the company's posters—advertised an event featuring the Chambers Brothers. It remains Neon Rose's most popular image.

© 1967 NEON ROSE #12

Mark DeVries [dates unknown] **and Hetty McGee** [1931–2011]. <u>THE CITY OF SAN FRANCISCO ORACLE</u>, NO. 7, 1967, 11½ X 15 IN. This underground tabloid was just one example of the sixties counterculture publishing that endorsed expanded political (and other types of) consciousness and the pursuit of alternative modes of living. Poet Allen Cohen—inspired by a dream about a newspaper covered with rainbows—launched <u>The City of San Francisco Oracle</u> in 1966. The publication became known for its prolific use of the rainbow-like split-fountain printing technique, which entailed filling the press's ink trough—or fountain—with a spectrum of colors that blended, during printing, on the paper. Utilized in nineteenth-century Japanese woodblock prints, split-fountain—which <u>Oracle</u> helped to popularized—ended up becoming a design signifier of the sixties and of California.[17] ¶ In commissioning work, the <u>Oracle</u> would give artists texts and invite them to "make an organic unity of the word and image," says Cohen, adding that many contributors were under the influence of substances that would induce "a visionary state of mind," anticipating that readers would be in a similar state. In targeting such New Age initiates, its reports and messages were more opaque than the message-to-receiver directness of conventional media communications. ¶ This photo collage for the cover of the paper's seventh issue commemorates the Houseboat Summit, a discussion among former Harvard professor and LSD evangelist Timothy Leary, philosopher Alan Watts, and poets Allen Ginsberg and Gary Snyder—patron saints of the political, social, and cosmic principles the <u>Oracle</u> sought to further. In this collaboration, the multiplied images of the four gurus nestle in a rainbow scene of ancient temples, lotus flowers, and Art Nouveau–inspired lettering. The lotus drawings

Tom Weir's full-page photomontage of a couple making love, with multiple sets of arms and legs in motion

THE CITY OF SAN FRANCISCO
ORACLE
25¢
VOL 1
NO 7
©1967 San Francisco
ORACLE Publishing
CO-OP

were likely McGee's, as was the split-fountain color: she recalls that upon first considering the Oracle, she commented that a newspaper for a psychedelic community shouldn't be black-and-white, and her input confirmed Cohen's initial vision: the rainbow motif became a regular design feature.[18] **RIGHT, TOP: Jim Phillips [b. 1944]. DOCTOR MOTO'S MEDICINE BUS, PUBLISHED IN THE CITY OF SAN FRANCISCO ORACLE, NO. 6, 1967, 11½ x 15 IN.** Phillips enrolled at the California College of Arts and Crafts but lost his scholarship when administrators discovered he didn't have a high school diploma. This drawing was the result of a trip (in every sense) that started out at a Santa Cruz crash pad with a monkey for a roommate and ended, via hitchhiking, in the San Francisco digs of an advertising-agency artist. Phillips decided to use his host's drawing materials to make him a thank-you present, but the project became more elaborate once he was offered a tab of acid. A friend suggested he submit the completed work to the Oracle. The newspaper added the rainbow effect.[19] ¶ **BOTTOM, LEFT: Rick Griffin [1944–1991]. GRATEFUL DEAD, PUBLISHED IN THE CITY OF SAN FRANCISCO ORACLE, NO. 6, 1967, 11½ x 15 IN.** Griffin was considered one of the "Big Five" psychedelic poster designers, along with Alton Kelley, Victor Moscoso, Stanley Mouse, and Wes Wilson. Having decamped for San Francisco from Southern California and his staff-artist gig at Surfer magazine, Griffin brought his comic surfer-dude "Murphy" to arenas including posters, Zap Comix, and the pages of the Oracle. A skilled draftsman who studied at the Chouinard Art Institute in Los Angeles (which later merged with CalArts), he shows his chops in this Egyptian-themed tribute to the original jam band. ¶ **BOTTOM, RIGHT: Paul Kagan [1943–1993]. AMERICAN TANTRIC #2 (YAB-YUM), PUBLISHED IN THE CITY OF SAN FRANCISCO ORACLE, NO. 7, 1967, 11½ x 15 IN.** Yab-Yum epitomizes the Oracle's dedication to the ideal of achieving unity between body and soul. A lacelike paisley print overlays Kagan's photograph, combined with the newspaper's signature split-fountain color treatment.

SIXTIES ALT SIXTIES

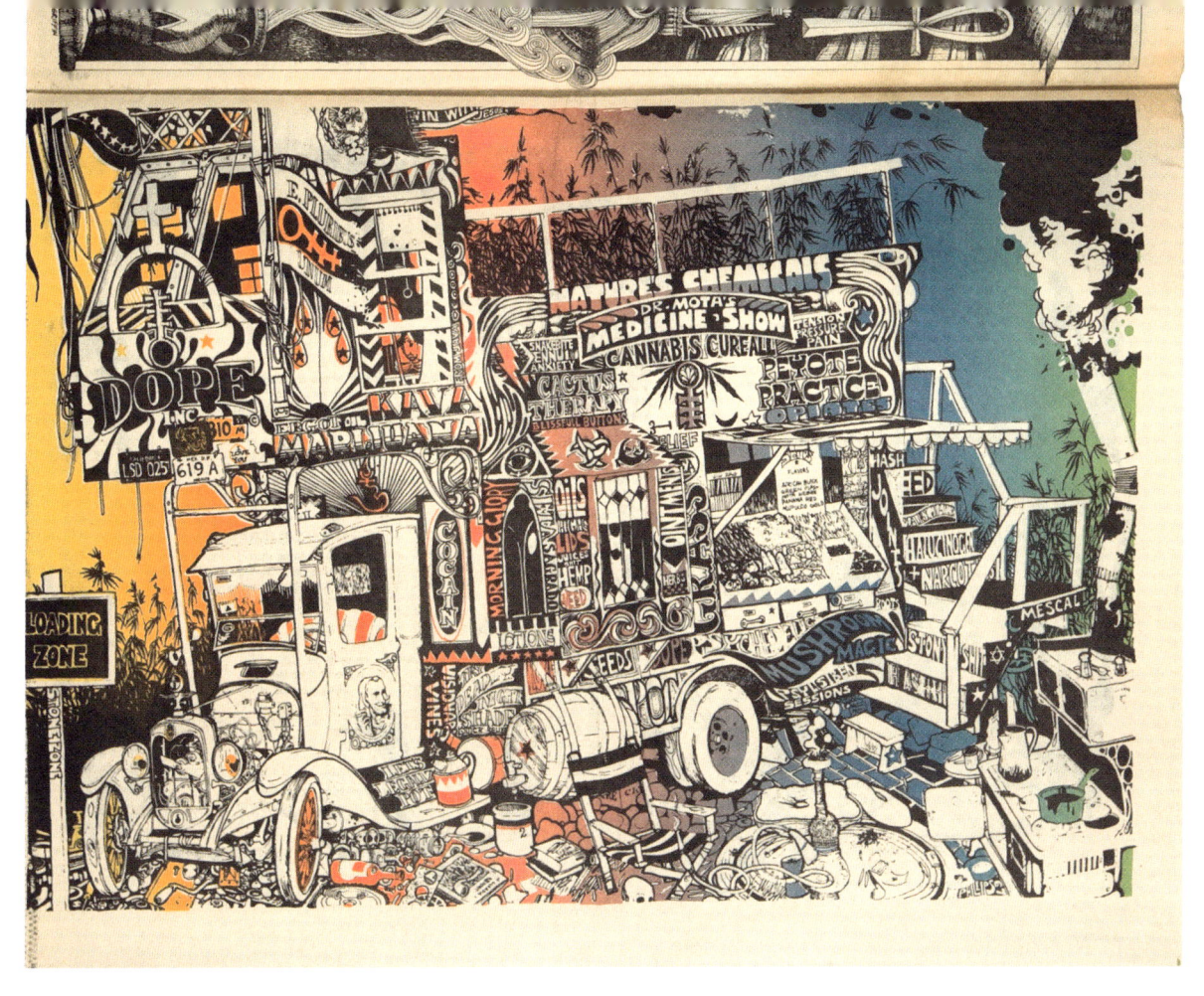

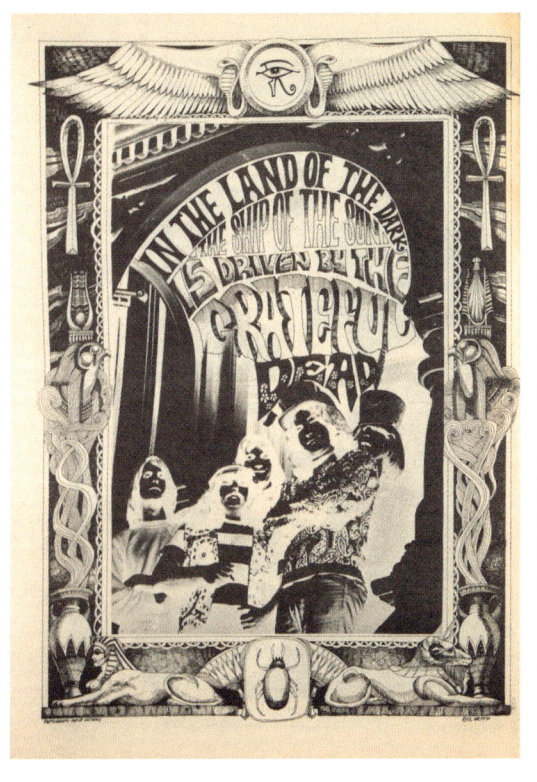

Anonymous. HAIGHT STREET IS OURS TO PLAY ON…, 1967, 8½ x 11 IN. In 1963, Claude Hayward moved to California in search of what he called "the door to the underground." Three years later, he met science-fiction writer Chester Anderson, a denizen of the psychedelic mecca that was San Francisco's Haight-Ashbury. With a mutual vow to provide people the means "to compete with the Establishment press for public opinion," they acquired the latest stencil-cutting and -duplication equipment for small print runs, allowing them to produce up to 10,000 reasonable-quality color copies, up to 8½ by 14 inches in size, in just a few hours. Thus, they launched the Communications Company.[20] "Love is communication" was their policy, an agenda Joan Didion viewed with a cold eye in her description of the group in her famous, and famously skeptical, essay "Slouching Towards Bethlehem," about the social shifts in San Francisco at the time.[21] ¶ Known as Com/Co, the group operated for just six months, starting in January 1967, but estimates that during this short span it printed more than 900 small posters featuring slogans or announcing events. Much of this work was done for the Diggers, a utopian collective born of the San Francisco Mime Troupe. The Diggers believed everything should be free and therefore provided free food, free shelter, and free entertainment, hoping to inspire an alternative to a society they saw as shaped by worn-out values that left many dispossessed. Actor, writer, and ex-Digger Peter Coyote recalls that Com/Co worked energetically with no preconceived notions about design traditions or refinement. The goal was to spread the message—and do it fast. Yet despite the scrappy execution, Com/Co's output achieves a level of artistry and craft born of sheer enthusiasm.[22]

SUNDAY, APRIL 2, 1:00 p.m.

the communication company a member of the Underground Press Syndicate
(415) 626-2926

Haight Street is ours to play on till we feel it beautiful to stop.

THE DIGGERS

ॐ

यथाऽङ्कुलीनं लवणं न पश्ये
दग्धिा एव यदलभ्यमसीः ।
ग्राह्यं च बुद्ध्या विपर्ययुरूप
स्तं विश्वनाथ शरणं प्रपद्ये ॥

Dave Hodges [dates unknown]. **POSTER FOR THE INVISIBLE CIRCUS: A 72 HOUR ENVIRONMENTAL COMMUNITY HAPPENING, 1967, 14 x 8½ IN.** Peter Coyote remembers the Diggers' Invisible Circus as a "psychedelic blast" held on February 24 at Glide Church. During the event, novelist and poet Richard Brautigan used Communications Company equipment to print updates about activities, events, supplies, and the like. "It was the analogue equivalent of texting your friends and letting them know what was what," Coyote says. Most of the work Com/Co printed was anonymous, so this Invisible Circus poster is a rare exception in being attributed to an artist named Dave Hodges. Mostly, the Diggers and Com/Co produced emphatic messages, such as "The Government of the CITY OF SAN FRANCISCO is hereby declared NULL + VOID." Many of these works—at least, of the 45 or so that remain—use bold typography, energetic drawing, or hand-drawn type to strong effect, and appropriate photographs or graphic imagery in ways that transform their original meanings.

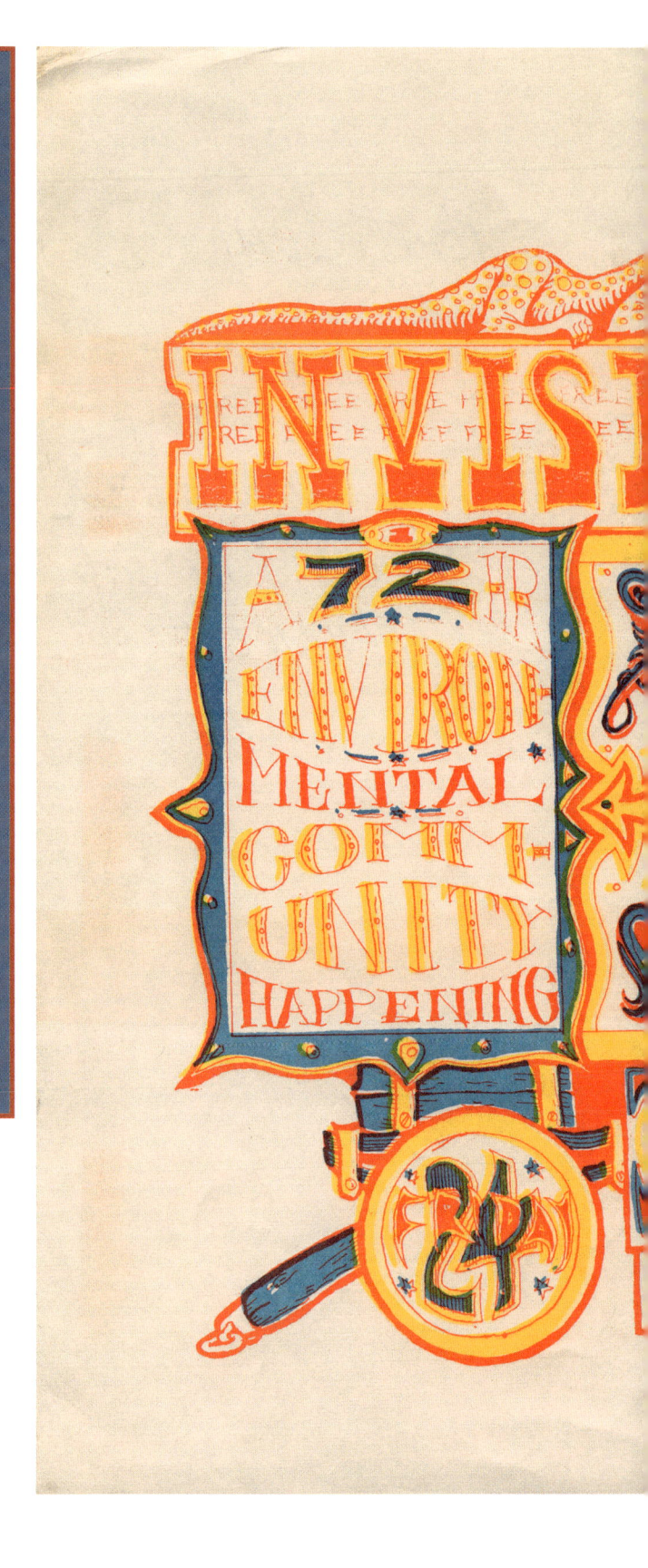

THE
BLE CIRCUS
FREE
SPONSORED BY
THE DIGGERS
ARTISTS LIBERATION FRONT
GLIDE
FOUNDATION
TIGER
Glide Church
AYLOR AT ELLIS
8 PM
POSTER © 1967 - DAVE HODGES

Anonymous. "1% FREE," AUGUST 1967, 8½ x 11 IN., ORIGINALLY 16¾ X 21 IN. The Digger Papers was a 24-page newsprint booklet containing the collected writings of Diggers founders and images from some of the group's posters and other printed materials. The publication, according to the anticapitalist group, was distributed free "as a gift to the world."[23] By June 1967, the Communication Company, which had produced many of the Diggers' ephemeral, throwaway graphics, had lost its momentum, so the Diggers took over Com/Co's state-of-the-art equipment and started publishing its own materials.[24] ¶ In its July 7, 1967, issue, Time magazine featured an article about the counterculture movement that conflated the Diggers with hippies in a way that the group felt misrepresented and trivialized its activities. To help correct the message, a New York City alternative publisher called the Realist reprinted The Digger Papers, including this image on the back cover. The Diggers saw the slogan "1% Free" as referring to themselves: in rejecting commerce, they were the liberated minority. Diggers cofounder Peter Berg says the Chinese figures came from a collection of photographs of the 1906 San Francisco Earthquake, and that the group liked the picture because it was "so outlaw, so San Francisco looking." Originally, the image was used on a poster pasted up around the city, where it caused confusion. "Merchants in the district thought it was extortion," Berg recalls. "They thought they were being asked to give up 1 percent of their profits."[25]

**Send Free $$$ Energy
To FREE CITY
c/o The Diggers
P.O. Box 31321
Diamond Hts. Sta.
San Francisco, Calif. 94131**

**Send Free $$$ Energy
To FREE CITY
c/o The Diggers
P.O. Box 31321
Diamond Hts. Sta.
San Francisco, Calif. 94131**

1% FREE

Emory Douglas [b. 1943]. **REVOLUTIONARY POSTERS AD, 1968, 11 x 17 IN.** Inspired by Malcolm X's edict of "self-respect, self-defense, self-determination," the Black Panther movement germinated as an arts initiative, the Black Communications Project, which aimed to bring black theater, poetry, and music events to college campuses.[26] The Panthers saw militancy as the sole response to the way the U.S. government ignored or compromised the human and civil rights of the black community. Over time, it moved toward addressing more pragmatic community needs, instituting health care, education, and food programs while still spreading awareness of government activities. Douglas—the movement's Minister of Culture—was responsible for the Panthers' visual communications platform. Introduced to printing and design during a teenage stint at a juvenile facility and trained in commercial art at City College of San Francisco, Douglas worked to unite the Panther membership—to align competing objectives and get everyone on the same page via emotionally rousing visual mission statements. Working with the organization from 1967 until the end of the seventies, Douglas created hundreds of posters and a weekly newspaper that brought messages of righteousness, indignation, and hope to an audience with varying degrees of literacy. ¶ Douglas's Revolutionary Posters offers a multileveled example of his early work: designed by him, this newspaper advertisement functions as a combination sampler/order form for eight of his posters, all for sale ("$1.00 each") to raise money for the party. Douglas used any means at hand—rub-on type, typewriter, pen and ink—to create these images of Black Panther leaders and the people they represented. Here, he arranges them not by a grid or other design formula but by a what-fits-where strategy.

Revolutionary Posters

By The Minister of Culture EMORY $1.00 each   EXCEPT FOR #4 and #6 WHICH ARE 75¢ EACH   25¢ EXTRA FOR OUT-OF-STATE DELIVERY

SEND CHECK OR MONEY ORDER TO EMORY DOUGLAS, P.O. BOX 8641, EMERYVILLE BRANCH, OAKLAND, CALIFORNIA 94608

ALL POSTERS ARE 17x22 EXCEPT FOR #4 and #6 WHICH ARE 8-1/2x22

1. No longer available

This space has previously been used for "Free Huey" posters. But now that the world is awaiting the verdict-Free Huey-or the sky is the limit!

2. PRIME MINISTER OF COLONIZED AFRO-AMERICA STOKELY CARMICHAEL

3. MINISTER OF JUSTICE H. RAP BROWN

4. BLACK STUDIES

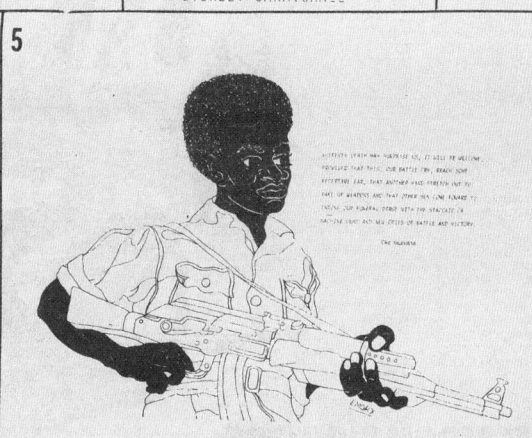

5. REVOLUTIONARY

6. MOTHER AND CHILD

7. BLACK POET AND PLAYWRIGHT LEROI JONES

8. HOPE

Check number of article(s) ordered and indicate quantity of each beside number:
FROM SEPTEMBER 28, 1968 ISSUE

REVOLUTIONARY POSTERS

___1 ___3 ___5 ___7   TOTAL NO.
___2 ___4* ___6* ___8   OF POSTERS

($1.00 each: $1.25 outside Calif.)
[*=.75¢ each:$1.00 outside Calif.)

TOTAL AMOUNT OF MONEY SENT-$
Send check or money order to
BLACK PANTHER PARTY, P.O. BOX 8641
EMERYVILLE BRANCH, OAKLAND, CALIF.

NAME
ADDRESS
CITY_____ STATE_____

Sätty (Wilfred Podreich) [1939–1982]. **McCARTHY POSTER, 1968, 23 x 35 IN.** A German trained as an engineering draftsman, Sätty arrived in San Francisco in the early 1960s. Known primarily for intricate collages that resembled those of the Surrealist Max Ernst, he was part of a Bay Area art scene in the late sixties known as the Visionaries. According to art historian Thomas Albright, this reactionary group of mostly trained artists sought a return to figurative work and "content," as opposed to the abstraction that prevailed before the upheaval of Pop.[27] Tapping the immense image archive he compiled from books and magazines, Sätty would create mystical, fantastical assemblages dominated by nineteenth-century etchings. He was immersed in the dance and counterculture scene, and dabbled in producing posters to publicize these events. This multilayered image for presidential hopeful Eugene McCarthy marked a rare foray for the artist into politics as well as poster making. The 1968 Democratic candidate appears behind a screen of Op Art–style flames with a white cutout shaped like a dove—the sign of peace. McCarthy's eyes seem to look through and merge with the dove, a design move that reflects the politician's antiwar platform: he appears as a perceptive presence amid the heated rhetoric and violence of Vietnam. The poster was printed by Orbit Graphic Arts, a small press in the Bay Area whose output included many counterculture and political posters.

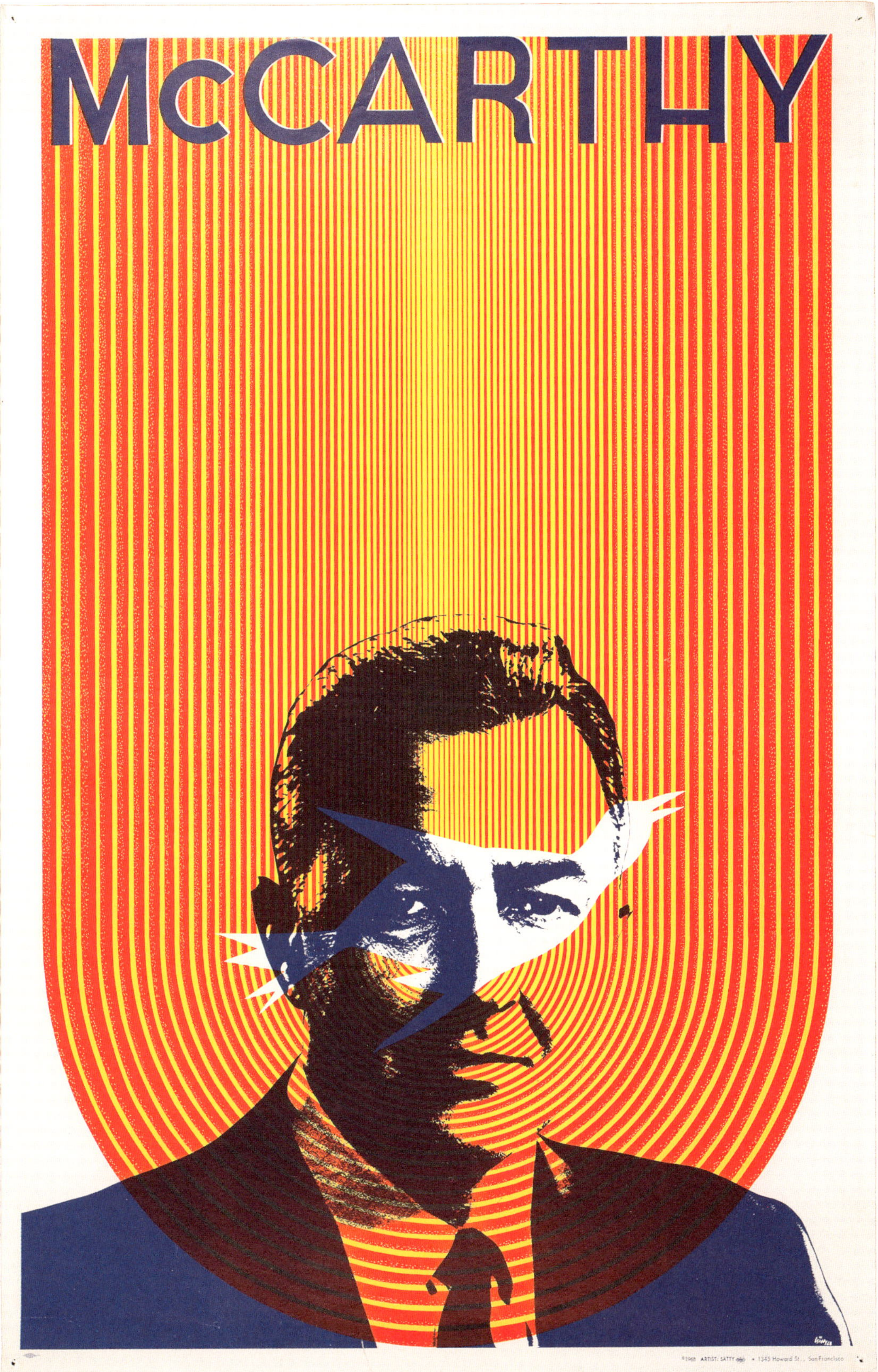
McCARTHY
©1968 ARTIST: SATTY • 1345 Howard St., San Francisco

John Van Hamersveld and Victor Moscoso. THE WHO (WITH FLEETWOOD MAC) SHRINE AUDITORIUM CONCERT POSTER, 1968, 22⅝ × 17½ IN. Seeing San Francisco give birth to the psychedelic scene inspired Los Angeles and other cities to create their own rock-dance-light-show extravaganzas—and distinctive graphic languages to go with them. Surfer-designer Van Hamersveld envisioned a Southern California counterpart to the happenings staged by Bill Graham and the Family Dog Collective, and he launched Pinnacle Productions in 1967 with the concert Amazing Electric Wonders, featuring Buffalo Springfield, Blue Cheer, and the Grateful Dead. Having just completed a stint as art director at Capitol Records, Van Hamersveld saw Pinnacle as a vehicle for artistic output as well as music promotion: poster production was integral to the events, and the Pinnacle office formed a social hub where art and music circles intersected.[28] ¶ Noted for his iconic image for the Endless Summer surfer documentary, Van Hamersveld created many posters for Pinnacle. His work exudes the skilled hand of a gifted, formally educated designer inspired by cartoons, a high-low mashup style that distinguished the L.A. poster look from the turn-of-the-century nostalgia and car culture affinities of psychedelic San Francisco. ¶ This poster for a Pinnacle event showcasing The Who—a major coup for such a new production company—was a north-south collaboration between Van Hamersveld and the San Francisco–based Victor Moscoso; the two shared a fondness for comics, something Moscoso would indulge later in his work with R. Crumb on Zap Comix but which manifests itself here in Van Hamersveld's strikingly dimensional type and Moscoso's electric use of offset color: the jarring effect is akin to something meant to be viewed through 3D glasses.

WHO
SHRINE
JUNE
28-29
FLEETWOOD
THE
BROWN
Tickets available at Wallichs Music City Stores and Mutual Agencies Free Press Book Stores · Either Or Store · Sound Spectrum.

Joni Mitchell [b. 1943] **and Ed Thrasher** [1932–2006]. **SONG TO A SEAGULL ALBUM COVER, 1968, 12⅜ x 12⅜ IN.** Until the cassette tape came along, album-cover design was a prized job. These canvases offered artists unparalleled freedom to invent new idioms and to collaborate with creative peers in expressing their music through visual and conceptual representations, whether photographic, illustrative, or both—what celebrated designer Paula Scher called "big-idea art direction."[29] So imaginative were the album covers of the time that some of their designs became sensations on their own. In the '60s, L.A. was home to many of the hottest rock groups. According to Jeri Heiden, former creative director at Warner Brothers Records, the L.A. music scene was more intuitive and relaxed compared to New York, and California designers relied more on a love of music and visuals than any formal training. "On the West Coast they were taking it to the beach instead of the streets."[30] Chief among this new breed of designers was California native Thrasher, who, as art director at Warner Brothers starting in 1964, was responsible for hundreds of album designs. This cover for Joni Mitchell's debut LP reflects his prowess for picking remarkable imagery—in this case, artwork by the musician herself. **Wayne Kimball** [dates unknown] **and Ed Thrasher. BIRTHDAY ALBUM COVER, 1968, 12⅜ x 12⅜ IN.** The Association recorded Top 40 hits such as "Never My Love," "Cherish," and "Windy." This California group couldn't have been further from the music that drove the tune-in-drop-out hippies of Haight-Ashbury. Yet the cover art for Birthday has a distinctly trippy vibe, an example of how the psychedelic look had become a commercial signifier of cool. **John Van Hamersveld and Ed Thrasher. A CHILD'S GUIDE TO GOOD AND EVIL ALBUM COVER, 1968, 12⅜ x 12⅜ IN.** Van Hamersveld had a New Age vision for this cover for the West Coast Pop Art Experimental Band: the black and white represented two sides of karma, the dark and the light. In his words, "The head is thinking of the butterfly image—freedom from the karma in the well of darkness."[31]

SIXTIES ALT SIXTIES

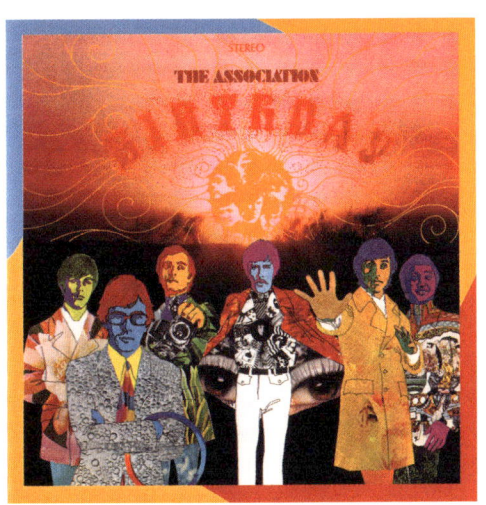

285

R. Crumb [b. 1943]. **CHEAP THRILLS ALBUM COVER, 1968, 12⅜ x 12⅜ IN.** Crumb got his commercial start doing cards for American Greetings at its Cleveland headquarters. He recalls the job as requiring "the simplest neutered little cartoon characters," an easy task for someone who grew up drawing comics but hard to reconcile with the out-there, supercrude, hypersexual content of Crumb's future work. His artistic transformation followed his first LSD experience, in 1965: he shifted from the lineage of the more sophisticated image-makers of the day—Jules Feiffer, Ronald Searle, or Ralph Steadman—toward the more pedestrian, everyperson look of 1940s-style cartoons: Krazy Kat, Little Orphan Annie, Popeye, and Pogo."[32] ¶ At the beginning of 1967—on a lark—he headed for San Francisco, where he worked for the alternative press before launching Zap Comix. By Zap's second issue, Rick Griffin, Victor Moscoso, and S. Clay Wilson had joined on and it spawned "comix"—a generic term for raunchy underground cartoons whose approach to topics such as race and sex flew in the face of what eventually would be called political correctness.[33] Zap was a kind of Mad magazine for the stoned and ultradepraved. ¶ One of Crumb's most iconic characters was Mr. Natural, a bearded guru-type who coined the hippie slogan "Keep on Truckin'." This album cover for Janis Joplin and her band, Big Brother and the Holding Company, brought him equal recognition. A fan of Crumb's comic work, Joplin asked him to create the art when the album still had the working title Sex, Dope, and Cheap Thrills.[34]

Stereo
CAN ALSO BE PLAYED ON MONO EQUIPMENT
COLUMBIA
CHEAP THRILLS
BIG BROTHER & THE HOLDING COMPANY
PLAYIN' AN' SINGIN' FER YEW THE FOLLOWING TUNES...
COMBINATION OF THE
(S. ANDREW) LEAD GUITAR: JAMES VOCAL: SAM
I Need A Man To Love
SUMMER-TIME
PIECE OF MY HEART
(Bert Berns, Jerry Ragamov) Vocal: Janis Lead Guitar: Sam
(Gershwin Bros.)
VOCAL: JANIS ARR.: S. ANDREW
ART: R.CRUMB
OH SWEET MARY
BALL and CHAIN
Vocal: Janis Lead Guitar: James
"Big Mama" Thornton
and featuring
JANIS JOPLIN VOCAL
AND HOW!
Vocal: Janis piano: John Simon guitar: Peter
TURTLE BLUES
(J. JOPLIN, P. ALBIN)
SAM HOUSTON ANDREW III!!
GUITAR & BASS!
SCREAM
SIGH
PANT PANT
PETER S. ALBIN, BASS, GUITAR
and,
DAVE GETZ, DRUMS
LIVE MATERIAL RECORDED AT BILL GRAHAM'S FILLMORE AUDITORIUM
TURTLE BLUES "VIBES" COURTESY OF BARNEY'S BEANERY
STONED OUT!
JAMES GURLEY, GUITAR.
SOCK IT TO US!
YAY
SPEED?
ACID?
LIDS?
SMACK?
TOO MUCH
FAR OUT!
SIKE-AY-DELIC!
Barney's Beanery
OPEN ALL NITE
TACOS CHILI
APPROVED BY HELL'S ANGELS FRISCO

Nicolas Sidjakov [1924–1993]. **SYMBOL FOR CONTINENTAL AIRLINES "CELEBRATION" AD CAMPAIGN, LATE 1960s.** Originally from Latvia, Sidjakov moved to the United States in 1956 with his American wife. Mostly self-taught, with some formal training in Paris, he became one of the "hot" designers of San Francisco in the '60s, particularly for his children's book designs. For this Continental Airlines symbol, he employs his bright sense of color and play to express the hipness and glamour of air travel at the time. Continental, whose original logo was designed by Saul Bass, was a major airline that advertised itself as "The Proud Bird with the Golden Tail." That slogan is recontextualized here as "The Year of the Proud Bird" and given the kind of groovy typographic stylization that came to characterize the era. **STAFFAN, 1970, 6¼ x 7⅜ IN.** This children's book, published by Parnassus Press in Berkeley, illustrates a folk song about Sweden's patron saint of horses.

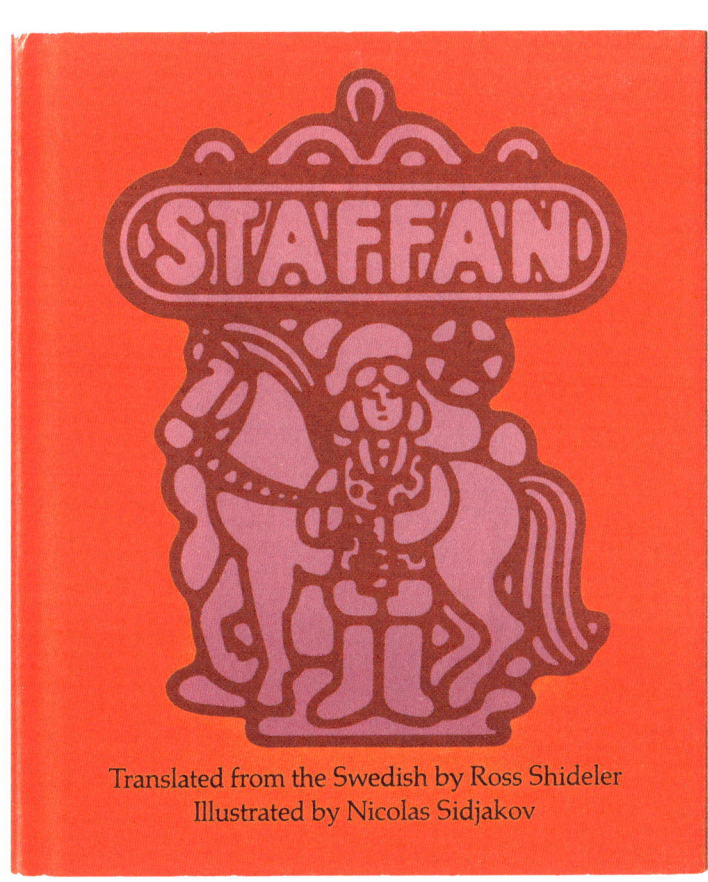

Translated from the Swedish by Ross Shideler
Illustrated by Nicolas Sidjakov

Corita Kent. AMERICAN SAMPLER, 1969, 12⅛ x 23 IN. In December 1967, Newsweek published a Christmas-themed cover story on the artist Sister Corita Kent titled, "The Nun: A Joyous Revolution." It was a testament to the popularity and renown of a woman who had come to symbolize efforts to modernize the Catholic Church. One year later, she was back on a magazine cover—this time, the Christmas/New Year edition of the Saturday Evening Post—but as the former Sister Corita Kent. No longer a nun, she had renounced her vows over her inability to reconcile her own politics with those of the Catholic Church. Corita embodied revolution in many respects—in art, activism, and how the Catholic faith was practiced. She was best known for the cheerful messages of faith and joy she crafted from pop-culture detritus such as bread wrappers and street signage, but Corita's soul by now was in political graphics. At a time of American social upheaval, with heated contention over Vietnam, she formed a beloved bridge between the divide. She was equally "there" for the angry antiwar protests and the "happening" celebrations of life, love, and God; and a poster insert she designed for the Post's holiday issue represented this gentle yet fervent negotiation. A gold-and-orange sun breaks forth from black-and-white photos of soldiers and combat, against which Corita's handwritten script reads, "Let the son shine in." Bold text declares "BOMBING HALTED," while demure italics advise "Remove Obstacles to Peace." American Sampler embodies a similar tension. Using her skill with color and semantics, Corita extracts words from within words to create political messages that both indict and question. "Nation" and "sin" emerge from "assassination." The refrain "I can, I can" embedded in the repetition of "American" becomes a kind of dual-edged mantra of optimism vs. obedience. The work's title references the practice of young ladies learning the alphabet and other rote lessons through embroidery. Corita both engages and subverts that tradition here, highlighting, through the process of craft, the potential within language for rebellion and change.

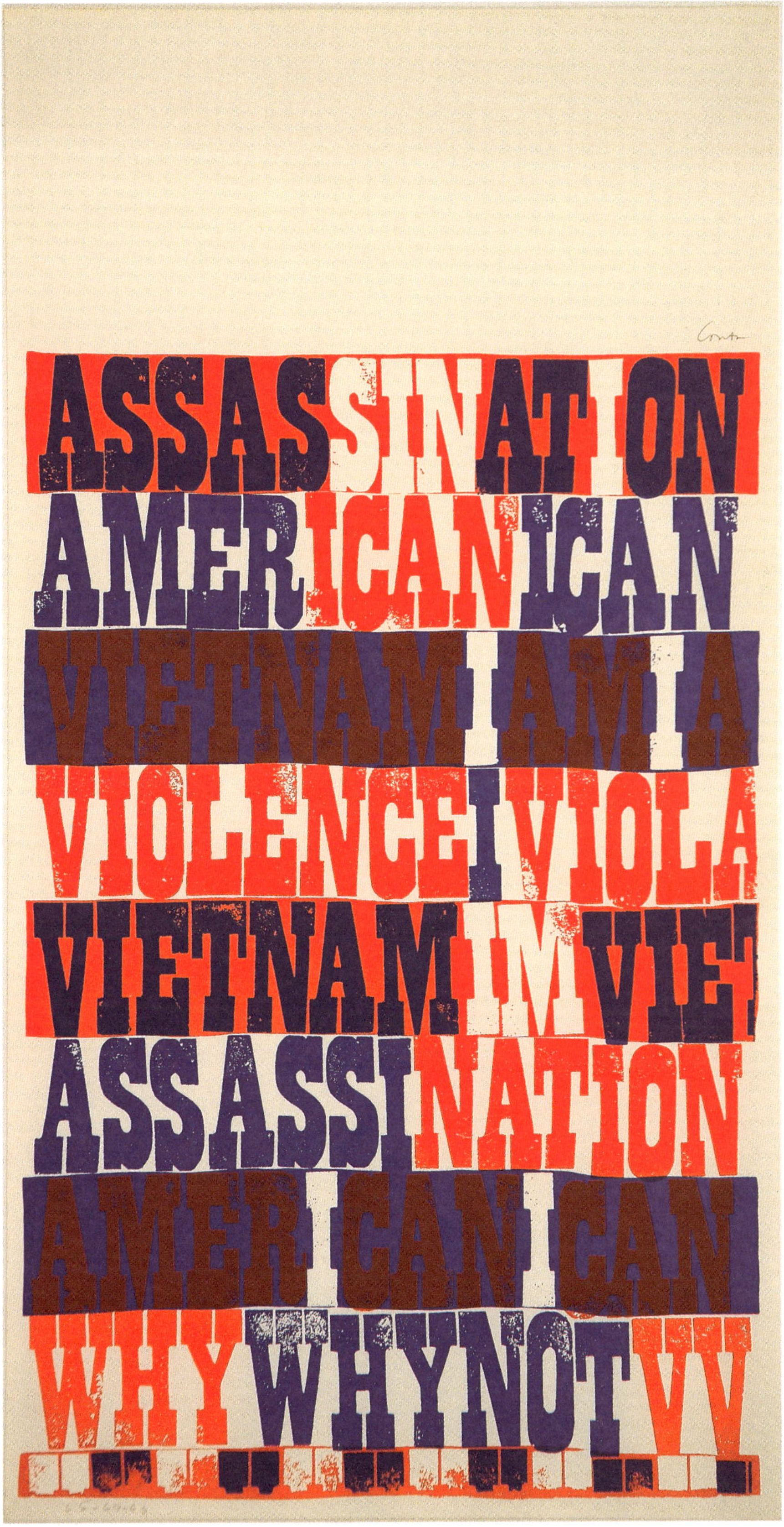

Anonymous. KALIFLOWER, VOL. 1, NO. 36, DECEMBER 25, 1969, 8½ x 11 IN. Many communes were inspired by the anticapitalist Diggers, a collective that envisioned—and briefly, in the late '60s and early '70s, realized—a postcompetitive version of free enterprise in which everything was, literally, free. These were utopia-minded artists who took their social concerns to the streets. One of the "free" communities that cropped up across the nation in 1967 was the Sutter Street Commune. Named for its San Francisco locale and inspired by the Diggers' publishing offshoot, the Communication Company, Sutter Street set up a press of its own called the Free Print Shop. Its best-known product was the newspaper Kaliflower: the title referenced both the Hindu concept of Kali Yuga, the last and most violent age of humankind, and a blossom arising from the ashes of destruction. A free weekly, Kaliflower served some 300 communes in San Francisco and elsewhere for three years, until 1972. The paper was printed on Wednesday nights, and every page received its own design. It was a radical and impractical process compared to the consistency and ease of conventional grids and limited typefaces, yet it liberated the energy and verve of some visionary makers. Once the pages were printed, members of other communes would gather on Thursdays for the finish work, using Japanese stab-stitch methods or staples to bind volumes for distribution.

KALIFLOWER No. 36
December 25, 1969
INTERCOMMUNAL
CHRISTMAS DAY
STREET
CHANT
with FLOATING LOTUS
MAGIC OPERA
bring instruments
2:00
end of Panhandle
Baker & Oak
God appears & God is Light
to those who dwell in Realms of Night
but does a Human Form display
to those who dwell in Realms of Day

Anonymous, KALIFLOWER, VOL. 2, NO. 39, JANUARY 21, 1971, 8½ x 11 IN.

The New Age weekly Kaliflower became so popular that people started referring to its publisher, the Sutter Street Commune, as the Kaliflower Commune. This hippie how-to and lifestyle paper offered the Bay Area's collective-living scene an alternative to mainstream news, covering such topics as the history of communes, the dangers of mass media, and the "difference between property in persons and property in things." It offered recipes and announced events including newcomer welcome receptions, spiritual gatherings, picnics, and, pictured here, a Christmas Day Street Chant. It also included public-service information, promoting a World Building and New Age Design class at the Messiah World Commune, or warning of a Newsweek reporter looking to infiltrate the communes. Each vivacious issue had a unique design, composed of drawing, handwritten text, and vintage and contemporary photography. Kaliflower exudes a distinct aesthetic of enthusiasm, thanks to anonymous artists whose desire for expression trumps any lack of design means or knowledge.

VOL. II
#39
JAN. 21 1971
WELFARE CREATE WELFARE PRESERVE WELFARE DESTROY WELFARE CAPITALIST WELFARE
DIG WELFARE
MAHĀ WELFARE
RAKṢĀ WELFARE
SYĀMĀ WELFARE
MAHĀ WELFARE
NITYA WELFARE
SMAŚĀNA WELFARE
KALIFLOWER

Steamboat. <u>WHOLE EARTH CATALOG</u>, FALL 1970, 10⅞ x 14¾ IN. When photographer Stewart Brand founded the <u>Whole Earth Catalog</u>, in Menlo Park in 1968, he envisioned a vehicle that would achieve a mass shift in consciousness and, in turn, transform society. His big idea: by providing broad access to new technologies and resources, and a wide range of knowledge and ideas, people with imagination and initiative could fashion an alternative way of living. At a basic level, he wanted to apply the achievements of the mainstream military-industrial complex to different ends. This counterculture vision of liberation through shared information and networking presaged his role in the development of the Internet: Brand cofounded the WELL (Whole Earth 'Lectronic Link), one of the first prototypical virtual communities. ¶ The <u>Catalog</u>'s "function," as described in the first issue, was to be an "evaluation and access device." Items included had to be "useful as a tool, relevant to independent education, high quality or low cost, and easily available by mail." Featuring the first photograph of our planet, the cover telegraphed hopes for a vast, interconnected audience. The NASA image not only celebrated the potential of new technologies but also depicted Earth as a single entity undistinguished by geographic and cultural boundaries. The message was one of optimism, that we might understand our world in new ways outside the established order. Published twice yearly until 1972 and then intermittently, the catalogue offered information ranging from books to tools to government documents to comics, much of it contributed by and solicited from readers in an early version of crowdsourcing. The hodgepodge layout, credited to a designer identified only as Steamboat, reflected both practicality and vitality: the DIY compositional equation was what-would-fit-where plus information density of text typed on an IBM Selectric Composer. In 1972, the <u>Whole Earth Catalog</u> won a National Book Award.

SIXTIES ALT SIXTIES

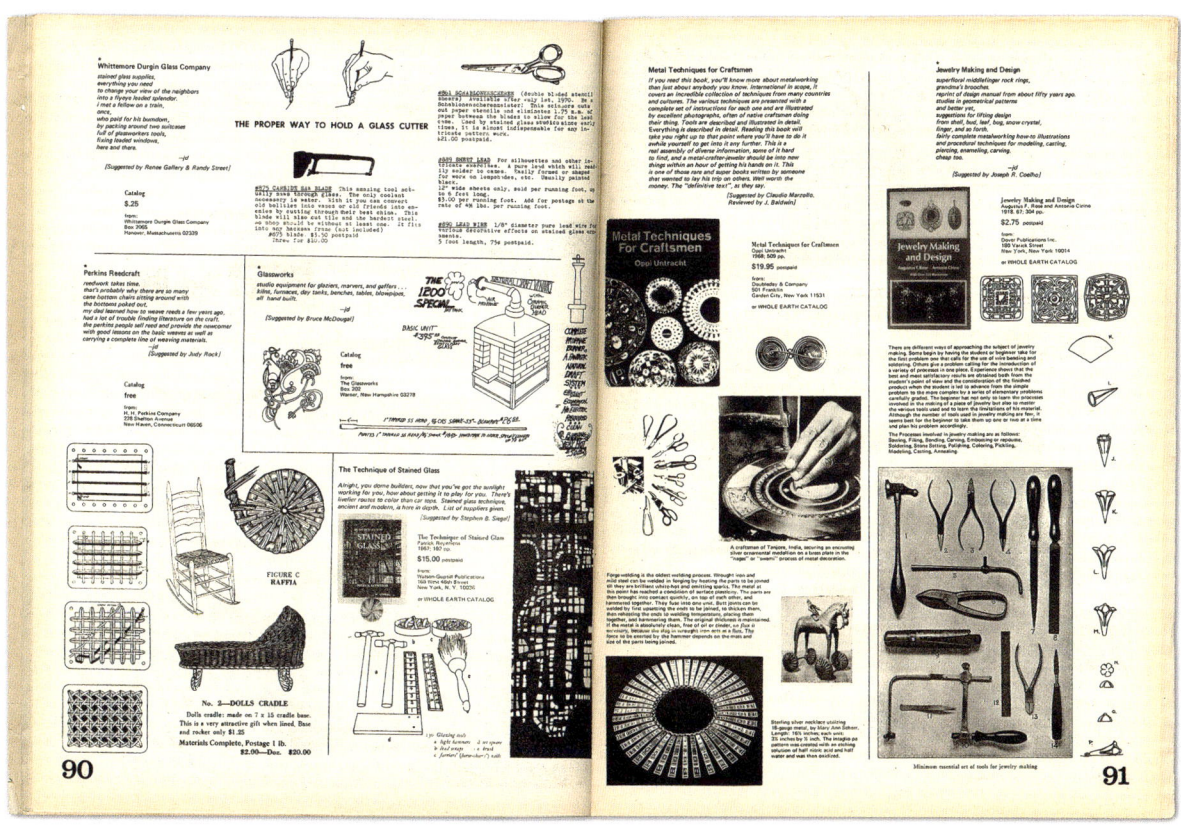

Emory Douglas. "PEACE WITH HONOR" POSTER, 1973, DIMENSIONS UNKNOWN. The sixties did not end with the decade. Continuing his design work with social and political vigilance into the seventies, Douglas went on producing powerful and compelling graphic communications for the Black Panthers. Throughout his career, the scope of his work reflected the shifting concerns of the Panther movement: his subject matter ranged from images of police aggression and activists in combat poses to lovingly dignified portraits of people in the black community. Wheat-pasted around the streets, his posters were intended to spread awareness about Black Panther social initiatives, such as health-care programs, while radicalizing the "brothers and sisters" of Oakland into a state of raised consciousness that would, in turn, strengthen the Panther mandate. ¶ Douglas's oeuvre was that of a "revolutionary artist," an identity the Panther leadership declared for him and one that artist Sam Durant acknowledges in comparing Douglas to the Russian Constructivists, artists and designers committed to social and political reform.[35] With a goal of ending "global capitalism and imperialism," the Panthers saw themselves as aligned with a worldwide revolutionary movement that equated U.S. government–mandated aggression at home, against its black community, with U.S. aggression overseas in Vietnam.[36] "Peace with honor" quotes a 1968 Richard Nixon campaign promise; once elected president, he intensified American involvement in the war.

"PEACE WITH HONOR"

MEDIA: BRUSH, PEN & INK

Notes

1 Leo Monahan, e-mail correspondence with the author, during which Monahan shared his own correspondence with Murray Garrett, March 31, 2014. **2** Art Chantry, "Judge by the Cover," Madame Pickwick Art Blog, January 22, 2012, www.madamepickwickartblog.com, accessed September 12, 2013. **3** Pat Kirkham, *Charles and Ray Eames: Designers of the Twentieth Century* (Cambridge, Mass.: MIT Press, 1995), 266. Kirkham writes, "The much-copied idea of using a 'time line' or 'history wall' to contextualize a subject originated in the Eames Office." **4** Ibid., 297. **5** This poster often has been attributed to the Colby Poster Printing Company. Jan Tumlir was the first to suggest that it was printed by Majestic. See Jan Tumlir, "Concrete Poetry," in Chris Michlig, Brian Roettinger, and Jan Tumlir, eds., *In the Good Name of the Company: Artworks and Ephemera, Produced by or in Tandem with the Colby Poster Printing Company* (Brooklyn, N.Y., and Los Angeles: Picture Box and For Your Art, 2013). **6** Eduardo Lipschutz-Villa, ed., *Wallace Berman: Support the Revolution* (Amsterdam: Institute of Contemporary Art, 1993), 169. **7** Mike Boehm, "Poster Boy for Bohemia," *Los Angeles Times*, September 25, 2004, www.latimes.com, accessed June 6, 2014. **8** John Van Hamersveld, e-mail correspondence with the author, September 16, 2012. **9** For a more complete description of Corita's technique, see Michael Duncan, "Someday Is Now," in Ian Berry and Duncan, eds., *Someday Is Now: The Art of Corita Kent* (Saratoga Springs, N.Y., Munich, and New York: Prestel, 2013), 18. **10** Booth Moore, "Fashion Designer Rudi Gernreich Defied Haute-couture Rules with Socially Aware Clothes that Said…," *Los Angeles Times*, September 28, 2001, www.latimes.com. **11** William Claxton and Peggy Moffit, *The Rudi Gernreich Book* (New York: Rizzoli, 1991), 214. **12** Archie Boston, e-mail correspondence with the author, January 29, 2013. See also Archie Boston, *Fly in the Buttermilk: Memoirs of an African American in Advertising, Design & Design Education* (Los Angeles: Archie Boston Graphic Design, 2001). **13** Boston, *Fly in the Buttermilk*, 151. **14** Thomas Albright, *Art in the San Francisco Bay Area, 1945–1980: An Illustrated History* (Berkeley: University of California Press, 1985), 170. **15** William Grimes, "Alton Kelley, 67, Artist of the 1960s Rock Counterculture, Dies," *New York Times*, June 4, 2008, www.nytimes.com, accessed June 17, 2014. **16** Gary Groth, "An Interview with Victor Moscoso," *Comics Journal* 246, February 9, 2011, www.tcj.com, accessed April 23, 2014. **17** Larry Clinton, "Sausalito Historical Society: 1967 Sausalito Houseboat Summit," *Marin Scope Sausalito*, January 8, 2014, www.marinscope.com, accessed May 30, 2014. **18** See Hetty McGee Maclise's website, Phantomly Oracula, www.phantomlyoracula.com, accessed June 10, 2014. **19** Jim Phillips, e-mail correspondence with the author, June 8, 2014. **20** David Hollander and Kristine McKenna, eds., *Notes from a Revolution: Com/Co, the Diggers & the Haight* (Santa Monica, Calif., and Rensselaerville, N.Y.: Foggy Notion Books and Fulton Ryder, 2012), 40. **21** Joan Didion, *Slouching Towards Bethlehem: Essays* (New York: Farrar, Straus and Giroux, 1968), 121. **22** Peter Coyote, "Making Visions Real," introduction to Hollander and McKenna, *Notes from a Revolution*. **23** "The Digger Papers," www.diggers.org, accessed June 10, 2014. **24** For information about Com/Co equipment, see Lincoln Cushing, "Cranking It Out, Old-School Style: Art of the Gestetner," October 19, 2010, www.aiga.org, accessed June 7, 2014. **25** Peter Berg, interview conducted August 2009, Internet Archive, https://archive.org/details/PeterBergOnOnePercentFree, accessed June 7, 2014. **26** For more about the Black Communications Project, see founder Amiri Baraka's essay "Emory Douglas: A 'Good Brother,' a 'Bad' Artist," in Sam Durant, ed., *Black Panther: The Revolutionary Art of Emory Douglas* (New York: Rizzoli, 2007). **27** Albright, *Art in the San Francisco Bay Area*, 176. **28** Paul D. Grushkin, *The Art of Rock Posters* from Presley to Punk (New York: Abbeville, 1999), 225. **29** Paula Scher quoted in Steven Heller, "Ed Thrasher, 74, Album Designer, Dies," New York Times, August 24, 2006, www.nytimes.com, accessed May 21, 2014. **30** Jeri Heiden, interview with the author, Los Angeles, December 2, 2008. **31** John Van Hamersveld, John Van Hamersveld: Fifty Years of Graphic Design (Berkeley: Gingko Press, 2012), 5. **32** Ted Widmer, "R. Crumb, The Art of Comics No. 1," Paris Review, no. 193, summer 2010, www.theparisreview.org, accessed May 22, 2014. **33** Albright, Art in the San Francisco Bay Area, 175, 269. **34** "R. Crumb: The Complete Record Cover Collection," Rolling Stone, rollingstone.com, accessed May 22, 2014. **35** Durant, Black Panther, 20. **36** Colette Gaiter, "What Revolution Looks Like," in Durant, Black Panther, 98.

↑ John Van Hamersveld in front of his
Pinnacle Indian prints, 1968
→ "Into the Port of San Francisco... beneath
the graceful span of the Golden Gate Bridge,"
from Beautiful California, 1971

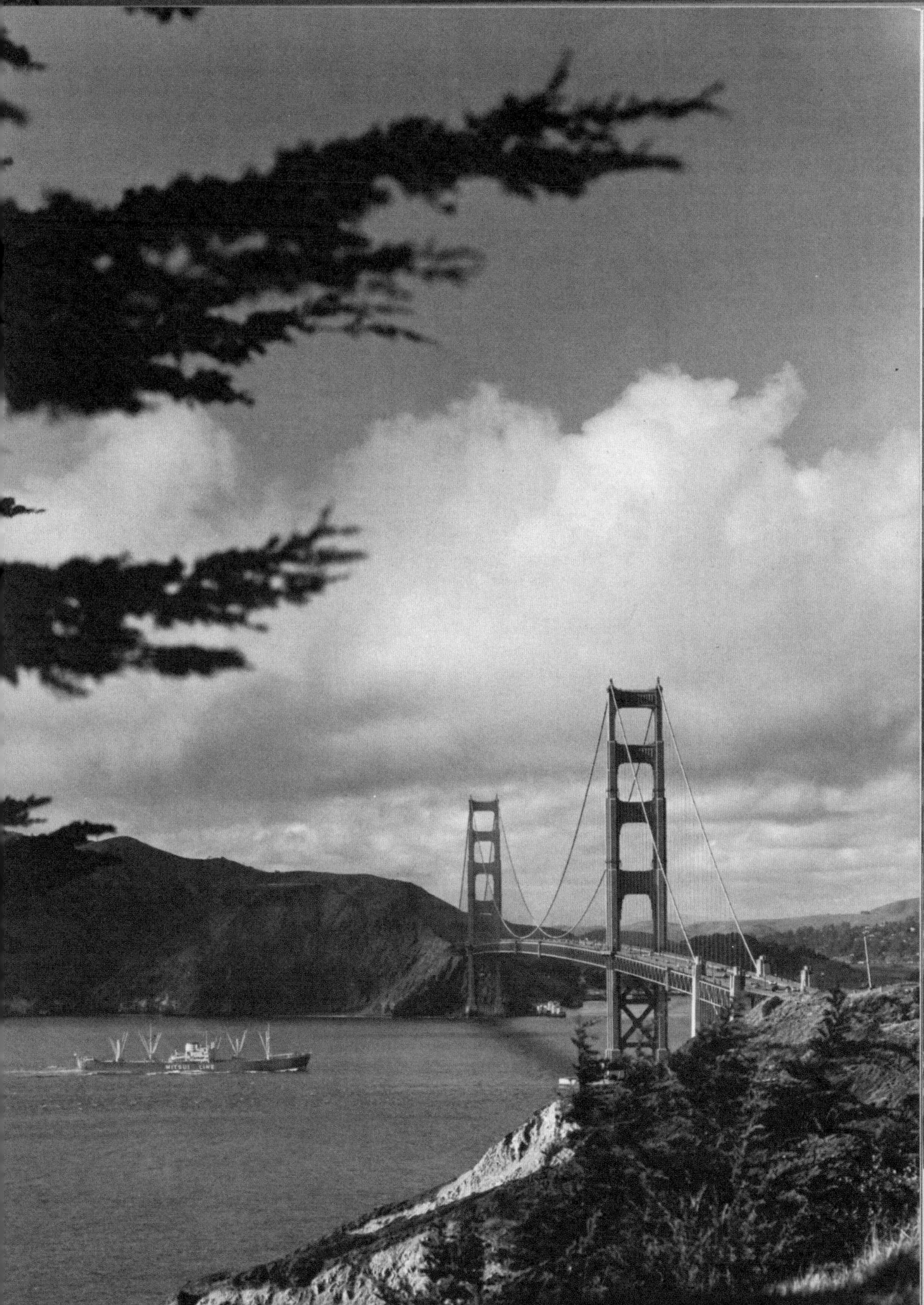

> "And so I was in California, on the lam, as it were, from the slam. Manifest Destiny, 1964. What was western expansion, after all, but a migration of malcontents and ne'er-do-wells, have-nots with no commitment to the stable society left behind, adventurers committed only to circumventing any society in their path."

JOHN GREGORY DUNNE

"EUREKA!"

1978

CALIFORNIA GIRLS

INTRODUCTION: VIEW FROM THE BROADS

On the phone one day, the inimical Gere Kavanaugh told me an outrageous story about an article she helped produce several decades ago intended to celebrate the exuberance of design in her beloved home of California. (For many in the field back then, California was, at best, a blind spot or, at worst, a backwater.) She sent her design approach to the publisher in New York and what came back—what got printed—was, to Kavanaugh's great dismay, nothing like what she had offered. Her work had been stripped to its modernist bones, shoveled into a grid, and drained of the color, messiness, delights, and sensations that represented everything vibrant and meaningful and delicious—everything her practice, and those of the designers she championed, embodied. The mill of an East Coast-cum-European aesthetic had churned up Kavanaugh's project and reduced it to a monotone of cool gray refinement. So NOT California. "Bad California design will not be tolerated here" was the message she received.

 It was a response so lacking in a vision of the way things might be instead of the way things were done by convention and rote, so antithetical to us here on the western edge of the continent—a place of experimentation and daring, a place whose character origins can be traced to an epic fantasy narrative produced by Spaniard Garci Ordóñez de Montalvo in 1510. According to California historian Kevin Starr, Montalvo's work contains the first mention of "California" as a place, albeit a mythical one that is home to a race of black Amazonians ruled by Queen Calafia, "the most beautiful of all of them, of blooming years, and in her thoughts desirous of achieving great things, strong of limb and of great courage."[1] This California was a land of women run by brave and powerful women for women. Now, that's what I call utopia! And maybe this myth isn't so far from reality, since it seems to me that more than anywhere else, California is a scene where women seem to thrive and prosper and—within this nonfiction narrative of graphic design—gain global influence in unusual numbers. Something in the water, something in the light, something in the air, something going on here facilitates liberation from tradition, from rules, and from the usual way of doing things.

 When I first came to California, in 1990, I was sure I had landed in some kind of promised land. I had just left a wintertime Boston, fresh from postmodernist and feminist studies and with substantial experience as a graphic designer (first for a small magazine, then a corporate studio). In contrast to Beantown, California really seemed ruled and galvanized by griffin-riding Amazons. No kindly old gentleman running the show. No "sweethahts" from the mouths of well-intentioned patriarchs who felt duty- and honor bound to help damsels they assumed could only be in distress. I was stunned by an environment that, had I not witnessed it myself, would have seemed as improbable as Disney's Tomorrowland. Call it Nopatriarchyland. Here, gender didn't carry the same stigmas and assumptions. And this freedom from convention also was going on within graphic design. Rather than following the rules, designers in California seemed to be making them up. For women designers, this meant a double whammy, a perfect storm, a jellyroll of change: once liberated from the conventions of the old misogynist social order, they were able to take the next step to unshackle themselves from the conventions of design.

From Grace Clements to Marget Larsen to April Greiman, a continuum of women designers in California defined their identities, their interests, and their professional output for themselves, forging new terrain rather than accepting the usual paths. Clements challenged Surrealism in search of something more real and tangible than dreams and the subconscious. Larsen reenvisioned fashion advertising and marketing as spirited, graphic, solid, and splashy. Greiman exploded onto the international scene by cultivating a new vision for a new tool—the Macintosh.

Yet even in New Amazonia, things weren't perfect. Like many young women of the 1960s and '70s, Barbara Stauffacher Solomon and Deborah Sussman strained against sexism and grappled with not being taken seriously. Still, they trailblazed on. With a combination of Manifest Destiny derring-do and a celebratory sense of showwomanship, these maverick designers often flew under the radar only to explode into the sky with bursts of color and joy. Small steps became big strides, and their confidence grew with the momentum. (I can relate!) And the resulting work, as well as the attitude, embodied the California spirit. In a 1966 article in the design trade publication <u>Print</u>, Sister Corita Kent reflected that her students' projects were "different from most people's concept of art" and, in comparison with the smooth, technical style of the staid East Coast, they reflected the "rugged Western atmosphere of free expression."[2]

In the end, the stories of these pioneers provided inspiration around the world, not only to other women but also to other designers, of both sexes. A whole generation of women who burst on the design scene starting in the 1980s thrived in and continued to cultivate the paradise created by their foremothers, mentoring the generations to follow. Think Anne Burdick, Margo Chase, Denise Gonzales Crisp, Laurie Haycock Makela, Jeri Heiden, Terry Irwin, Rebeca Mendez, Noreen Morioka, Jennifer Morla, Lucille Tenazas, and Lorraine Wild, to name just a few.

To frame this pink and sassy picture, this section offers a fresh reflection as well as three historical excerpts. The aforementioned Crisp envisions a fictional convergence of legendary women designers from across time and space, physics and dreams, and connects her ephemeral narrative to that enterprising ur-inventor Thomas Alva Edison. From the archives, a scrapbooklike spread gathers published observations about Corita from the mid-1960s; a 1971 article from Print delves into the motivations of supergraphics superstar Solomon; and Rose DeNeve's 1976 essay "A Feminist Option" examines the trajectory of Sheila Levrant de Bretteville from designer to activist.

1 Kevin Starr, California: A History (New York: Modern Library, 2005), 5. **2** Martha Monigle, "Sister Mary Corita: 'Be Aware! Be Curious! Be Joyous,'" Print, May/June 1966, 14–19.

INFLUENCES & INTERSECTIONS
California Girls

INFLUENCER → DESIGNER
EDUCATOR ↠ INSTITUTION/STUDENT
COLLABORATOR ⊸⊷ COLLABORATOR
EMPLOYER/COMMISSIONER ⋯▸ DESIGNER

- BETTY BRADER
- SISTER MAGGIE MARTIN
- SISTER CORITA KENT
- GERE KAVANAUGH
- JAN STEWART
- JOSEPH MAGNIN STORES
- ART/DESIGN EDUCATION
- IMMACULATE HEART COLLEGE ART DEPARTMENT
- DEBORAH SUSSMAN
- ARTS & ARCHITECTURE
- RAY (& CHARLES) EAMES
- GRACE CLEMENTS
- ALEXANDER GIRARD

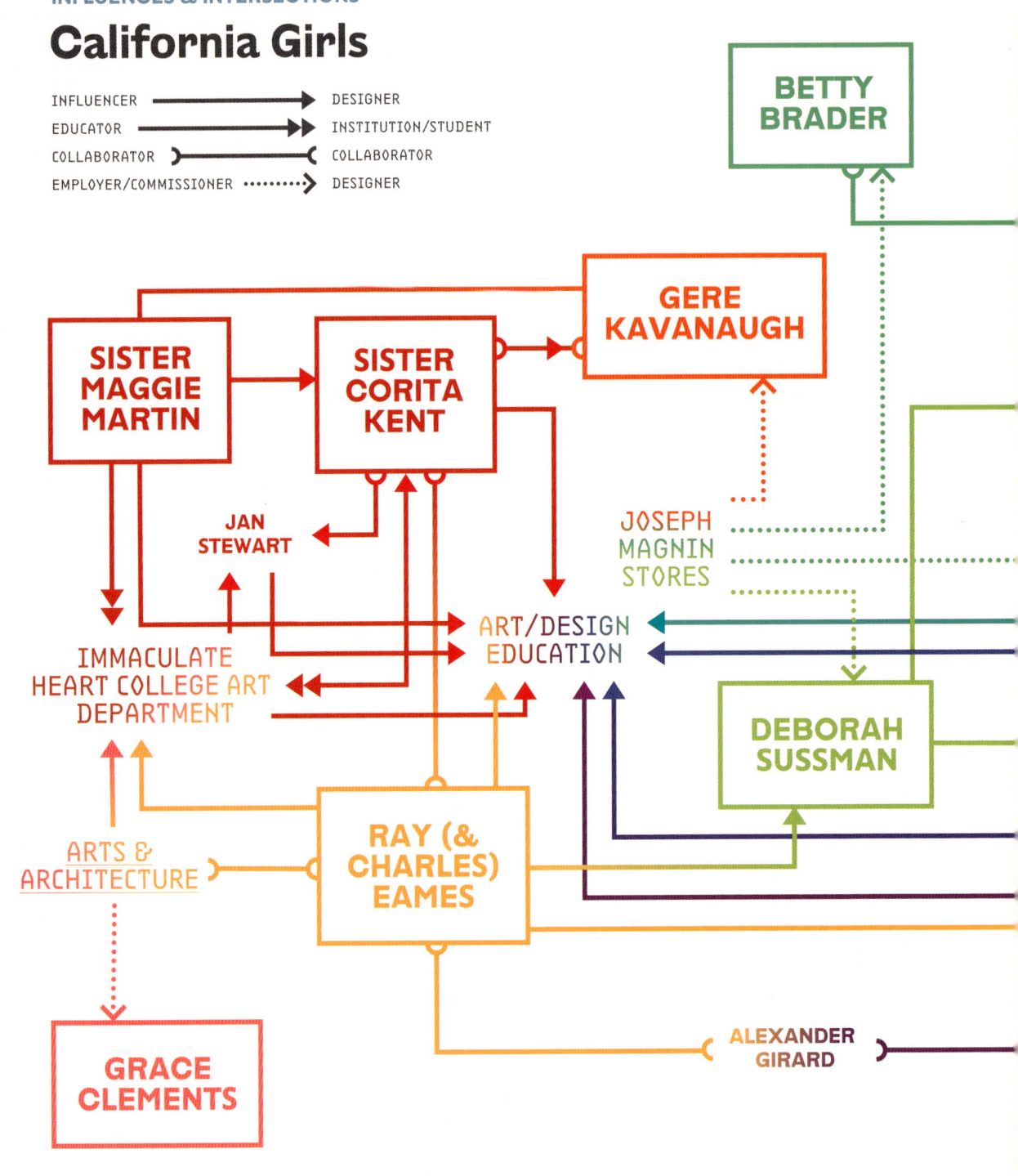

FRANCES BUTLER

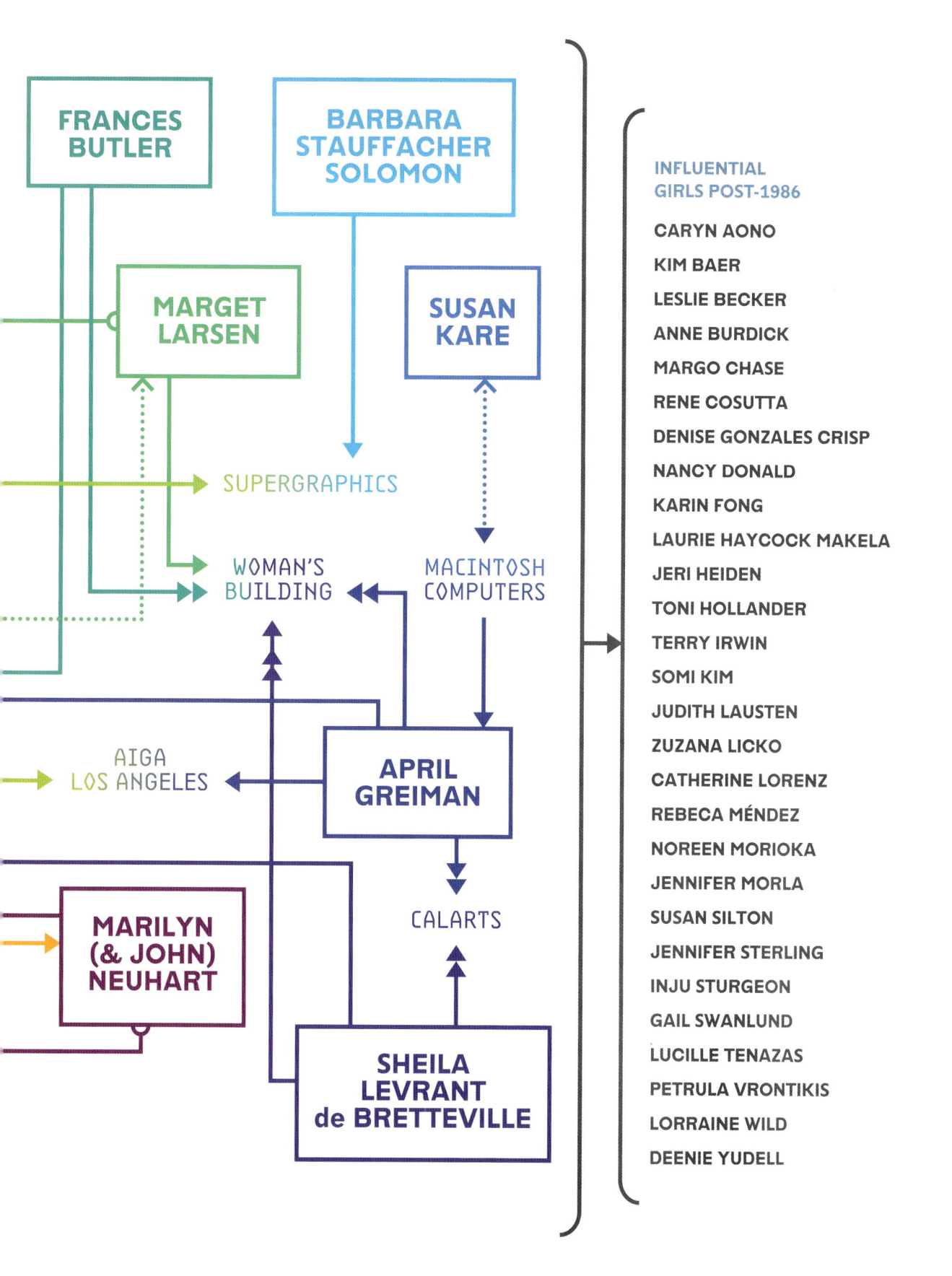

BARBARA STAUFFACHER SOLOMON

MARGET LARSEN

SUSAN KARE

SUPERGRAPHICS

WOMAN'S BUILDING

MACINTOSH COMPUTERS

AIGA LOS ANGELES

APRIL GREIMAN

CALARTS

MARILYN (& JOHN) NEUHART

SHEILA LEVRANT de BRETTEVILLE

INFLUENTIAL GIRLS POST-1986

CARYN AONO
KIM BAER
LESLIE BECKER
ANNE BURDICK
MARGO CHASE
RENE COSUTTA
DENISE GONZALES CRISP
NANCY DONALD
KARIN FONG
LAURIE HAYCOCK MAKELA
JERI HEIDEN
TONI HOLLANDER
TERRY IRWIN
SOMI KIM
JUDITH LAUSTEN
ZUZANA LICKO
CATHERINE LORENZ
REBECA MÉNDEZ
NOREEN MORIOKA
JENNIFER MORLA
SUSAN SILTON
JENNIFER STERLING
INJU STURGEON
GAIL SWANLUND
LUCILLE TENAZAS
PETRULA VRONTIKIS
LORRAINE WILD
DEENIE YUDELL

DENISE GONZALES CRISP

WATER AND POWER

WEDNESDAY, NOVEMBER 19, 1980, 2:30 PM,
VERMILLION VALLEY

Southern California Edison Company formed the lake to commemorate the 75th anniversary of the incandescent light bulb," the pamphlet explains. I pause to draw a light bulb, attempting perfect symmetry, miserably. "Completed in 1954 with the construction of Vermillion Valley Dam, the lake was…"

"More?" The waitress hovers a coffee pot over my cup. I nod.

"You're in art?" she asks.

"Graphic design."

"We get a few artists up here. Is graphic design like art?"

I look up and smile politely. "I couldn't tell you."

"I see." The waitress isn't leaving. "We get all sorts here. Backpackers mostly, down from the trails for a zero day. Khaki asses, we call them." She waves the coffee pot limply at the room. "Not much action in winter though." The fire in the woodstove releases a sudden pop to testify. "I'm Lucy, if you need anything. I'll be over there," she gestures to the stool behind the register, "interminably."

I turn my attention back to the pamphlet. "The lake was constructed to store water and generate hydroelectric power. The name of Thomas Alva Edison was given to the lake in honor of… "

But I know all this. The history is in part what drew me to this valley. I was born the same year the lake opened, which means that tomorrow, my twenty-sixth birthday, it and I will celebrate together, each in our solitude. I am retreating here for a few days because it's exactly halfway between my home in Los Angeles and my birthplace, San Francisco. And because of Edison, the inventor.

I put the pamphlet down and turn to the next page in my notebook. A sweep of my palm across the blank surface begins a quest, on this, the last day of my first quarter-century.

11/19—near Edison Lake:

I've been reading about Edison's inventions. I'm attracted to them because, in an era of prolific global invention of every sort, the apparatuses that he imagined and produced made human thought physical in completely unfamiliar ways. He (and his collaborators) perfected existing inventions, and introduced new ones that expanded how the written word, sound, and images could, and would, be seen and heard forevermore. Edison devised the "fluoroscope" (precursor to the X-ray machine), a more efficient stock ticker…

A woman bursts into the café stomping leather boots, aubergine. She looks to be in her late forties.

"C-c-c-cold!" she announces to no one. Lucy and I fix on the shivering emerald green coat.

"Vermillion Lodge, right?" the woman asks breathlessly, peeling off leather gloves.

"We call it a resort," Lucy corrects. "This is the café. Can I h…"

"Brandy. And coffee." The green woman charges toward the woodstove as if trying to outpace the chill behind her. Her silver case bangs on the slate hearth as she settles into the nearest table.

"Ma'am?" Lucy calls apologetically, "We only have beer and wine."

"Wine, then. Red. Whatever you have."

So much for solitude. I return to my notebook.

…the cylinder phonograph, Kinetophone, Kinetoscope, and Vitascope opened the floodgates for future movie cameras, tape recorders, and now VCRs. And the "autographic printer" (an early mimeograph) foretold the office copier (mem: research Eastman and Xerox). Shining light on them all is the first long-lasting light bulb. Surely these very real manifestations were fantasies prior to the inventions. Yet to witness fantasies materialize before your eyes is to experience something otherworldly. Sound recordings, moving photographs, and information from faraway places all seem to simply appear, as if out of the clouds. We call Edison an inventor, but there must have been a moment when he was seen as a magician, or maybe an imaginator…

Movement from the archway leading to the reception office distracts me once again. Another woman comes in. A head of cropped hair appears to hover above a jacket covered in black and white checks. She scans the small café, sees the green woman, and shrieks, **"MARGET?"**

"FRANCES?" the Marget person returns the surprise. Frances glides past my table toward the woodstove. On the back of the jacket the checks frame a surreal orange face in full Cheshire cat smile. Globs of red flowers dot a marigold field. Marget asks what Frances is doing 500 miles from the bay.

"I'm meeting someone," says Frances, taking off her jacket. The lining is yellow. "And you?"

"Sierra Club campaign… a last-minute deal. No crew even," Marget explains, pointing to her case. "Just me and the Leica. Who are you meeting?"

"SHEILA from the Woman's Building in L.A. Poltroon is putting together a book about the Feminist Studio Workshop, and we're spending a couple of days together to get it started."

I think I know these women. I haven't been working as a designer for long, but these names are unusual and vaguely familiar. I'm almost certain I've seen them in photos. (A bit of a nerd, I spend a lot of time at the UCLA Arts Library, in the design and architecture stacks). Green coat might be Marget Larsen, who designed the Joseph Magnin advertising and collectible gift packaging, which became all the rage in the sixties. The wild jacket lady has to be Frances Butler, the textile-printing artist turned paper-printing-and-book artist. She and Alastair Johnston founded Poltroon Press in Berkeley. And I will recognize Sheila. She was our commencement speaker (but you'd have to be in a coma to not notice her). Plus, the FSW's Woman's Building is famous, at least to me.

They must be them! I try to shake myself from eavesdropping and return to pondering the weighty implications of stock tickers and phonographs. My thoughts, though, drift back rebelliously to these women, to their work. I can see Marget's in my mind's eye: bold, colorful, playfully decorative, clever. It seemed to anticipate an emerging consumer—Summer of Love baby boomers maturing into steady paychecks. Frances's work as a textile printer is cool: naked women and graphic flowers and grids and patterns, all at once. Now she brings those images to books and posters. I don't think she had made books before starting Poltroon.

I am aware of a slight lift, my weight on the chair lightening. I poise my pen over my notebook in an attempt to anchor myself, but my ears have already floated away toward the women's voices.

WEDNESDAY, NOVEMBER 19, 1980, 2:10 PM,
VERMILLION VALLEY

"Yes, I left the city at six-ay-em!" BARBARA laughed into the phone at the front desk. The clerk, busy collecting key, towels, pamphlet, and soap into a neat pyramid, looked askance at the new guest.

"Yes, yes. No traffic. Listen, I forgot the Sea Ranch photos." She paused, then covered the mouthpiece and whispered to the clerk, "Do you get UPS up here?" He shook his head.

"Shit. No, no, not you. They don't have it here. Anyway, yes, fine…. I will. Bye." Barbara returned the handset to the wall and drummed red fingernails on the pinewood counter.

"We've put you up in the yurt, at David's request." The clerk pointed out the door and to the left. "I turned on the heater already. The café is just there, through that arch."

"Splendid."

Barbara's cousin, David—a holdover from the Haight-Ashbury heyday—had roped her into meeting with his fellow members of the Vermillion Valley Business Association. They hope to attract San Joaquin Valley suburbanites without alienating the backpackers and fishermen who comprise the majority of their lodgers. Even though Barbara had opted out of design practice three years ago, she agreed to consult for a day. Surveying the yurt's interior, with its curved pine-paneled perimeter and calico bedspread, she questioned whether they needed her. They might rather need a bulldozer.

She retrieved her suitcase from the car and pulled out jeans, a wool Alpine sweater, and the city version of hiking boots to change into. Once dressed for the rugged wilds, she zipped her orange goose-down coat to the neck and stepped out into the cold to begin assessing the raw material. A 30-minute drive around the area and a walk through the town to the ferry dock told her all she needed to know. She headed back. "I hope this café has a decent wine list. Yeah, sure it will."

WEDNESDAY, NOVEMBER 19, 1980, 3:15 PM,
VERMILLION VALLEY

A bracing draft suddenly steadies me. Glancing up, I recognize her instantly. She is formidable in all black: trench coat, slacks, turtleneck, gloves, boots. Black hair is swept into a ponytail. She lifts her arms and seems to part the air before her as she sails by. "Fran!"

"Sheila, you found it!" Frances gets up. Cheek kisses, the way Europeans greet each other.

"A little later than I had hoped. Problems getting one of the presses to the Woman's Building."

"Do you know Marget Larsen?"

"I don't. Wonderful work, truly wondrous."

"Thank you. And your work!… Well, thank you." Marget gestures to a chair. "Join us?"

Still standing, Sheila regards Frances. "Reluctantly, we should get started, don't you think, Fran? Not much time." After a few more polite exchanges, Frances and Sheila excuse themselves, and set up at a table across the room.

I cannot help but stare. Sheila Levrant de Bretteville is one of the founders of the Feminist Studio Workshop, a kind of alternative school for women painters, sculptors, printmakers, and performance artists, and later of the Women's Graphic Center. My design studio class took a field trip there once, and I remember feeling a little uncomfortable. But that was some time ago. I think she also started a program up at CalArts.

"Can I get you anything to eat?" Lucy asks me, suddenly energized by the rush of customers.

I realize that the lightness in my body persists, and is rising steadily to my head. "I should eat, yes. I'll have an omelet. Oh, and a glass of white wine, please."

"You got it." Lucy spins and nearly rams into another patron. "OH! Sorry, didn't see you there! Please, sit anywhere."

The woman's nose is pink, and she's wrapped in a puffy orange coat. The café erupts once again with a colliding "Barbara!" and "Marget!" Sheila and Frances raise their heads for a moment but quickly resume their huddle. The orange coat, the Barbara, walks over and warms her hands at the woodstove. She and Marget tell each other why they're here, and the term "sea ranch" flips a switch in my memory. I think I know of this woman, too. She transformed typical wall graphics into what we now call supergraphics.

Supergraphics are as common as light bulbs these days (as are graphic sweatshirts, an idea Marget came up with using an etching of Beethoven, of all things). But back then how wild it must have been to be immersed in language and colorful shapes sprawled brazenly across walls and ceilings and in stairwells. A silent yet vital personality that tells people, "You are here and nowhere else but here."

"Imaginator," I say, loudly enough to prompt Marget and Barbara to look over and offer me forgiving smiles. I sheepishly retreat to my notebook.

Is Barbara an imaginator? Or any of them? Would seeing their work for the first time have been as fantastic as seeing text spill into one's hands (the vast world of stock prices captured on a paper ribbon)? Or as incredible as seeing moving pictures in a Kinetoscope? (I came here seeking inspiration from conjured proximity to Edison. Instead I find myself among these women—lights that are, to me, as bright as stars.)

MONDAY, NOVEMBER 17, 1980, 2:50 PM,
VENICE BEACH

The plane approached LAX from the south, flying over the harbor where the engineered Los Angeles River empties into the Pacific. No evidence of the rising tide that threatened to flood Long Beach last winter, a story CORITA followed closely in the L.A. Times delivered daily to her South Boston home. The concrete river is a barren slash, while the freeways trickle cars.

Corita picked up a taxi at the terminal curb. "Venice, please. Take Lincoln to Washington to Abbott Kinney?"

"You must be from here," the driver observed.

"I am of here, yes."

The taxi windows framed shallow green lawns fronting flat-roofed houses, their Spanish tile awnings and painted archways mimicking the grander constructions of Los Feliz, her former neighborhood. Here, newly minted Thai restaurants, Latino markets, nail salons, and parking lots interrupted residences and small manufacturing businesses. Corita savored flashes of rude, glorious color trapped amid ivory stucco or wood, weathered to taupe. She pulled her eyes away from the abundance streaming by when the cab stopped suddenly at 901 Washington Boulevard.

Corita let herself in and set down her things in the front office. "RAY?"

The spaces felt bigger than they did during Corita's visit so many years ago. She tried to recall when that was. Has it been 10 years? Twelve? Innumerable visual treasures still crowded every surface, as they did before, but they appeared more settled now, as if they had already yielded the depth of their mysteries. Or perhaps they were respectfully quiet, in memory of Charles. Corita found Ray in the graphics room leaning over a light table, her black pinafore and cotton blouse sweetly amplified by the glow.

"THERE you are!" Ray squealed, opening her arms and walking toward her friend, dark eyes gleaming with pleasure. They embraced and swayed. "Oh my GOOD-ness how heavenly it is to lay eyes on you!" Ray pulled away to survey Corita. "You look a bit worn out, my dearest," she concluded, troubled.

"And your hair is as gray as mine!" Corita deflected, laughing and pointing to Ray's familiar bun bound by a black bow. "The trip out here might have added more than a few to my own head, I can say. We were very delayed in Chicago."

"You poor thing. Of course you're exhausted."

Within a few quiet moments, the long hiatus of their friendship condensed and finally evaporated inside the small space that separated them. "Come!" Ray blurted, breaking the silence. She pulled Corita by the hand to the light table, bubbling, "You must look at these. You will <u>love</u> them."

TUESDAY, NOVEMBER 18, 1980, 8:30 AM,
WEST LOS ANGELES

DEBORAH answered the buzzing telephone as she zipped the presentation boards into a leather portfolio. "You're gone, I know," the receptionist asserted, "But Ray's on line two."

Deborah switched lines. "Ray, is everything all right?"

Ray twittered brightly on the other end, "Oh, fine, quite fine. Guess what? Corita is here and we're leaving today for a watercolor painting excursion. On a lark! And we're… "

"That's lovely, Ray." Deborah gently cut her off, explaining in rapid fire that she's heading for meetings in Fresno and how murderous the traffic will be and that she must leave this instant.

"Yes, well, you get going, dear. I just wanted to say that I'm bringing Corita by your studio this morning."

"Okay. Paul's here."

"You're going to Fresno?" Ray piped. "We're stopping there for the night, and heading up tomorrow to the Vermillion, um, I have it here somewhere… Ah, here. Vermillion Valley Resort."

Deborah pulled on her coat and leaned into the phone. "Where?"

"An old fisherman friend of Corita's told her about it."

"Do be careful driving. Love to Corita. I'll tell Paul. I really must go."

Deborah ran down the stairs, waded through a mass of new drafting tables, and stopped at the door to the project room. "I'm off. Ray's coming by this morning."

Paul looked up. "Why? To smell paint fumes?"

"Corita's in town. Wants to see the new venture." Deborah blew a kiss, then scurried out to the car.

TUESDAY, NOVEMBER 18, 1980, 11:50 AM,
DOWNTOWN LOS ANGELES

As APRIL stepped off the elevator of One Bunker Hill and walked toward the rotunda, she turned her thoughts from the meeting to the squish and squeak of her white, rubber-soled brogans hitting the marble steps. Stopping in the rotunda—walls lined in yet more, ornately tiled, marble—she absorbed the reverberating clack and click of other soles passing through and imagined them as unbridled bits of sound querying each other in search of a shared rhythm.

Once outside, she squinted up at the three reliefs carved above the entrance, her hand shielding the noon sun from her eyes. Her client—housed on the twelfth, and topmost, floor—had explained that the building was erected in 1930 to be Southern California Edison's headquarters, and so the carvings depict hydroelectricity, light, and power. The building's genesis had come up because they'd been joking about earthquakes. The client had told her that the structure was the first in L.A. engineered to resist imminent catastrophe. "But," he added, "that was 50 years ago."

April crossed a crowded Fifth Street and headed to the Central Library to start background work. Before going inside, she turned back to the Edison facade, as if it had voiced a call that she alone could hear above the din of idling cars and screeching bus brakes. She froze for a long moment, listening.

The stairs to the library's second floor led her to the high rotunda covered in concentric patterns of intricate gold and sun-sea-sand–inspired color. The graphic sunburst at the dome's apex shimmered, and the walls seemed to vibrate. The flood of light animated the solid surfaces into semi-liquid. Ambient brightness dulled the globe chandelier alight overhead, yet the zodiac symbols encircling it glinted. The 12 murals expressing California's history just beneath the dome prompted a thought, unexpected and urgent. Energy. In an instant, April determined to take the next few days off. She usually escapes to the desert, but this day the words "hydroelectricity," "light," and "power" swam in her consciousness. Instead of driving east, she would drive north.

WEDNESDAY, NOVEMBER 19, 1980, 4:30 PM,
VERMILLION VALLEY, CALIFORNIA

I know that molecules—including those of humans—migrating or transforming each other is not magic. This phenomenon is merely the convergence or collision or dispersion of particles through some exchange of energy. It's like lightning (what little I know about it). Opposing negative and positive charges in water droplets and ice—clouds—interact with a charge introduced by the electrons of water evaporating from the ground. Or something like that. It's plain physics.

And yet I can't keep my body from bobbing, as if the room is a pool and I float near the ceiling above us all. I see myself sitting at a table, near April Greiman. She was as surprised as I to see the women gathered here, but she seems to know almost everyone. Now, she is eating a salad and reading. April is my design heroine. Her iconoclastic composition and typography shocked me into visual consciousness. And there is Ray Eames, the maker and curator of delight, sitting with Corita Kent, formerly known as Sister Corita. She, like Sheila, uses design to educate, inspire, agitate, and activate. Deborah Sussman seems to be telling them a story. She worked with Ray at the Eames Office back in the fifties and sixties, and I hear she's started a new studio that does environmental graphic design. Deborah punctuates her tale with a smack on the table. Ray catches Corita's hand, and they all throw their heads back, laughing. Frances and Sheila are sorting photographs. Barbara Stauffacher Solomon, there at a corner table, is writing on a yellow pad. Marget is inspecting her camera gear. I see myself turn the page of my notebook, and begin to write.

The sun has descended well beyond the trees. The room glows a low vermillion. I stand almost weightless and move to April's table, touch her shoulder and say that the ferry is ready. I move to Sheila and Frances, touch their shoulders and say that the ferry is ready. I do the same for Deborah, Ray, Corita, Marget, and Barbara. We gather our things and together walk into the evening frost.

The helmsman standing on the dock waves a lantern, although it's not quite dark. We board the ferry, and it glides away from shore. Soon we are in the middle of a lake, and the ferry stops. We stand on the bow looking out across the lake, whispering to each other in shared amazement. Our voices travel out over the water, and small ripples echo back, catching the twilight. Sheila and Corita say, "How incredible it is to hear voices in the air, as if from other worlds, or from heaven itself." Ray and Deborah say, "How incredible it is to see a pavilion on a chilly evening, blazing lights mirrored on the water." We peer deep into the lake and see fish and plants, all the way down to the rocks lining the bottom. April and Frances say, "How incredible it is to see bright bones exposed onto film." At the tip of the bow I see a large metal ball reflecting the aqua horizon. I ask the women what it is. Marget says she thinks it is imagination. Barbara says she thinks it is consciousness. We approach it cautiously. I pick the ball up. It is dense and heavy. I move to the rim of the bow and cup the ball in my hands over the water, prepared to release it. All the women say, "Go. Just go."

THURSDAY, NOVEMBER 20, 1980, 9:30 AM,
VERMILLION VALLEY

Lucy brings coffee to my table. "Sleep okay?"

"Yes, I did, thanks. I had a funny dream."

"Oh, yeah? Funny how?" She sits in the chair across from me.

"I dreamt a dream that Edison had dreamt during a vacation on the shore. He wrote it down."

"That Edison?" she asked, pointing toward the dam up the mountain.

"Yes, that one. I dreamt the exact dream, as I had read it: The air was filled with millions of perfectly formed, translucent cherubs, each the size of a fly. They all swept down to the surface of the sea and cupped both tiny hands to take a very small drop. Then they all flew up together and released their droplets to form a cloud."

"That's not funny. That's kind of beautiful."

"The best part is that Edison came up to me and said, 'That method of forming clouds is very different from the method described in Ganot's Physics.' And then he congratulated me for having learned the true method."

"What's Ganot's Physics?"

"Some old book about how things work."

Lucy got up and headed to her stool behind the register. She paused halfway and turned back to me. "So, if cherubs make clouds, who makes lightning?"

11/20—near Edison Lake. Birthday:

I've read somewhere that Edison slept in short intervals—lying on a narrow bed, his hands holding in place a large steel ball perched just below the sternum. When his body softened, the ball would escape, thud to the hardwood floor, and shock him into mortal consciousness. Before coming here, I had also heard that if you were to heave a solid metal ball into the lake, it wouldn't sink. Rather, it would smash against the water, skitter briefly, then subdue into slow rotation—a continuous curve working surface tension against its mass. I didn't think it possible. But in California many such impossible things occur routinely. I know. I have seen them with my own eyes.

EXCERPT FROM Sister Corita Kent, daisy with all the petals yes (Los Angeles: Immaculate Heart College, 1966)

THE NEW YORKER

Sister Corita herself arrived the next week—a one-woman *aggiornamento*, pretty, cheerful, gentle, and dynamic. The Morris Gallery, at 174 Waverly Place, was displaying her latest serigraphs, which, like all her others, are built around quotations. "I take things out of context and play with them," she told us when we looked her up. The show included such diverse sources as advertisements for Wonder Bread and words by Rabbi Abraham Heschel and Father Daniel Berrigan, who recently became co-chairmen of Clergy Concerned About Vietnam. An example of Sister Corita's penchant for varied sources can be seen in a short article called "Art and Beauty in the Life of the Sister," which she wrote for a book called "The Changing Sister." In it she quotes or refers to Albert Camus, Federico Fellini, John Cage, Peanuts, Cardinal Suenens, William James, an ad for Del Monte catsup, John Dewey, George Bernard Shaw, J. D. Salinger, Little Red Riding Hood, Pope Paul VI, and James Baldwin. She has taught art at Immaculate Heart College for the past sixteen years.

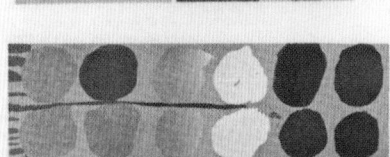

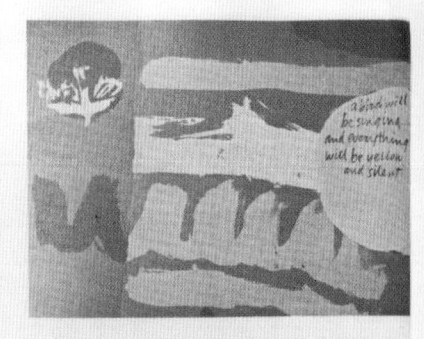

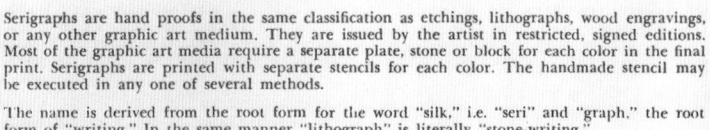

Serigraphs are hand proofs in the same classification as etchings, lithographs, wood engravings, or any other graphic art medium. They are issued by the artist in restricted, signed editions. Most of the graphic art media require a separate plate, stone or block for each color in the final print. Serigraphs are printed with separate stencils for each color. The handmade stencil may be executed in any one of several methods.

The name is derived from the root form for the word "silk," i.e. "seri" and "graph," the root form of "writing." In the same manner "lithograph" is literally "stone-writing."

Serigraphs are produced entirely by hand by the artist in his own studio and are actually "stencil" prints. Because this particular stencil-making method allows tremendous flexibility, the medium is suited to almost every form of artistic expression. Prints can be designed with flat areas of color or with parts broken in both color and texture.

A piece of finely-woven silk is stretched on a rigid frame hinged to a board. In the *tusche resist* method of making a stencil, the parts to be printed with a certain color are painted or drawn in with the greasy substance called "tusche." The silk is then coated with glue and the *tusche* removed with a solvent, thus carrying the glue away from the areas to be printed and leaving only the clear silk.

Because one stencil is destroyed in the making of the next, it is impossible to exactly reproduce a serigraph. Another edition, if one is attempted, actually produces another print. Thus, serigraphs differ from etchings, or from any other techniques.

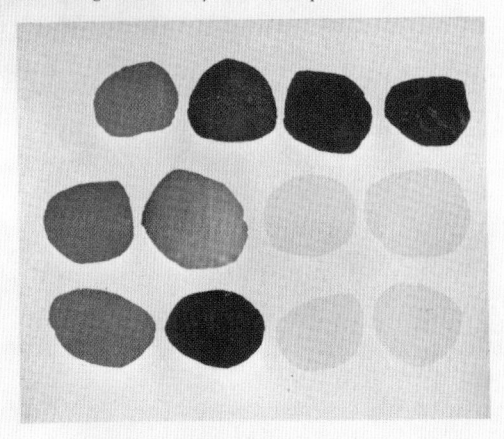

Some of the liveliest and most beautiful graphic design being created today is the loving work of a lively and gifted nun called Sister Mary Corita. A member of the order of the Sisters of the Immaculate Heart of Mary, and professor of art at the Immaculate Heart College in Los Angeles, Sister Mary Corita has won an international reputation for her serigraphs (silk screen prints), many of which hang in our most distinguished art museums. But her art is not just for the cloister, whether of convent or gallery. Her commercial projects include an advertisement for the Container Corporation (below), a line of gift-wrap paper for Neiman-Marcus, the Dallas department store, and some foil wrap for the Reynolds Metals Company. At present she is working on a poster design for New York's trash wagons, as part of the city's clean-up campaign.

If these seem to be renderings unto Caesar, Sister Mary Corita doesn't mind, although it is a distinction she doesn't much concern herself with in her art. Most of her work is joyfully religious, whether it ends up in a liturgical journal or wrapped around a Texan's birthday present. "We have this horrible need to measure everything," she says, "and we are so busy measuring objects that we often miss their true beauty." When asked recently to discuss the distinction between fine art and applied art, she dismissed the matter thoughtfully but quickly with the statement, "I don't think there is one, really."

But it may be as misleading to take one of Sister Mary Corita's remarks out of context as it is to take *her* out of context. Her context—the garden in which her prints, banners, and fame grow—is the Immaculate Heart College art department. This department has developed one of the most widely known and highly praised art curricula in the nation. It is responsible for what is now called "the Immaculate Heart style," a style characterized by nothing so much as the precious individuality of the artist. This in itself is rare enough (just look through any modern art gallery), and it would seem to be impossible to teach (just look through any ordinary college art department). Yet they teach it.

The force of the habit

Dr. Samuel Johnson once said to Boswell: "Sir, a woman preaching is like a dog's walking on his hind legs. It is not done well, but you are surprised to find it done at all." Unquestionably some of Sister Mary Corita's success stems from the same phenomenon: our interest in novelty and incongruity. One is reminded of all the prizefighters — Mickey Walker, Tony Canzoneri, Rocky Graziano—who were publicized as painters not because they had talent, or even much skill, but because it was so remarkable that they painted at all. A nun who creates modern art, some of it commercial art at that, is so curious to behold that, in Sister Mary Corita's case, the shock of her habit tends to obscure how really good she is.

Her serigraphs are at once disciplined and uninhibited, personal without being private, and celebrative in a way that is as unexpectedly catholic as it is expectedly Catholic.

Ralph Caplan

The two wonder cards are from labels for bread wrappers and have an obvious relationship to the kind of action the Spirit specializes in. Fr. Häring says that the Holy Spirit is the principle of wonder.

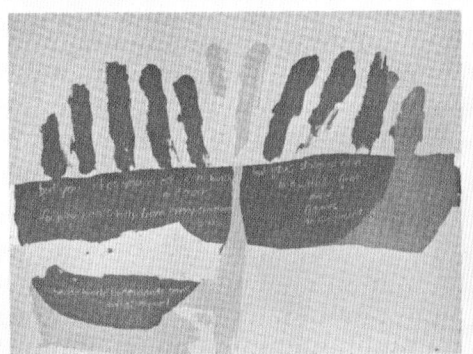

SISTER MARY CORITA, SERIGRAPHS, Comara: The walls are abloom with colored delights, bon-bons of the soul abound. The shapes are unshaped by freedom flowing from the heart — they lilt, they squeak, they scamper, and at times they just sit and jiggle. The colors, light as a breath, clear as a whistle, sassy as a jay, and sometimes ripe, roam the walls. The words—psalms and sayings and parts of poems—file through the colored forests, or duck around the corner just in the nick of time, or glide by with a dignity that is unmindful of all the din. Sister Mary Corita has fielded a team of sprites that say words with pictures that pop questions and each one is an enactment of her own particular, playful celebration. More and more her work defies the usual critical handles, not because it is beyond art in the sense of configuration — she is an enthusiastic borrower of forms — but because her impulse to express soars weightlessly above problems of style. Her mission seems to be to surprise us into awakening to delight, using our eyes like pleasantly greedy children. In these works she does not insist we also use our minds. D.M.

CALIFORNIA GIRLS

Signing for Sea Ranch.

Interior of bath house.

"No, kid, make it happy!"

Mention "Swiss Graphics" to anyone even remotely familiar with design and he is likely to respond with a description consisting of words like severe, cerebral, cold, joyless, refined and/or synonyms thereof.

Swiss-trained supergraphic* designer Barbara Stauffacher Solomon is herself the exact antonym of all those words; and, with the exception of "refined", so is her work.

To be sure, her typographic vocabulary is, with very few deviations, limited to Helvetica; and she does stick to the simple geometric forms that the Swiss school (in this case the *Kunstgewerbeschule* of Basel, Switzerland) insists upon. But it is precisely within this tight circle of discipline that her most successful graphic art is located.

Indeed, it seems as if Mrs. Solomon thrives on limitations. The work for which she is still best known (and for which she recently, and belatedly, was awarded the AIA Industrial Arts Medal) was done in 1966 for Sea Ranch, a chic "r & r" compound for the reasonably well off, located on a wildly beautiful section of northern California coastline.

BSS was commissioned by the architects to bail them out of a potential design disaster. As the budget shrank the bath house did likewise. To this dilemma she brought a few cans of paint, some charcoal to sketch on walls with, and two sign painters.

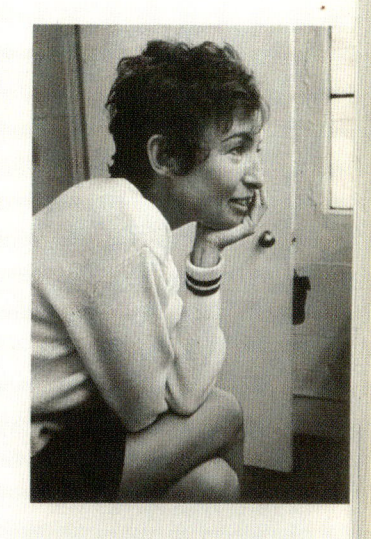

---

*The general style of architectural graphics referred to by this banal and ambiguous term undoubtedly originated with Mrs. Solomon. Happily, another must take discredit for coining the bastard name itself. The fact that it is in wide use only indicates to me that our language, particularly within the specialized dialects, has fallen to a deeper circle of semantic Hell. I have reluctantly used the term here for the questionable purpose of sub-categorization only, and will not offend the reader in that particular manner again.

(Incidentally the designer herself uses the remarkably humble but eloquent term "signing" (after sign painting) when describing some of her work.)

There is another distinction that should be made within this footnote; this one between the *style* of architectural graphics represented by the work of BBS, and the historical precedences for the purposes and applications of the graphics themselves.

In a real sense, architectural graphics preceded architecture (cave paintings), and comes down through time in a continuity unequaled by any other cultural form in history. I won't belabor this beyond pointing out that Pope Julius had precisely the same motives in commissioning Michelangelo as the architects of Sea Ranch had in hiring Mrs. Solomon. Only the scale was different: the ceiling was too big and the bath house was too small.

BARBARA STAUFFACHER SOLOMON

Three days later, according to legend, Sea Ranch was richer by one superbly conceived and executed mural wrapped around the interior of a bath house, and the design groupies had yet another embryonic trend to name and follow.

It occurs to me that a major point has been missed by nearly all of the critics who have written about BSS's work since Sea Ranch. It is simply that she gives her clients an awful lot of invented atmosphere for their money. It's not that she doesn't enjoy, or do a good job for, a client with unlimited funds and space. There aren't too many of that kind floating around, so she has succeeded where most of her colleagues have failed. When handed a lemon she makes damn good lemonade.

Anybody opening up anything, from a state fair to a boutique to a laundromat, in any dumpy, drab setting, can, for a decent fee and an absurdly low investment in time, labor and materials, transform his establishment into an inviting circus of colored circles, stripes, arrows, stars, sexy hearts and gigantic birds—whatever seems right at the time.

And, since it can easily be painted over and revised, it is at once a most viable, powerful and inexpensive form of point-of-purchase/billboard advertising as well. This ephemeral nature of her work is seen by her as a positive value; unusual enough in a field dominated by the vain search for immortality.

There is no evidence of esoteric graphic "Newspeak" about her. Her speech, like her symbols, is simple and candid. She has tempered her talents with graceful humor, pragmatism, pride in her well-learned craft, and a finely honed sense of simplicity.

Mrs. Solomon told me that she really enjoys doing all of the paste-up for the print material which comprises the bulk of her work. "In fact," she said, "I design all of it in finish."

"What happens if a client wants to see a layout?" I asked.

"No one has," she replied.

Dugald Stermer

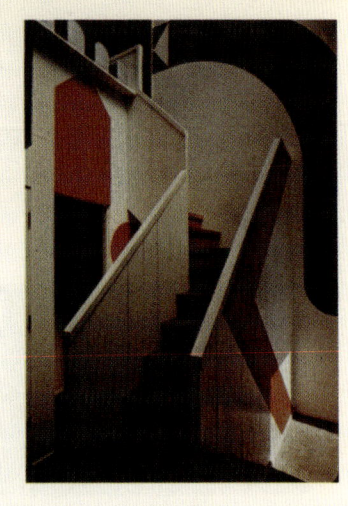

"Whenever I'd ask Sea Ranch's builder, Mattie Silva, if it was getting to be too much, he'd say, 'No, kid, make it happy!'"

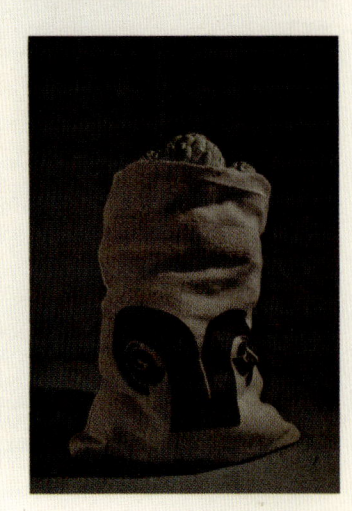

Left: interior views of bath house at Sea Ranch and the logo on burlap bag.

Sea Ranch sheep used in restaurant lounge and mermaid illustration for announcement of events.

Interiors for HearHear Record Store in Ghiradelli Square. Artist's husband, Daniel Solomon, was the architect.

A Feminist Option

By Rose DeNeve

Sheila de Bretteville's evolution as a woman who is a designer has led to her present founding role with the Woman's Building in Los Angeles.

In the languid atmosphere of Los Angeles, Sheila Levrant de Bretteville seems out of place. She is at once serious and vivacious, her wit and energy being carefully directed, her life and work being more a matter of artful discipline than flashy self-indulgence. Nor does her work fit comfortably into any "California school"; rather it reflects the various influences that have shaped her thinking. Indeed, as a spokesperson for the women's movement, and as a founder of and designer for the Woman's Building in Los Angeles, de Bretteville has inextricably bound together her work and her life into the kind of contiguous whole few designers are able to achieve.

But de Bretteville didn't always consider herself a feminist. In her undergraduate years at Barnard, she recalls, despite the fact that it was an all-women's college, the focus of her energy was not the female but the scholarly environment. Her training at Yale and in jobs immediately following reinforced the disciplined and controlled esthetic that had captured her eye since her youth. The work she produced in this time is pure design, employing grids and symbols to relate varying levels of abstract thought; her books and book advertisements use "clean, clear forms that stand for something else," systems of design that are totally supportive of their content. While not denying an interest today in abstract thought, she notes that her work then "meant finding a level of complexity that is hard to make elegant and simple. To some extent," she says, "the esthetic I aspired to was oversimplified. But there was a lot happening then—the primary structure in art was popular, for example—that made what I was doing seem right."

Indeed, timing has had a great import in de Bretteville's development as a designer. Because of her abstract bent, Olivetti hired her to design corporate brochures and advertising in the firm's Milan office, and for the first time she felt a sense of alienation from her studio and her work. "I saw people who had been excited about their work suddenly not care anymore," she recalls. "I saw work being taken from someone who had done the image and saw someone else do the typography, awards being given to the director of the studio and no credit being given to the person who actually generated the idea. I had never seen these things in the U.S. because of the very cultural and supportive environment in which I had grown up as a designer, in which you were given credit the moment you did something in a book, in which your feeling of being responsible was acknowledged. And that acknowledgment of responsibility is very important, especially in the U.S. where we have a very strong individualist training."

De Bretteville was in Milan during a time of serious political upheaval all over the world. In the U.S., Robert Kennedy was assassinated. There were student revolts in Paris and Milan. "I began to feel a stranger at Olivetti," de Bretteville continues, "pushing type around, while down below there were people in the streets. I felt connected with the attitudes of the 'revolution'—I'd heard a lot of fake communism from my colleagues who were talking about the U.S. in deprecating terms and then collecting new fixtures for their Nikons, without validating their own culture's richness. I began to see the complexity between what people say and what people do."

De Bretteville's stint abroad freed up a lot of stereotypes and attitudes for her. She began looking in the streets for other ways to communicate, not to rip off another culture, but to learn more about people and their vernacular forms. "I realized all my references were from art and painting," she notes. What caught her eye in the streets were the brightly colored, inexpensively produced posters used to announce what was going on in the schools and communes. "I had been used to using black and white or very subtle color relationships—the Albersian heritage of Yale. But I saw these posters, so vibrant and full of life, and said, Ah, RED! and YELLOW! Not primary, but that highway safety yellow that's the same all over the world, and that lipstick red. It's as good as black and white. They became my colors."

De Bretteville's work from this point exhibits a surprising number of pieces using "her colors." True, there are still the more formally resolved letterheads and posters with their grids and Garamond and Helvetica, but there are also posters designed on her own time and printed from huge, wooden letterforms in black and yellow and red. "I wondered what my friends in the States were thinking had happened to me in that change," she muses. "The things

---

1. Cover of program/order form for American Symphony Orchestra.
2-8. De Bretteville's designs for Olivetti included advertising for business machines and brochures detailing their application in various industries.

1.

2.

3.

4.

Olivetti Programma 101 in cantiere

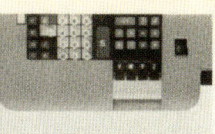

Olivetti Programma 101 nell'ufficio

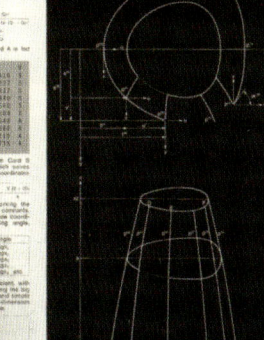

Olivetti Programma 101 nell'officina

Olivetti Programma 101 at SKF Ball Bearing Co.-Göteborg

Olivetti Programma 101 in operation with SAAB Co. Sweden

Olivetti Programma 101 in operation at Götaverken, Shipbuilders and Engineers

5.

6.

7.

8.

> If the designer is to make a deliberate contribution to society, he must be able to integrate all he can learn about behavior and resources, ecology and human needs; taste and style just aren't enough.

For information regarding admission, graduate & undergraduate study, and financial aid write:

School of Design
California Institute of the Arts
2404 West 7th Street
Los Angeles, California 90057

opening fall 1970

9.

California Institute of the Arts: Valencia California 91355

California Institute of the Arts: Admissions Bulletin 1973–1974

10.

California Institute of the Arts: Admissions Bulletin 1973–1974

11.

School of Film/Video

12.

I'd previously sent them were on really incredible paper and really finely printed. But I felt a need to make a statement as a designer about what I believe."

It was this sense of responsibility that de Bretteville brought back with her to the U.S. when she returned with her architect husband, Peter, in 1969. "I was concerned about doing work in which the content spoke about the problems and possibilities I saw in society," she declares. "I wanted to do work that had more content than my work previously. And I was looking for a way to make money at it, since I had to support myself." The prospect of finding someone else—be it designer or corporation—whose content she believed in, and then getting herself hired to give graphic form to that content, was dismal indeed. It was a period when many designers were likewise concerning themselves with the possibility of doing "relevant art," and the opportunities to do so were rare.

Fortunately for de Bretteville, the newly formed California Institute of the Arts was at the same time staffing its Valencia, CA, campus. Conceived in the '60s amidst the first tides of change that swept college campuses, Cal Arts posed a challenge in design education—and a challenge in design thinking. Suddenly, the medium became as or more important than the message; designers and design educators were being asked to examine very carefully every aspect of the communications process. De Bretteville gladly accepted a position.

"It happened at such a potent time," she declares. "I had gained a real understanding of the ways in which one could become connected to or alienated from one's work, and I had participated in the whole '60s reassessment of society. Now I was coming to Cal Arts as a professional designer, and I was being validated for challenging the profession, for asking where it could go, what does it really serve, what do I really want to serve. Here was a content, an effort of trying to build a community, looking for ways to merge the boundaries between the various arts, and to really challenge design in a very basic way—and I was getting paid to do all of these things. It was pretty terrific."

Besides teaching courses in design, de Bretteville was charged with selecting and

13.

14.

**Arts in Society
volume 7 no. 3
fall-winter 1970
2 dollars
California Institute
of the Arts: Prologue
to a Community**

15.

9. De Bretteville's designs while at California Institute of the Arts were geared to what she calls "mass reproduction of the vernacular sort." This poster is lightweight packaging cardboard, printed in yellow and orange, with three-dimensional objects shrink-wrapped in. It cost less to produce than the same poster conventionally printed.

10-12. 1974 Cal Arts admissions bulletin is a pocket book printed on newsprint.

13-15. Spreads and cover from Arts in Society magazine, which de Bretteville guest-edited and designed. Subject was founding of Cal Arts as an artists' community; limitations were three: the book had to be produced for one dollar per copy, had to measure 7" by 10" and could weigh no more than 15 ounces. De Bretteville designed a splashy, mixed-media magazine with a corrugated cover, the totality of which she felt represented the challenge of Cal Arts.

16. Poster/envelope sent to design schools to announce Cal Arts advance study program. Inside envelope is plentiful supply of return order cards for information and applications, to be used by interested students.

16.

California Institute of the Arts

Advanced Study

Scene Design

Technical

Print

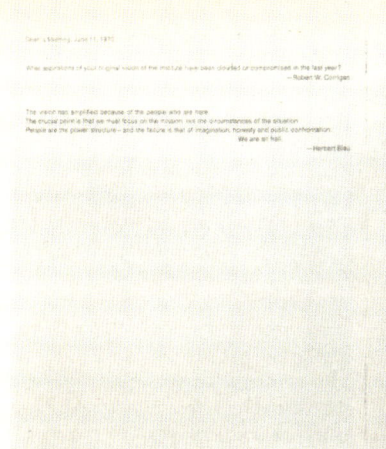

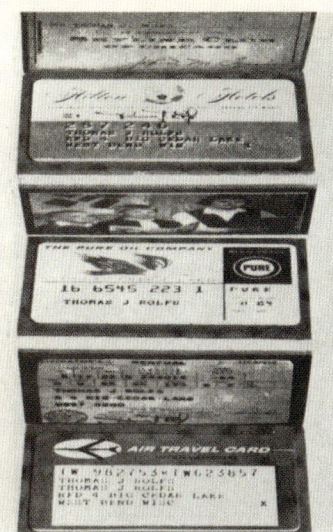

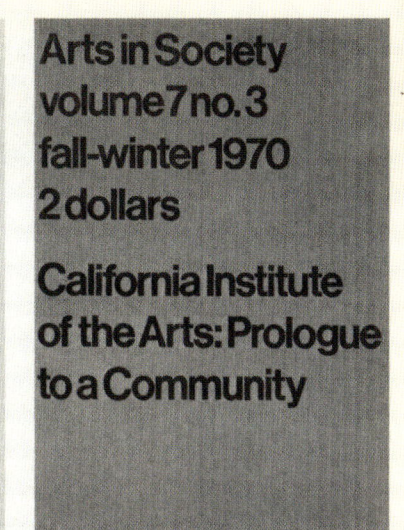

17. *Designs executed by de Bretteville as director of the Woman's Building in Los Angeles bear a feminist consciousness. This poster announces a conference entitled "Women in Design," makes use of a tooled object—the eye bolt—which is explicitly feminist.*

18. *De Bretteville designed this poster at the invitation of the AIGA to appear in a show whose theme was "Color." She chose pink because she wanted the poster to be feminist; she divided the poster into 30 squares, which she gave away to other women in order to see their reactions to this traditionally "feminine" color—and she reassembled their responses to make a statement for them all.*

purchasing equipment and furnishings for the school's workshops and studios, designing the school's graphics, and devising a curriculum. In all of these roles, she welcomed her position as a challenger of the status quo. "If someone told me, Sheila, we need publicity for this event," she continues, "I could say, do I believe in that event? Should that event take place? Should that publicity take the form of a radio announcement, or a performance in public centers, or is it a poster? If it's a poster, what size does it need, who is the audience, what printing processes are appropriate to it? It allowed me to ask questions much farther back down the line in the communication process."

The fruits of de Bretteville's explorations are self-evident. When she was asked to design a poster about the Cal Arts design school to be sent to other colleges, and there were to be 15,000 printed, she had the latitude to use the mass-production methods employed by supermarket packagers. Thus, she produced a two-color, three-dimensional, shrink-wrapped poster costing less than the same poster printed on paper. It was what de Bretteville calls plugging into "mass-production methods of the vernacular sort," rather than fine art production methods.

As Cal Arts changed its policies and reverted to a more traditionally structured design school, de Bretteville became aware that there were elements in Cal Arts' very structure that would prevent it from being the progressive enclave it had set out to be. Moreover, as the school's values and point of view changed, so would the context of de Bretteville's work—and hence its meaning. She became concerned with her precarious position as a designer whose livelihood was solely at the whim of the school's hiring and firing politics, and more and more wanted to be a controlling factor in the structure that made the context of her work.

Again, timing was on de Bretteville's side. During this period of growing alienation from Cal Arts came a connection with the women's movement. In 1971, she founded the Women's Design Program at Cal Arts, and began a period of feminist examination culminating in the founding of the Woman's Building in Los Angeles with artists Arlene Raven and Judy Chicago. "I learned a lot about myself," she says, "and

19.

about how I had been seeing women professionals in the past, about what kind of woman professional I wanted to be myself, and how I could modify my choices." The decision to leave Cal Arts and work full time at the Building was a matter of evolution.

That the Woman's Building—a learning and doing center primarily for women but not sexually exclusive—happened in Los Angeles was a matter of the fortunate joining of many independent forces. There was first the heritage of risk-taking endemic to California since the '60s, and the concomitant optimism that risk-taking will succeed. Women artists had already begun to organize in Los Angeles, essentially to get their work shown, and in a very vocal way. Their collusion as artists and women gave the movement a good deal of positive energy—and the motivating force to hurdle the obstacles confronted in such an undertaking.

At last de Bretteville was a team member whose vision helped shape the "product" and whose job it was to give graphic expression to the product. Her duties included finding and buying equipment—a cause to which she donated her first year's salary—and planning use of space in the Building's three loft floors. She also designed graphics and signing for the Building's entrance/reception area, and she continues to produce posters and announcements of various Building events between teaching classes in photography and graphics in the Building's Feminist Studio Workshop.   *Continued on page 88*

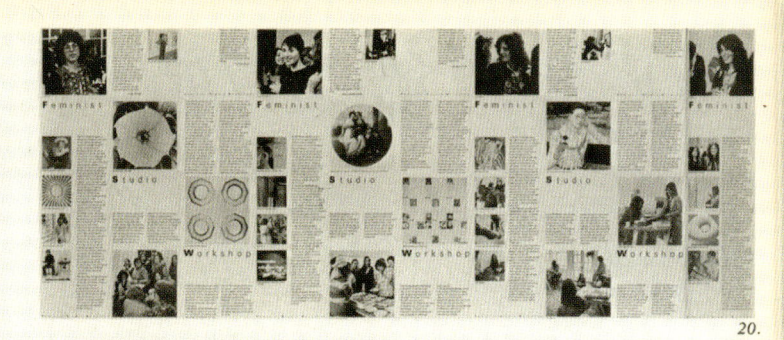

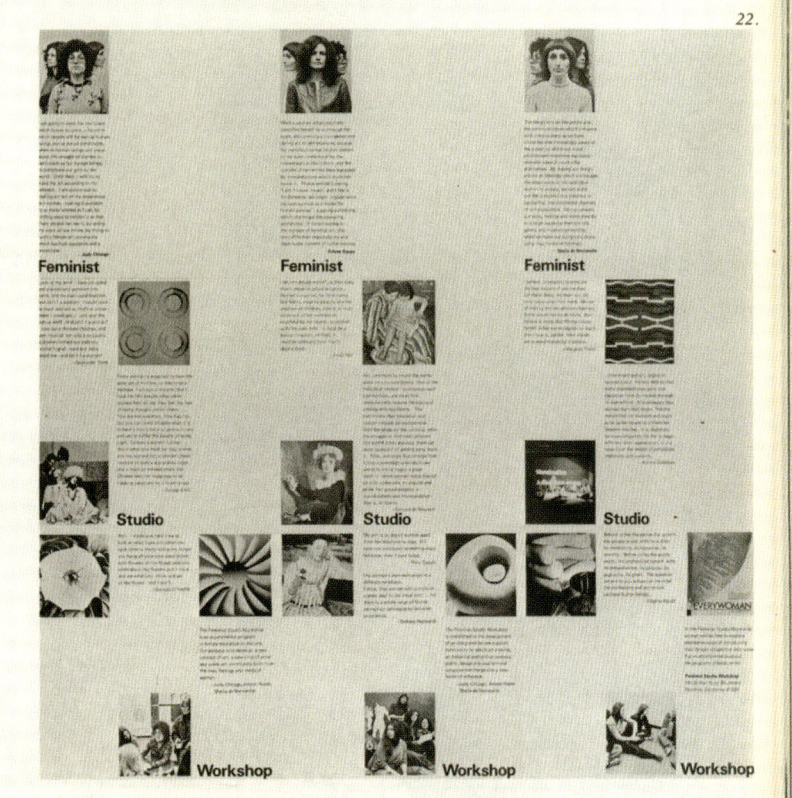

20.
21.
22.

19. Reception area of the Woman's Building is purposely low key. Wall graphics, designed by de Bretteville and painted with student Cher Martin, are executed in pinks and lavenders, read "The Woman's Building, a public center for women's culture, welcomes you." De Bretteville is third from left.

20-22. Promotion posters for the Woman's Building and the Feminist Studio Workshop.

59   Print

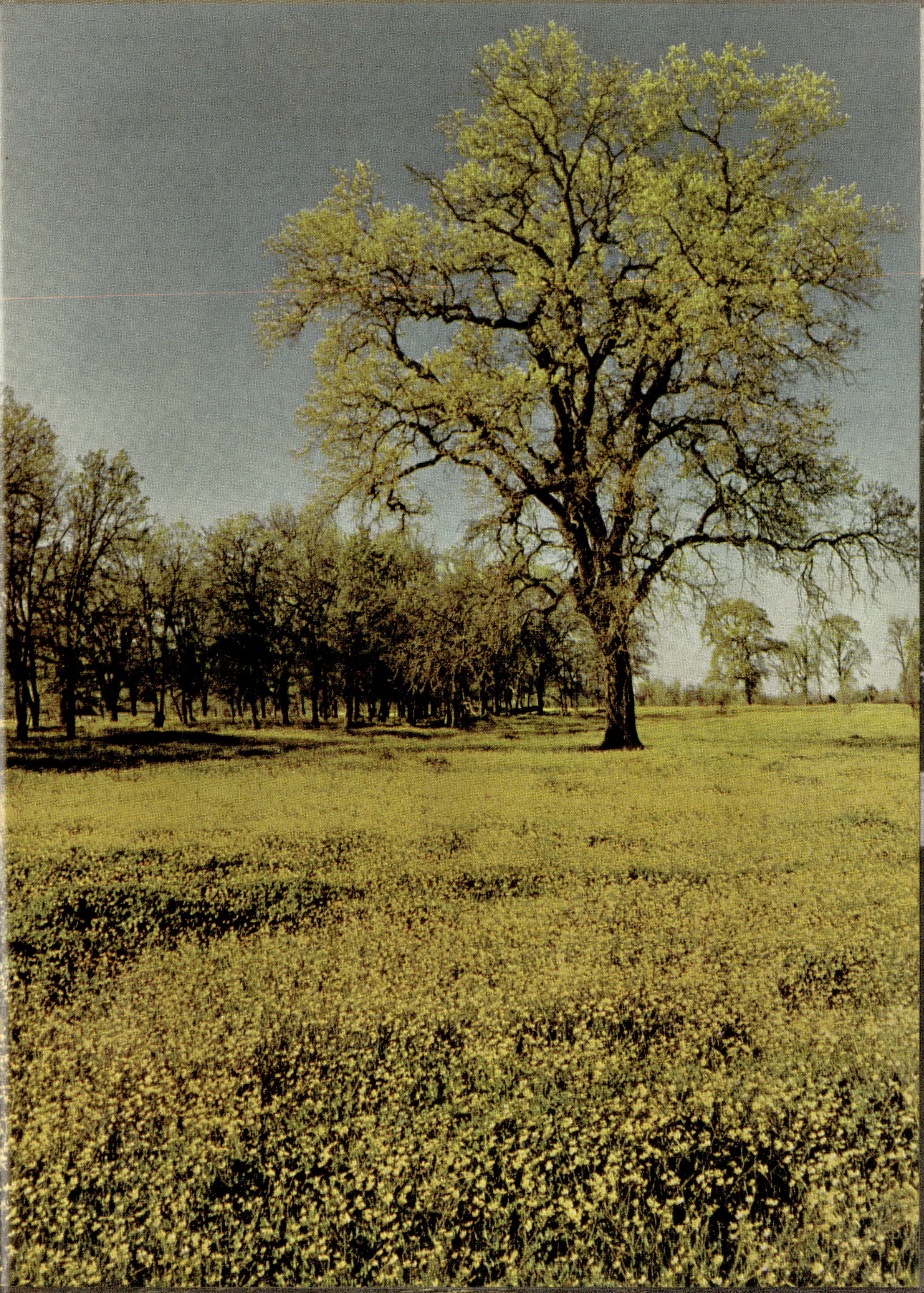

↑ Deborah Sussman (left) at the
Eames Office, mid-1950s
← "In Sutter County [Central Valley],
acres of golden buttercups,"
from Beautiful California, 1971

Grace Richardson Clements [1905–1969]. COMMUNICATION (AVIATION AND NAVIGATION) MOSAICS, DRAWING SHOWING LAYOUT OF MOSAICS ON FLOOR, AND MURALS, LONG BEACH AIRPORT, 1942.

Artist, designer, critic, and California native Grace Clements was a founding member of the Postsurrealists, a contrarian art movement. In the group's manifesto, titled "New Content–New Form," published in the leftist journal Art Front in March 1936, she argued for art to address social concerns not through academic formalism but through a language ordinary people could understand. To this end, she advised artists to emulate the populist techniques of movies.[1] Clements was also a prolific contributor to Arts & Architecture, the Los Angeles–based magazine that helped bring global attention to West Coast art, architecture, and design from 1929 until 1967. ¶ Her elaborate Works Progress Administration project for the Long Beach Airport involved ceramic mosaics on the floors and painted murals on the walls, which together occupied more than 4,300 square feet.[2] Art historian Michael Duncan describes the murals as centering on themes of land, water, and air, with interlocking areas depicting technical equipment, maps, scientific diagrams, and landscape, as well as methods of transportation and communication including ships, aircraft, and the telephone. This combination of motifs, says Duncan, echoed the early experimental film technique of montageand thus infused the murals with the spirit of Postsurrealism.[3]

CALIFORNIA GIRLS 341

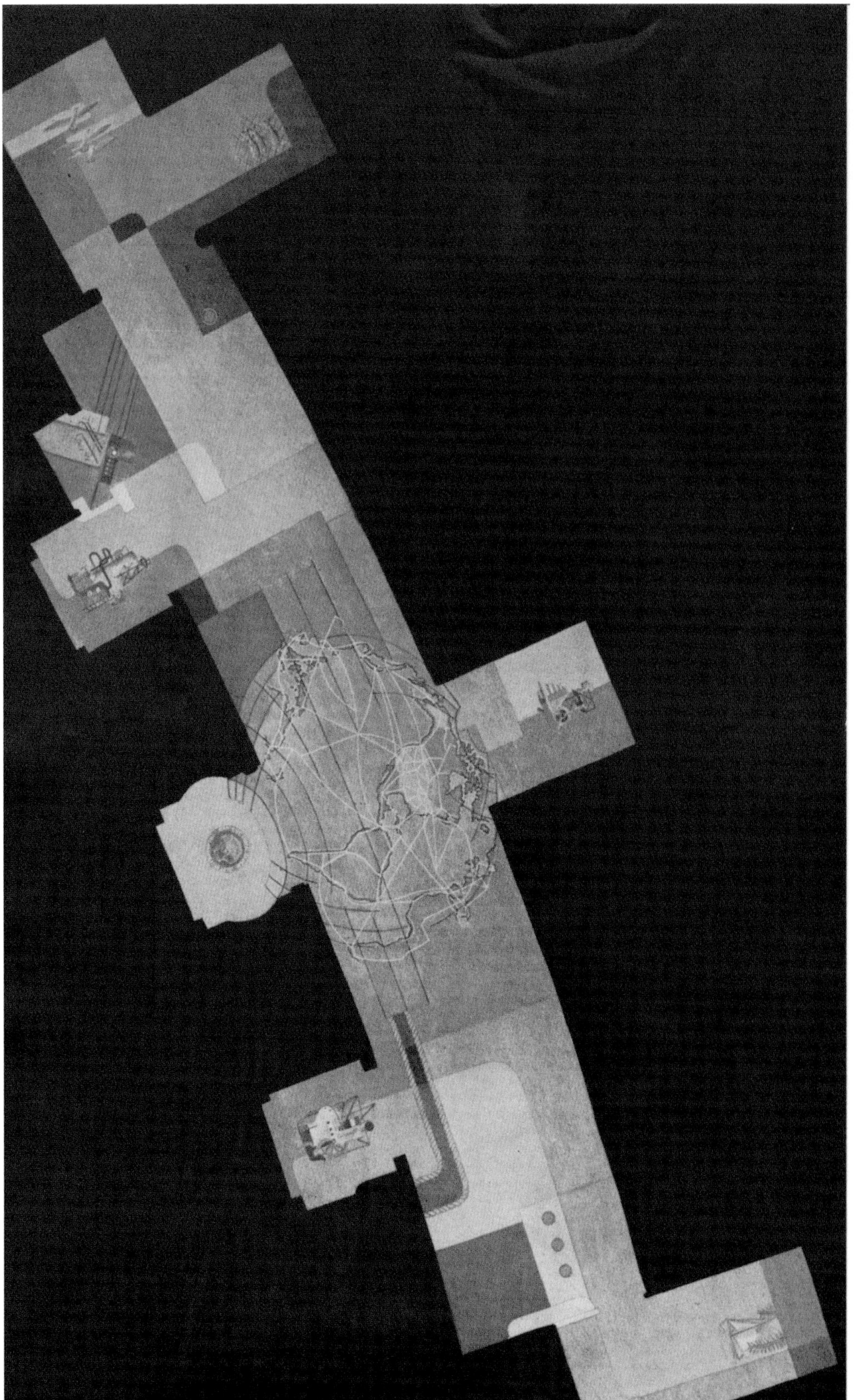

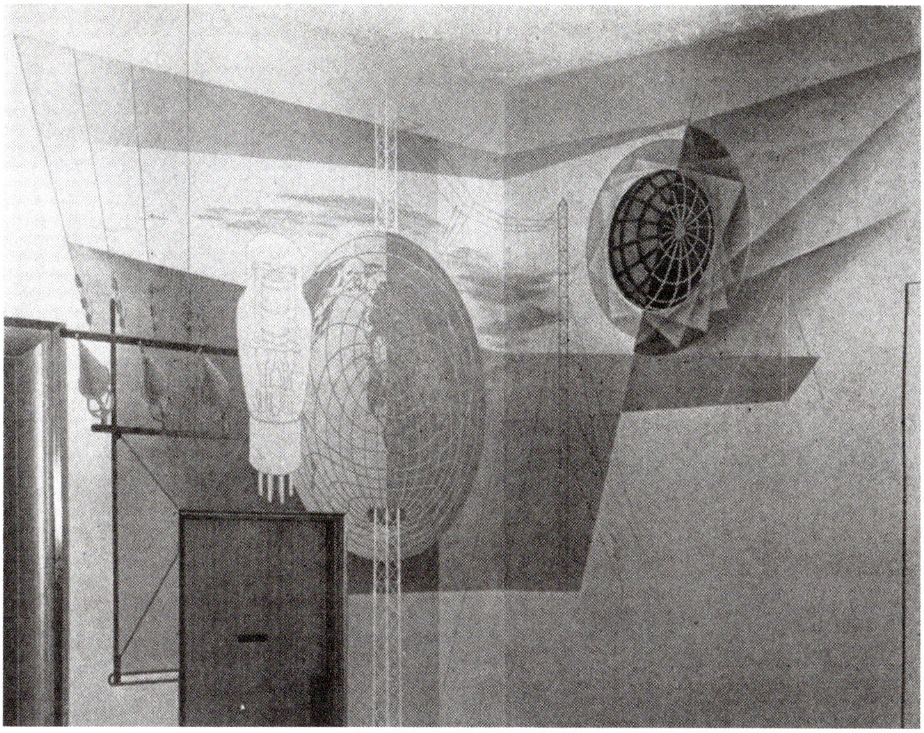

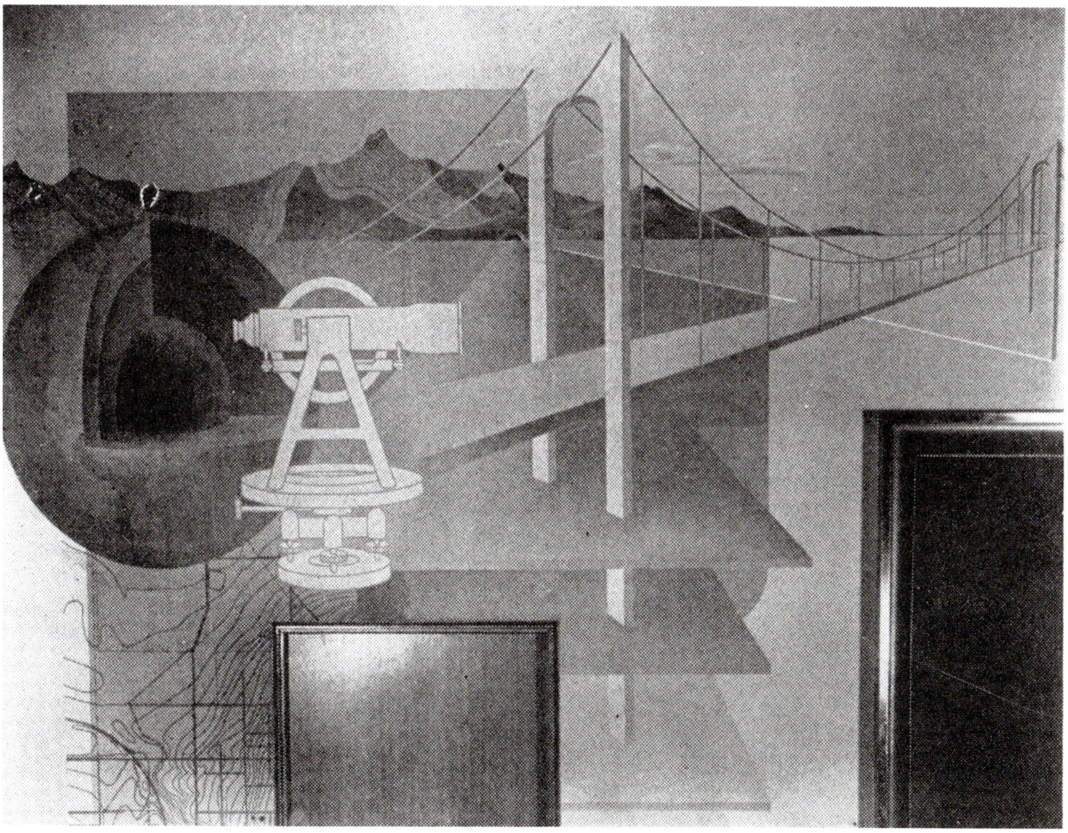

Ray Kaiser Eames [1912–1988]. For many years, people assumed Ray Eames was Charles Eames's brother. And despite all obvious indications of her importance, it wasn't until Pat Kirkham's 1995 biography, Charles and Ray Eames: Designers of the Twentieth Century, that Ray's role in the Eames studio and her contributions to design became more widely understood. Although originally interested in engineering, Bernice "Ray" Kaiser studied painting with Hans Hoffmann in New York.[4] With a commitment to modernism, she next attended Cranbrook Academy, in Bloomfield Hills, Michigan, where the curriculum combined handcraft with industrial forms of production. There, she met Charles Eames (on a fellowship at the time but eventually an instructor and a collaborator of Cranbrook's president, architect Eliel Saarinen). The couple married and, in the summer of 1941, moved to Ray's native California. They saw Los Angeles as a place where they could enjoy a casual lifestyle and where, free of the social and professional distractions of their community back in Michigan, they could focus on their work.[5] ¶ **ARTS & ARCHITECTURE COVER, MARCH 1947, 10 x 12¾ IN.** This was the penultimate cover Ray Eames conceived for Arts & Architecture; in total, she designed 26, some during the magazine's early incarnation as California Arts & Architecture.[6] It departs from her earlier covers, which featured more drawn or painted imagery, collage, biomorphic shapes, and/or combinations of these approaches, sometimes with the inclusion of hastily hand-drawn type. This one also marks the end of Ray's solo graphic design work, before she turned her exclusive focus toward collaborations with Charles.[7]
¶ **SEA THINGS SKETCH AND PRINTED FABRIC, 1945.** Ray submitted this design to the Museum of Modern Art's 1947 "Competition for Printed Fabrics." MoMA gave it an honorable mention, and in the early 1950s Waverly Products used the motif for a serving tray

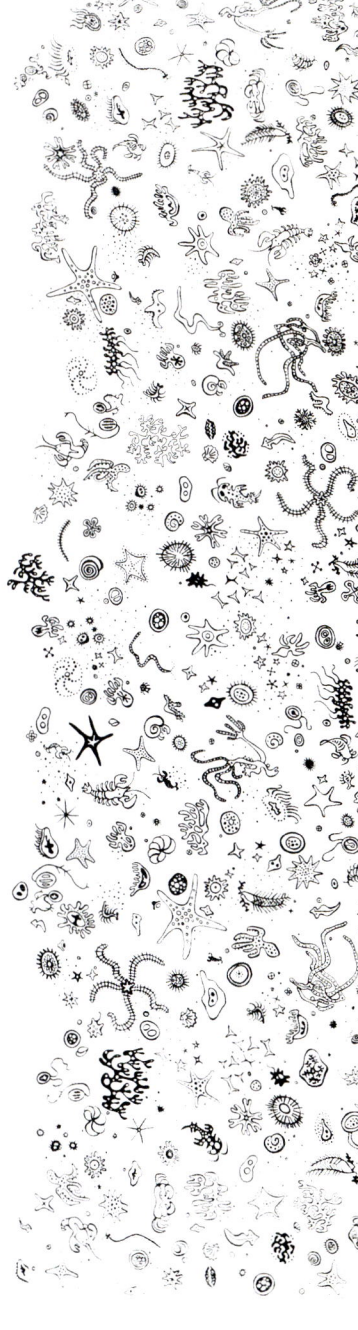

CALIFORNIA GIRLS

345

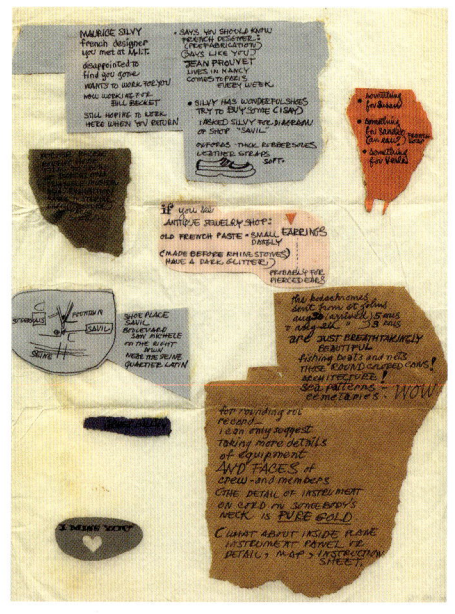

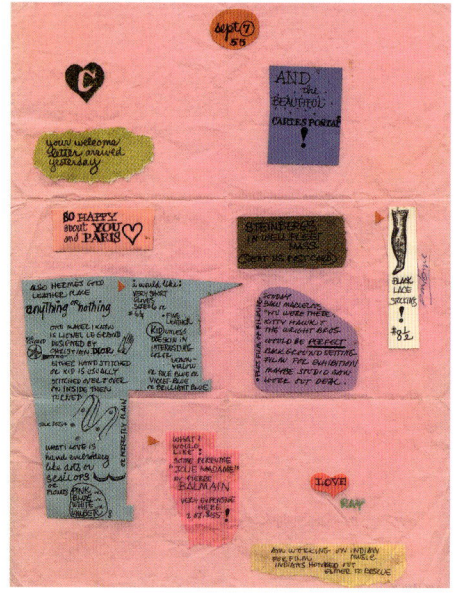

in various color combinations. Unlike her other fabric designs, many of which were produced commercially, this one employs organic, natural shapes with a complex charm and whimsy. ¶ **LETTERS TO CHARLES EAMES,** ABOVE, **1955;** RIGHT, **1953. EACH 8½ x 11 IN.** With her sharp eye for color, shape, texture, letterforms, and composition, Ray also applied a loving hand to her many activities and creations, professional or personal. These letters to Charles are just one such example.

Dearest C

happy happy happy happy happy happy happy happy

o june 17th

of 1953

to the BIRTHDAY CHILD
who · can · do · no · wrong

goes All Love and Honours and HUGS + KISSES

Marget Larsen [1922–1982] **and Betty Brader** [1923–1986]. **"EYE SHADE!" AD FOR JOSEPH MAGNIN DEPARTMENT STORE, LATE 1950s OR EARLY 1960s.** Design historian Steve Reoutt remembers that every few years, Larsen would reinvent her look, becoming "a completely different person." One year, her hair was black, shiny, and short; the next, it might be long and blond.[8] The Bay Area–native saw this mobility of personae as a way of acting and being in the world, and she applied this approach to her design projects, too. In the 1950s, she took a job at Joseph Magnin—or JM, as it came to be known—the "hip" department store that was responding to, if not helping to create, the mod, young, postwar, baby-boomer consumer. Larsen was hired by JM's visionary founder, Cyril Magnin (a renegade scion of the more staid I. Magnin department store), who teamed her with in-house advertising manager Toni Harley and illustrator Betty Brader. Together, they transformed bland, tasteful retail fashion advertising into bold, colorful, dynamic ads that made both shoppers and designers look twice. The threesome answered to no one—not even Cyril Magnin himself—in terms of which merchandise to push or how to do it. Whim, fancy, and inspiration ruled. Larsen left JM in 1964 to work independently, collaborating on rebellious visions for commercial and activist messages with admen Howard Gossage and Robert Freeman. The team created irreverent, long-winded ads that flouted the current trend for big pictures with snappy slogans.
¶ This JM mascara ad features a drawing by Brader using the striking visage of Larsen during one of her many incarnations, this time, dark haired and green lashed. The women's memorable graphic compositions garnered praise from the design community and the fashion trade and were prized, pinned-up, and republished by their many fans.

altogether now
everybody
put on their
EYE
SHADE!

the best thing
since the invention
of eyelashes!
REVLON'S
revolutionary
new eye shade
ROLL ON
it's a mascara that
you actually roll on
your lashes. but,
perish the thought,
once it's applied
it won't 'roll off'
(it's waterproof)
comes in a handsome
'gold' case. and in
addition to the
green eye shade
it's available also in
black, light brown,
dark brown, light
blue, and dark blue.
2.00 plus federal tax
in all joseph magnin
cosmetic
departments

JOSEPH MAGNIN

25!!!

JM JOSEPH MAGNIN

XMAS

M MERRY

CHRISTMAS

XXXX
OOOO

CALIFORNIA GIRLS

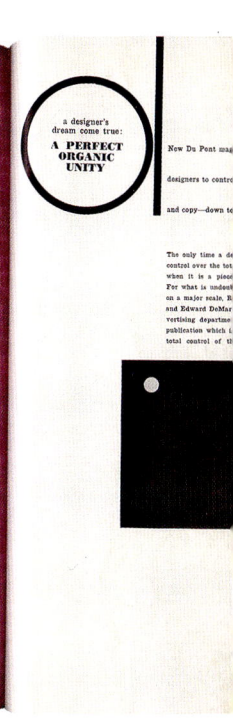

351

Marget Larsen. PAGES 350–51, LEFT: **JM CHRISTMAS WRAPPING PAPER, 1963;** RIGHT, BOTTOM: **JM CHRISTMAS BOXES, MID-1960s.** At first, there were concerns about the possible expense of this new-fangled Christmas packaging, but it turns out Larsen's innovation was economic as well as formal: her designs halved the cost of the store's usual boxes. And, as JM manager and Magnin family member Walter Newman remembers, the campaign "took off like a rocket. People just adored these things, and they came in to buy the merchandise just to get the boxes, to put the boxes under their Christmas trees." PAGE 351, TOP: **DUPONT "COLOR ON COLORED STOCK," TWO-SIDED AD FOR PRINT, 1959, 9 x 12 IN.** RIGHT: **"IT'S A LEG WATCHER'S YEAR!" FULL-PAGE JOSEPH MAGNIN AD, 1967**

Joseph Magnin
FIRST, SHORTER SKIRTS, MORE LEG IN VIEW. NOW, FASHION BRIGHTENS THE PICTURE EVEN FURTHER WITH VIVID OPAQUE
HUDSON HOSIERY'S NUDE-HEELED, SEAMLESS PURPLE, GREEN, GOLD, NAVY, RED, MAROON, WHITE AND OFF-WHITE ONES
IT'S A LEG WATCHER'S YEAR!
4.00

PRETTY, PLEASE. ALEXANDRA DE MARKOFF is romantically inclined. her new concept couture make-up complements fashion's newly found fondness for the fragile lady look. she begins by brightening lips deliciously with three new lipsticks: couture pink, a delectable bon-bon, couture red, a luscious raspberry, and couture orange, not-quite pumpkin, not-quite mango, but quite, quite wearable, 3.50. she makes eyes light up softly with couture shadowcreme, either paled, whitened couture blue or brightened couture green packaged with the subtlest neutral, couture taupe, 5.00. and she continues giving the entire face a most delicate air with the illuminating countess isserlyn make-ups, 20.00, 30.00 and 50.00. for the prettiest look of the year, pretty please visit alexandra de markoff's personal emissary, miss mildred gay, tomorrow through friday in the jm cosmetic salon, first floor, stockton and o'farrell. for further enhancement, look to the jm jewelry's variety of neck encirclers, 3.00 to 12.00, and the big-news wrist enveloper 10.00. **JOSEPH MAGNIN**

LEFT: Marget Larsen and Betty Brader. "PRETTY, PLEASE," FULL-PAGE JOSEPH MAGNIN NEWSPAPER AD, 1967. JM's dynamic graphics helped take the store to a new level of hipness, and its unique design signature set a high bar for the competition. Art director Larsen, with her boundary-pushing vision, was responsible, as was fashion illustrator Brader, with her bold drawings. ¶ **ABOVE: Betty Brader. CAL TJADER QUINTET ALBUM COVER, 1956, 12⅜ x 12⅜ IN.** Self-taught, Brader started her career in Los Angeles working for various department stores and other clients before joining the JM team in the 1960s.

Sister Corita Kent [1918–1986]. <u>BE, OF LOVE, (A LITTLE) MORE CAREFUL, THAN OF EVERYTHING, 1967. EACH APPROX. 18 x 15 IN.</u> Introduced to silk screening at the University of Southern California in 1951, Corita quickly earned acclaim for dense, color-laden compositions of religious iconography that departed radically from the usual Christian-themed depictions of crucifixes and Madonnas. In 1954, she began to combine typographic elements in the form of inspirational phrases—religious and secular—with her formally sensitive and playfully abstract imagery. Artist Ben Shahn declared that she "joyously revolutionized all type design."[9] As for her style, it seemed inspired early on by a folk vernacular, surely reinforced by the folk art she and her teaching colleague and mentor at Immaculate Heart College, Sister Magdalen Mary Martin, voraciously collected, not only because they could afford it but also because they loved the humble acts of its producers.[10] Yet to come would be the revelation of including another vernacular—that of advertising. Corita took this flotsam and jetsam of daily life and invested its seemingly banal messages with the spiritual and profound. She also was deeply influenced by Charles Eames, whom she credited with inspiring her to live out the Balinese credo "We have no art, we do everything as well as we can" and to make connections between unrelated ideas.

BE OF LOVE (A LITTLE) MORE CAREFUL THAN OF EVERYTHING

CALIFORNIA GIRLS

PHOTOGRAPH OF MARY'S DAY EVENT, 1964. COMMENT NEWSPAPER SPREAD DESIGNED BY SISTER CORITA KENT'S STUDENT DIAN COBLENTZ, 1964, 17 x 22 IN. As a teacher, Sister Corita inspired many in Los Angeles and beyond with her nonjudgmental approach to what constituted art and her sense that passion and curiosity ruled art-making. When, in 1961, she took over Immaculate Heart's annual Mary's Day event, she transformed a staid May Day church procession into a counterculture-style happening, with flower-bedecked and colorfully dressed participants carrying equally colorful placards. In 1964, she introduced pop graphics into the Mary's Day signage in the form of appropriated images from food packaging and marketing; this coincided with the event's sounding a new political note, with a plea for peace and for feeding the hungry. ¶ Corita's use of food packaging and concern for "the stuff of life" is echoed in this spread for the school's newspaper, Comment, designed by Coblentz, one of her students, for Mary's Day 1964. Coblentz used a set of Helvetica rubber stamps that Corita had purchased in Italy, along with hand-lettering and layout skills acquired in Corita's class. Considered an example of the artist-nun's activities and influence, Coblentz's layout was reproduced, as seen here, in the December 1965 issue of Motive, a progressive Methodist magazine for which Corita designed the cover, as well as in the catalogue for daisy with all the petals yes, an exhibition of Corita's printmaking held at the Municipal Art Gallery, Los Angeles, in 1966.[11]

AND THE VIRGIN HAS BORN A GIVEN PEACE TO THE WORLD

the function of such a day
is to provide a day of no functioning
a day of general feasting and rejoicing
a day of being with our friends
for one day to show ourselves
as a visible community
on a campus marked with extra colors
and extra sounds
a community playing
and singing
and worshipping
and feasting
after which we go back to our work
refreshed and inspirited

it is also a day to pull loose ends
together
about the theme of the school year

PACEM IN TERRIS

an earthly peace
(this will on earth is worked by men)

to make this more tangible
we focus on food
in our own market places
where the stuff of life is sold
and bought
we take time out to celebrate
the ordinary stuff of life

WE LIFT THE COMMON STUFF — GROCERIES AND SIGNS ABOUT GROCERIES — OUT OF THE EVERY DAY

and give it a place
in our celebration

when we put them back
into our everyday life
they will be somehow ennobled
on our grocery shelves

HAPPY ARE THOSE WHO MAKE

CHILD WHO IS GOD AND MAN — GOD HAS BY UNITING IN HIMSELF HEAVEN AND EARTH — ALLELUIA

and in our kitchens
when we see them every day
they will remind us
of this good day
and our good Lord
and heaven and earth
will not be so far apart
for us

ORDINARY THINGS WILL BE SIGNS FOR US

of our neighbor's needs
of our own responsibility
as Christ's now
to be concerned
of gratitude
for our plenty
of our need for
daily bread
and of a heavenly Father
who provides

we bring food
and carry it in a friendly walk
and place it around the altar
a way of giving our life
is giving away what makes our life
our gift of ourselves thru our food
is taken during the mass
and changed into the Body of Christ
and given back to us
as new food
to nourish a divine life in us
this is why we call the mass a banquet
at the last supper
Christ gathered his friends
to feast with him
a sign of brotherliness
and said do this

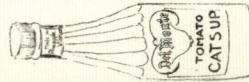

on may 19th
we gather together
to celebrate the mass
Christ invites us to
a banquet
and helps us
worship the Father
in the spirit
of love

and we extend
this feast

TO OUR ORDINARY EATING

keeping the two connected

after lunch
we will see
in our own times
art
a film
to experience how great
a power
is love
in the midst of great hunger
and poverty

at the end of the day
we will take the
food
not eaten at mass
to people who need it
in the centers
where IHC students
have been working
this year
to St Vibiana's
and St Thomas
and Watts

SONS OF GOD

PEACE FOR THEY WILL BE KNOWN AS

Marilyn Neuhart. HANDMADE DOLLS FOR TEXTILES & OBJECTS, 1960–67, 3–14 IN. TALL. Neuhart began making these dolls in 1957, first for her sons and nieces and then for friends. Initially simple forms, they became more embellished over the next few years, and it was one of these later dolls that Neuhart gave to Ray Eames, her husband's employer, for Christmas in 1959. According to Neuhart, Eames declared in a letter the following September that "Sandro has to see these for the T&O shop!"—a reference to designer Alexander Girard, who was preparing to open his legendary New York–based store, Textiles & Objects, which combined folk art and other handmade goods with the modern designs of the Michigan-based Knoll company. Girard responded by asking Neuhart to create a hundred dolls in time for Christmas. Shocked at first by the size of the order, Marilyn agreed, with the understanding that each doll would be different. She met her deadline and the dolls sold out, becoming popular enough to appear in many magazine articles and—in the highest form of flattery—be copied by other producers. Eventually, Neuhart developed 19 different dolls. ¶ During the late 1950s and through the '60s, she continued to produce dolls in her home studio while running a small graphic design practice, the Hand Press, with her husband, John (who worked in the Eames Office until 1961). In 1980, they opened Neuhart Donges Neuhart, offering graphic- and exhibition design services for corporate and cultural clients until the end of the decade.[12] **PAGES 362–63: "CALIFORNIA SANTA," CA. 1959, 12¼ x 15½ IN. (NEVER PUBLISHED); GALLERY PROMENADE POSTER AND INVITATION FOR JUNIOR ART COUNCIL, LOS ANGELES COUNTY MUSEUM OF ART, MID-1960s, 11¾ x 17½ IN.**

CALIFORNIA GIRLS

noel noel noel

THE JUNIOR ART COUNCIL OF THE LOS ANGELES COUNTY MUSEUM OF ART
CORDIALLY INVITES YOU TO A

GALLERY PROMENADE

ON LA CIENEGA BOULEVARD

SPECIAL EXHIBITIONS AND SELECTIONS FROM PRIVATE COLLECTIONS - COCKTAILS - MUSIC - REFRESHMENTS

SUNDAY, MAY FIFTH 5-9:00 PM

$7.50 PER PERSON - TAX DEDUCTIBLE

RESERVATIONS CLOSE APRIL 29th

Gere Kavanaugh [b. 1929]. **GERE KAVANAUGH HOME, LOS ANGELES, LATE 1970s.** Kavanaugh recalls her father registering her at the Memphis College of Art like this: "He turned to me—and I will never forget it…—and he said, 'I don't expect you to do anything with this, but I do expect your life to be enriched.' And it has."[13] She went on to attend Cranbook Academy, and became the third woman to receive a master's in fine art from that venerable institution. Kavanaugh then worked for architect Eero Saarinen on a project for real estate developer and architect Victor Gruen, which led to a choice of plum jobs: one with Saarinen in Detroit, another with Gruen in Los Angeles. Kavanaugh went west, a decision influenced by something like divine intervention. She had met artists Sister Corita Kent and Sister Magdalen Mary Martin at a barbeque back in her hometown of Memphis. When she traveled to Los Angeles on Gruen's dime to consider his job offer, she rang up the nuns. Their response to her call: Hello, how are you? Do you have a job out here? We have a house for you. And so Gere—pronounced "Jerry"—moved, ignoring the concerns of some her friends. As one of them later quipped, "If the earthquakes don't get you, the mudslides will. And if not that, it's the fires and the riots."[14] ¶ Kavanaugh, imaginative and skilled in all realms of design—product, interior, textile, exhibition, graphic—whether mass-produced or handcrafted, festooned her L.A. residence, which also served as her studio, with products she designed, crafts by native producers (particularly from Latin America), and her own decorative wall treatments in nooks and around doors and windows. Around the telephone nook, she used rubber stamps to create leaves, which she then outlined in black marker. For her bedroom, she appliquéd fabric with black felt and metal buttons.[15]

CALIFORNIA GIRLS

ABOVE: TOYS BY ROY, ALBUQUERQUE, NEW MEXICO, CA. 1961. Kavanaugh designed the graphics and interiors for this store, part of the Winrock Shopping Mall, for her employer, architect Victor Gruen—a pioneer of mall develoment. **RIGHT, TOP: TOYS BY ROY WRAPPING PAPER, CA. 1961.** Graphics that Kavanaugh created for the store include this paper design. She cut the shapes out of tire rubber and then glued them onto plywood to create the pattern. The design was later produced as a fabric—one of many textiles that Kavanaugh designed and for which she was celebrated. **RIGHT, BOTTOM: BOB MITCHELL DESIGNS, LOS ANGELES, WALLPAPER, CA. 1970.** To produce this design for the fashionable wallpaper company, Kavanaugh cut the individual flowers from paper; these were used to create screens for printing using a silk-screening process, with each blossom printed in a different color to create the overlapping composition.[16]

CALIFORNIA GIRLS

Barbara Stauffacher Solomon [b. 1928]. **MONTHLY CALENDARS FOR SAN FRANCISCO MUSEUM OF MODERN ART, 1965–71, 7 x 7 IN.; 21 x 28 IN. UNFOLDED.** A second-generation California native, Solomon fled the Golden State in the 1950s. She needed a break from the familiarity and expectations of the land of promise and was grieving the death of her first husband, Frank Stauffacher (whose SFMOMA Art in Cinema series helped introduce experimental film to the West Coast). She found solace and a graphic design education in Switzerland, where she studied with modernism evangelist Armin Hofmann. When she returned to the United States, she brought with her the Swiss font Helvetica, ubiquitous today but a stark contrast back then to the serif fonts favored in San Francisco for their nostalgic appeal. Yet Solomon was not really interested in the one-style-fits-all orthodoxy of that storied typeface; she chose instead to experiment, through pristine hand-drawn letters, with how the look of a word might change its meaning. ¶ **PAGES 370–71: THE SEA RANCH, ATHLETIC CLUB INTERIOR GRAPHICS AND EXTERIOR SIGNAGE, SEA RANCH, CALIFORNIA, 1966–67.** The supergraphics that began to appear in the late '60s—billboard-scale designs applied to architectural surfaces to produce volume-expanding optical effects—were among the many formal expressions of the changing times. Architectural critic and historian C. Ray Smith, who coined the term, was emphatic about the significance of supergraphics as spatially disruptive, writing that the technique was "not a decorative device, repeat, not a decorative device."[17] Solomon is considered one of the first to introduce supergraphics, a strategy that marked an early and radical postmodern

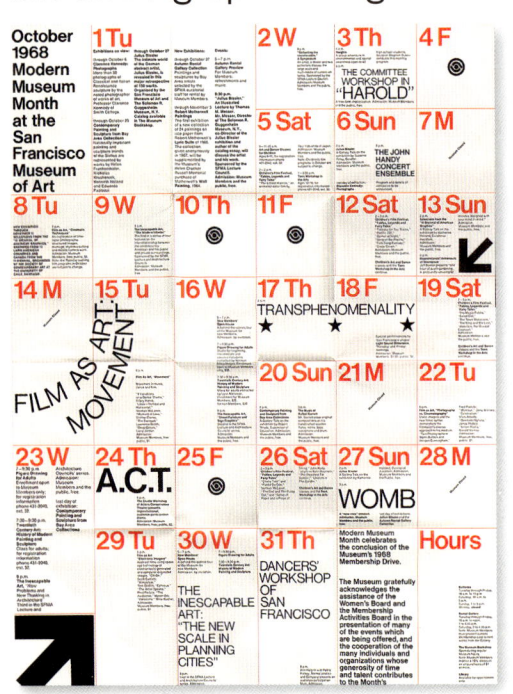

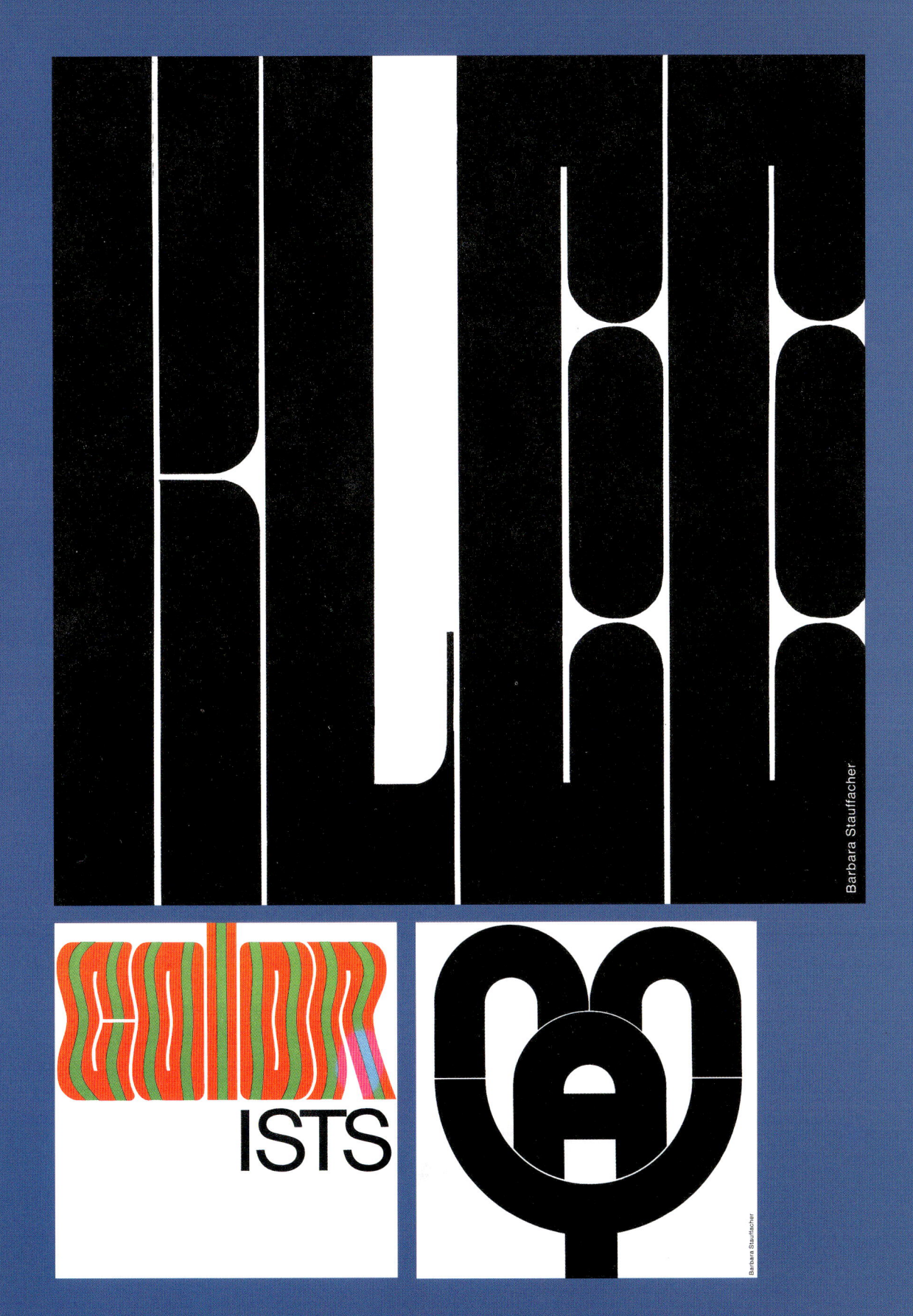

CALIFORNIA GIRLS

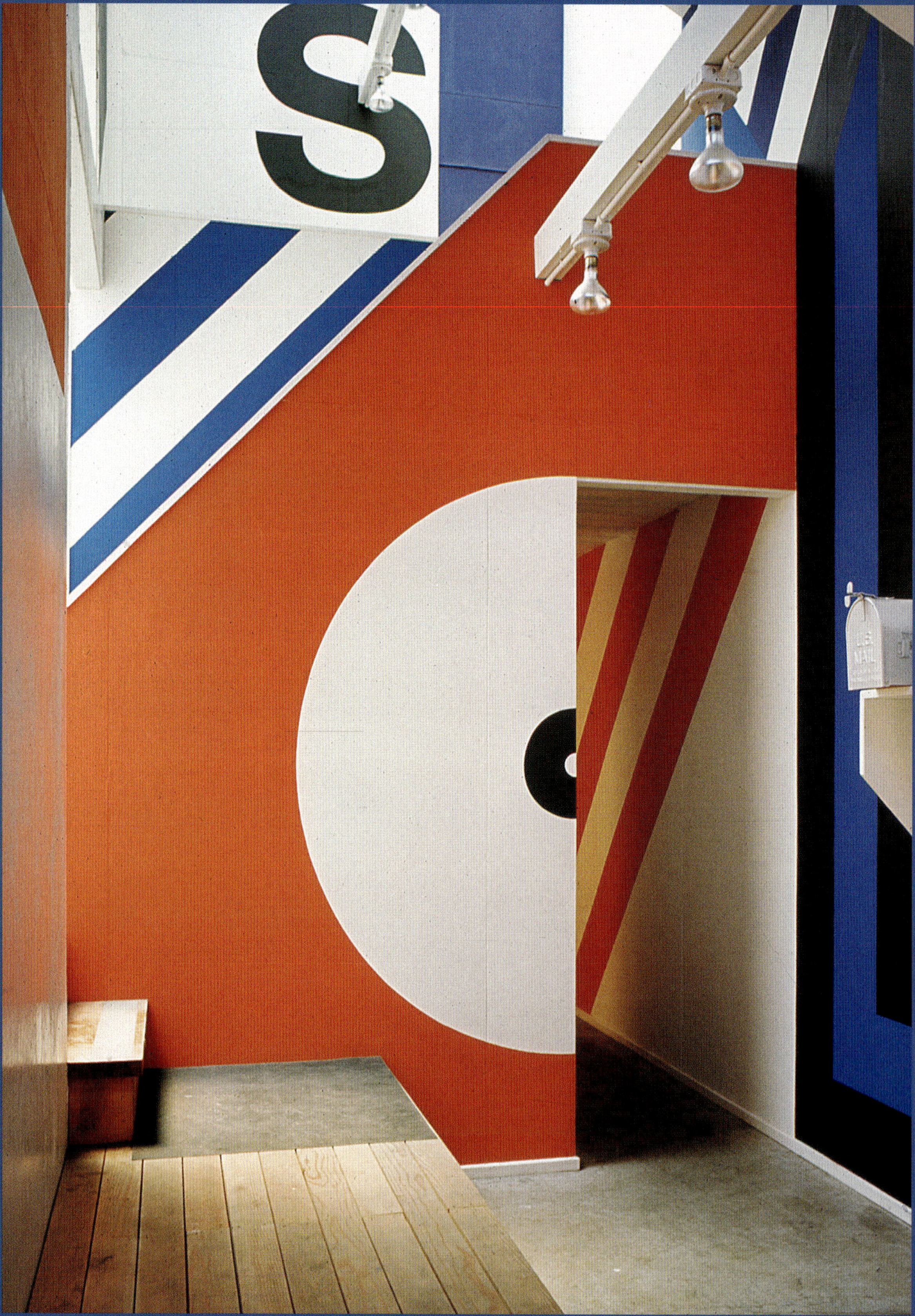
S

CALIFORNIA GIRLS

confrontation to the dictates of traditional modernist architecture. (Rock concert light shows also offered superscale graphic images, with a similar aim of enhancing our spatial experience.) ¶ Supergraphics became known and embraced through the wide publication of Solomon's designs for The Sea Ranch—a wilderness-conservation-minded coastal residential development north of San Francisco. At first, Solomon had no social-reformist agenda: she simply relished the opportunity to realize her work as an artist at a large scale. As she reflects in her autobiography, "In this superworld, supercharged and superintense, with my 1960s superwoman exuberance, I combined my training in supersized California abstract expressionism with my training in hard-edged Swiss graphics and ended up with, however superfluous and superficial, supergraphics."[18] Ironically, as Solomon became famous as a designer for The Sea Ranch, she began to take a more critical position toward her work, to question modernism and its goals of achieving a universal visual language that would unite humanity. She came to the realization that The Sea Ranch, despite its environmentalist intentions, was actually a showplace for affluence and leisure, and in her autobiography she criticizes its architects for their "urge to build trophy second homes in which [God's] chosen few could admire the view over martinis."[19] No longer able to believe that good design could somehow save the planet, she closed her practice and in 1976 went back to school—this time, as an architecture student at University of California, Berkeley, where she reexamined her understanding of design. **ABOVE AND RIGHT: HEAR-HEAR RECORD STORE, SAN FRANCISCO, 1969.** This project for a Ghirardelli Square building by Solomon's second husband, architect Daniel Solomon, earned praise from Smith as "one of the most successful and boldest of the supergraphic shop interiors."[20]

CALIFORNIA GIRLS 373

Deborah Sussman [1931–2014]. **ZODY'S DISCOUNT DEPARTMENT STORE, LOS ANGELES, 1971.** Sussman had a diverse education: she attended Black Mountain College, studying with John Cage, Merce Cunningham, Franz Kline, and others; spent time at Bard and the New Bauhaus, in Chicago (later, the Illinois Institute of Design); and worked for Ray and Charles Eames from 1953 to 1957. A Fulbright took her to the Ulm School of Design, in Germany, and she returned to the Eames Office afterward. It was, she remembers, "the greatest school you could go to." She also valued what she saw as Charles Eames's respect for talent regardless of a person's sex, especially when she encountered gender bias later in her career. With some clients, she remembers, "she's so passionate" really meant "get that woman out of here." ¶ Armed with this prodigious training, Sussman opened her own practice in 1968. The yet-to-be-legendary architect Frank Gehry gave her free space in the former painting studio he occupied with product and interior designer Gere Kavanaugh. In the early 1970s, she formed Sussman-Prezja and Company with her husband, Paul Prezja; their projects ranged from the stage set for a Rolling Stones Fourth of July concert to the landmark graphics program for the 1984 Summer Olympics, held in Los Angeles. ¶ The signage and interior graphics that Sussman created for Zody's were intended to fit cozily among the other marquee-laden theaters of downtown Los Angeles.

CALIFORNIA GIRLS 375

JOSEPH MAGNIN STORES, ALMADEN AND COSTA MESA, CALIFORNIA, 1968–69. Employing her special zing, Sussman crafted a typographic wonderland for the cutting-edge department store of its day. She says it was likely Magnin couldn't afford 3-D lettering for its multiple signage needs, so she faked it with playful trompe-l'oeil sculptural letterforms placed throughout the Gehry and Associates–designed space. ¶ **PAGE 378: HOLLYWOOD BOWL PROGRAM, 1970.** An incidental group effort resulted in this Sussman design: She met the client, Los Angeles Philharmonic director Ernest Fleischmann, through his friend Frank Gehry. And fellow designer Fred Usher suggested she use a shell motif—it was a summertime band shell after all, with the beach just down the road. ¶ **PAGE 379: H. C. WESTERMANN EXHIBITION CATALOGUE, LOS ANGELES COUNTY MUSEUM OF ART, 1968, 7¾ x 9¾ IN.** Opportunities for graphic design firms, as opposed to advertising agencies or renowned individuals, were still hard to come by when the LACMA curatorial group decided to hire local designers including Sussman and Lou Danziger. After meeting with Westermann, Sussman received a note from the artist that included a cartoon of an animal doing a handstand. It was signed, "Respectfully, Cliff." Sussman saw the drawing as a means to capture the essence of the wacky-spirited Westermann, an exercise buff. After taking a photo of him in the handstand pose, she adapted it with rainbow coloring, and added the artist's salutation and a bright yellow background.[21]

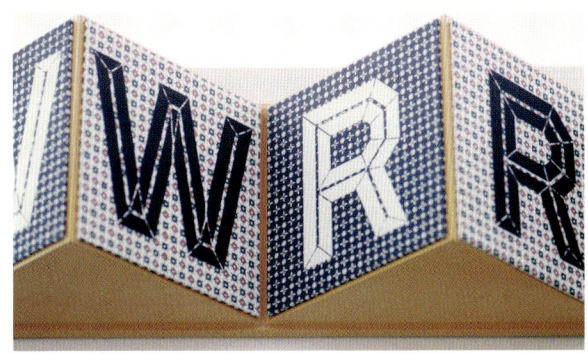

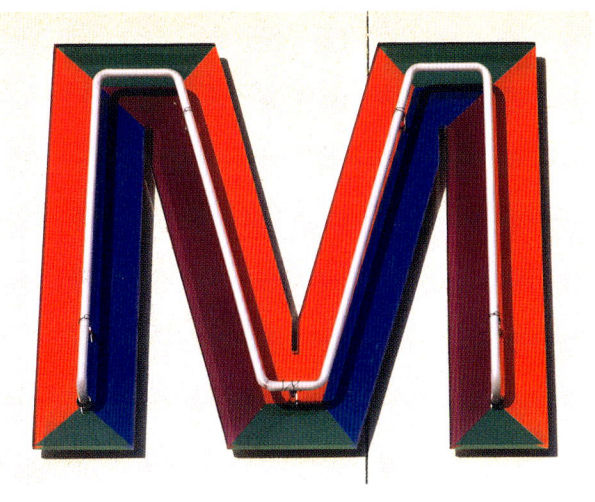

CALIFORNIA GIRLS

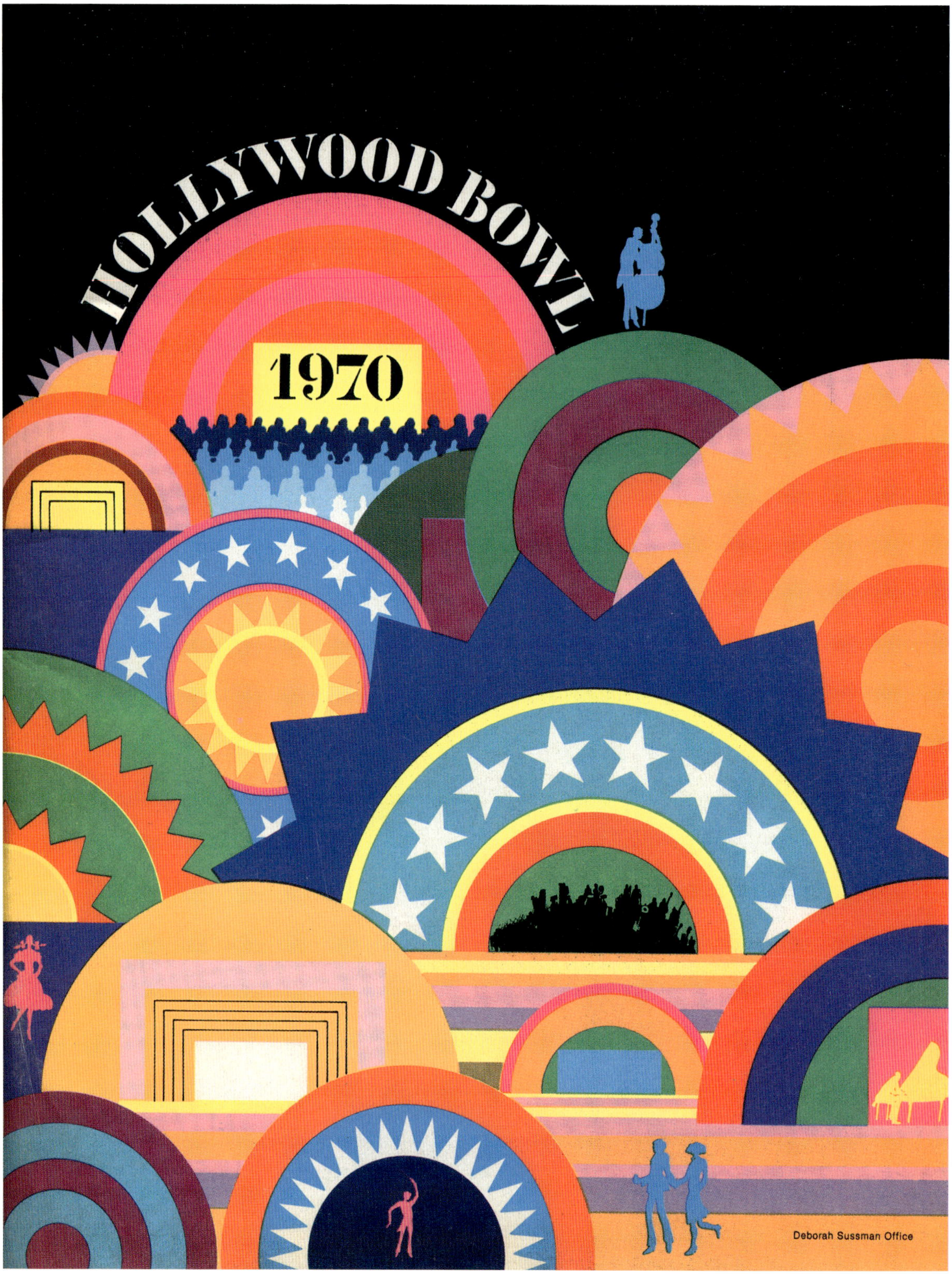
HOLLYWOOD BOWL
1970
Deborah Sussman Office

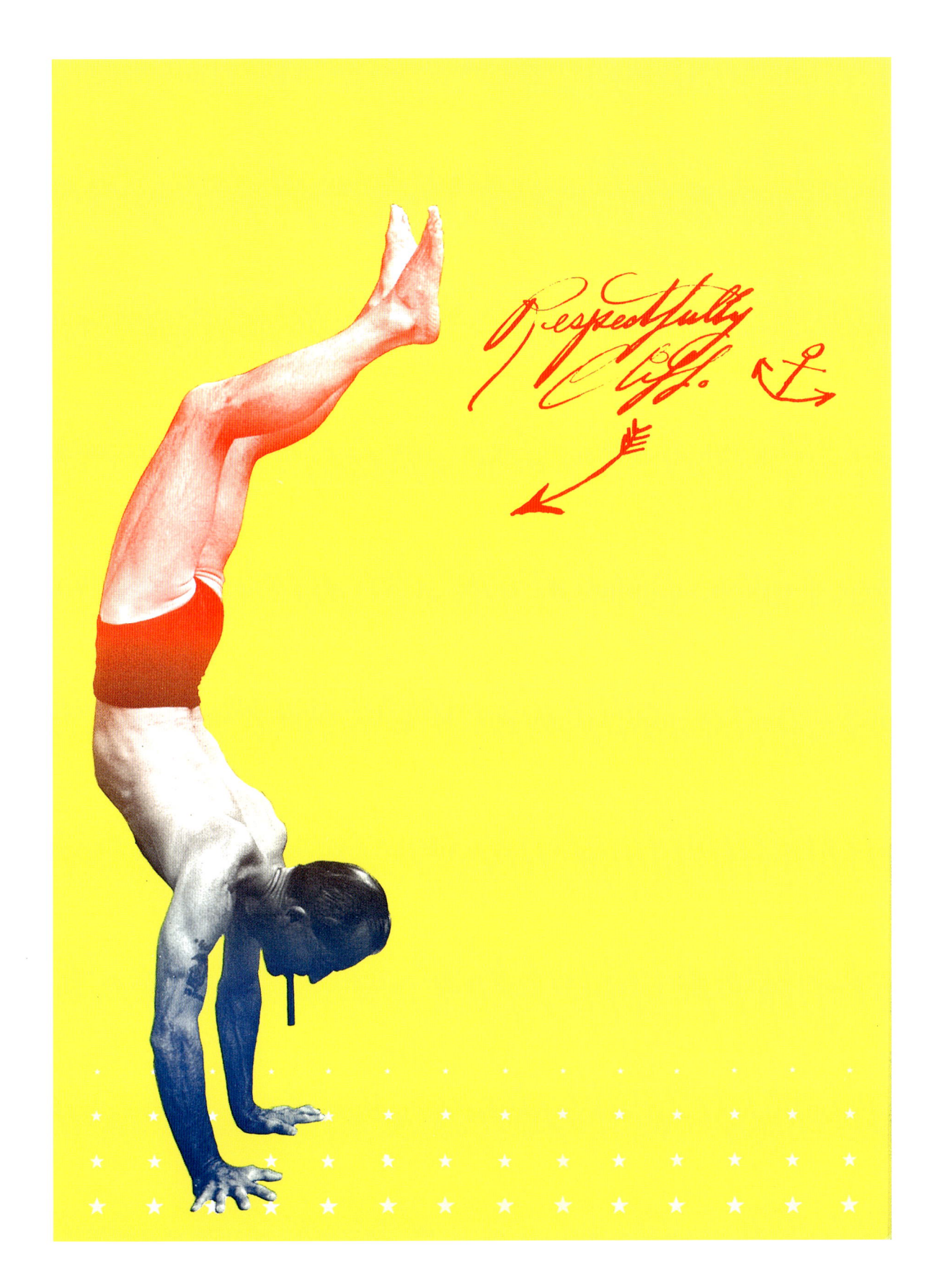

CALIFORNIA GIRLS

Frances Butler [b. 1940]. **BANANAMAN IN SWITZERLAND, 1972, 21½ × 16 × 4 IN.; 192 × 16 IN. UNFOLDED.** Bulter's design impulses lie at the margins rather than the heart of commercial production. Trained in history at the University of California, Berkeley, and at Stanford, she taught herself book design, calligraphy, and printing and then returned to Berkeley, where she earned a master's in typography in 1964. She became an instructor there and, in 1975, set up Poltroon Press with writer and typographer Alastair Johnston; together, they made books and posters.[22] ¶ Butler had already been printing her imagery on fabric, and it was after forming Poltroon that she began to consider combining textiles with the reading experience.[23] Bananaman was one of a number of soft-sculpture books Butler printed using four-color-process silk screen on cotton fabric. She originally intended these as a pun on the erotic literature known as "pillow books" produced by female Japanese authors. In the end, though, Butler was more interested in a contrarian juxtaposition of form to content: soft, fluffy pillow-like books that contained, in her words, "garishly colored stories of inspiration and racial prejudice."[24] Folded into an accordion-pleated volume of stuffed pages, the comic-book-like format of the Bananaman narrative is, as Butler describes it in her monograph, Colored Reading, "a muscular 'primitif'… converted to a sweet roll, typifying 'Swiss Style' (Helvetica type used in an asymmetric grid system) as kitsch (sans options). Stylish Swiss cheese then consumed the dog biscuits."[25]

BANANAMAN IN SWITZERLAND

Sheila Levrant de Bretteville [b. 1940]. RIGHT AND PAGE 384: "CALIFORNIA INSTITUTE OF THE ARTS: PROLOGUE TO A COMMUNITY," ARTS IN SOCIETY, VOL. 7, NO. 3, FALL/WINTER 1970, 7 x 10 IN. Described by Deborah Sussman as "a force that developed into a tornado," de Bretteville has galvanized artists and designers with work driven more by content than aesthetics. And from the beginning, writes design critic Rose DeNeve, her interests and stars seemed to align with the "heritage of risk-taking endemic to California since the '60s."[26] De Bretteville launched her now-legendary career at a new West Coast arts institution born of a nontraditional vision that emphasized conceptual thinking over formal skill: the California Institute of the Arts. She joined the design school faculty in 1969 and worked in-house as a designer for CalArts itself. One of her early projects was to co-edit and design an issue of Arts in Society, an interdisciplinary journal of the University of Wisconsin that was published irregularly, between one and four times a year, but always with a theme. De Bretteville chose to create a record of the conversation between CalArts provost Herb Blau and one of his friends during the 10-year development period after the school opened, in 1961. Visually, the outcome reflects tensions between de Bretteville's modernist design training at Yale (her use of Helvetica, for example) and her interest in a more quotidian vernacular (belied by casually Xeroxed documents and a corrugated cardboard cover). Through letters and other correspondence, combined with photographs of noteworthy characters and current events, including civil-rights activism and the Altamont rock concert, de Bretteville presented a portrait of the cultural landscape that helped shape CalArts and its students.[27]

Arts in Society
volume 7 no. 3
fall-winter 1970
2 dollars

California Institute of the Arts: Prologue to a Community

YESTERDAY
ructivists
ematists
s circle
ucas circle
stilj bauhaus
lenin trotsky gramsci
lang stroheim vigo clair
chaplin eisenstein griffith
RATIONALIZATION
CLASS STRUCTURE
TRADITION OF THE NEW
DISENCHANTMENT
DISSOCIATION OF SENSIBILITY

If the designer is to make
a deliberate contribution to society,
he must be able to integrate
all he can learn about
behavior and resources,
ecology and human needs;

taste and style just aren't enough.

For information regarding admission,
graduate & undergraduate study, and financial aid
write:

School of Design

California Institute of the Arts
2404 West 7th Street
Los Angeles, California 90057

opening fall 1970

California Institute of the Arts: Admissions Bulletin 1973-1974

California Institute of the Arts: Admissions Bulletin 1973–1974

PAGE 385, TOP: ANNOUNCEMENT POSTER FOR THE CALARTS SCHOOL OF DESIGN, 1970, 7¾ x 10 IN. De Bretteville again merged "high" and "low" vernaculars and deployed a raw aesthetic for this CalArts poster, applying a modernist typographic treatment—along with symbols of nature (a pinecone), play (a jack), and technology (a transistor)—to cardboard packaging, which was then shrink-wrapped. **PAGE 385, BOTTOM: CALARTS 1973–74 ADMISSIONS BULLETIN, 1973, 3½ x 5¼ IN.** Pocketsize and printed on newsprint in black and white, this publication veers far from the large-format glossy "authority" of the typical school admissions catalogue. **RIGHT: PINK, 1973, 30 x 30 IN.** In 1971, feeling that the CalArts School of Design was becoming more conventional, de Bretteville formed the Women's Design Program within the institution. Two years later, her engagement with feminism and her interest in design's potential for inclusiveness led her to cofound the landmark Woman's Building in Los Angeles, dedicated to women's education and culture. The environment and programming there allowed de Bretteville to focus on developing a graphic language that was less about satisfying the designer's aesthetic interests and more geared toward giving voice to the aesthetics and interests of others. ¶ This broadsheetlike poster was a commission from the American Institute of Graphic Arts, which asked 100 designers to explore the theme of color. Wanting to reinvest pink with more positive and diverse meanings beyond the usual "sugar and spice," de Bretteville invited women ages 13 to 80 to draw or write about this deeply gendered color. The designer assembled these points of view into a single poster, which she printed at the Woman's Building and pasted up around Los Angeles.[28]

CALIFORNIA GIRLS

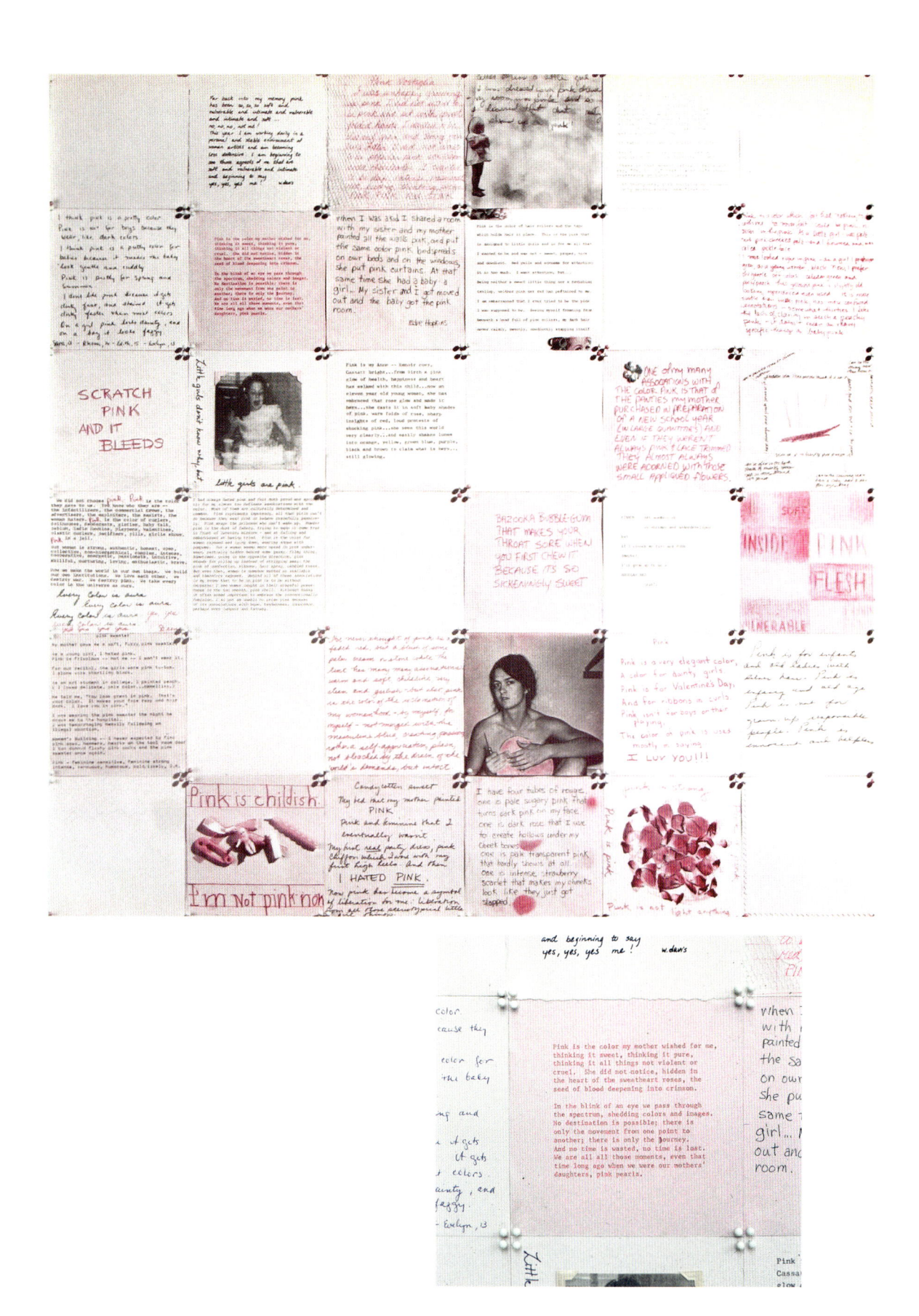

Susan Kare [b. 1954]. With a degree in art history, a bit of graphic-design experience, and a high-school-buddy connection, Kare landed a job with Apple just before the Macintosh computer debuted in January 1984. She was to help construct the graphic interface language of icons and fonts that would allow us humans to navigate this formidable device with ease. ¶ Kare used old-school graph paper to create her "bitmapped" Apple icons, and had to type on a keyboard until her friend and colleague Andy Hertzfeld generated icon-editor software that allowed her to design on the screen. Multiple sources, from folk to fine art, informed Kare's explorations in this uncharted territory. She refined the designs of others and worked with metaphors to develop new symbols. Inspiration also came from her understanding "bitmap graphics [as being] like mosaics and needlepoint and other pseudodigital art forms, all of which I had practiced before going to Apple." ¶ **CONTROL PANEL FOR MACINTOSH 1.0, 1983.** An original accessory for the Mac, the control panel featured Kare's clever iconography, including the tortoise and the hare to indicate the speed of program responses to keyboard commands. **MACPAINT INTERFACE FOR MACINTOSH, 1983.** Kare had a hand in designing the overall look of MacPaint. The program included her icons and introduced Chicago, the font she designed that appeared on all subsequent Macintosh products.[29] **MACINTOSH SYSTEM AND APPLICATION ICONS, 1983–84.** When Kare joined Apple, some icons were already in place, such as the one for "documents" (the paper with the folded corner). Kare embraced this literal language, in which icons looked like the things they stood for, but she also faced the more complex task of inventing forms to communicate applications, which required users to do something and thus needed to appear more directive. For the category "application," Kare created an icon of a hand holding a pencil against a diamond; with this gesture and others like it, she introduced the whimsy and humor that helped define the Macintosh personality.[30]

CALIFORNIA GIRLS 389

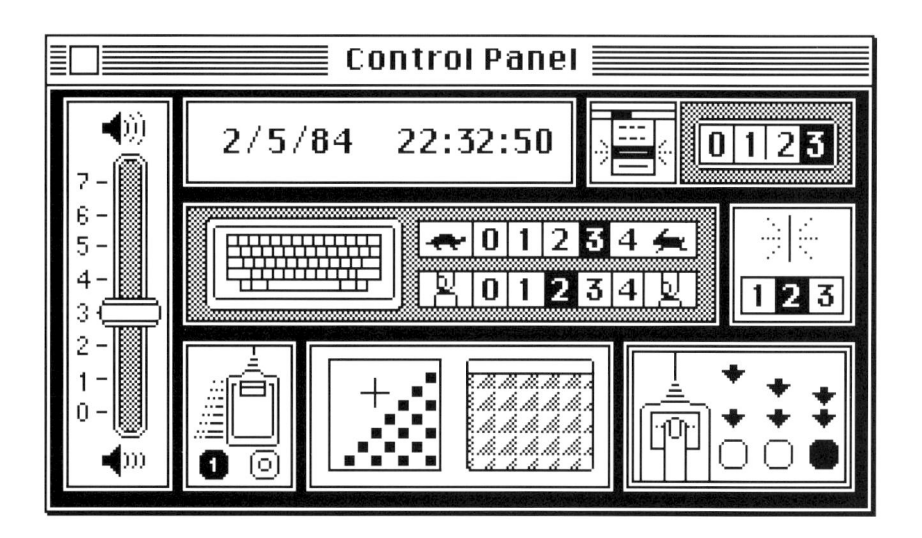

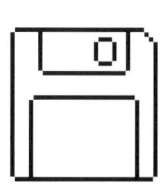

April Greiman [b. 1948]. Greiman arrived in Los Angeles in 1976, after an education in Switzerland and some time in New York. Her priority was to avoid Hollywood, to find the non-tinsel parts of the town. She visited the offices of the Eameses and Saul Bass and met with Lou Danziger, introducing them to a Swiss-honed, postmodern aesthetic of bright colors, squiggles, splashes, and fragments. Greiman's style—soon to be known as West Coast "new wave"—was a blast of shock and awe heard round the world. Yet beneath the bluster in L.A., she remembers, she found a city still trying to define itself, a place where she could escape that right-brain, right-coast world of corporate design, marketing, and planning. She could be bedazzled by the Southern California light, be it from the cathode rays of the computer screen or the sunshine streaming across new horizons.[31] ¶ **POSTER FOR ART IN LOS ANGELES: SEVENTEEN ARTISTS IN THE SIXTIES, 1981, 21½ x 34 IN.** The layered production of this exhibition poster for the Los Angeles County Museum of Art—first spray-painted, then photographed, with type added before it was printed in four-color offset—forecasts Greiman's collagelike work with the computer.

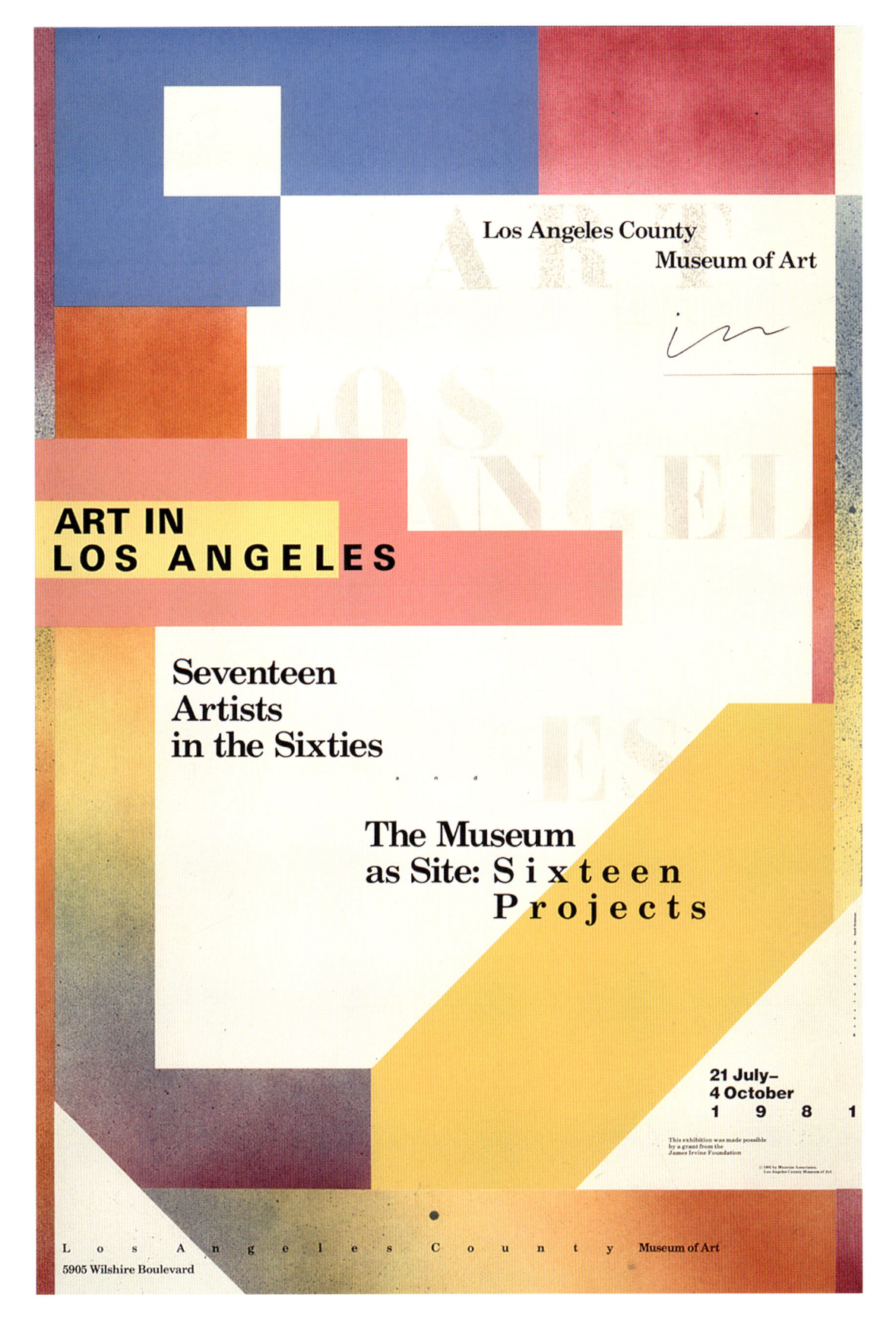

Los Angeles County
Museum of Art

ART IN LOS ANGELES

Seventeen
Artists
in the Sixties

The Museum
as Site: Sixteen
Projects

21 July–
4 October
1 9 8 1

This exhibition was made possible
by a grant from the
James Irvine Foundation

© 1981 by Museum Associates,
Los Angeles County Museum of Art

Los Angeles County Museum of Art
5905 Wilshire Boulevard

¶ **IRIS LIGHT POSTER, 1984, 35 x 47 IN.** This silk-screened promotional poster for Ron Rezek Lighting and Furniture was one of Greiman's early forays into working with electronic imagery. The top and bottom images were created from video stills. Not just a mash-up, the result manages a kind of digital-analogue mirroring: the misaligned, awkward use of the print screen creates a sense of the glow and shimmer of images when viewed on the electronic screen. ¶ **PAGES 394–95: "DOES IT MAKE SENSE?" DESIGN QUARTERLY 133, WALKER ART CENTER, MINNEAPOLIS, 1986, 8½ x 11 IN.; 76½ x 25½ IN. UNFOLDED.** This publication—a giant folded poster, as opposed to the usual 32-page journal—hit designers' desks just two years after Apple released the first mass-market computer. Few had embraced the Macintosh with optimism, much less artistic vision and imagination. Greiman showed us the design potential of this new digital tool, as well the strange beauty of the pixel applied to organic forms. Her Design Quarterly poster issue features a life-size representation of her own body, scanned in sections and rendered in dark purple, juxtaposed with an atomic particle diagram, layered with cave drawings, and surrounded and overlapped by luridly colored ambiguous images and texts that leap from the metaphysical to the mundane. The subject was, in essence, the part representing the whole, a concept the audience encounters literally and figuratively with texts that shift in scale and pixelated details that intrigue as much as the image they compose. Here, we see a designer who, in taking herself as her subject, revealed the beauty in an unfamiliar aesthetic.

RON REZEK
LIGHTING + FURNITURE

CALIFORNIA GIRLS

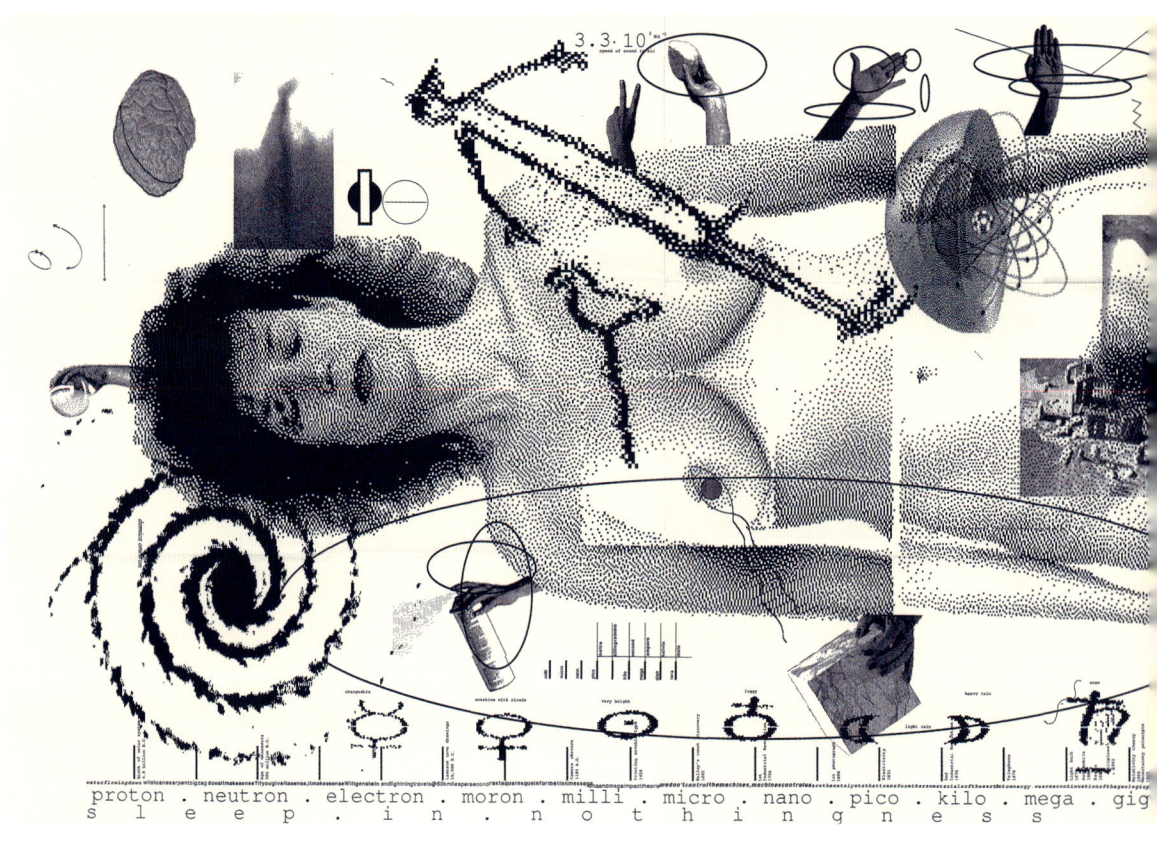

proton . neutron . electron . moron . milli . micro . nano . pico . kilo . mega . gig
s l e e p . i n . n o t h i n g n e s s

and so I'm walking through the English Garden with Andreas--and I mention the idea (duality) of order and chaos. So, he tips me off to the latest philosophical twist--chaos is simply a man/mind-made invention that frankly doesn't exist! I think about this and I say...yea, come to think about it, in seeing a computer model of fractal geometry, things that appear without structure, such as clouds and mountains, are in fact orderly processes. While on the surface, things seem irregular and chaotic, when you break down the parts, in reality they are more and more modular and ordered. The more finitely we perceive them, the more their inherent order becomes apparent.

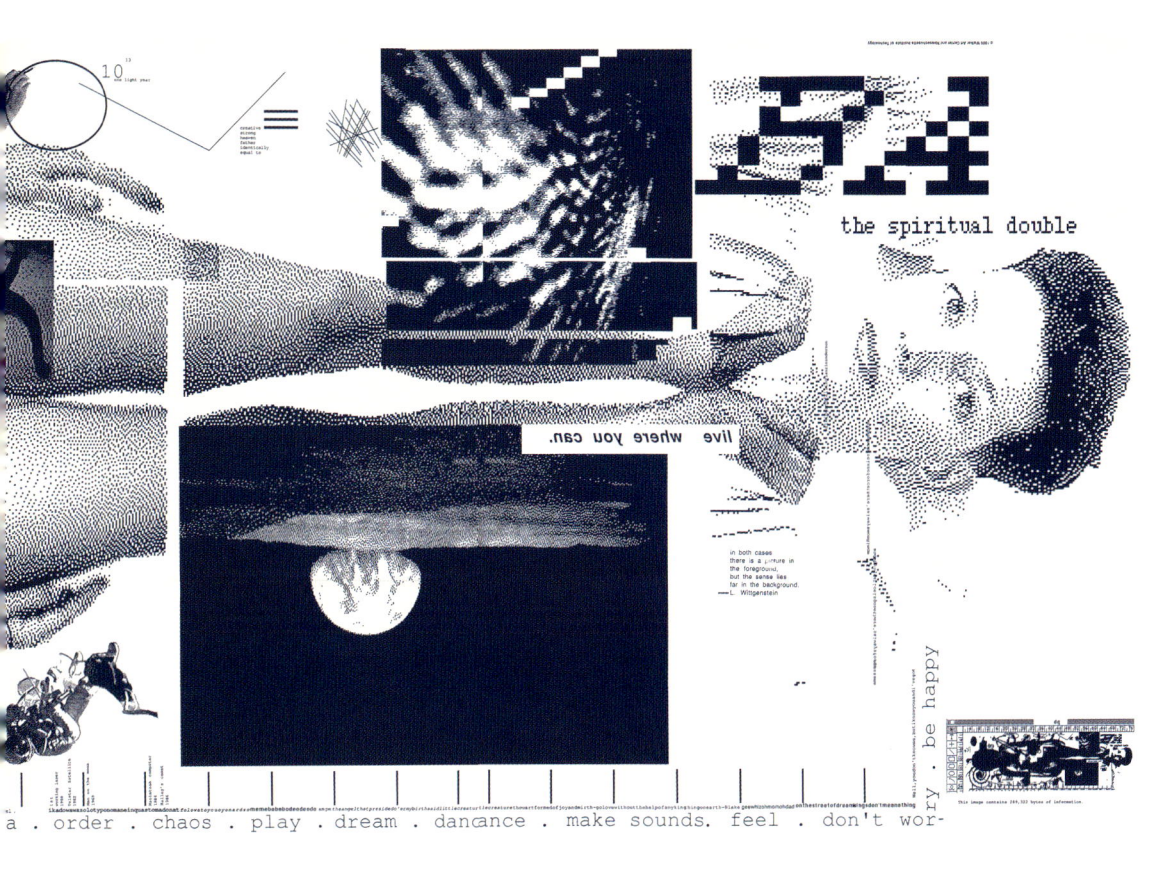

a . order . chaos . play . dream . danc·ance . make sounds . feel . don't wor-

CALIFORNIA GIRLS

395

Notes

1 Paul J. Karlstrom and Susan Ehrlich, Turning the Tide: Early Los Angeles Modernists 1920–1956 (Santa Barbara: Santa Barbara Museum of Art, 1990), 53. **2** Kendra Ablaza, "Art And Architecture: Retracing the Long Beach Airport's History Through Its Art Deco Design," Long Beach Business Journal, January 29, 2013, http://issuu.com/longbeachbusinessjournal/docs/longbeachairport90thanniverary. **3** Michael Duncan, "Post Surrealism: Genesis and Equilibrium," in Post Surrealism, exh. cat. (Logan: Utah State University, 2002), 7, 13, http://digitalcommons.usu.edu/artmuseum_cat/7. **4** Ray Eames, interview with Ruth Bowman, Venice, Calif., July 28–Aug. 20, 1980, oral history, Archives of American Art, Smithsonian Institution, http://www.aaa.si.edu/collections/interviews/oral-history-interview-ray-eames-12821#transcript, p. 3; and Pat Kirkham, Charles and Ray Eames: Designers of the Twentieth Century (Cambridge, Mass.: MIT Press, 1995), 28. **5** Interview with Ray Eames, 2–4. **6** Arts & Architecture Collection: Designers, http://artsandarchitecturecollection.com/design/designers/index.html. **7** Kirkham, Charles and Ray Eames, 41. **8** Steve Reoutt, interview with the author, San Francisco, March 15, 2008. **9** Michael Duncan, "Someday Is Now," in Ian Berry and Duncan, eds., Someday Is Now: The Art of Corita Kent (New York: Prestel, 2013), 14. **10** Corita Kent might also have been influenced by her UCLA silk-screening teacher, Mexican native Maria Sodi de Ramos Martínez. See oral history compiled by Alexandra Carrera, in Berry and Duncan, Someday Is Now, 35. **11** Alexandra Carrera (director, Corita Art Center, Los Angeles) and Mickey Myers (student, friend, and colleague of Corita), e-mail correspondence with the author, May 28–29, 2014. **12** Marilyn Neuhart, interviews with the author, September 28–December 6, 2012; Marilyn Neuhart, e-mail correspondence with the author, December 12, 2012–July 15, 2013. **13** Steven Kurutz, "If It Has a Shape…," New York Times, Real Estate section, May 8, 2013, www.nytimes.com. **14** Gere Kavanaugh, interview with the author, Los Angeles, March 12, 2012. **15** Gere Kavanaugh, conversation with Jessica Fleischmann, June 23, 2014. **16** Ibid. **17** See C. Ray Smith, Supermannerism: New Attitudes in Post-Modern Architecture (New York: Dutton, 1977). **18** Barbara Stauffacher Solomon, Why? Why Not? 80 Years of Art & Design in Pix & Prose, Juxtaposed (San Francisco: Fun Fog Press, 2013), 77. **19** Ibid., 72. **20** Smith, Supermannerism, 284. **21** Deborah Sussman, conversation with the author, May 2008; Holly Hampton, Paul Prejza, and Deborah Sussman, interview with the author, October 18, 2012; Deborah Sussman, phone conversation with the author, February 11, 2014. **22** Frances Butler, "Biographical Notes," Colored Reading: The Graphic Art of Frances Butler (Oakland: Lancaster-Miller, 1979). **23** Clara Database of Women Artists, National Museum of Women in the Arts, Washington, D.C., www.clara.nmwa.org, accessed December 12, 2012. **24** Frances Butler, e-mail correspondence with the author, March 2013. **25** Butler, Colored Reading. **26** Rose DeNeve, "A Feminist Option," Print, May/June 1976. **27** Sheila Levrant de Bretteville, interview with Jenni Sorkin, June 22, 2010, oral history, "Woman's Building," Art Spaces Archive Project, www.as-ap.org, downloaded July 15, 2012. **28** DeNeve, "A Feminist Option." **29** The Japanese figure came from a woodcut (purchased by Steve Jobs) that the Apple team used for early scanning experiments. **30** Susan Kare, interview with Alex Pang, September 8, 2000, in Susan Kare, oral history, "Making the Macintosh: Technology and Culture in Silicon Valley," Stanford University Libraries and Academic Information Resources, http://www-sul.stanford.edu/mac/primary/interviews/kare/index.html. **31** April Greiman, interview with the author, Los Angeles, August 14, 2012.

↑ Gere Kavanaugh with
wrapping paper and display for
pilot Hallmark store, late 1970s
→ "The pinnacled castle of
Sleeping Beauty [Disneyland],"
from Beautiful California, 1971

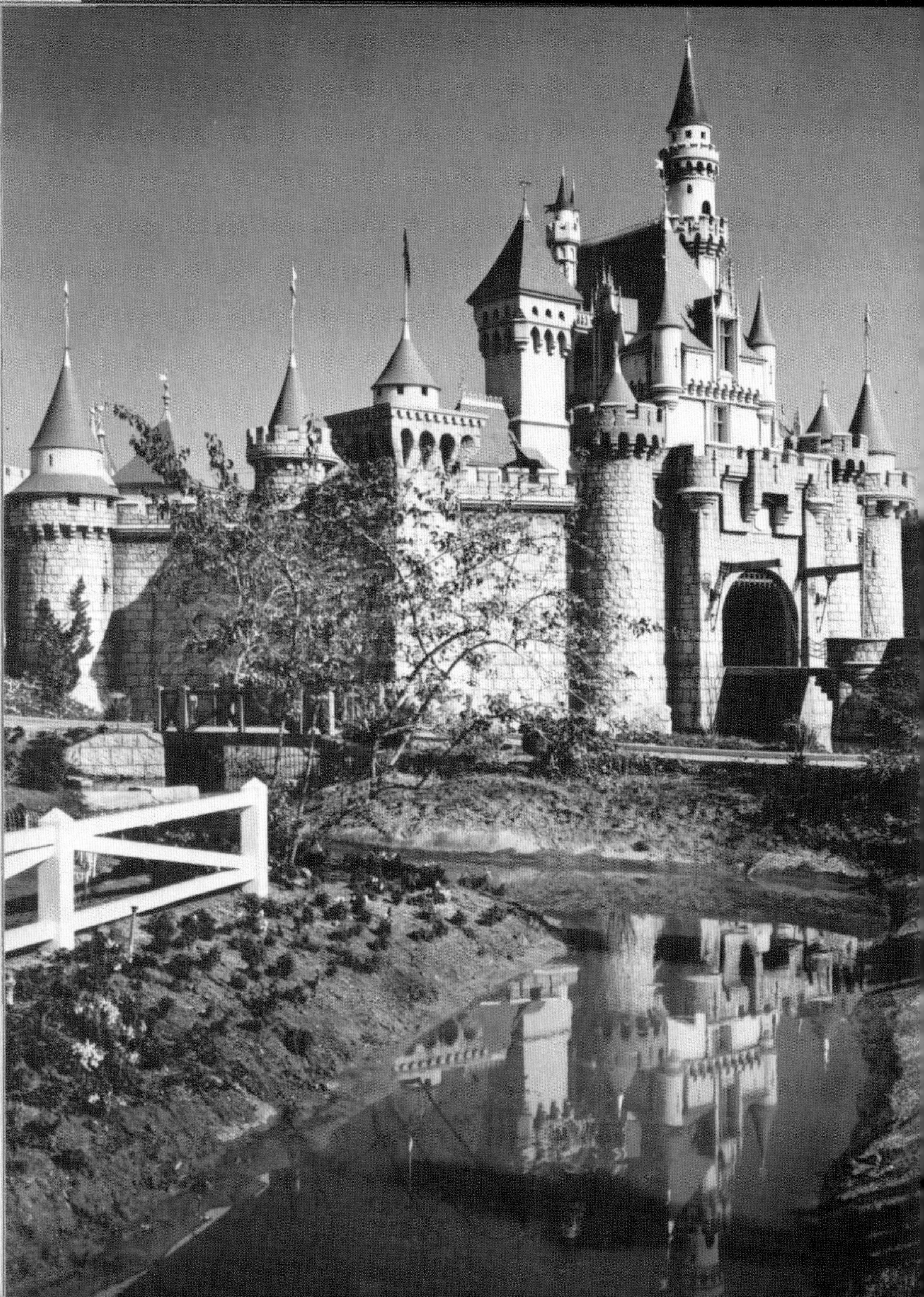

ACKNOWLEDGMENTS

This book started with a conversation that turned into a collaboration with my friend, professional colleague, and mentor Lorraine Wild. It is to her that I owe this book. She watered the initial seed, and one of her most important contributions was in helping me decide how to frame the vast expanse of this unwieldy subject into its four themed sections. Her encouragement, suggestions, feedback, and connections kept the project going, and her two brilliant essays give this volume heft. Lorraine also connected me to Diana Murphy, the publisher of Metropolis Books, who became the champion this project required to see it through to completion. Without Diana's unrelenting faith in this crazy endeavor, her cheer, backbreaking work, and friendship, there would have been no book at all, or maybe a sad shadow of its lively final outcome. Diana and Lorraine are the true heroines of the story of this project—each is a refined combination of Queen Calafia, the mythological Amazon from whom California derives its name, and Wonder Woman. Two other superheroes—the Robins to Diana's Batman—are Anne Thompson and Gideon Brower. Anne's wordsmithery spun gold from crude floss; she mind-melded with me to create coherent and compelling texts worth the ink. Gideon spent several years communicating with the numerous copyright-holders and others who generously gave permission for the use of images in this book and, in many instances, supplied print-ready files. I thank Kristine McKenna not only for the introduction to Gideon but also for her encouragement and assistance in taking up the phone or pencil. Elaine Farris transcribed disembodied voices into the concrete words on which writing depends. At ARTBOOK | D.A.P., Sharon Gallagher, the indefatigable president and publisher, and Jane Brown, vice president and national accounts director, were also unfailing advocates of the book.

The initial research and design support that turned the project from a notion into a reality was carried out by Derrick Schultz. He laboriously pored over old annuals and dusty periodicals in search of overlooked gems of California graphic design; he also set in motion the book's playful approach to showcasing these examples. Former students who are now professional colleagues joined along the way and their contributions to the book's design are immeasurable. Christopher Morabito designed the brilliant grid and typographic direction. Jens Gehlhaar originally designed the font family used throughout the book, CIA Compendium, as his CalArts graduate thesis; he then tailored the font to suit the particular needs of this project, for example, the quotation page at the front of each section.

Many current and former students bolstered this book's development. Thomas Kracauer and Hayden Smith came to the rescue as the project drew to a close, putting themselves at my beck and call for production and design help. Their hard work, smarts, and enthusiasm kept the project going when it most needed them. Katherine Catmur and Benjamin Woodlock cheerfully slogged through the Influences & Intersections diagrams, giving an elegant readability to complicated networks among a variety of people, media, and cultures. Cameron Ewing, Manuel Garcia, Teira Johnson, Jessica Kao, Kaoru Matsushita, Randy Nakamura, Michelle Park, Joe Potts, Jennifer Schanen Rider, and Evan Schoninger lent their hands on research and design. Edwin Alvaregna, in the heat of his graduate studies, did the heavy lifting of research on motion designers that became integral to the section "Industry & the Indies."

Behind every historian (or, in my case, "historian") are great archivists and librarians: Jan-Christopher Horak and Mark Quigley of the UCLA Film and Television Archive; Casey Blake, Anne Coco, and May Hadoung of the Academy of Motion Picture Arts and Sciences; and Alexandra Carerra, director of the Corita Art Center. Then, there were those colleagues and sources who lent their ears and shared their personal and professional knowledge, their wisdom, and sometimes even their hearts—all with exceptional generosity: Caryn Aono, David Asari, Jennifer Bass, Juliette Bellocq, Tosh Berman, Barbara Bestor, Michael Betancourt, Andrew Blauvelt, Denise Bratton, Chuck Bryne, Cathy Callahan, Michael Carabetta, Art Chantry, Louise Coffey-Webb, Chris Cooper (COOP), Patrick Coyne, Victoria Dailey, Eames Demetrios, Mike Dooley, Jeff Doud, Michael Duncan, Nancye Ferguson, Allen Ferro, Karin Fong, Jim Ford, Valentina Ganeva, Elizabeth Guffey, Holly Hampton, Jeri Heiden, Jim Heimann, Steven Heller, Billy Ingram, Alastair Johnson, Kevin Jones, Geoff Kaplan, Wendy Kaplan, Jeff Keedy, Cindy Keefer, Michael Leon, Felipe Lima, Peter Lunenfeld, Elaine Lustig Cohen, Joe Molloy, Leo Monahan, Susan Morgan, Gerard O'Brien, Pat O'Neill, Mike Neal, Andrew Neuhart, Ellen Newman, Stephen Nowlin, Andrew Perchuk, Billy Pittard, Alida Post, Paul Prejza, Chistopher Pullman, Brian Roettinger, Marvin Rubin, Janet Sager, Arnold Schwartzman, Adrian Shaughnessy, Rani Singh, Lynn Spigel, Staci Steinberger, Bill Stern, Robert Taylor, Scott Taylor, Frank Terry, Bobbye Tigerman, Frederick Usher, Xochil Usher, Michael Vanderbyl, Rudy VanderLans, Jonathan Wells, James Whitney, John Whitney, Jr., Holly Willis, and Gregory Zinman.

An enormous, special thank you goes to the devoted people whose work is included in these pages. Unrelenting in giving their time, talents, insights, and necessary first-hand perspectives were Lou Danziger, April Greiman, Gere Kavanaugh, Harry Marks, Kenny Mirman, Marilyn Neuhart, Barbara Stauffacher Solomon, Deborah Sussman, Richard Taylor, and John Van Hamersveld. Generous in providing specific insights and information on their work were Chris Blum, Archie Boston, Frances Butler, Mike Davies, Chris Dawson, Heidi Endemann, Barbara Fairbrother Singh, Pablo Ferro, Wayne Fitzgerald, Keith Godard, Bill Ham, Franz Lanzinger, Sheila Levrant de Bretteville, Victor Moscoso, Earl Newman, Dan Perri, Jim Phillips, Jan Steward, and Fred Usher.

This book is dedicated not only to these designers but also to the designers they inspired—those located just off these pages, in the ripples and pools formed in the wake of a great tide. This group includes my students and all that they contribute to California design of the present and future.

Special gratitude goes to David Mayes and Typecraft Wood and Jones for donating the production of sample spreads that provided the first glimmer of the book in paper and ink; Thomas Lawson, dean of the School of Art, California Institute of the Arts, for supporting the project with several grants that kept the ball rolling; and the Los Angeles Department of Cultural Affairs for its 2008 C.O.L.A. Individual Artist Fellowship, which helped propel the project further by providing its first public airing.

Friends cannot be underestimated. Kim Baer, Jessica Fleischmann, Lynda Kahn, Kali Nikitas, and Julia Paull deserve recognition for championing the project throughout and kindly enduring my absence for far too long. But it was my husband, Michael Shapiro, whom I met during the long journey of this endeavor, who patiently rode the trails and weathered the travails by my side. With his love and support everything seems possible. It all begins and ends with him.

ABOUT THE CONTRIBUTORS

Louise Sandhaus is the former director and a current faculty member of the graphic design program at the California Institute of the Arts. Her design office, LSD (Louise Sandhaus Design), in partnership with others, has designed museum exhibitions on California art and artifacts for the Los Angeles County Museum of Art, the Hammer Museum, and the Los Angeles Natural History Museum. She is an AIGA Los Angeles Fellow and recently completed a term on the AIGA national board.

Denise Gonzales Crisp is a graphic designer and professor of graphic design at the College of Design, North Carolina State University. She is the author of Typography: Graphic Design in Context, and her design and writing have appeared internationally in many magazines, exhibitions, and anthologies. She divides her time between Los Angeles and Raleigh.

Lorraine Wild is a graphic designer whose practice, Green Dragon Office, focuses on collaborations with artists, architects, curators, editors, and publishers. She is a faculty member at CalArts and is the creative director for the design department of the Los Angeles County Museum of Art. Recent projects include publications for LACMA, the Hammer Museum, and the Stedelijk Museum, and ongoing work for the Edible Schoolyard. In 2006, Wild was awarded the Gold Medal of the AIGA.

Michael Worthington is a founding partner of Counterspace, a graphic design studio that specializes in editorial and identity work for cultural clients. His writing has been published, and his work exhibited, widely. He has taught at CalArts since 1995; he is co-director of the school's graphic design program and in 2012 initiated the school's MFA specialization in motion graphics.

HENRY DREYFUSS
Hybrid Imagery
The fusion of technology and graphic design
April Greiman
L.A.'S EARLY MODERNS
GENE YOUNGBLOOD
Introduction by R. BUCKMINSTER FULLER
SUPERMANNERISM
New Attitudes in Post-Modern Architecture
C. RAY SMITH
ART IN CINEMA
SAN FRANCISCO MUSEUM OF ART
Someday is Now
The Art of Corita Kent
INTRODUCTION BY BOB WEIR
A HISTORY BY CHARLES PERRY
THE HAIGHT-ASHBURY
LOS ANGELES
THE ARCHITECTURE OF FOUR ECOLOGIES
REYNER BANHAM
SPECTACULAR VISUAL AND ORAL HISTORY
THE ART OF ROCK
Architectural Signing and Graphic
CARTOON MODERN
STYLE AND DESIGN IN FIFTIES ANIMATION
BY AMID AMIDI
Colored Reading: The Graphic Art of Frances Butler

SELECTED BIBLIOGRAPHY

Adam Abraham, When Magoo Flew: The Rise and Fall of Animation Studio UPA (Middletown, Conn.: Wesleyan University Press, 2012)

"Airport with Murals and Mosaics by Grace Clements," California Arts & Architecture, December 1942

Thomas Albright, Art in the San Francisco Bay Area, 1945–1980: An Illustrated History (Berkeley: University of California Press, 1985)

Jeffrey Altshuler, "Robert Abel: Video Surrealist," Print, November/December 1975

Amid Amidi, Cartoon Modern: Style and Design in 1950s Animation (San Francisco: Chronicle, 2006)

Merle Armitage, Accent on Life (Ames: Iowa State University Press, 1964)

———., Notes on Modern Printing (New York: Wm. E. Rudge's Sons, 1945)

Elizabeth Armstrong et al., Birth of the Cool: California Art, Design and Culture at Mid-Century (Newport Beach, Calif., Munich, and New York: Prestel, 2007)

Julie Ault, Come Alive! The Spirited Art of Sister Corita (London: Four Corners, 2007)

Suzanne Baizerman and Jo Lauria, California Design: The Legacy of West Coast Craft and Style (San Francisco: Chronicle, 2005)

Georgette Ballance and Steven Heller, Graphic Design History (New York: Allworth Press, 2001)

Reyner Banham, Los Angeles: The Architecture of Four Ecologies (New York: Harper and Row, 1971)

Stephanie Barron, Sheri Bernstein, and Ilene Susan Fort, Made in California: Art, Image, and Identity, 1900–2000 (Berkeley: University of California Press, 2000)

Jennifer Bass and Pat Kirkham, Saul Bass: A Life in Film and Design (London: Laurence King, 2011)

Saul Bass and Associates, Saul Bass and Associates (Tokyo: Seibundo Shinkosha, 2003)

Ian Berry and Michael Duncan, eds., Someday Is Now: The Art of Corita Kent (Saratoga Springs, N.Y., Munich, and New York: Prestel, 2013)

Michael Betancourt, The History of Motion Graphics: From Avant-Garde to Industry in the United States (Rockville, Md.: Wildside Press, 2013)

David Bianculli, Dangerously Funny: The Uncensored Story of "The Smothers Brothers Comedy Hour" (New York: Touchstone, 2009)

Archie Boston, Fly in the Buttermilk: Memoirs of an African American in Advertising, Design & Design Education (Los Angeles: Archie Boston Graphic Design, 2001)

———., 20 Outstanding L.A. Designers (1986), DVD (Los Angeles: Archie Boston Graphic Design, 2008)

Susan Braybrooke, Print Casebooks 3: 1978/79 Edition: The Best in Environmental Graphics (Washington, D.C.: RC Publications, 1978)

Kerry Brougher, Jeremy Strick, Ari Wiseman, and Judith Zilczer, Visual Music: Synaesthesia in Art and Music Since 1900 (New York: Thames and Hudson, 2005)

Frances Butler, Colored Reading: The Graphic Art of Frances Butler (Berkeley: Lancaster-Miller, 1979)

Giorgio Camuffo and April Greiman, Pacific Wave: California Graphic Design (Udine: Magnus, 1987)

William Claxton and Peggy Moffit, The Rudi Gernreich Book (New York: Rizzoli, 1991)

Allen Cohen, ed., The San Francisco Oracle: The Psychedelic Newspaper of the Haight Ashbury, facsimile edition, digital version (Berkeley: Regent Press, 2009)

Edie Cohen, "Welcome to 1969 Pix: That's When Alexander Girard Put His Upbeat Modernist Imprimatur on a Northern California House by Don Knorr," Interior Design, March 1, 2007, www.interiordesign.net, accessed January 18, 2014

Victoria Dailey, Michael Dawson, William Francis Deverell, and Natalie W. Shivers, LA's Early Moderns: Art, Architecture, Photography (Los Angeles: Balcony Press, 2003)

Eames Demetrios, An Eames Primer (New York: Universe, 2001)

Rose DeNeve, "A Feminist Option," Print, May/June 1976

Joan Didion, Slouching Towards Bethlehem: Essays (New York: Farrar, Straus and Giroux, 1968)

Emory Douglas, Black Panther: The Revolutionary Art of Emory Douglas, ed. Sam Durant (New York: Rizzoli, 2007)

Paul Drury, "The Making of Tempest," Retro Gamer, issue 105, 2012

Michael Duncan, "Post Surrealism: Genesis and Equilibrium," in Duncan, ed., Post Surrealism, exh. cat. (Logan: Utah State University Press, 2002)

Ray Eames, interview with Ruth Bowman, Venice, Calif., July 28–Aug. 20, 1980, oral history, Archives of American Art, Smithsonian Institution, http://www.aaa.si.edu/collections/interviews/oral-history-interview-ray-eames-12821#transcript

Russell Flinchum, Henry Dreyfuss, Industrial Designer: The Man in the Brown Suit (New York: Rizzoli, 1997)

John Follis, Architectural Signing and Graphics (New York and London: Watson-Guptill, 1950)

Martin Fox and Janet Vrchota, "Can a British-Born Yale-trained Designer Find Happiness and Fulfillment in Southern California?" Print, March/April 1972, 57–59

Thomas Frank, The Conquest of Cool: Business Culture, Counterculture, and the Rise of Hip Consumerism (Chicago: University Of Chicago Press, 1998)

Mildred Friedman and Joseph Giovannini, eds., Graphic Design in America: A Visual Language History (Minneapolis and New York: Walker Art Center and Abrams, 1989)

Rudi Gernreich, Rudi Gernreich: Fashion Will Go out of Fashion (Philadelphia: Institute of Contemporary Art, 2001)

Howard Luck Gossage, The Book of Gossage (Chicago: Copy Workshop, 1995)

April Greiman, Hybrid Imagery: The Fusion of Technology and Graphic Design (New York: Watson-Guptill, 1990)

Christoph Grunenberg and Jonathan Harris, eds., The Summer of Love: Psychedelic Art, Social Crisis and Counterculture in the 1960s (Liverpool: Liverpool University Press, 2006)

Paul D. Grushkin, The Art of Rock Posters from Presley to Punk (New York: Abbeville, 1999)

Daniel Handke and Vanessa Hunt, Poster Art of the Disney Parks (New York: Disney, 2012)

Harry Marks, Broadcast Designer, Creative Inspirations series, produced by www.lynda.com

Steven Heller and Elaine Lustig Cohen, Born Modern: The Life and Design of Alvin Lustig (San Francisco: Chronicle, 2010)

David Hollander and Kristine McKenna, eds., Notes from a Revolution: Com/Co, the Diggers & the Haight (Santa Monica, Calif., and Rensselaerville, N.Y.: Foggy Notion Books and Fulton Ryder, 2012)

Institute of Graphic Designers, Graphic Design: San Francisco (San Francisco: Chronicle, 1979)

David James, "Expanded Cinema in Los Angeles: The Single Wing Turquoise Bird," Millennium Film Journal 43/44, summer 2005, 9–31

David E. James, The Most Typical Avant-Garde: History and Geography of Minor Cinemas in Los Angeles (Berkeley: University of California Press, 2005)

Geoff Kaplan, Power to the People: The Graphic Design of the Radical Press and the Rise of the Counter-Culture, 1964–1974 (Chicago: University Of Chicago Press, 2013)

Wendy Kaplan, ed., California Design, 1930–1965: Living in a Modern Way (Los Angeles and Cambridge, Mass.: Los Angeles County Museum of Art and MIT Press, 2011)

Susan Kare, interview with Alex Pang, September 8, 2000, in Susan Kare, oral history, "Making the Macintosh: Technology and Culture in Silicon Valley," Stanford University Libraries and Academic Information Resources, http://wwwsul.stanford.edu/mac/primary/interviews/kare/index.html

Cindy Keefer and Jaap Guldemond, eds., Oskar Fischinger (1900–1967): Experiments in Cinematic Abstraction (New York: Thames and Hudson, 2013)

Pat Kirkham, Charles and Ray Eames: Designers of the Twentieth Century (Cambridge, Mass.: MIT Press, 1995)

Roy Laughton, TV Graphics (London and New York: Studio Vista and Reinhold, 1966)

Sylvia Lavin and Kimberli Meyer, eds., Everything Loose Will Land: 1970s Art and Architecture in Los Angeles (Nürnberg: Verlag für Moderne Kunst, 2014)

Esther Leslie, Hollywood Flatlands: Animation, Critical Theory and the Avant-Garde (London: Verso, 2004)

Sheila Levrant de Bretteville, interview with Jenni Sorkin, June 22, 2010, oral history, "Woman's Building," Art Spaces Archive Project, www.as-ap.org, accessed July 15, 2012

Sheila Levrant de Bretteville, Barry Hyams, and Marianne Partridge, eds., "California Institute of the Arts: Prologue to a Community," Arts in Society, vol. 7, no. 3, fall/winter 1970

Eduardo Lipschutz-Villa, ed., Wallace Berman: Support the Revolution (Amsterdam: Institute of Contemporary Art, 1993)

Alvin Lustig, The Collected Writings of Alvin Lustig, ed. Holland R. Melson (New Haven: H. R. Melson, Jr., 1958)

Chris Michlig, Brian Roettinger, and Jan Tumlir, eds., In the Good Name of the Company: Artworks and Ephemera Produced by or in Tandem with the Colby Poster Printing Company (Brooklyn, N.Y., and Los Angeles: PictureBox and ForYourArt, 2013)

William Moritz, "Digital Harmony: The Life of John Whitney, Computer Animation Pioneer," Animation World, August 1997

———., Optical Poetry: The Life and Work of Oskar Fischinger (Eastleigh, U.K.: John Libbey, 2004)

John Neuhart, Marilyn Neuhart, and Ray Eames, Eames Design: The Work of the Office of Charles and Ray Eames (New York: Abrams, 1989)

Andrew Perchuk and Rani Singh, Harry Smith: The Avant-Garde in the American Vernacular (Los Angeles: Getty Research Institute, 2010)

Charles Perry, The Haight-Ashbury: A History (New York and London: Wenner, 1985)

Ward Ritchie, Of Bookmen and Printers: A Gathering of Memories (Los Angeles: Dawson's Book Shop, 1989)

———., A Tale of Two Books (Los Angeles: The Book Collectors, 1985)

Elias Romero, 3 Films by Elias Romero (1968–1972), DVD (Los Angeles: Center for Visual Music, 2008)

Pierluigi Serraino, NorCalMod: Icons of Northern California Modernism (San Francisco: Chronicle, 2006)

"SFMOMA 75th Anniversary: Jack Stauffacher," interview with Lisa Rubens, 2006, Regional Oral History Office, Bancroft Library, University of California, Berkeley, copyright San Francisco Museum of Modern Art, 2008, transcript, 2

C. Ray Smith, Supermannerism: New Attitudes in Post-Modern Architecture (New York: Plume, 1977)

Lynn Spigel, TV by Design: Modern Art and the Rise of Network Television (Chicago and London: University of Chicago Press, 2009)

Kevin Starr, California: A History (New York: Modern Library, 2005)

Frank Stauffacher, ed., Art in Cinema: A Symposium on the Avantgarde Film (San Francisco: San Francisco Museum of Modern Art, 1947)

Barbara Stauffacher Solomon, Why? Why Not? 80 Years of Art & Design in Pix & Prose, Juxtaposed (San Francisco: Fun Fog Press, 2013)

Bobbye Tigerman, ed., A Handbook of California Design, 1930–1965: Craftspeople, Designers, Manufacturers (Cambridge, Mass.: MIT Press, 2013)

David F. Travers, ed., Arts & Architecture, 1945–1967: The Complete Reprint, vol. 1 (Cologne: Taschen, 2008)

Marc Treib, "Design in Two and a Half Dimensions," Print, November/December 1975

John Van Hamersveld, My Art, My Life, ed. David Lynn Clucas (South Bend, Ind.: St. Augustine's Press, 2010)

John Van Hamersveld and Coolhous Studio, Fifty Years of Graphic Design (Berkeley: Gingko Press, 2013)

John Whitney, "Animation Mechanisms," American Cinematographer, January 1971

Ted Widmer, "R. Crumb, The Art of Comics No. 1," The Paris Review, no. 193, summer 2010, www.theparisreview.org, accessed May 22, 2014

Gene Youngblood, Expanded Cinema (New York: Dutton, 1970)

INDEX

White page numbers refer to illustrations.

ABC Television, 152, 166, 172, 180, 184
Abel, Robert: The ABC Friday Night Movie promo, 1970, 174, 175; Altshuler on, 121, 140–43; Berger Paint TV commercial, 1977, 192, 193; photographs of, 140, 206; 7UP "Bubbles" commerical, 1975, 121, 174, 184, 185; Tron, 1982, 14, 198, 199. See also Robert Abel and Associates
Abstract Expressionist painting, 162, 170
advertising: broadcast advertising, 164, 184; and graphic design, 24–25, 27, 72; and Kent, 224; and Larsen, 312, 348; and sixties, 224
Advertising Designers: "The Art of 'Instantaneous Communication,'" 1959, 84, 84–85; A Dictionary for Moderns, 1956, 76, 77; graphic designers working for, 14
Albers, Joseph, 223, 266
alternative press: and The City of San Francisco Oracle, 268; and color combinations, 224–25; and sixties, 219
Altshuler, Jeffrey, "Robert Abel: Video Surrealist," 121, 140–43
American Institute of Graphic Arts (AIGA), Los Angeles chapter, 64, 315, 386
American National Exhibition, Moscow, 1959, 120, 154
Amidi, Amid, 119, 160
Anderson, Cal: Invitation, 1956, 78, 79; and modernism, 27
Anderson, Chester, 272
animation: and motion graphics, 119, 120, 122, 126–27; Whitney on, 121, 134–39
annual-report design, 24, 76
anonymous: Haight Street Is Ours to Play On..., 1967, 272, 273; Kaliflower, vol. 1, no. 36, December 25, 1969, 292, 293; Kaliflower, vol. 2, no. 39, January 21, 1971, 294, 295; "1% Free," August 1967, 276, 277
Aono, Caryn, 315
Apple Macintosh: and Greiman, 13, 312, 392; and Kare, 388, 389
arcade video games, and motion graphics, 119, 121, 123, 196, 200, 202
Armitage, Merle: and book design, 25, 48; Igor Stravinsky, 12, 13, 48, 49; Looking Backward, 32, 52, 53; Ritchie on, 25, 42–45
Aronson, Bjorn: Autopia poster, 1955, 60, 63; Disneyland Hotel poster, 1956, 60, 61; Skyway poster, 1956, 60, 62
Art Center College of Design, Pasadena: and Cal Anderson, 78; and Danziger, 23, 68, 72; and Fitzgerald, 182; and Follis, 23; and Kratka, 23, 94; and Lustig, 23, 66, 72, 78, 88, 94, 222; and Perri, 190; and Dean Smith, 86; and Usher, 23, 66; and Van Hamersveld, 254
Art Deco, 30, 31, 32
art/design education, 314. See also specific schools
Art Directors Club, 64
Art Nouveau, 215, 231, 268

Arts & Architecture magazine: ads in, 68; and Clements, 340; cover designs for, 24, 32, 58, 66; Ray Eames's covers for, 344, 345; Follis's covers for, 24, 58, 64, 65; and high-contrast ads, 223; Matter's covers for, 24, 58, 58, 59; style-less typography of, 32; Usher's cover sketch for, 66, 67
Asian cultures, 24, 224, 226
Association, The, 284
avant-garde: and Art Deco, 30; and political and social activists, 256; and Jack Stauffacher, 102
Baer, Kim, 315
Banham, Reyner: autopia, 60; California lineage of, 14; Los Angeles: The Architecture of Four Ecologies, 11; Reyner Banham Loves Los Angeles documentary billboard, 5
Barton's Bonbonniere, 226
Bass, Elaine: Seconds title sequence, 1966, 168, 169
Bass, Jennifer, 164
Bass, Saul: Apples and Oranges, 1962, 164, 165; and color relations, 223; and Continental logo, 288; and Danziger, 72; The Frank Sinatra Show titles, 1957, 152, 153; Installation for XIV Milan Triennale, 1968, 98, 99; The Man with the Golden Arm movie titles, 119–20, 152, 182, 223; and New York design community, 222; Seconds title sequence, 1966, 168, 169; and Dean Smith, 86; Vertigo movie titles, 1958, 158, 223; and Whitney, 106, 158; Why Man Creates, 98
Bauhaus, 25, 223
Baumfeld, Rudi, 226
Beat culture, 54, 162, 215, 219, 250
Becker, Leslie, 315
Bellamy, Edward, Looking Backward, 32, 52, 53
Bengston, Billy Al, 12, 13
Berman, Wallace: Second Los Angeles Film-Maker's Festival poster, 1963, 248, 249; and sixties, 216, 219
Big Brother and the Holding Company, 286
Big Five, 216, 270
Birrell, Don: and modernism, 23, 24, 26; Nut Tree, 34, 47; Nut Tree graphics and environmental design, Vacaville, California, 74, 74, 75
black arts movement: Black Communications Project, 278; and sixties, 219
Black Panthers, 35, 215, 219, 225, 298
Blum, Chris: Levi's "Evolution" commercial, ca. 1975, 186, 187; photograph of, 206
book design, 25, 48. See also alternative press
Boston, Archie: photograph of, 241; self-promotional posters, 1966–67, 215, 260, 261, 262
Boston, Brad: photograph of, 241; self-promotional posters, 1966–67, 215, 260, 261, 262
Boston, David, 241
Boston and Boston, office of, 241
Brader, Betty: Cal Tjader Quintet album cover, 1956, 355, 355; Dupont "Color on Colored

Stock," ad for Print, 1959, 351; "Eye Shade!" ad for Joseph Magnin Department Store, late 1950s or early 1960s, 348, 349; "It's a Leg Watcher's Year!" Joseph Magnin ad, 1967, 353; JM Christmas boxes, mid-1960s, 351, 352; JM Christmas wrapping paper, 1963, 350–51, 352; "Pretty, Please," Joseph Magnin newspaper ad, 1967, 354, 355
Brand, Stewart: and sixties, 219, 262; Whole Earth Catalog, 33, 296
Burdick, Anne, 312, 315
Butler, Frances: Bananaman in Switzerland, 1972, 380, 380, 381; Colored Reading, 380
CA (Communication Arts), 217, 229
CalArts: Corrigan on, 217, 239; and Danziger, 72; and de Bretteville, 320, 334, 336, 382; Disney on, 217, 238; and Godard, 72, 104; and Greiman, 225; history of graphic design courses, 24; and postmodern graphics, 13
California College of Arts & Crafts, 27, 78
California graphic design: European traditions in, 13; history of, 10–15, 32–35; and modernism, 12–13, 23–25, 26–27, 31–32, 36–41, 221, 222; and motion graphics, 13, 119–21, 122–23, 125–29; and sixties, 13–14, 215–17, 218–19, 221–26; and women, 13, 14, 311–13, 314–15, 317–25
California Institute of Technology, Pasadena, 106
California Institute of the Arts. See CalArts
California State University, Long Beach, 23
Candela, Felix, 66
candy-apple neon effect, 140, 184
Catalina Design Conference (1962), 119
CBS Television, 152, 172, 180
Chase, Margo, 312, 315
Chouinard Art Institute, 23, 74, 270
CIA Compendium, 11
The City of San Francisco Oracle, 219, 268, 269, 270, 271
Clements, Grace Richardson: Communication (Aviation and Navigation) mosaics, 340, 340, 341; drawing showing layout of mosaics on floor, 342; murals, Long Beach Airport, 1942, 340, 343
Coblentz, Dian, Comment newspaper spread, 1964, 358, 359
Cohen, Allen, 268, 270
Colby Poster Printing Company, 1, 219, 246
color: and alternative press, 224–25; color vector drawing, 196; and counterculture, 221, 224, 226; and East Coast design, 216, 221, 225, 311; and psychedelia subculture, 221, 223, 224, 262; and sixties, 216, 221, 226
Columbia Pictures, 150
comix culture, and sixties, 218, 270, 282, 286
Communications Company: and Diggers, 14, 272, 276, 292; and Hayward and Anderson, 272; and Invisible Circus, 274; and sixties, 219
computer technology: as aesthetic, 13; and bitmapping, 35, 200, 388; and Danziger, 106; and Greiman, 13, 312, 392; and

410

motion graphics, 24, 106, 120, 121, 125–26, 128, 129, 176, 198; and Whitney, 106, 121

Connections exhibition (UCLA's Wight Gallery, December 1976), 90

Corrigan, Robert, 217, 239

Cosutta, Rene, and women in California graphic design, 315

counterculture: and authenticity, 262; and Brand, 296; and color combinations, 221, 224, 226; and Diggers, 276; and hippie modernism, 86; and historical typography, 34; and Nielson, 259; and Sätty, 280; and sixties, 216, 219; and Stermer, 217. See also alternative press; psychedelia subculture

Coyote, Peter, 272, 274

Cranbrook Academy, 70, 344, 364

Crisp, Denise Gonzales, 14, 312, 313, 315

Crumb, R.: Cheap Thrills album cover, 1968, 286, 287; and sixties, 218; and Zap Comix, 282, 286

Danziger, Louis: cover of A Report on the Art and Technology Program of the Los Angeles County Museum of Art, 1967–1971, 32–33, 33; Earth Quake album cover, 1971, 106, 107; Gelvatex Paint ad, 1956, 25, 72, 73; General Light ad, December 1949, 68, 69; and high contrast ads, 223; and Los Angeles County Museum of Art, 376; and Lustig, 23, 54, 72; and New York design community, 222; and Parkhurst, 76; Xybion logo, 1975, 106, 107

Dawson, Chris, 178

Day of the Dead (film and exhibition; 1957), 34, 82, 83

de Bretteville, Sheila Levrant: American Symphony Orchestra program cover, 332; Announcement Poster for the CalArts School of Design, 334, 385, 386; and CalArts, 320, 334, 336, 382; CalArts 1973–74 Admissions Bulletin, 1973, 334, 385, 386; California Institute of the Arts, Arts in Society, 217, 238–39, 335, 382, 383, 384; "Color" poster, 336; DeNeve on, 313, 332–37, 382; and Feminist Studio Workshop, 320; Olivetti designs, 332, 333; Pink poster, 1973, 386, 387; and Woman's Building, 332, 336–37, 337, 386; "Women in Design" poster, 336

DeNeve, Rose, "A Feminist Option," 313, 332–37, 382

Depression, 30, 31

DeVries, Mark, The City of San Francisco Oracle, no. 7, 1967, 268, 269, 270

Didion, Joan, 14, 272

Diggers: and Communications Company, 14, 272, 276, 292; The Digger Papers, 276; and Invisible Circus, 274; publications of, 225; and sixties, 215, 219; and typography, 35

Disney, Walt, 104, 217, 238

Disneyland, Aronson's posters for, 60, 61, 62, 63

Donald, Nancy, 315

Dorfsman, Lou, 164, 172

Douglas, Emory: "Peace with Honor" poster, 1973, 298, 299; posters for Black Panthers, 215; Revolutionary Posters ad, 1968, 278, 279; and sixties, 219

Dreyfus Agency, 25, 27, 72

Eames, Charles: Case Study House No. 8 (1949), 225; and Danziger, 72; and Disney's graphics, 60; Ray Eames's collaborations with, 344; and functional decoration, 34, 35; and Girard, 82, 100, 225, 226; House of Cards, 1952, 70; Kent influenced by, 356; and Kratka, 94; and Mathematica, 244; and Sussman, 374; and upper case fonts, 82; and vernacular, 225; and Whitney, 106

Eames, Ray Kaiser: Arts & Architecture cover, March 1947, 344, 345; Case Study House No. 8 (1949), 225; and Danziger, 72; and functional decoration, 34; and Girard, 82, 100, 225, 226; House of Cards, 1952, 70; letters to Charles Eames, 346, 346, 347; and Marilyn Neuhart, 360; Sea Things sketch and printed fabric, 1945, 344, 345, 346; and vernacular, 225; and Whitney, 106

Eames Office: and color combinations, 225, 226; Day of the Dead title card, 1957, 82, 83; Giant House of Cards, 1953, 70, 70, 71; Glimpses of the U.S.A., 1959, 120, 154, 155, 158; Kaleidoscope Jazz Chair, 1960, 120, 156, 157; and Kratka, 94; math game and multiplication cube for Mathematica, 1961, 215, 244, 245; and Matter, 58; and midcentury modern, 34; Nut Tree furnishings, 74; and Sussman, 34, 324, 339, 374; and Whitney, 120, 154, 158

Earth Quake (rock group), 106; album cover, 107

East Coast design: California graphic design compared to, 12–13, 66, 125, 222, 312; color palette of, 216, 221, 225, 311; standards of, 23, 50

E.A.T. (Experiments in Art and Technology): and motion graphics, 121, 122; Pepsi Pavilion at Expo '70, Osaka, Japan, 1970, 121, 178, 178, 179

Edison, Thomas Alva, 313, 317–18, 321, 324–25

8th Annual Exhibition of Advertising Art (San Francisco, 1956), 78

Elise (Cavanna), 32, 52

Endemann, Heidi, Levi's "Evolution" commercial, ca. 1975, 186, 187

Envirolab: and motion graphics, 121, 122; Pepsi Pavilion at Expo '70, Osaka, Japan, 1970, 121, 178, 178, 179

environmental design, 24, 64

European design: California graphic design compared to, 12–13, 125, 222; color palette of, 216, 221, 311; standards of, 23, 50

expanded cinema, and motion graphics, 122, 176

Family Dog: and Ham, 170; and Moscoso, 266; and Mouse and Kelley, 264; and Phillips, 262; and sixties, 218; and Van Hamersveld, 282

fashion culture: and color combinations, 224; and Gernreich, 258–59; and Larsen, 312, 348; and sixties, 219

Feminist Studio Workshop, 318, 319, 320, 337

Ferro, Pablo: Citizens Band titles, 1977, 194, 195

Fillmore Ballroom, 224, 231, 262

films and filmmaking: and Art Deco, 30; independent films, 119, 120; and motion graphics, 119, 120, 122, 123, 125–27, 170, 176; Youngblood on, 130–33

film titles: and motion graphics, 123, 128. See also specific designers

Fischinger, Oskar: Allegretto, 1936–43, 146, 147; in his Hollywood studio, 145; and modernism, 12; and Harry Smith, 148

Fitzgerald, Wayne: McMillan & Wife titles, 1971, 182, 183

Follis, John: Arts & Architecture covers, 24, 58, 64, 65; and Lustig, 23, 54, 58, 64

Fong, Karin, 315

Francis, Ed, 242

Frank Wiggins Trade School, 96

Free Print Shop, 219, 292

Frimkess, Louis, 76

Garrett, Murray, 242

Garrett-Howard, 215, 242

Gehlhaar, Jens, 11

Gehry, Frank, 374, 376

Gehry and Associates, 376

German Expressionists, 250, 262

Gernreich, Rudi: Cream, Brown, and Orange Triangle Print Scarf and Astrology Print Scarf, both mid-1960s, 258–59, 258, 259; and sixties, 219

Getty Research Institute, 23, 222

Girard, Alexander: and Charles and Ray Eames, 82, 100, 225, 226; main entrance door for Scoren House, Woodside, California, 1969, 100, 100, 101; and John and Marilyn Neuhart, 88, 100; Textiles & Objects, 74, 88, 360

Girard, Susan, 88

Godard, Keith: and Danziger, 72; proposed commemorative poster for opening of California Institute of the Arts, 1972, 104, 105

Goodman, Art, 168

Gossage, Howard, 348

Graham, Bill, 262, 282

graphic design: and advertising, 24–25, 27, 72; definitions of, 14; and futurism, 30, 31, 32; history of, 10, 24, 29–31, 72; and modernism, 10, 29. See also California graphic design

Graphic Design in America exhibition (Walker Art Center; 1989), 10

Greiman, April: and Apple Macintosh, 13, 312, 392; and color combinations, 225; "Does It Make Sense?" Design Quarterly, 12, 13, 392, 394–95; Iris Light poster, 1984, 392, 393; poster for Art in Los Angeles:

Seventeen Artists in the Sixties, 1981, 390, 391; Wet magazine covers, 225
Griffin, Rick: Grateful Dead, published in The City of San Francisco Oracle, no. 6, 1967, 270, 271; and sixties, 216, 218; and Zap Comix, 286
Group Five, 215, 242
Gruen, Victor, 226, 364, 366
Gruen Associates, 226
Hal Stebbins Inc., 26, 72, 76, 84, 84–85
Ham, Bill: projection set-up for live video performance for Marin County Public Access TV, 1977, 170; and sixties, 218; Spontaneous Painting of Projected Imagery, 1966–69, 170, 171
Hand Press, 360
happenings, 121, 170, 274, 290
Heiden, Jeri, 284, 312, 315
Heller, Steven, 10, 160
Helms, Chet, 264
Henry Dreyfuss and Associates, 25, 26, 96
hippie culture, 86, 215, 224, 232, 254, 262, 276. See also counterculture; psychedelia subculture
Hodges, Dave: poster for the Invisible Circus, 1967, 274, 274–75; posters of, 215
Hodgetts, Craig, 104
Hollander, Toni, 315
Honig, Cooper, and Harrington, 186
hot rod/car culture, 218, 264, 282
Howard, Gene, The Swingin' Eye!!!!!!!! album cover, 1960, 242, 243
IBM, 215, 244
IBM Selectric Composer, 296
Immaculate Heart College Art Department: and Kent, 216, 228, 356; photograph of Mary's Day Event, 1964, 358, 359
International Style, 222, 225
Irwin, Terry, 312, 315
Janss, Larry, 176
Johnston, Alastair, 319, 380
John Urie and Associates, ABC 1964–65 fall season promo, 1964, 166, 167
Joplin, Janis, 286
Joseph Magnin stores: and Larsen, 34, 226, 319, 348, 352
Jugendstil, 262
Kagan, Paul, American Tantric #2 (Yab-Yum), published in The City of San Francisco Oracle, no. 7, April 1967, 270, 271
Kaliflower: as collective enterprise, 14; publications of, 225, 292, 293, 294, 295; and sixties, 219
Kare, Susan: control panel for Macintosh 1.0, 1983, 388, 389; Macintosh system and application icons, 1983–84, 388, 389; MacPaint interface for Macintosh, 1983, 388, 389
Kavanaugh, Gere: Bob Mitchell Designs, Los Angeles, wallpaper, ca. 1970, 366, 367; Gere Kavanaugh home, Los Angeles, late 1970s, 364, 365; photograph with Hallmark store wrapping paper and display, late 1970s, 398; and Sussman, 374; Toys by Roy, Albuquerque, New Mexico, ca. 1961, 366, 366; Toys by Roy wrapping paper, ca. 1961, 366, 367
Kelley, Alton: Celestial Moonchild, 1967, 264, 265; photograph of, 232; posters of, 216, 232, 264, 270; and sixties, 218
Kelley/Mouse Studios, 232
Kent, Sister Corita: American Sampler, 1969, 290, 291; Be, of Love, (A Little) More Careful, Than of Everything, 1967, 356, 357; on California graphic design, 312; Circus Alphabet series, 224; Daisy, 1966, 256, 257; daisy with all the petals yes exhibition and catalogue, 313, 326–27, 358; "Immaculate Heart College Art Department Rules," 216, 228; and Kavanaugh, 364; repurposing of common advertising language, 224; and sixties, 219; visual works of, 216
Kepes, György, 98, 164
Kim, Somi, 315
Kimball, Wayne, Birthday album cover, 1968, 284, 285
Kingrey, Kenneth, 88
Kirkham, Pat, 154, 156, 164, 344
Koblick, Harry, 23, 27
Koelker, Mike, 186, 206
Kratka, Charles: Giant House of Cards, 1953, 70, 71; and Lustig, 23, 54, 94; murals for the Los Angeles International Airport, 1961, 24, 94, 95
Kubrick, Stanley, 120, 172, 194
Lanziger, Franz X.: Crystal Castles, Atari arcade video game, 1983, 200, 201
Larsen, Marget: Dupont "Color on Colored Stock," ad for Print, 1959, 351; "Eye Shade!" ad for Joseph Magnin Department Store, late 1950s or early 1960s, 348, 349; and fashion advertising, 312, 348; "It's a Leg Watcher's Year!" Joseph Magnin ad, 1967, 353; JM Christmas boxes, mid-1960s, 351, 352; JM Christmas wrapping paper, 1963, 350–51, 352; and Joseph Magnin stores, 34, 226, 319, 348, 352; "Pretty, Please," Joseph Magnin newspaper ad, 1967, 354, 355
Lausten, Judith, 315
Lebrun, David, 176
Lee, Robert Tyler, Lassie and The Gale Storm Show interstitial cards, 1958, 80, 81
Lemonado de Sica: Flatt and Scruggs Avalon Ballroom concert poster, 1967, 262, 263; and sixties, 218
letterpress, 24, 76, 82, 90, 248
Licko, Zuzana, 315
light shows: and motion graphics, 119, 121, 122, 162, 170, 176, 184; and sixties, 262; and supergraphics, 372; and Van Hamersveld, 216
Locks, Seymour, 162
Long Beach City College, 88
Lord, Denny, 178
Lorenz, Catherine, 315
Los Angeles County Museum of Art: Art in Los Angeles exhibition, 390, 391; Gallery Promenade poster and invitation for Junior Art Council, mid-1960s, 360, 363; H. C. Westermann exhibition, 376, 379; Made in California exhibition, 12; A Report on the Art and Technology Program of the Los Angeles County Museum of Art, 1967–1971, 32–33, 33
Los Angeles Olympics (1984), Sono Tube temporary signage, 225–26
Lustig, Alvin: Arts & Architecture logo, 58; and book-cover design, 24, 56; "California Modern" essay, 25, 36–41; Camino Real book cover, 56, 57; The Day of the Locust book cover, 56, 57; as educator, 23, 66, 72, 78, 88, 94, 222; Flowers of Evil book cover, 56, 57; and Follis, 23, 54, 58, 64; The Ghost in the Underblows, 50, 51; graphic pattern, 1950, 54, 55; Mister Magoo titles, ca. 1950, 150, 151; Neurotica logo, 1947, 54, 55; New Directions book covers, 12, 56, 57; and Parkhurst, 76; on strictures of style, 32, 33; Three Lives book cover, 56, 57; UPA logo, 1946, 54, 55, 150; The Wanderer book cover, 56, 57
Made in California exhibition (Los Angeles County Museum of Art; 2000–2001), 12
Majestic Poster Press: New Painting of Common Objects exhibition poster, Pasadena Art Museum, 1962, 246, 247; and sixties, 216, 219
Makela, Laurie Haycock, 312, 315
Marks, Harry: The ABC Friday Night Movie promo, 1970, 174, 175; ABC Movie of the Week promo, 1969, 120, 172, 173, 174
Martin, Sister Magdalen Mary, 314, 356, 364
Mathematica exhibition (1960), 34
Matter, Herbert: Art & Architecture covers, July 1945 and May 1948, 24, 58, 58, 59; tourist brochures of, 68
McCann Erickson, 72, 86
McGee, Hetty, The City of San Francisco Oracle, no. 7, 1967, 268, 269, 270
Mead, Syd, Tron, 1982, 14, 198, 199
Méndez, Rebeca, 312, 315
midcentury-modern, 31, 32, 33, 34
Miller, Herman, 88
Miller, Stanley George. See Mouse, Stanley
Mirman, Kenneth, Tron, 1982, 14, 121, 198, 199
Mitchell, Joni, Song to a Seagull album cover, 1968, 284, 285
Moderne, 30, 32
modernism: and California graphic design, 12–13, 23–25, 26–27, 31–32, 36–41, 221, 222; corporate modernism, 13; folk modernism, 24, 225, 226; and graphic design, 10; and Solomon, 372; visual syntax of, 222
Morioka, Noreen, 312, 315
Morla, Jennifer, 312, 315
Moscoso, Victor: and Big Five, 216; Neon Rose #12, 1967, 266, 267; photograph of, 233; posters of, 10, 232, 266, 270; psychedelic colors, 10, 223, 224, 266, 270, 282; and sixties, 218, 223; The Who

412

(with Fleetwood Mac) Shrine Auditorium concert poster, 1968, 282, 283; and Zap Comix, 282, 286

motion graphics: and E. Bass, 123; and S. Bass, 119–20, 123, 129, 158, 172, 190; and California graphic design, 13, 119–21, 122–23, 125–29; and computer technology, 24, 106, 120, 121, 125–26, 128, 129, 176, 198; and films, 119, 120, 122, 123, 125–27, 170, 176; and Ham, 122, 176; history of, 119–20, 125–29; and Marks, 123, 166, 184; and Norman, 122; and Perri, 123; and Romero, 122, 170, 176; and Single Wing Turquoise Bird, 122; and TV production, 119, 120, 121, 123, 127, 176, 180; and Urie, 123; and Whitney, 24, 106, 119, 121, 122, 158, 190, 196, 198

Motion Graphics (Whitney's company), 158

Mouse, Stanley: Celestial Moonchild, 1967, 264, 265; photograph of, 232; posters of, 216, 232, 233, 264, 270; and sixties, 218

Mouse Studios, 264

Museum of Modern Art, New York, 254

Music industry: album covers, 242, 284; and color combinations, 224; rock posters, 217, 230–33; and sixties, 218; and Van Hamersveld, 282. See also specific designers

NBC Television, 182

Nelson, George, 154

Neuhart, John: birth announcement for Lisa Ferreira, 1960, 90, 90; birth announcement for Peter Ferber, 1958, 90, 91; and Eames Office, 34, 154; "A Fourth Greeting," 1957, 92, 93; "Greetings, Greetings, Greetings," mid-1960s, 92, 92; and Hand Press, 360; Hand Press logo, 1957, 88, 88; House of Cards, 1952, 70; Junior Art Council Newsletter covers, early 1960s, 90, 91; and Neuhart Donges Neuhart, 110; opening announcement for Textiles & Objects, 1961, 88, 89; poster for Textiles & Objects, 1961, 34; wedding announcement for Marilyn Marqua and John Neuhart, 1957, 90, 91

Neuhart, Marilyn: birth announcement for Lisa Ferreira, 1960, 90, 90; birth announcement for Peter Ferber, 1958, 90, 91; "California Santa," ca. 1959, 360, 362; and Eames Office, 34; "A Fourth Greeting," 1957, 92, 93; Gallery Promenade poster and invitation for Junior Art Council, Los Angeles County Museum of Art, mid-1960s, 360, 363; "Greetings, Greetings, Greetings," mid-1960s, 92, 92; handmade dolls for Textiles & Objects, 1960–67, 360, 361; and Hand Press, 360; Hand Press logo, 1957, 88, 88; House of Cards, 1952, 70; Junior Art Council Newsletter covers, early 1960s, 90, 91; modernist take on rag doll, 90; and Neuhart Donges Neuhart, 110; opening announcement for Textiles & Objects, 1961, 88, 89; wall hanging composed of dolls, 74; wedding announcement for Marilyn Marqua and John Neuhart, 1957, 90, 91; Neuhart Donges Neuhart, 110, 360

New Age, 268, 292, 294

New Bauhaus, Chicago, 68, 374

New Directions, New York, 27

Newman, Earl: Circus, ca. 1965, 253, 253; Hiroshima, 1966, 250, 252; Insomniac poster, ca. 1965, 250, 251; and sixties, 219; and typography, 250, 250

New Painting of Common Objects exhibition (Pasadena Art Museum, 1962), 216

New York Worlds Fair of 1964–65, 158

Nielson, Layne, Cream, Brown, and Orange Triangle Print Scarf and Astrology Print Scarf, both mid-1960s, 258–59, 258, 259

Norman, Phill: various title graphics for UPA, late 1950s–early 1960s, 160, 161; Wonder Woman titles, season one, 1976, 188, 189

Olden, Georg, Lassie and The Gale Storm Show interstitial cards, 1958, 80, 81

orange, and sixties, 216, 221, 226

Orbit Graphic Arts, 280

Pacific Standard Time: Art in L.A., 1945–1980 exhibition program (Getty Research Institute), 23, 222

Pacific Title and Art Studio, 182, 186

Paramount, 120, 146

Parkhurst, Ken, 24, 27, 76

Pate, Bill, The Swingin' Eye!!!!!!!! album cover, 1960, 242, 243

Pate/Francis, 215, 218, 242

Pederson, Con, Berger Paint TV commercial, 1977, 192, 193

Perri, Dan: Star Wars franchise logo, 190; Taxi Driver titles, 1976, 190, 191

Phillips, Ardison, 178

Phillips, Doyle, Flatt and Scruggs Avalon Ballroom concert poster, 1967, 262, 263

Phillips, Jim, Doctor Moto's Medicine Bus, published in The City of San Francisco Oracle, no. 6, 1967, 270, 271

Pinnacle Productions, 176, 216, 282

Podreich, Wilfred. See Sätty

political and social activists: and The City of San Francisco Oracle, 268; and Douglas, 298; and Kent, 256, 290, 358; and sixties, 215, 219

Poltroon Press, 318, 319, 380

Pop Art, 216, 246

Porter, Allen: Gruen Lighting ad, October 1952, 68, 69

Portfolio of Western Advertising Art, 84

posters: psychedelic posters, 34–35, 215, 216, 223, 224, 264, 266, 270; rock posters, 230–33, 254. See also specific designers

postmodern theory, 13, 35

Pratt Institute, 86

Prezja, Paul, 225–26, 374

psychedelia subculture: and album covers, 284; colors of, 221, 223, 224, 262; and Communications Company, 274; and Haight-Ashbury, 272; and Ham, 170; place in California graphic design, 215; and posters, 34–35, 215, 216, 223, 224, 264, 266, 270; and sixties, 218, 262; and TV advertising, 184; and Whitney's Catalog, 158

rainbow roll technique. See split fountain technique

Rand, Marvin, 68

Rand, Paul, 29, 152, 166

Reagh, William, Shelly's Manne-Hole, 250

Reoutt, Steve, 78, 348

Ritchie, Ward: on Armitage, 25, 42–45; The Ghost in the Underblows, 50, 51; Of Bookmen & Printers, 42–45

Robert Abel and Associates: Berger Paint TV commercial, 1977, 192, 193; offices of, 206; 7UP "Bubbles" commerical, 1975, 121, 174, 184, 185; Tron, 1982, 14, 198, 199

Romero, Elias: Stepping Stones, 1968, 162, 163

Rosenthal, Herb, 98

Ruscha, Ed: New Painting of Common Objects exhibition poster, Pasadena Art Museum, 1962, 246, 247; Twentysix Gasoline Stations, 216, 218

Saarinen, Eero, 364

Saarinen, Eliel, 344

San Francisco Mime Troupe, 219, 272

San Francisco Museum of Modern Art, 148

San Francisco State College, 162

Sätty: McCarthy Poster, 1968, 280, 281; and sixties, 218

science fiction, 30, 120, 121

Scoren, Robert, 100

screens, and motion graphics, 119, 121

Scroggins, Michael, 176

The Sea Ranch, 328, 329, 330, 330, 331, 368, 370–71, 372

Sidjakov, Nicolas: and sixties, 218; Staffan, 1970, 288, 289; symbol for Continental Airlines "Celebration" ad campaign, late 1960s, 288, 289

Silton, Susan, 315

Singh, Barbara Fairbrother: Crystal Castles, Atari arcade video game, 1983, 200, 201

Single Wing Turquoise Bird: re-creation of performance, ca. 1969, 176, 177; and Van Hamersveld, 176, 216

sixties, and California graphic design, 13–14, 215–17, 218–19, 221–26

slit-scan technique, 120, 190

Smith, C. Ray, 368

Smith, Dean: Ahwanee Resort Ads, 1959, 86, 87

Smith, Edd, 76

Smith, Harry: Film #5: Circular Tensions (Homage to Oskar Fischinger), 1947, 148, 149; still from Film #2: Message from the Sun, ca. 1946-48, 148; still from Film #10, 1957, 148

Smothers Brothers Summer Show promo, 1970, 180, 181

Society of Contemporary Designers, 64

Solomon, Barbara Stauffacher: Hear-Hear Record Store, San Francisco, 1969, 331, 372, 372, 373; monthly calendars for San Francisco Museum of Modern Art,

1965–71, 368, 368, 369; The Sea Ranch, Sea Ranch, California, 1966–67, 328, 329, 330, 331, 368, 370–72; and sexism, 312; Stermer's "Barbara Stauffacher Solomon," 313, 328–31; and supergraphics, 329, 368, 372
Solomon, Daniel, 331, 372
split-fountain technique, 1, 250, 268, 270
sponsored and commercial films, and motion graphics, 123, 164, 194
Spungbuggy, 186
Stanton, Alan, 178
Stauffacher, Frank, 102, 148, 368
Stauffacher, Jack: G2, 1969, 102, 103; and modernism, 24, 25; The Rebel Albert Camus, 1969, 102, 102
Steamboat, Whole Earth Catalog, fall 1970, 296, 297
Stebbins, Hal: A Dictionary for Moderns, 76, 77; promo for agency, 84, 84–85
Sterling, Jennifer, 315
Stermer, Dugald: "Barbara Stauffacher Solomon," Print, vol. 13, no. 3, 1971, 313, 328–31; "Rock Posters," 217, 230–33
Stewart, Jan, 314
still photography, and motion graphics, 119, 126, 194
Stravinksy, Igor, Armitage on, 12, 13, 48, 49
Streamlined style, 30, 31, 35
Sturgeon, Inju, 315
supergraphics: and Girard, 100; and Solomon, 329, 368, 372
surf culture, 12, 160, 216, 218, 246, 254, 255, 282
Sussman, Deborah: on Danziger, 72; Day of the Dead film titles, 82; on de Bretteville, 382; on Disney's graphics, 60; and Eames Office, 34, 324, 339, 374; Giant House of Cards, 1953, 70, 71; H. C. Westermann exhibition catalogue, Los Angeles County Museum of Art, 1968, 376, 379; Hollywood Bowl program, 1970, 376, 378; Joseph Magnin stores, Almaden and Costa Mesa, California, 1968–69, 376, 377; and Los Angeles Olympics, 225–26, 374; Mathematica, 244; and John and Marilyn Neuhart, 88; and New York design community, 222; Reyner Banham Loves Los Angeles documentary billboard, 5; and sexism, 312, 374; Zody's Discount Department Store, Los Angeles, 1971, 374, 374, 375
Sussman-Prejza and Company, 374
Sutter Street Commune, 219, 292, 294
Swiss graphics, 329, 372
Taylor, Henry, dinner party poster-size invitation, 1
Taylor, Richard: photographs of, 206; 7UP "Bubbles" commercial, 1975, 121, 174, 184, 185; Tron, 1982, 14, 198, 199
technological innovation. See computer technology
Technology Entertainment and Design (TED) conference, 172
Teletype machine, 96

Tenazas, Lucille, 312, 315
Textiles & Objects, New York, 24, 26, 34, 74, 88, 89, 360
Theurer, Dave: I, Robot, Atari arcade video game, 1983, 202, 203; Tempest, Atari arcade video game, 1980, 196, 197
Thrasher, Ed: Birthday album cover, 1968, 284, 285; A Child's Guide to Good and Evil album cover, 1968, 284, 285; and sixties, 218; Song to a Seagull album cover, 1968, 284, 285; Southern California poster, 3; West Coast Pop Art Experimental Band album cover, 216
Trumbull, Doug: ABC Movie of the Week promo, 1969, 120, 172, 173, 174; "Star Gate" interdimensional travel sequence for 2001: A Space Odyssey, 120, 172
TV branding and promos, and motion graphics, 123, 152, 164
TV commercials, and motion graphics, 123, 180
TV production: and motion graphics, 119, 120, 121, 123, 127, 176, 180; relocation to California, 80; titles, 123. See also specific designers
typography: and Armitage, 48; and Berman, 248; and Butler, 380; and Colby Poster, 246; commercial wood typography, 34, 82, 90, 102; and Communications Company, 274; and counterculture, 34; and Danziger, 106; and de Bretteville, 332, 386; and Greiman, 225, 323; historical typography, 34–35; IBM Selectric, 33, 296; and Kare, 388; and Kent, 256, 356; and Majestic Poster, 246; and Marks, 172; and midcentury modern, 34; and modernism, 32, 222; and Moscoso, 266; and motion graphics, 119, 128–29, 158, 160, 190; and Newman, 250, 250; and pictorial intensity, 34, 35; and psychedelia subculture, 262; and Solomon, 329, 368; and Stauffacher, 102; and Sussman, 82, 376; Swiss typographic style, 33; and Van Hamersveld, 160, 282; and Whitney, 158; and Whole Earth Catalog, 296; and Young, 25, 96
UCLA Hammer Museum, World from Here, 13
United Productions of America (UPA): logo of, 54, 55, 150; and Norman, 160, 188; and Urie, 166; and Whitney, 158
University of California, Los Angeles, 23, 88, 178, 184
Usher, Frederick: Arts & Architecture cover sketch, 1950, 66, 67; and Eames Office, 34; Felix Candela: Shell Forms exhibition catalogue, 1957, 66, 67; and high contrast ads, 223; and Lustig, 23, 54, 66; Monterey Bay Aquarium logo, 1950, 66, 67; and Sussman, 376
U.S. State Department, 120, 154
Vacaville, California, 24, 74
Van Hamersveld, John: A Child's Guide to Good and Evil album cover, 1968, 284, 285; The Endless Summer poster, 12, 160, 246, 254, 255, 282; photograph with his Pinnacle Indian prints, 1968, 302; and Single Wing

Turquoise Bird, 176, 216; and sixties, 218; Southern California poster, 3; The Who (with Fleetwood Mac) Shrine Auditorium concert poster, 1968, 282, 283
Vrontikis, Petrula, 315
Ward Ritchie Press, 26, 52, 76
Warner Brothers Records, 216, 284
Weir, Tom, photomontage of couple making love, 268
Weston, Edward, Stravinsky portraits, 48, 49
Whitney, James, 120, 184
Whitney, John: and Abel, 184; "Animation Mechanisms," 121, 134–39; Bob Hope Show titles, 158; Catalog, 1961, 158, 159; The Dinah Shore Show titles, 158; and Eames Office, 120, 154, 158; and Fischinger, 120; The Glass Bottom Boat movie titles, 120; To the Moon and Beyond, 158
Whole Earth Catalog: "Communications" section, 217, 234–37; designer of, 14; fall 1970 issue, 296, 297; and sixties, 219
Wild, Lorraine, 14, 25, 86, 216, 312, 315
Wilson, Wes: and color combinations, 224; photograph of, 232; posters of, 232, 233, 262, 270; and sixties, 218
Wired magazine, 13, 226
wireframes, 196, 202
Woman's Building, Los Angeles: and de Bretteville, 332, 336–37, 337, 386; reception area, 337
women: and California graphic design, 13, 14, 311–13, 314–15, 317–25; and feminism, 313, 318, 319, 320, 332–37, 337, 382
Women's Graphic Center, 320
Works Progress Administration, 340
Works West, 104
Worthington, Michael, 14, 121
Young, Doyald: and modernism, 24, 25, 26; Teletype Monocase font, 1965, 96, 97
Youngblood, Gene: "The Artist as Design Scientist," 121, 130–33; on motion graphics, 176
Yudell, Deenie, 315
Zap Comix, 270, 282, 286

ILLUSTRATION CREDITS

The author has made her best efforts to locate and credit the sources and copyright holders of all the illustrations in this book.

Courtesy of Academy Film Archive, used with permission of CBS, 165; ©American Broadcasting Companies, Inc., 167 (courtesy of UCLA Film & Television Archive), 167, 173 (center, archival still provided by Oddball Films), 175; ©Anthology Film Archives, 148–49; Courtesy of Arts & Architecture Archives, ©David Travers, used with permission, 58, 59, 65, 69; Courtesy of Atari Interactive, Inc., all rights reserved, used with permission, Tempest®, ©1980, 197, Crystal Castles®, ©1983, 201, I Robot®, ©1983, 203; Courtesy of Jennifer Bass, 153, 169; Courtesy of Archie Boston, 241, 260–61; Courtesy of Stewart Brand, 297; Courtesy of Bruce Brown Films, LLC, all rights reserved, 255 (photograph courtesy of John Van Hamersveld); Courtesy of Frances Butler, 381; Courtesy of California Historical Society, Friends of Perfection Collection, 1968-1972, MS 4008, 293, 295; Used with permission of CBS, 81; ©Center for Visual Music, 145, 147; Trouble Indemnity, ©1950, renewed 1977 Columbia Pictures Industries, Inc., all rights reserved, courtesy of Columbia Pictures, 151; Courtesy of Classic Media, LLC, 161; Courtesy of the Estate of Allen Cohen and Regent Press, 268, 269 (photograph courtesy of University of Connecticut, Archives and Special Collections), 271 (top and bottom left, courtesy of Geoff Kaplan); Taxi Driver, ©1976, renewed 2004 Columbia Pictures Industries, Inc., all rights reserved, courtesy of Columbia Pictures, 191; Reprinted with permission of Communication Arts, ©Coyne & Blanchard, Inc., 99; Courtesy of Concord Music Group, Inc., 355 (photograph courtesy of Los Angeles County Museum of Art); Used with permission of the Corita Art Center, Immaculate Heart Community, Los Angeles, 70, 257 (photograph by Joshua White), 291 (photograph by Joshua White), 357 (photograph by Arthur Evans), 359; Courtesy of Mike Davies, 178–79 (photography by Mike Davies); Courtesy of Sheila Levrant de Bretteville, 83–87 (383–85 used with permission of California Institute of the Arts; 384 photography by Scott Taylor), 385; Courtesy of Disney Enterprises, Inc., ©Disney, 60–63, 199; ©2013 Emory Douglas/Artists Rights Society (ARS), New York, 279, 299; Permission of DuPont, 351 top; ©Eames Office LLC, used with permission, 71, 83, 155, 157, 245, 345–47; Esther McCoy Papers, Archives of American Art, Smithsonian Institution, 67 top; Courtesy of Keith Godard, 105; Courtesy of April Greiman, 391–95, (394–95 courtesy of the Walker Art Center, Minneapolis); ©Bill Ham, all rights reserved, 171 (top right photograph by Lawrence Lauterborn); Courtesy of the Indianapolis Museum of Art, Nancy Foxwell Neuberger Acquisition Endowment Fund, 2012.151, 258–59; ©Estate of John and James Whitney, courtesy of John Whitney, Jr., 159; Courtesy of Susan Kare Design (kare.com and kareprints.com), used with permission from Apple, Inc., 389; Courtesy of Gere Kavanaugh, 365–67, 398; ©Eric Laignel, used with permission, 100–101; Used with permission of Los Angeles World Airports, 95; Reprinted by permission of New Directions Publishing Corp.: Gertrude Stein, Three Lives, ©1945 by Alvin Lustig, Alain Fournier, The Wanderer, ©1946 by Alvin Lustig, Charles Baudelaire, Flowers of Evil, ©1947 by Alvin Lustig, Nathanael West, The Day of the Locust, ©1950 by Alvin Lustig, Tennessee Williams, Camino Real, ©1953 by Alvin Lustig, 57; Courtesy Elaine Lustig Cohen, 51, 55; Thomas McConville for the Long Beach Business Journal, 341; Courtesy of Kristine McKenna, 273–77; Courtesy of Monterey Bay Aquarium, 67 center left; Courtesy of Victor Moscoso and John Van Hamersveld, ©Pinnacle Productions 1968, used with permission from John Van Hamersveld and Victor Moscoso, 283; Nelson Hackett Papers, D-152, Special Collections, University of California Library, Davis, 1; ©Neon Rose 1967, www.victormoscoso.com, all rights reserved, 267; Courtesy of Marilyn Neuhart, 89–93, 361 (top photograph by John Neuhart), 362–63 (photographs by Andrew Neuhart ©ANeuhart 2012); ©Earl Newman, used with permission, all rights reserved, 251–53; Courtesy of Ellen Magnin Newman, all rights reserved, 349 (courtesy of Steve Reoutt), 350, 351 (bottom, courtesy Steve Reoutt), 353–54 (photographs by Benjamin Blackwell); Courtesy of the Oakland Museum of California, All Of Us Or None Of Us Archive, Fractional and promised gift of The Rossman Family, 281; Seconds, Citizen's Band ©Paramount Pictures Corp, all rights reserved, 169, 195; Photograph by William Reagh, courtesy of Los Angeles Public Library Photo Collection, 250; Courtesy of Steve Reoutt, 79; ©Rhino Entertainment Company, used with permission, all rights reserved, Artwork by Limonada de Sica 263, Artwork by Stanley Mouse and Alton Kelley 265; Courtesy of Rhino Entertainment Company, A Warner Music Group Company, 285; Courtesy of RIT Graphic Design Archives, Wallace Library, Rochester Institute of Technology, permission of Louis Dangizer, 73, 107 (top, permission of Universal Music Enterprises); ©Andy Romanoff from original art by Single Wing Turquoise Bird, all rights reserved, 177; Courtesy of Christopher Romero, 163; Courtesy of San Francisco Museum of Modern Art, Accessions Committee Fund purchase, ©Jack W. Stauffacher, 102 (photograph by Don Ross), 103; Courtesy of Barbara Stauffacher Solomon, 368–69 (reproduced with permission from the San Francisco Museum of Modern Art), 370–71, 372–73 (courtesy Adrian Shaughnessy); Used with permission of the Smothers Brothers, 181; Courtesy of Sony Music Entertainment, 287; Courtesy of Steve Reoutt Collection, California College of the Arts, Simpson Library, San Francisco, California, 87; Courtesy of Sussman/Prejza & Co., Inc., 5, 339, 374–79; Courtesy of Charles Swaney (photograph by Charles Swaney), 340; Courtesy of Richard Taylor, 206; Used with permission from United Continental Holdings, Inc., 289; Used with permission from Universal Music Enterprises, 243; ©1971 Universal Television, courtesy of Universal Studios Licensing LLC, used with permission of Dr Pepper/Seven Up, Inc. The 7UP ad shown was used in the United States; and in the USA 7UP is a registered trademark of Dr Pepper/Seven Up, Inc. The 7UP brand is used under different ownership in the rest of the world, 185; Courtesy Frederick Usher III and Xochil Usher, 55 center, 67; Courtesy of Vacaville Museum, A Center for Solano County History, 47; Courtesy of John Van Hamersveld, 3, 302; Courtesy of Michael Kohn Gallery, ©The Estate of Wallace Berman, used with permission, 249; Courtesy of William Andrews Clark Memorial Library, University of California, Los Angeles; 49, 51, 53; Courtesy of James Whitney, 97

EARTHQUAKES, MUDSLIDES, FIRES & RIOTS

First published in the United States by Metropolis Books, ARTBOOK | D.A.P., 155 Sixth Avenue, New York, N.Y. 10031

First published in the United Kingdom in 2014 by Thames & Hudson Ltd, 181A High Holborn, London WC1V 7QX

Earthquakes, Mudslides, Fires & Riots: California and Graphic Design, 1936–1986 is copyright ©2014 Louise Sandhaus. The essays by Denise Gonzales Crisp, Lorraine Wild, and Michael Worthington are copyright ©2014 the authors.

PROJECT DIRECTOR: Diana Murphy
EDITOR: Anne Thompson
DESIGN: LSD (Louise Sandhaus Design) with Thomas Kracauer, Kaoru Matsushita, Christopher Morabito, Derrick Schultz, Hayden Smith
TYPEFACE: CIA Compendium by Jens Gehlhaar
QUOTATION PAGES DESIGN: Jens Gehlhaar
DIAGRAM DESIGN: Katherine Catmur with Benjamin Woodlock
PRODUCTION: Echelon Color, Santa Monica, California
PRINTING: Oceanic Graphic International, Hong Kong, China

All Rights Reserved. No part of this publication may be reproduced or transmitted in any form or by any means, electronic or mechanical, including photocopy, recording or any other information storage and retrieval system, without prior permission in writing from the publisher.

British Library Cataloguing-in-Publication Data
A catalogue record for this book is available from the British Library

ISBN 978-0-500-51796-3

Printed and bound in China by Oceanic Graphic International

To find out about all our publications, please visit www.thamesandhudson.com. There you can subscribe to our e-newsletter, browse or download our current catalogue, and buy any titles that are in print.

Pages 46, 111, 144, 207, 240, 303, 338, 399: From Paul C. Johnson, ed., Beautiful California (Menlo Park, Calif.: Lane, 1971). Pages 130–33: From Gene Youngblood, Expanded Cinema (New York: Dutton, 1970); reprinted with permission of Gene Youngblood. Pages 134–39: From John Whitney, "Animation Mechanisms," American Cinematographer, January 1971; reprinted with permission of American Cinematographer. Pages 140–43: From Jeffrey Altshuler, "Robert Abel: Video Surrealist," Print, November/December 1975; reprinted with permission of Print Magazine and the Estate of Robert Abel. Page 228: "Immaculate Heart College Art Department Rules," created by a class of Sister Corita Kent's, 1965, calligraphy by David Mekelburg, 1968; reprinted with permission of Corita Art Center, Immaculate Heart Community, Los Angeles. Page 229, cover of CA, vol. 9, no. 1, 1967, and pages 230–33, from Dugald Stermer, "Rock Posters," CA, vol. 9, no. 1, 1967, reprinted with permission of Communication Arts, ©Coyne & Blanchard, Inc. Pages 234–37: From "Communications," Whole Earth Catalog, fall 1970; courtesy of Stewart Brand. Pages 238–39: From Sheila Levrant de Bretteville, Barry Hyams, and Marianne Partridge, eds., "California Institute of the Arts: Prologue to a Community," Arts in Society, vol. 7, no. 3, fall/winter 1970. Pages 326–27: From Sister Corita Kent, daisy with all the petals yes, 1966; reprinted with permission of Corita Art Center, Immaculate Heart Community, Los Angeles. Pages 328–31: From Dugald Stermer, "Barbara Stauffacher Solomon," Print, vol. 13, no. 3, 1971; reprinted with permission of Print Magazine and Barbara Stauffacher Solomon. Pages 332–37: Rose DeNeve, "A Feminist Option," Print, May/June 1976; reprinted with permission of Print Magazine and Sheila Levrant de Bretteville.